PRAISE FOR
Understanding Worship

A few sentences can't do this book justice. It is theologically potent, refreshingly honest, and desperately needed in this generation. This is more than wisdom; it's a catalyst for action. Every worship leader and disciple maker should keep this book in their arsenal.

—**CHLOE MACK,** Circuit Riders

God is clearly using Sam Storms to address a common ditch in the church. This book will challenge every believer to have a passionate, joyful, and biblically rooted heart in worship and to understand that our love for him and joy in him are never to be disconnected from the worship of him. I believe it is a key contribution to the body of Christ in this hour.

—**JUDAH DAWKINS,** worship pastor and elder,
Revolution Church, Lone Tree, Colorado

Sam effectively tackles a subject as vast as worship and makes it accessible to all believers. His point about glorifying God by enjoying him is alone worth the price of the book. The way he frames this dimension of enjoyment in our worship has the potential to take us to a new level in our personal relationship with God and will infuse new life into our gatherings. I believe this book can unleash an explosive and compelling element that will enable us to worship the Lord in the way he intended it from the beginning.

—**DANIEL BRYMER,** worship leader

UNDERSTANDING WORSHIP

BIBLICAL FOUNDATIONS
FOR DELIGHTING IN AND
FEASTING ON GOD

SAM STORMS

ZONDERVAN
REFLECTIVE

ZONDERVAN REFLECTIVE

Understanding Worship
Copyright © 2025 by Sam Storms

Published by Zondervan, 3950 Sparks Drive SE, Suite 101, Grand Rapids, MI 49546, USA. Zondervan is a registered trademark of The Zondervan Corporation, L.L.C., a wholly owned subsidiary of HarperCollins Christian Publishing, Inc.

Requests for information should be addressed to customercare@harpercollins.com.

Zondervan titles may be purchased in bulk for educational, business, fundraising, or sales promotional use. For information, please email SpecialMarkets@Zondervan.com.

ISBN 978-0-310-17116-4 (audio)

Library of Congress Cataloging-in-Publication Data

Names: Storms, C. Samuel, 1951- author
Title: Understanding worship : biblical foundations for delighting in and feasting on God / Sam Storms.
Description: Grand Rapids, Michigan : Zondervan Reflective, [2025] | Includes index.
Identifiers: LCCN 2024060666 (print) | LCCN 2024060667 (ebook) | ISBN 9780310171140 paperback |
    ISBN 9780310171157 ebook
Subjects: LCSH: Worship--Biblical teaching | God--Biblical teaching | Holy Spirit
Classification: LCC BS680.W78 S76 2025 (print) | LCC BS680.W78 (ebook) | DDC 248.3--dc23/eng/
    20250318
LC record available at https://lccn.loc.gov/2024060666
LC ebook record available at https://lccn.loc.gov/2024060667

Cover design: LUCAS Art & Design
Cover image: Adobe Stock
Interior design: Sara Colley

Printed in the United States of America
25 26 27 28 29 LBC 5 4 3 2 1

Dedicated to my favorite worship leaders
with profound gratitude for the many ways each of you
has awakened me to the greatness and glory of God:
Daniel Brymer
David Brymer
Judah Dawkins
Chris DuPré
Charity Gayle
Abigail Ginsterblum
Steffany Gretzinger
Kent Henry
Dennis Jernigan
Chloe Mack
Jeremy Riddle
Phil Wickham

Contents

Acknowledgments

Gratitude must first be expressed to Ryan Pazdur and Matt Estel for their belief in this project and the excellent way in which this book was edited. No one should blame them for any errors or theological missteps, as these would surely be mine.

Perhaps the greatest debt of gratitude for my perspective on worship is due to my friend, John Piper. The reader will notice a considerable dependence on Piper throughout the book. John's God-centered, Christian Hedonist approach to worship has exerted a tremendous influence on how I think about God and why I believe that we must worship him for the joy to be found in who he is and what he has done for us in Jesus. Thanks, John!

Introduction

Worship Is Feasting on God! So Come Hungry!

I suspect that the title to this introduction strikes many of you as inordinately odd, perhaps even a bit irreverent. Worship is *feasting on God*? Really? So, to make sense of this, let's begin with a question: *Why do you worship?* What is your motivation in investing so much time and making such great sacrifices to expend your energy in the praise of God? Some of you immediately know the answer to that question, and it strikes you as silly that I should even dare to ask it. Others of you, quite honestly, are more than a little unsure. You're confused and don't fully understand your motives. Perhaps you worship from a sense of duty. You tell yourself, "Worshiping God is like studying the Bible and praying and witnessing. God commanded it, so here I am reporting for duty. I don't know if I really like it all that much, but being willing to obey God even when I don't feel like it is what being a Christian is all about. Right?"

Whenever I hear someone say something like that, a fascinating verse in the book of Deuteronomy comes to mind: "Because you did not serve the LORD your God *with joyfulness and gladness of heart*, because of the abundance of all things, therefore you shall serve your enemies whom the LORD will send against you" (28:47–48).

I always responded to that verse, "Wait a minute, Lord. Isn't it enough just to serve and obey you?" "No," says God. "It is because they didn't serve me *with joyfulness and gladness of heart* that I will discipline them." This passage in Deuteronomy 28, along with scores of others in both the Old and

New Testaments, alerts me to the fact that *why* we do something for God is absolutely fundamental in determining whether what we do is good, pleasing, and glorifying to our heavenly Father. Now, let's apply this to worship.

This may initially sound strange, but consider this proposition: if you come to worship for any reason other than the joy, pleasure, and satisfaction that are to be found in God, you dishonor him. This means worship is principally a feasting on all that God is for us in Jesus. This is because, as John Piper has so often said, "God is most glorified in you when [you] are most satisfied in him."[1] Or again, you are his pleasure when he is your treasure. Which is to say that God's greatest delight in you is your delight in him.

I want you to consider that you and I must come to worship *hungry*! We must not come with hands or hearts full of goodies and gifts, thinking that worship is fundamentally where we serve and feed God. God is not in need of us. We are desperately in need of him. Don't come to God with your well-ordered life, serving up your best efforts to feed God as if he were hungry. Come with open hands, an empty belly, and a hungry heart. Let him honor himself by filling you. If you've ever wondered if God can be sarcastic, consider this claim:

> For every beast of the forest is mine,
>   the cattle on a thousand hills.
> I know all the birds of the hills,
>   and all that moves in the field is mine.
>
> If I were hungry, I would not tell you;
>   for the world and its fullness are mine. (Ps. 50:10–12)

This sentiment was echoed by Paul in his sermon on Mars Hill:

> The God who made the world and everything in it, being Lord of heaven and earth, does not live in temples made by man, nor is he served by human hands, as though he needed anything, since he himself gives to all mankind life and breath and everything. (Acts 17:24–25)

---

1. John Piper, *Desiring God: Meditations of a Christian Hedonist* (Colorado Springs: Multnomah, 2011), 10.

Worship is a feast in which God is the host, cook, waiter, and the meal itself.

It's not unusual for people to voice an objection at this point: "But I thought worship was all about glorifying God. You seem to say it's all about my delight and satisfaction." But this is a false dichotomy. To say that worship is *either* about glorifying God *or* finding personal satisfaction in him is to put asunder what God has joined together. His glory and your gladness are not antithetical impulses moving in opposite directions. Rather, *his glory is in your gladness in him*. Take a moment and read over that last sentence again, and let its liberating truth sink into your soul.

Years ago, if you had asked me why I chose to show up on a night devoted to worshiping the Lord, I would have said something like, "I've come to give glory to God." Today I would push back on my earlier self and wonder how it is that a broken, finite, sinful man like me could ever hope to "give" God anything. After all, as someone once said to me, "We're talking about the God who has Genesis 1 on his résumé!" This God, the only God, the creator and sustainer of all that exists, lacks nothing. He is entirely self-sufficient. To suggest that any creature could give anything to God, adding what he otherwise lacks, is nothing short of blasphemous.

At this point, I might have responded with a question of my own. "Worship is all about glorifying God, isn't it?" The answer, of course, is yes. But precisely how do we glorify God? Isn't it by receiving from him all that he graciously provides for us in Jesus? Didn't the psalmist declare that "he satisfies the longing soul, and the hungry soul he fills with good things" (Ps. 107:9)? When God overflows in love to you and me, when he blesses and empowers us and forgives, heals, and fills us with delight, when he satisfies the deepest needs of our souls, he is exalted as the only all-sufficient supply for his people. God—not we—is the one who gives. And when he does, we see him as the only all-sufficient treasure in whom we find "fullness of joy" and "pleasures forevermore" (Ps. 16:11). That is why *worship is all about glorifying God by finding or gaining personal satisfaction in him. When you worship, you glorify God through glad-hearted getting of all he gives!*

When people first hear this, they mistakenly think that I'm saying worship is principally about our enjoyment. In fact, it is about our enjoyment *of God*. It is not merely about our pleasure or delight or satisfaction. It is about our pleasure, delight, and satisfaction *in God*. We glorify God in worship by feasting on him and enjoying him.

The issue is not whether worship is concerned with glorifying God. Everyone agrees it is. The issue is, *how* does one best glorify God? Is it by coming to enrich an impoverished God with what we think we have to offer, or is it by becoming enriched by an all-sufficient God as he overflows in goodness to us? Are we to come in our alleged wealth, intending to lavish it upon God, thereby alleviating his poverty? Or do we come in our abject spiritual deprivation to the God who owns everything, asking for help and hope and happiness? Clearly, we best glorify God by enjoying him forever, by drinking our fill from the abundance of his house and from the river of his delights (Ps. 36:8).

I am indescribably grateful for the Christian atmosphere provided by my parents while growing up. I was raised in Southern Baptist churches until I arrived at seminary in the fall of 1973. Until then, and for several years following, I believed that coming into a worship service conscious of my need for joy and satisfaction was sinful and selfish. I was led to believe that worshiping with the hope of finding personal joy ruined or undermined the moral value and virtue of praise. "Come and focus on God, not your need," I was told (quite sternly most often). But what if I come and focus on *my need for God* and exalt him by declaring that he alone satisfies my soul and fills the emptiness of my heart? Listen to how David described his own experience of God in Psalm 63:1–5.

> O God, you are my God; earnestly I seek you;
> my soul thirsts for you;
> my flesh faints for you,
> as in a dry and weary land where there is no water. (v. 1)

Should we respond to this with a rebuke, chastising David for fixating on his thirst? David unabashedly spoke not simply of seeking God but "earnestly" seeking him. His flesh didn't merely yearn for God, but he was on the verge of fainting from spiritual exhaustion. He was more than needy; he was desperately needy. Should someone have called his hand on this and demanded that he repent? Was his hunger and thirst for God misguided and self-centered? Certainly not! There is no hint of sin in being thirsty or in his desire to have it quenched. He continued:

> So I have looked upon you in the sanctuary,
>   beholding your power and glory.
> Because your steadfast love is better than life,
>   my lips will praise you. (vv. 2–3)

People often say that we should only "praise" the Lord because he deserves it. Yes, he deserves all our praise and adoration. But David made no apology for justifying his praise by appealing to the fact that it is "because" God's "steadfast love is better than life." He exalted the Lord precisely because the Lord's covenant lovingkindness filled the emptiness of David's heart. David found acceptance and security in God's steadfast love that nothing in life could remotely match. I don't believe David sinned in speaking this way. I don't believe that his hunger for God detracted from the latter's well-deserved glory. Indeed, it was precisely when David saw God's "power and glory" and felt his "steadfast love" deeply in his soul that God was honored and extolled. David affirmed something similar in Psalm 4:7, saying of God, "You have put more joy in my heart than they have when their grain and wine abound."

We see this theme repeated often in the Psalms. The psalmist's soul longed for the courts of the Lord (Ps. 84:2), and his deepest desire was to be found in God's dwelling place. Why? Because he found it altogether "lovely" (v. 1). The beauty and sweetness of God's courts transcend the most sublime of earthly locales. The sons of Korah undertook a comparative study as they prepared to worship. They looked at the sweetest and most sublime that this world could offer and drew this profound conclusion: "A day in your courts [O God] is better than a thousand elsewhere. I would rather be a doorkeeper in the house of my God than dwell in the tents of wickedness" (v. 10).

All of life is inescapably competitive. Every choice we make is a decision between competing pleasures. Even if we are unaware of it, such choices demand a comparative evaluation of rival claims. These crossroad decisions in life don't spring up *ex nihilo*. They aren't causeless. The psalmist declared that he chose God and the pleasures of life in his courts *because* "the LORD God is a sun and shield" (84:11). The world, on the other hand, leaves us scorched and defenseless. "The LORD bestows favor and honor" while the passing pleasures of sin lead only to misery and despair. "No good thing does

xvi | UNDERSTANDING WORSHIP

he withhold from those who walk uprightly" (v. 11). People, however, demand their pound of flesh. This is precisely what we see yet again in Psalm 63.

> So I will bless you as long as I live;
>   in your name I will lift up my hands.
>
> My soul will be satisfied as with fat and rich food,
>   and my mouth will praise you with joyful lips. (vv. 4–5)

I trust that by now you can see how finding satisfaction for our souls in God is precisely what magnifies him and puts him on display as incomparably greater than all this world has to offer. It was because David's soul was satisfied as if he had just concluded a meal of the richest and most exquisite food that he didn't simply praise God but did so "with joyful lips."

When we worship God merely from a sense of moral duty, the greatness and abundant supply that he provides us is obscured. To say that God is pleased with worship that lacks a relentless passion and hunger for him is to say that he endorses hypocrisy. How can one ever forget the stinging rebuke Jesus made of the Pharisees in this regard (another text we'll look at in detail later in this book)?

> You hypocrites! Well did Isaiah prophesy of you, when he said:
>
> "This people honors me with their lips,
>   but their heart is far from me,
> in vain do they worship me,
>   teaching as doctrines the commandments of men."
>   (Matt. 15:7–9)

This verse is at one and the same time the most frightening statement in Scripture and the most encouraging. I'm terrified that I might pretend to honor God by singing his praise while my heart is disengaged and indifferent. I might have every hymn memorized since childhood and sing with the best of the religious leaders of our day, only to discover that all my worship is utterly in vain.

When realizing that God's Word insists that for worship to be honoring to the Lord, it must be a passionate expression of our longing for God, many recoil in fear and dread. They know the condition of their souls, and they honestly confess that all they feel within is pain, brokenness, and devastation. The words of Jesus in Matthew 15 are frightening. But it is precisely here that we all need to be reminded that even our pain and spiritual emptiness are, in a very real sense, passions. They may be passions we would rather live without, but they are expressions of our desperation without God. We may feel only the anguish of longing and anticipation for what we don't have in God, but we know we must have it if we will survive.

Look at things from God's point of view. You come into his presence as one who has been redeemed, forgiven, and justified by the blood of his own Son. And you say, "God, I'm not overly thrilled with being here right now. To be perfectly honest, I don't feel a thing for you right now. You leave me high and dry. I'm not moved by a spontaneous affection for you as a person. I'm not particularly overwhelmed by your beauty. Your splendor and glory really leave me cold and lifeless. But I'm going to worship anyway. I'm going to declare your worth anyway because you've commanded me to do so in Scripture and because you are God." I seriously doubt if God is going to be thrilled with that. Extracting some form of praise from your soul while in that mindset is hardly the sort of "worship" (if we can even call it that) that honors him.

So, what should we do when we feel nothing, when we are bored and indifferent and dead on the inside, when we are downcast and can barely move our mouths to sing? What should we do when we've lost our sense of intimacy with the Lord, when we feel nothing of his presence, when there is but a haunting echo of his distance? Some of you struggle to attend church. You find little appealing in it but feel obligated to go because a friend or family member pressured you into coming. Can you still glorify God in worship? Yes!

Here's the good news. Even though you may not now feel any joy or satisfaction in God's presence, *you want to*. There comes to mind days past when your heart was aflame and your spirit ablaze with passion for God and with a sense of his presence. You delighted in his goodness, and praise was easy and natural and free. You want it. You are desperate for it. You cry for it. But it's not there, for now.

Perhaps you are in a place of extreme emotional brokenness. Your life is crumbling all around you. Nothing has worked out the way you hoped. All that you've strived to achieve is disintegrating before your eyes, and you are helpless to stem the tide. All that you once valued is vanishing. You feel nothing. Your spirit is dry and barren, and you sense an ugly anger and bitterness rising up in your heart. Can you worship in a way that honors and glorifies God? Yes. So, what should you do?

Sing anyway. Worship anyway. Praise God for his matchless worth and his unexcelled beauty.

"Wait a minute, Sam. That sounds like you're encouraging me to be a hypocrite. I thought I heard you moments ago denounce the very thing you now seem to endorse. I'm confused."

I can appreciate that. But what I'm advocating isn't hypocrisy, because God is glorified by your longing for the joy that is to be found in him even if you are not yet experiencing it. God is honored by what John Piper calls "the spark of anticipated gladness" that leads you to praise him even when you don't feel like it.[2]

In your brokenness, you know that only God can heal and bind up your wounds. In your spiritual weariness, you know that only God can bring refreshment and renewal to your arid soul. In your coldheartedness, you know that only God can bring life-giving warmth. In your joylessness, you know that only God can restore delight to your spirit. And it is precisely this deep and desperate desire in your spiritual desert that so profoundly honors God.

Consider the imagery from Psalm 42:1–2, where David envisioned himself as "a deer" panting in desperation for the "flowing streams" of God's presence and love. David thought of God as a desert oasis while he was that thirsty deer "in a dry and weary land where there is no water" (Ps. 63:1). As I see it, the deer (David or you) can magnify an oasis in either of two ways. The most obvious way is by jumping into its refreshing, cool, life-giving waters and drinking to your heart's delight. But you can also honor the oasis by the painful sorrow you feel in not yet having reached it as you continue to press on in the spiritual desert. When you ache for the refreshment of the oasis even though you're still hot and dry and thirsty, when you grieve because of

---

2. Piper, *Desiring God*, 97.

the absence of its life-giving waters in your life, you magnify the oasis even before you have opportunity to enjoy it. So, too, with God.

So, if you went to church last weekend feeling nothing for God, feeling that he's a million miles away, you could and should have worshiped him anyway. Isn't this what we see in Psalm 42:1–2? What honors the water: the deer bent over drinking after a long journey in the desert, or the deer diligently panting for the water while yet in the desert? Both! Actually, drinking is the best and most satisfying way to honor the water; but until you get there, continue to thirst for it.

In the Meantime

Come to God in worship to enjoy the satisfying richness of all that he is for you in Jesus. Press through reading this book even if you struggle to turn a single page. If you are not yet enjoying God, here are a few words of practical advice.

Don't downplay or minimize the absence of joy in your heart. Am I saying that joylessness is a sin? Yes. To live without joy is to say that God cannot elicit the excitement and delight that honors him from your heart. To find joy in the victory of your favorite football team or in the flavor of well-prepared filet mignon but not in God is an insult to him. Acknowledge the coldness and indifference of your heart. Don't pretend that it doesn't matter how you feel. It matters not only to you but especially to God.

Pray for a revelation of God's splendor, beauty, majesty, sweetness, and all-satisfying, all-sufficient goodness. Ask the Holy Spirit to grant you spiritual ears that you might hear the Father rejoicing over you with loud and boisterous singing (Zeph. 3:17). Ask the Holy Spirit to grant you spiritual eyes that you might again see the goodness of the Lord in the land of the living (cf. Eph. 1:15–23).

Begin to take those steps set forth in Scripture to renew your joy—Bible reading and meditation and memorization, prayer, participation in the Lord's Supper, remembering God's past deeds of kindness, focusing on the cross, fellowshipping with those who *are* enjoying God, reading a book on worship (whether it is this one or another you find more edifying), and so on. Rarely will God reignite a fire in your soul apart from those means of grace he has provided for us in Scripture.

Think about hell! Yes, you read it right. Think about hell. I realize that may not be an appetizing thought. It may strike you as a bit morbid. Among his personal resolutions, Jonathan Edwards included the following: "Resolved, when I feel pain, to think of the pains of martyrdom, and of hell."[3] You'll be amazed at how a brief time of meditation on the agonies of hell, from which you have been so graciously delivered, will serve to increase and deepen your joy and gratitude!

Finally, worship God anyway. Pursue the outward dimension of your duty in prayerful hope and expectation that it will help to rekindle the inward delight. Again, this is not hypocrisy because you are doing the outward act *hoping* to regain the inward joy, not as a substitute for it or as a disguise to convince others you mean it when, in fact, you don't.

In conclusion, don't come to God in times of worship arrogantly presuming to give. Come humbly, yearning to get, for God always feeds the hungry heart. In the next chapter, I'll explain how God led me into the experience of finding complete satisfaction in him, by which he is most honored and glorified in me.

---

3. Jonathan Edwards, *The Works of Jonathan Edwards: Letters and Personal Writings*, vol. 16, ed. George S. Claghorn (New Haven, CT: Yale University Press, 1998), 754.

PART 1

WORSHIP IS WHY THE WORLD EXISTS

CHAPTER 1

My Journey into the Joy of Worship

The most powerful catalyst in my spiritual transformation, second only to the sanctifying power of Scripture, was the discovery of God's beauty, power, and love during times of worship. I had always worshiped God. I had always loved music, especially the great hymns of the church. Both my mother and sister were classically trained pianists. Hardly a day passed in our house without one or both of them playing "My Savior's Love" ("I Stand Amazed in the Presence"), "How Great Thou Art," "The Love of God," "At the Cross," or any number of other hymns, accompanied by the singing of my dad and me.

Sadly, though, as time passed and my intellectual pride increased, worship became little more than singing songs *about* God. Of course we ought to sing about him. But I rarely had any expectation of meeting God, experiencing his presence, engaging my heart with his, or, far less, *enjoying* him. Over time I was drawn to songs that let me keep God at arm's length and kept my emotions intact. In terms of musical excellence, they were superb compositions. But something about them (or perhaps something about me) made it possible for my affections to be kept in check. I never had to fear being seen as weak, sentimental, or anti-intellectual. God was more a distant object of my admiration than a Father who delights in me. I avoided being seen as cherishing and delighting in him. I foolishly believed that was for weaklings, not theologians whose goal was to be known as smart and in control.

I can't recall how it happened or through whom, but in late 1986–87 I began to listen to new expressions of praise and worship. Tapes produced by Hosanna Integrity and the Vineyard somehow made their way into my office cassette player and the tape deck in my car.[1] It was more than just a new style of music. I have never stopped loving or singing the traditional hymns of the church. But something was happening in times of worship that had never happened before. It's difficult to describe, but I'll try.

The Birth of a Christian Hedonist

When people hear the words *Christian hedonism* for the first time, they instinctively conclude that if ever there was a contradiction in terms, this is it. Christian hedonism falls into the same illogical category as fried ice or a square circle. But my "conversion" to Christian hedonism occurred at almost the same time as the transformation in my experience of worship. Before reading *Desiring God* by John Piper, I thought the verb *enjoy* and the noun *God* should never be used in the same sentence. I could understand *fearing* God and *obeying* God, even *loving* God. But *enjoying* God struck me as inconsistent with the biblical mandate to glorify God and deny myself. How could I be committed to seeking God's glory if I was concerned about my own joy? My gladness and God's glory seemed to cancel each other out. They were on different tracks, racing in opposite directions, destined never to meet, much less be reconciled to each other. I had to choose one or the other, but embracing them both struck me as out of the question. Worse still, enjoying God sounded a bit too lighthearted, almost casual, perhaps even flippant, and I knew that Christianity was serious business.

Then I read Jonathan Edwards (1703–58), the one theologian from the past who had influenced me most. Something he said hit me like a bolt of lightning. I'm not a Christian hedonist because of Jonathan Edwards. Scripture always has and will remain the final authority in my life. But Edwards helped me see that God's glory and my gladness were not antithetical. He helped me see that at the core of Scripture is the truth that my heart's passion for pleasure (which is God-given and not the result of sin) and God's passion for praise converge in a way that alone makes sense of human existence. Outside of the Word of God, it may well be the most significant and life-changing utterance I've ever read:

---

1. If you are too young to know what a cassette player or tape deck is, let Google inform you!

> Now what is glorifying God, but a rejoicing at that glory he has displayed? An understanding of the perfections of God, merely, cannot be the end of the creation; for he had as good not understand it, as see it and not be at all moved with joy at the sight. Neither can the highest end of creation be the declaring God's glory to others; for the declaring God's glory is good for nothing otherwise than to raise joy in ourselves and others at what is declared.[2]

Here it is again, stated in slightly different words:

> God is glorified not only by his glory's being seen, but by its being rejoiced in. When those that see it delight in it, God is more glorified than if they only see it. God made the world that he might communicate, and the creature receive, his glory . . . both [with] the mind and the heart. He that testifies his having an idea of God's glory [doesn't] glorify God so much as he that testifies also his approbation [i.e., his heartfelt commendation or praise] of it and his delight in it.[3]

Edwards's point is that *passionate, heartfelt enjoyment of God, and not merely acknowledgment or intellectual apprehension, is the aim of our existence.* If God is to be supremely glorified in us, we must be supremely glad in him and in what he has done for us in Jesus. Enjoying God is not a secondary, tangential endeavor. It is central to everything we do, especially worship. We do not do other things, hoping that joy in God will emerge as a by-product. Our reason for pursuing God and obedience to him is precisely the joy found in him alone. To worship him for any reason other than the joy that is found in who he is, is sinful.

Helpful Insights from C. S. Lewis

I don't know how familiar C. S. Lewis was with Edwards, or whether he ever read anything by the famous Puritan pastor. But Lewis's discovery of the true nature of worship runs along a path similar to the sentiments of Edwards.

---

2. Jonathan Edwards, *The Miscellanies [Entry Nos. a–z, aa–zz, 1–500]*, The Works of Jonathan Edwards, vol. 13, ed. Thomas A. Schafer (New Haven, CT: Yale University Press, 1994), no. 3, 200.

3. Edwards, *The Miscellanies*, no. 448, 495.

The struggle that tore at Lewis's heart was one that perhaps you share. He was extremely puzzled, even agitated, by the recurring demand by Christians that we all "praise God." That was bad enough. What made it even worse is that *God himself* called for praise of *God himself*. What kind of "God" is one who incessantly demands that his people tell him how great he is? This was almost more than Lewis could stomach. He described his struggle and how he worked through it in an enlightening passage in his essay "The Problem of Praise in the Psalms."[4] As you read this (and I hope you do read it), observe how Lewis worked step-by-step to the same conclusion this chapter draws about our motivation in the worship of God. Said Lewis:

> We all despise the man who demands continued assurance of his own virtue, intelligence or delightfulness; we despise still more the crowd of people round every dictator, every millionaire, every celebrity, who gratify that demand. Thus a picture, at once ludicrous and horrible, both of God and His worshippers, threatened to appear in my mind. The Psalms were especially troublesome in this way—"Praise the Lord," "O praise the Lord with me," "Praise Him." . . . Worse still was the statement put into God's own mouth, "whoso offereth me thanks and praise, he honoureth me" (50:23). It was hideously like saying, "What I most want is to be told that I am good and great." . . . It was extremely distressing. It made one think what one least wanted to think. Gratitude to God, reverence to Him, obedience to Him, I thought I could understand; not this perpetual eulogy.

I suspect this strikes us as problematic, as it did Lewis, because we want to think that God is preeminently concerned with us, not himself. We want a God who is man-centered, not God-centered. Worse still, we can't fathom how God could possibly love us the way we think he should if he is so unapologetically obsessed with the praise and glory of his own name. How can God love *me* if all his infinite energy is expended in the love of *himself*? Part of Lewis's problem, as he himself confessed, was that he did not see that

---

4. C. S. Lewis, *Reflections on the Psalms* (New York: Harcourt, Brace, 1958), 90–98, emphasis added.

it is in the process of being worshipped that God communicates His presence to men. It is not of course the only way. But for many people at many times the "fair beauty of the Lord" is revealed chiefly or only while they worship Him together. Even in Judaism the essence of the sacrifice was not really that men gave bulls and goats to God, but that by their so doing God gave Himself to men; in the central act of our own worship of course this is far clearer—there it is manifestly, even physically, God who gives and we who receive. The miserable idea that God should in any sense need, or crave for, our worship like a vain woman wanting compliments, or a vain author presenting his new books to people who never met or heard him, is implicitly answered by the words, "If I be hungry I will not tell *thee*" (50:12). Even if such an absurd Deity could be conceived, He would hardly come to *us*, the lowest of rational creatures, to gratify His appetite. I don't want my dog to bark approval of my books.

Lewis was addressing, somewhat indirectly, the question that I raised earlier: Why do you worship a God who needs nothing? If God is altogether self-sufficient and cannot be served by human hands as if he needed anything (Acts 17:24–25; Rom. 11:33–36), least of all glory, why does he command our worship and praise of him? Lewis continued:

But the most obvious fact about praise—whether of God or anything—strangely escaped me. I thought of it in terms of compliment, approval, or the giving of honour. I had never noticed that *all enjoyment spontaneously overflows into praise unless* . . . shyness or the fear of boring others is deliberately brought in to check it. The world rings with praise—lovers praising their mistresses [Romeo praising Juliet and vice versa], readers their favourite poet, walkers praising the countryside, players praising their favourite game—praise of weather, wines, dishes, actors, motors, horses, colleges, countries, historical personages, children, flowers, mountains, rare stamps, rare beetles, even sometimes politicians or scholars. . . . Except where intolerably adverse circumstances interfere, praise almost seems to be inner health made audible. . . . I had not noticed either that just as men spontaneously praise whatever they value, so they spontaneously urge us to join them in praising it: "Isn't she lovely? Wasn't it glorious? Don't you think that magnificent?" The Psalmists in telling everyone to praise God are doing what all men do when they speak of what they care about. My whole, more general, difficulty about the praise of God depended on my absurdly denying to us, as regards the supremely Valuable, what we delight to do, what indeed we can't help doing, about everything else we value.

Lewis was touching on how God's love for sinners like you and me is ultimately made manifest. God desires our greatest good. But what greater good is there in the universe than God himself? So, if God is truly to love us, he must give us himself. But merely giving us of himself is only the first step in the expression of his affection for sinners. He must work to elicit rapturous praise and superlative delight from our hearts because, as Lewis said, "all enjoyment spontaneously overflows into praise." That's the way God made us. We can't help but praise and rejoice in what we most enjoy. The enjoyment itself is stunted and hindered if it is never expressed in joyful celebration. Here's how Lewis explained it:

I think we delight to praise what we enjoy because *the praise not merely expresses but completes the enjoyment; it is its appointed consummation.* It is not out of compliment that lovers keep on telling one another how beautiful they are; the delight is incomplete till it is expressed. It is frustrating to have discovered a new author and not to be able to tell anyone how good he is; to come suddenly, at the turn of the road, upon some mountain valley of unexpected grandeur and then to have to keep silent because the people with you care for it no more than for a tin can in the ditch; to hear a good joke and find no one to share it with....

If it were possible for a created soul fully ... to "appreciate," that is to love and delight in, the worthiest object of all, and simultaneously at every moment to give this delight perfect expression, then that soul would be in supreme beatitude.... To see what the doctrine really means, we must suppose ourselves to be in perfect love with God—drunk with, drowned in, dissolved by, that delight which, far from remaining pent up within ourselves as incommunicable, hence hardly tolerable, bliss, flows out from us incessantly again in effortless and perfect expression, our joy is no more separable from the praise in which it liberates and utters itself than the brightness a mirror receives is separable from the brightness it sheds. The Scotch catechism says that man's chief end is "to glorify God and enjoy Him forever." But we shall then know that these are the same thing. Fully to enjoy is to glorify. In commanding us to glorify Him, God is inviting us to enjoy Him.

So, if I understand Lewis correctly, he's telling us that God's pursuit of my praise is not weak self-seeking but the epitome of self-giving love! If my satisfaction in him is incomplete until expressed in praise of him for satisfying me with himself (note well: with *himself*, not his gifts or blessings, but the intrinsic beauty and splendor of God as God), then God's effort to elicit my worship (what Lewis before thought was inexcusable selfishness) is both the most loving thing he could possibly do for me and the most glorifying thing he could possibly do for himself. For in my gladness in him (not his gifts) is his glory in me.

Whew! If you can, go back and read it again. It's not the sort of statement one can fully digest in one sitting. Lewis has here forged the link that makes sense of it all.

I know how strange this sounds the first time one hears it (it can sound strange for a long time thereafter as well!). So, permit me to look elsewhere for help in making sense of it. In an article on the Desiring God website, we find the following explanation of Christian hedonism:[5]

A "Christian Hedonist" sounds like a contradiction, doesn't it? If the term makes you squirm, we understand. . . . We're not heretics (really!). Nor have we invented another prosperity-obsessed theology by twisting the Bible to sanctify our greed or lust. We are simply stating an ancient, orthodox, Biblical truth in a fresh way.

"All men seek happiness," says Blaise Pascal. "This is without exception. Whatever different means they employ, they all tend to this end. The cause of some going to war, and of others avoiding it, is the same desire

5. John Piper, "We Want You to Be a Christian Hedonist!," Desiring God, August 31, 2006, https://www.desiringgod.org/articles/we-want-you-to-be-a-christian-hedonist.

in both, attended with different views. The will never takes the least step but to this object. This is the motive of every action of every man, even of those who hang themselves." We believe Pascal is right. And, with Pascal, we believe God purposefully designed us to pursue happiness.

Does seeking your own happiness sound self-centered? Aren't Christians supposed to seek God, not their own pleasure? To answer this question, we need to understand a crucial truth about pleasure-seeking (hedonism): *we value most what we delight in most*. Pleasure is not God's competitor, idols are. Pleasure is simply a gauge that measures how valuable someone or something is to us. Pleasure is the measure of our treasure.

We know this intuitively. If a friend says to you, "I really enjoy being with you," you wouldn't accuse him of being self-centered. Why? Because your friend's delight in you is the evidence that you have great value in his heart. In fact, you'd be dishonored if he didn't experience any pleasure in your friendship. The same is true of God. If God is the source of our greatest delight then God is our most precious treasure; which makes us radically God-centered and not self-centered. And if we treasure God most, we glorify Him most.

Does the Bible teach this? Yes. Nowhere in the Bible does God condemn people for longing to be happy. People are condemned for forsaking God and seeking their happiness elsewhere (Jeremiah 2:13). This is the essence of sin. The Bible actually commands us to delight in the Lord (Psalm 37:4). Jesus teaches us to love God more than money because our heart is where our treasure is (Matt. 6:21). Paul wants us to believe that gaining Christ is worth the loss of everything else (Phil. 3:8) and the author of Hebrews exhorts us to endure suffering, like Jesus, for the joy set before us (Heb. 12:1–2). Examine the Scriptures and you'll see this over and over again.

Christian Hedonism is not a contradiction after all. It is desiring the vast, ocean-deep pleasures of God more than the mud-puddle pleasures of wealth, power or lust. We're Christian Hedonists because we believe Psalm 16:11, "You show me the path of life; in Your presence there is fullness of joy, in Your right hand are pleasures for evermore."

Join us in this pursuit of satisfaction in God, because God is most glorified in us when we are most satisfied in him.

Some find the next step difficult. Here it is: our glad-hearted passion for God is exceeded only by *God's* glad-hearted passion for God. If the chief end of man is to glorify God by enjoying him forever, the chief end of *God* is to glorify *God* and to enjoy *himself* forever!

What is the preeminent passion in God's heart? What is *God's* greatest pleasure? In what does *God* take supreme delight? I want to suggest that the preeminent passion in God's heart is his own glory. God is at the center of his own affections. The supreme love of God's life is God. God is preeminently committed to the fame of his name. God is himself the end for which God created the world. Better still, God's immediate goal in all he does is his own glory. God relentlessly and unceasingly creates, rules, orders, directs, speaks, judges, saves, destroys, and delivers to make known who he is and to secure from the whole of the universe the praise, honor, and glory of which he and he alone is ultimately and infinitely worthy.[6]

I distinctly recall the reaction to this from one young lady who took a course I offered on the doctrine of God. She was livid, to say the least. Her face turned red and she began to weep, more in anger than sadness. If she had been physically capable of doing so, I think she would have picked up her chair and thrown it at me. To her way of thinking, I had just destroyed her relationship with God.

The bottom line for her was this: If God loves himself preeminently, how can he love me at all? How can we say that God is for *us* and that he desires *our* happiness if he is primarily for *himself* and his own glory? This was her stumbling block, not unlike that which Lewis himself almost tripped over. But what Edwards, Lewis, and Piper all came to see is that it is precisely because God loves himself that he loves you and me.

This theological digression is important because it articulates the transformation in my perspective on worship. There's no other way to say it: I suddenly felt the freedom to *enjoy God*. I actually *felt* his presence. I actually *felt* his enjoyment of me in my enjoyment of him (cf. Zeph. 3:17). I began to sense a *power* and *spiritual intensity* that, at first, was a bit frightening. Although I have always been a romantic of sorts, when it came to worship, especially in a public setting, I was diligent to rein in my emotions. I felt compelled to

---

6. The most cogent and biblical defense of this proposition is found in Jonathan Edwards's treatise, "Dissertation concerning the End for Which God Created the World," in Edwards, *Ethical Writings*, ed. Paul Ramsey (New Haven, CT: Yale University Press, 1989).

preserve a measure of so-called dignity and religious sophistication. After all, I was determined to protect my image as an in-control and profoundly insightful theologian. If that sounds sinfully prideful and arrogant, it was!

But God *visited* me in worship! As I drew near to him, he drew near to me (James 4:8). I began to experience an intimacy and warmth of relationship with God that reminded me of Paul's prayer for the Ephesians:

> [I pray] that according to the riches of his glory he may grant you to be strengthened with power through his Spirit in your inner being, so that Christ may dwell in your hearts through faith—that you, being rooted and grounded in love, may have strength to comprehend with all the saints what is the breadth and length and height and depth and to know the love of Christ that surpasses knowledge, that you may be filled with all the fullness of God. (3:16–19)

David wrote that in God's presence there is "fullness of joy" and at his right hand are "pleasures forevermore" (Ps. 16:11). I began to move beyond affirming this truth to tangibly enjoying it. It suddenly dawned on me that, whereas I had trusted God with my mind, confident that he was sufficiently sovereign to protect my theology, I had not trusted him with my emotions. A few years later, I came across a statement in one of Jack Hayford's books that perfectly expresses what I was sensing at that time:

> It began to dawn on me that, given an environment where the Word of God was *foundational* and the Person of Christ the *focus*, the Holy Spirit could be trusted to do *both*—enlighten the intelligence and ignite the emotions. I soon discovered that to allow Him that much space necessitates more a surrender of my senseless fears than a surrender of sensible control. God is not asking any of us to abandon reason or succumb to some euphoric feeling. He is, however, calling us to trust Him—enough to give *Him* control.[7]

Several people played a significant role in my life at this time. I will never forget a particular Sunday morning in our church in Oklahoma when I saw something I had never seen before. A young lady and her husband

---

7. Jack Hayford, *A Passion for Fullness* (Dallas: Word, 1990), 31, emphasis added.

were visiting our church for the first time. During the singing of one of the hymns, I looked up and saw her. Unlike everyone else in the congregation, whose faces were either bored or buried in the hymnbook, she was gazing toward heaven, her eyes aglow and a smile of "joy . . . inexpressible and filled with glory" (1 Peter 1:8) spread across her face. I was deeply moved. I know it sounds odd, but I couldn't get over how much she appeared to be *enjoying* God. There was an openness, a vulnerability, a childlike confidence in her countenance that I couldn't help but envy. I can remember saying to myself, "I wish I felt like that about God. I wish I could be free enough to express my joy like she did." Both wishes (prayers) were to come true.

Not long after that Sunday morning, I obtained a videotape of a worship service led by Jeanne Rogers, who had been associated with the ministry of James Robison for many years. Virtually every night I watched and listened to the hour-long service. I saw people lifting their hands, dancing, weeping, rejoicing, and singing not simply *about* God but *to* God. Each time I was led away from merely watching the video into my own personal worship of the Lord. I sensed God draw near to me. I felt as if he were saying, "Sam, don't be afraid. Open your heart to me. Lift your hands to me. I want you to enjoy me. I want to enjoy you. I want to flood your spirit with mine" (cf. Rom. 5:5).

I immediately undertook an in-depth study of the Scriptures. I wasn't about to pursue anything that didn't have the explicit endorsement of the Word of God. I preached a twelve-week series on worship in the Bible. I read every book I could find on the subject. My life has never been the same since.

About this time, someone told me of a man named Dennis Jernigan, then worship leader at Western Hills Church in Oklahoma City. Soon many of us in Ardmore, Oklahoma, began making the short drive each month to the Night of Praise, a three- to four-hour worship celebration led by Dennis. That may sound a bit excessive for those of you accustomed to, at most, fifteen minutes of singing the first, third, and fifth verses of two hymns on Sunday morning. But it was in those services that God enlarged my heart to embrace him, freely and fully, without regard for what people might think. The music and message of Dennis Jernigan have contributed immeasurably to my growth as a Christian. It was Dennis, in fact, who first made me aware of Zephaniah 3:17 and the shocking discovery that God loves me so much that he *sings* over me!

Other worship leaders were unwittingly used by God to expand my enjoyment of God and the freedom with which I expressed that delight. On numerous occasions, I would find some excuse to drive to Dallas, Texas, only to end up attending a worship celebration that encouraged me to express my joy and satisfaction in God in ways that were as yet unacceptable (or at least extremely unfamiliar) to my church in Ardmore. On more than one occasion, I actually traveled to St. Louis, Missouri, to attend a marathon worship service led by Kent Henry, one of the most anointed worship leaders I know. My friend Jack Deere contributed in his own way to my growth by sending me every new Vineyard worship tape as soon as it was produced.

I still sing *about* God—I always will—but there's something different about singing to God. Yes, I still join with others and sing, "We love him." After all, we must never lose sight of the fact that we are a community of worshipers. But I much prefer engaging God one-on-one, my heart touching his, and singing, "*I* love *you!*"

I should briefly mention yet another related discovery I believe is repeatedly found in Scripture. Unfortunately, whereas I read it, I never experienced the reality of it. I'm referring to the outpouring of divine *power* during times of praise. When God's people exalt and enjoy him, he releases his power to heal them, encourage them, and enlighten them, among other things, in a way that is somewhat unique. When God's people worship, he goes to war on their behalf (see 2 Chron. 20). When God's people worship, he enthrones himself in their midst (Ps. 22:3). When God's people worship, he speaks to them and guides them (see Acts 13:1–3). When God's people worship, he delivers them from their troubles or comforts and sustains them in the midst of hardship (see Acts 16:19–40). He breaks the bonds of depression and anxiety and delivers his people from sinful addictions. In this way and countless others, he is put on display as the one and only God who delights in blessing his redeemed children.

Thus began my journey into the joy of worship.

CHAPTER 2

Do You Know Why You Exist? I Do

Why is there something rather than nothing? That question has baffled philosophers and theologians for centuries. Several years ago, I found a fascinating book titled *Why Does the World Exist? An Existential Detective Story.*[1] I won't delve into the author's complicated attempt to explain why there is something rather than nothing. I only want to draw your attention to the answer to its question. *The world exists for worship!* Worship is the end for which God created the world. I say this based on numerous texts of Scripture, one of which is 1 Peter 2:9–10: "You are a chosen race, a royal priesthood, a holy nation, a people for his own possession, that you may proclaim the excellencies of him who called you out of darkness into his marvelous light. Once you were not a people, but now you are God's people; once you had not received mercy, but now you have received mercy."

There's a quote often attributed to Mark Twain that goes like this: "The two most important days in your life are the day you were born and the day you find out why." Twain probably never said that, but the quote seems right. We all know the day we were born. That day for me was February 6, 1951. It is equally important—no, it is immeasurably more important—that we "find out why." I know why I was born on February 6. And if you know Jesus Christ as Lord and Savior, I also know why *you* were born. We were born physically and then born again spiritually, as Peter said in 1 Peter 2:9, in order that we might "proclaim the excellencies of him who called [us] out of darkness into his marvelous light." In other words, I was born to worship God! So, too, were you.

---

1. Jim Holt, *Why Does the World Exist? An Existential Detective Story* (New York: Liveright, 2012).

Now, be certain that you don't confuse what you *do* with the ultimate reason why you were both born and born again. When someone asks you what you "do," you immediately assume they mean: How do you earn a living? Your response is typically something along the lines of "I am a schoolteacher," "I am a housewife and mother of three wonderful children," "I am an attorney," "I am a salesman," or "I don't really do anything yet because I'm still in school to study and figure out what I'm supposed to do later on in life."

But what you *do* in terms of a job or career is not *why* you exist. There is something far more ultimate for which you were born and born again, and it can't be reduced to how you earn a living. Peter said that we were born and then born again to "proclaim the excellencies" of God. In other words, *we exist to worship*. This is why there is something rather than nothing. The end for which God created the world is worship!

What is worship? Here is my definition:

> Worship begins in the mind with deep, biblical thoughts about God, robust and expansive truths about who he is, his greatness and glory. Anything that passes itself off as worship that is not based on the biblical revelation of what God is truly like is nothing less than idolatry. This in turn inflames the heart and awakens passionate affections for God, such as yearning, joy, gladness, delight, reverence, gratitude, admiration, love, fear, zeal, awestruck wonder, brokenness for sin, and deep satisfaction in all that God is for us in Jesus. These in turn find expression in all of life, whether in singing or speaking or serving or sacrificing or acting or dancing or kneeling, as well as in the decisions we make or the way we live life in general.
>
> Worship happens when the *mind* is gripped with the revelation of great truths about God and the *heart and affections* are set on fire with joy, satisfaction, gratitude, gladness, and admiration, and the *mouth* explodes in songs of praise and proclamations of the incomparable greatness of God.

If you look closely at this attempt to define worship, you'll notice the absence of anything relating to style or type of music. Rather, my focus is on three key elements. The absence of any one of these elements undermines true worship. To say that worship begins in the mind is to say that a person must undergo *education* or *enlightenment* about who God is. Knowing who God is sets on fire the affections of the soul, leading to *exultation*.

To say that the mouth—indeed all of our lives—explodes in praise means a person is engaged in *exaltation* of God himself. There you have them: education–exultation–exaltation.[2]

And these elements *must* occur in that order. Each leads into the next. If you don't know who God is and are ignorant of what he has done to save your soul and reconcile you to himself through the person and work of Jesus, you can't exult in him. To exult (note: it is spelled with a *u*) is to enjoy, to relish, to take deep delight in someone. To exult is to celebrate and be satisfied. To exult is to find joy in someone. Exultation (again, with a *u*) happens when your heart, soul, mind, and spirit—your affections—are elevated and set on fire, and you find in God your deepest treasure and most enjoyable friend.

But if your exultation is not informed by your education, you may end up worshiping the wrong god! If the so-called god in whom you hope to exult is not the triune God of the Bible, your exultation is idolatry! If the so-called god in whom you delight isn't the God described in Scripture, your so-called exultation is little more than empty-headed, misguided, ill-informed, and deluded infatuation. That is why I say that before exultation can happen, education or enlightenment must occur.

Sadly, far too many professing Christians think worship begins and ends with education. They live under the illusion that simply knowing facts about God is the same as worshiping God. These folks can be quite unpleasant. They are fine if you want information. They can set you straight on what you should think and believe about God. But they are largely devoid of joy. They are often arrogant and elitist. They are frequently filled with pride because they believe they are better "educated" about God than you are. They are also *afraid of their affections.* They suppress their emotions. When a song, prayer, or biblical text stirs their feelings, they shut them down. They are terrified of emotions, fearing that feeling is antithetical to knowing and will lead to a mushy mind.

Then, of course, some Christians are afraid of education and dismiss it as unnecessary or dangerous. They are all about exultation. All they desire is to rejoice and feel passionately about God. Don't burden them with biblical truth about God. That only gets in the way of feeling good about him.

2. Thanks to John Piper for first articulating the nature of worship in this way.

The problem comes when they discover, much to their dismay, that the "god" in whom they exult isn't the God of the Bible.

The point is that both education and exultation are essential to true worship. And they must come in that order. Jonathan Edwards would often say that for there to be heat in the heart (exultation), there must first be light in the mind (education).

But education and exultation are not enough. They must produce exaltation (note: it is spelled with an *a*). To exalt is to lift up. To exalt is to elevate, extol, proclaim, make known, and draw attention to how wonderful and glorious the object of your worship really is. To exalt is to praise, honor, and declare for all to know that God is worthy of all adoration.

How does exaltation happen? It happens as a result of exultation! Again, God is most exalted in and by you when you exult supremely in and because of him. That is, God is most glorified in you when you are supremely glad in him. Your delight in God, your joy, happiness, satisfaction, and excitement in God are what serve to make him known as more worthy than anything else in the universe to receive your praise. If you want to praise God (exalt him), find pleasure in God (exult in him). The most effective pathway to praising God is enjoying God. To elevate God, enjoy God. To be enthralled and captivated and altogether satisfied with God is to exalt him.

In an otherwise excellent book, theologian John Frame defines worship as "the work of acknowledging the greatness of our covenant Lord."[3] So, what could possibly be wrong with that, you ask? It's not so much wrong as inadequate. Merely "acknowledging" the greatness and goodness of God is insufficient. We must both acknowledge and *rejoice in* the greatness of our Lord. No one expressed this better than eighteenth-century pastor Jonathan Edwards. We looked at this statement in the previous chapter, but it will do us well to read it again. To those of you who would argue that "acknowledging" or even "understanding" God's greatness is the most effective way to glorify him, Edwards asked,

Now what is glorifying God, but a *rejoicing* at that glory he has displayed? An understanding of the perfections of God, merely, cannot be the end of

3. John M. Frame, *Worship in Spirit and Truth: A Refreshing Study of the Principles and Practice of Biblical Worship* (Phillipsburg, NJ: P&R, 1996), 1.

the creation; for he had as good not understand it, as see it and not be at all moved with joy at the sight. Neither can the highest end of creation be the declaring God's glory to others; for the declaring God's glory is good for nothing otherwise than to raise joy in ourselves and others at what is declared.[4]

Here is how you most effectively honor God. It is when you give expression to truths such as this:

Oh, God, you are my greatest and most satisfying treasure. You are the most precious prize in all the universe. I value you above all earthly wealth and fame and power.

Oh, God, you satisfy my soul infinitely beyond what anyone or anything else in all the universe could possibly achieve.

Oh, God, you supply my soul with joy that is inexpressible and filled with glory.

Oh, God, it is in your presence—not in sex or alcohol or drugs or political power or respect or money or any other such thing—that I find fullness of joy and pleasures forevermore.

What this means is that, regardless of the mood or atmosphere of the service, our aim is to glorify God by enjoying him and all that he is for us in Jesus. True biblical worship happens anytime the mind is filled with exalted thoughts about God, the heart is inflamed with joy and love for God, and Jesus is treasured as preeminent in our souls.

This is far too important to rush through quickly, so let me slow down and say it again in slightly different terms. I want to be certain that you understand what I'm saying. Worship begins with our minds being enlightened by the truth of Scripture through the ministry of the Holy Spirit.

4. Jonathan Edwards, *The Miscellanies [Entry Nos. a–z, aa–zz, 1–500]*, The Works of Jonathan Edwards, vol. 13, ed. Thomas A. Schafer (New Haven, CT: Yale University Press, 1994), no. 3, 200, emphasis added.

That is why I care so much about theology. That is why I preach verse by verse through books of the Bible. If we hope to worship passionately, we must first think precisely about who God is and what he has done for us in Jesus. However, we must never forget that the ultimate purpose of theology isn't knowledge. It's worship. We learn to laud!

Simply put, worship that truly honors God must never stop with big ideas that fill our minds about who God is. These ideas must inflame our affections, stir our feelings, ignite our passions, and intensify our feelings of love, joy, awestruck wonder, brokenness for sin, longing for God, gratitude for what he's done, and hope in what he has promised. Truth is designed to take our breath away. *Education leads to exultation.*

These truths that fill our minds and then inflame our affections often are then expressed physically and externally in a variety of ways: singing, shouting, kneeling, bowing, lying prostrate on the ground, raising of our hands, weeping, dancing, trembling, and yes, even sitting still in our chairs! They are expressed in the Lord's Supper, baptism, public prayers, Scripture reading, and serving the needy or generously giving to them financially. The education that leads to exultation issues in the exaltation of God and all that he is for us in Jesus. This is why there is something rather than nothing. This is the end for which God created the world. This is the end for which God created you!

The mistake, then, is in conceiving of worship as if it's all about "thoughts" or all about "feelings" when the Bible insists it must be about both. Listen to what Jesus said in an important text about true worship. Of the religious leaders of his day, he declared, "You hypocrites! Well did Isaiah prophesy of you, when he said: 'This people honors me with their lips, but their heart is far from me; in vain do they worship me, teaching as doctrines the commandments of men'" (Matt. 15:7–9). You can say and sing all the right things and never truly worship God! You can walk into your church every Sunday morning with every song memorized so that you never have to look at the screen or the hymnbook or even open your eyes and still not truly worship God. You can move your lips, raise your hands, sit, sway, dance, or kneel, and never truly worship God.

What makes worship genuine and Christ-exalting? Jesus says it is *the engagement of the heart!* By this I think he means the totality of who we are: our thoughts and especially our affections and feelings for God. That is why

I said earlier that true worship always requires both exalted thoughts about God and passionate affections for God. One without the other is a disaster.

Every Sunday countless churches are filled with people who are passionate, emotional, energetic, and excited. Tears flow, laughter fills the air, dancers twirl and sway, the music is loud, hands are raised, and *God is offended*. Why? Because they worship a prefabricated "god" of their own making, a product of their own imaginations, a "god" who bears little to no resemblance to the God of the Bible. They come to church because they love the euphoric feeling of the music, the elevated emotions of the atmosphere, and the sheer fun of celebrating with other people. But they have very little grasp of who is being celebrated. Their affections, feelings, and the physical sensations that course through their bodies are unrelated to anything in the mind, and their thoughts about God are distorted and wrongheaded.

Some of them are even afraid of biblical truth, believing that thinking is a Spirit-quenching endeavor. To be fair, they aren't opposed to the Bible; they're just careless and even a bit indifferent about it. If they feel elevated emotions and their bodies tremble, and there is a tangible warmth and freedom to move about and shout, all is well.

And there are just as many churches today where people are thinking in perfect harmony with what the Bible says about God. Their theology is spot-on accurate. They love the thrill of intellectual enlightenment. They wouldn't be caught dead entertaining the slightest heretical thought about God. They can quote Scripture accurately. They can debate anyone on any doctrinal issue and win. And just as with the other folks, *God is offended*!

Why? Because, according to Jesus, their "hearts" are far from him. They feel little or nothing for him. God is at most a big idea in their minds. They believe they have successfully worshiped if they have been able to bring their thoughts into line with Scripture, if their ideas about God corresponded perfectly with the Bible. After it's over, they can confidently say, "I did it right!" They revel in mental satisfaction. But they don't really love the God about whom they've been singing. They don't rejoice and delight in him. He is not the preeminent treasure of their souls. They feel no zeal or longing for him. They accurately recite God's Word but do not tremble at it. They have no awe or fear or sorrow for sinning against him. Theirs is a coldhearted intellectualism.

It terrifies me to think that we would build a spiritual culture at my church in which anyone could "honor" God with their lips while their heart remained unaffected, lifeless, joyless, and distant from him. God forbid! We can't prevent anyone from doing that, but we want to make it extremely painful and uncomfortable for you should that be your choice. And if you are the sort who soars, being caught up in an ecstatic rush of emotional euphoria unrelated to biblical truth, we will do everything we can to grab you by the feet and pull you back to earth and tie your affections to the written Word of God.

Simply put: *God is not honored by heartless orthodoxy. Nor is he honored by joyful heresy.* It isn't enough to think correctly or to feel passionately. To worship God truly, we must have our heads aligned with truth *and* our hearts on fire with love and joy inexpressible and full of glory! Only then shall we worship in a way that honors God and brings spiritual enrichment to our own souls.

We Exist to Proclaim His Excellencies

You are a chosen race, a royal priesthood, a holy nation, a people for his own possession, that you may proclaim the excellencies of him who called you out of darkness in his marvelous light. Once you were not a people, but now you are God's people; once you had not received mercy, but now you have received mercy. (1 Peter 2:9–10)

Let's begin with how we got here. The apostle Peter described us as God's special and personal possession. To whom or what do we attribute the fact that we are a chosen race and a holy priesthood?

First, we are who we are because although we were once immersed in darkness, blind to the beauty of Christ and insensitive to the grandeur of God, he called us and brought us into the light of knowledge and forgiveness and understanding and joy (1 Peter 2:9). In sovereignly choosing us for life, God determined to deliver us from moral, spiritual, intellectual, social, and relational "darkness" (v. 9). Apart from grace, we don't see spiritual things; they are invisible to us. We call good evil and evil good. We are ignorant of and disdainful toward what is of infinite value and beauty, namely, God. We fail or refuse to see how splendid, majestic, and all-sufficient he is. We are blind to the beauty of Jesus, his excellency, glory, and power.

To be born again is to be brought out of such darkness into light, by which Peter meant understanding and enjoyment. It isn't enough to have the former without the latter. God has delivered us so that we might experience a new sight, a new taste. God's shining of his light into the soul doesn't merely awaken us to the existence or reality of spiritual things, of God and Christ and the Holy Spirit. It shows the excellency, glory, and beauty of such and imparts a new taste for them.

No one, in my opinion, has explained this with greater clarity than Jonathan Edwards. I have in mind what I consider to be his most important sermon. No, it wasn't "Sinners in the Hands of an Angry God." That was certainly his most famous sermon, but not the most important one he ever preached. That distinction must be reserved for "A Divine and Supernatural Light," which he delivered to his congregation in Northampton, Massachusetts, in 1734. The full title of this message is "A Divine and Supernatural Light Immediately Imparted to the Soul, by the Spirit of God, Shown to be Both a Scriptural and Rational Doctrine." The sermon was based on Matthew 16:17, where Jesus said to Peter, "Blessed are you, Simon Bar-Jonah! For flesh and blood has not revealed this to you, but my Father who is in heaven."

Edwards was quick to explain what the "divine and supernatural light" is not. It is not to be identified with the conviction of sin that unregenerate people experience. The Spirit can act upon the soul of the unregenerate without communicating himself to or uniting himself with that person. It is not to be identified with "impressions" made upon the "imagination." It has nothing to do with seeing anything with one's physical eyes. The divine and supernatural light does not suggest or impart new truths or ideas not already found in the written Word of God. Finally, it is not to be identified with those occasions when the unregenerate are deeply and profoundly affected by religious ideas. One may be moved or stirred or emotionally impacted by a religious phenomenon without believing it to be true.

So, what then, is the divine and supernatural light that God imparts to the souls of his elect? To use Edwards's own words, it is "a true sense of the divine excellency of the things revealed in the Word of God, and a conviction of the truth and reality of them, thence arising."[5] Edwards's Puritan prose is

---

5. Jonathan Edwards, "A Divine and Supernatural Light," in *A Jonathan Edwards Reader*, ed. John E. Smith, Harry S. Stout, and Kenneth P. Minkema (New Haven, CT: Yale University Press, 1995), 111.

odd, I admit. But don't let it obscure the truth of what he is saying. Again, it is the "apprehension of the divine excellency of things revealed" or "a true sense of the divine and superlative excellency." Edwards argued that a person doesn't "merely rationally believe that God is glorious, but he has a sense of the gloriousness of God in his heart."[6]

Edwards drew this critically important distinction between "rationally" believing that God is glorious and having a "sense of the excellency" of God's glory. This is the difference between knowing that God is holy and having a "sense of the loveliness" of God's holiness. It is not only a "speculatively judging that God is gracious" but also "a sense how amiable God is upon that account" or sensing the "beauty" of God's grace and holiness. This new "sense" or experience of the heart is not a new faculty of the soul but a new capacity wherein the soul finds lovely, sweet, excellent, and pleasing what before was regarded as ugly and unappealing. This, I contend, is absolutely essential to Christ-exalting worship.

Edwards based this distinction on the difference between two ways of knowing: there is, first, a merely speculative, notional, or cognitive awareness of some truth, which is to be differentiated, second, from "the sense of the heart" in which one recognizes the beauty or amiableness or sweetness of that truth and feels pleasure and delight in it. It is the difference between knowing or believing that God is holy and having a "sense" of or *enjoying* his holiness. "There is a difference," said Edwards, "between having a rational judgment that honey is sweet, and having a sense of its sweetness."[7]

This new sense of the heart that is supernaturally imparted to the soul enables one to be sensible "of the beauty and amiableness of a thing." Whenever this happens, the soul "necessarily feels pleasure in the apprehension."[8] So far from being afraid of such feelings or affections, Edwards would go on to locate the essence of all true religion and God-honoring worship in the experience of sanctified emotions (or better still, sanctified affections).

So how does this "new sense" come about? It may be imparted indirectly, and that in two ways. First, when the divine excellency of God is revealed to a person, it "destroys the enmity, removes those prejudices, and sanctifies the

---

6. Edwards, "A Divine and Supernatural Light," 111.
7. Edwards, "A Divine and Supernatural Light," 112.
8. Edwards, "A Divine and Supernatural Light," 112.

reason, and causes it to lie open to the force of arguments for their truth."[9] Second, it not only removes hindrances but positively helps reason; it causes the notion to be more lively and enables the mind to focus, think, and concentrate with more intensity on what is known.

This new sense of the heart may also be imparted directly. What Edwards meant is that this divine and supernatural light enables the mind and heart, by "a kind of intuitive and immediate evidence," to be convinced of the truth of the superlative excellency of such things. In other words, this light is given directly by the Spirit of God and not by means of natural phenomena. This is why unregenerate people can have the truths of the Word of God in their heads but find no pleasure, delight, or beauty in them. It is also why they can engage in what they believe to be acceptable worship of God when in fact it is anything but.

Men and women often experience a great deal of pleasure in learning something new. They delight in the study of nature and revel in the insights gained from observation and comparison. But, said Edwards, "this is nothing [in comparison] to that joy which arises from this divine light shining into the soul. This light gives a view of those things that are immensely the most exquisitely beautiful, and capable of delighting the eye of the understanding. This spiritual light is the dawning of the light of glory in the heart."[10]

In his message at the Jonathan Edwards Conference on October 12, 2003,[11] John Piper reminded those present that "sinners, left to themselves, will never see the beauty of the gospel. Christ crucified for sinners will always be foolishness to the natural man. There is only one hope—a divine and supernatural light immediately imparted to the soul by the Spirit of God." He added, "The natural mind—the fallen, worldly mind—does not want the glory of Christ as its treasure. And we all have this fallen mind by nature. We wouldn't mind escaping from hell. And we wouldn't mind the healing of our bodies and removal of guilt feelings and the reunion with our relatives [and] with our loved ones in heaven. All that is natural. But treasuring

9. Edwards, "A Divine and Supernatural Light," 112.
10. Edwards, "A Divine and Supernatural Light," 123.
11. John Piper, "A Divine and Supernatural Light Immediately Imparted to the Soul by the Spirit of God," Desiring God 2003 National Conference, Desiring God, October 12, 2003, https://www.desiringgod.org/messages/a-divine-and-supernatural-light-immediately-imparted-to-the-soul-by-the-spirit-of-god.

Christ above all, enjoying the glory of Christ above all joys—for that we have no taste."

So how do we gain this "taste" or "sense" for the sweetness and beauty of Christ Jesus? Piper answers, "Being converted to Christ—being saved—is a supernatural work of God. It is being born again by the Spirit of God—being given a new nature, a new spiritual taste, and a new way of seeing, and by that, an awakening of joy in Christ that you never knew before." This is the new birth. It brings us "a new taste for reality. The created things that we thought were the fountain of pleasure turn out to be empty, and the one we thought was a boring, bloody fool turns out to be a beautiful treasure chest of holy joy."

Thus, our only hope, says Piper, via Edwards, "is that something supernatural must happen in my heart that causes me to see Christ as the image of God, and see God in the face of Christ, and see the cross as the wisdom and power of God, and see Jesus as a treasure so valuable that I count everything as rubbish in comparison with him. A divine and supernatural light must shine in my heart so that Christ appears as compellingly glorious. That is, I must be born again. I must be regenerated by the Holy Spirit." And in this way, we truly honor God with our worship and adoration.

Second, Peter tells us in 1 Peter 2:10 that we are who we are because although there was a time when we were not God's people, we were made the recipients of divine mercy. In other words, God acted to impart his mercy to us and make us his own. So, the answer to the question of how we got this identity is that God gave it to us. He gave it to us by virtue of his irresistible call that brought us out of horrific and indescribable darkness into glorious and indescribably marvelous light! He gave it to us by showering us with saving mercy, showing compassion on spiritual fornicators and making us the pure bride of his Son. We are now enveloped in his marvelous light; we are now God's people because of what God has done! So, who are we? What is our identity? Peter singles out four things.

We are a chosen race. Whether Jew or Gentile, Greek or Roman, from Cappadocia, Bithynia, Russia, or Zambia, though from many races, colors, and ethnicities, we have been united by faith in Jesus to be a new people, a new race. But don't think of the word "race" here as you normally would in conversation today. This kind of race has nothing to do with ethnicity precisely because this race is comprised of *every* ethnicity! This chosen race is not solely black or exclusively white or only red or yellow or brown. It is comprised of each and every color and is therefore no single color in particular. It is a spiritual race, a chosen race!

We are a royal priesthood. Elders, pastors, staff, musicians and singers, nursery workers and sound technicians, each and every one of us regardless of title or function, are the priests of this new spiritual house, and our privilege now as priests is to draw near to God with spiritual sacrifices. The priests brought the sacrifices into the tabernacle in the Old Testament. But now that tabernacle is replaced by the Christian church. The atoning altar is replaced by Jesus Christ and his shed blood. And the priests are replaced by you, those who believe in Christ. Every believer is a part of this priesthood. This priesthood is not made up of those who wear special clothing, whether clerical collars or robes. It is not made up only of those who are called "Pastor" or who attended seminary.

We are a holy nation. This isn't talking about America! This can't be said about any geopolitical nation on earth. You are not merely part of the world anymore. You are set apart for God. You exist for God. And since God is holy, you are holy. Your ultimate allegiance isn't to any particular country. As much as I love the United States, and I do love it deeply, my loyalty is first and foremost to the church, the body of Christ, regardless of the geopolitical identity of those who comprise it.

Finally, *we are a people for his own possession.* Although God owns everything (Ex. 19:5), we are special! We are unique. But we aren't God's people because we are special and unique. We are special and unique because we are God's people! Don't ever reverse it!

We've now come to our third and final question. We learned both who we were and how we got to be who we are. Now we look at the most important question of all: *Why* are we? What was God's purpose in choosing us, showering us with mercy, and causing us to be born again so that Christ would be precious to our souls? Peter tells us the answer in verse 9: so that "you may proclaim the excellencies of him" who saved you. The word translated "excellencies" most likely refers to two things: God's attributes and God's activities.

God's attributes refer to his moral virtues, the greatness of his being, the splendor of his character; in a word, his *beauty*! Consider how perfectly harmonious in God are certain characteristics that in us often prove contradictory or at least in competition, such that we struggle to be both: God is both tenderhearted and firm, good and great, forgiving and just, humble and exalted, transcendent and immanent, gracious and holy, powerful and self-sacrificial, loving and severe, kind and royal, compassionate Father and conquering King, merciful and moral.

By God's actions, I have in mind his deeds, chief among which are calling us out of darkness into light, showering us with saving mercy, and making us his people.

To "proclaim" or make known this aspect of God's excellency means we are to tell of how he did this for us individually. Make your testimony known. Tell of his greatness and grace in your life. Seize every opportunity to brag on what he's done for you!

- Proclaim the excellency of his power in lifting you out of a pit of sin and self-destruction and exalting you to his right hand together with Christ!
- Proclaim the excellency of his redemptive purpose in Jesus in making provision for your ransom from slavery to sin and death.
- Praise the excellency of his self-emptying as seen in the willingness of the Son to put aside the glory of heaven and humble himself as a man who lived as a servant to others so that they might become the children of God.
- Praise the excellency of his immeasurable strength in raising Jesus from the dead, thereby conquering death for us all.
- Praise the excellency of his wisdom in making a way for the Righteous One to suffer and die for the unrighteous so that the unrighteous would be made righteous themselves and never die!
- Praise the excellency of his omnipresence such that he is always with you, at the same time he is always with me, at the same time he is always with everyone else who calls on him in faith!
- Praise the excellency of his triunity, in that he is mysteriously only one God but also three distinct persons.
- Praise the excellency of his eternal purpose that will be consummated when Christ returns, delivers the creation from its curse, and transforms our lowly bodies into glorified and resurrected bodies like Christ's!

To proclaim his excellencies: that is why we exist; that is the end for which God created the world. Worship is the reason why there is something rather than nothing.

Worship Is an End in Itself

The worship we read about here in 1 Peter 2 and everywhere else in Scripture is unlike every other Christian experience. It is eternally unique in one critically important respect: worship is an end in itself. In other words, worship that glorifies God must be expressed in conscious awareness that this is the ultimate goal for which we were created and redeemed. We do not worship God to attain some higher end, accomplish some greater goal, or experience a more satisfying joy.

Every other ministry or activity of the Christian serves some higher end. A "so that" is appended to everything we do except for worship. We preach so that. . . . We evangelize so that. . . . We cultivate fellowship in the body of Christ so that. . . . We study the Bible so that. . . . We make use of our spiritual gifts so that. . . . But when it comes to glorifying God by enjoying him and all that he is for us in Jesus, we can never say we do it so that . . . as if worship is simply a step on the path to something more ultimate, or as if worship is merely a door through which we proceed into something more important, or as if worship is merely one experience we pursue for the sake of yet another higher and more satisfying experience.

"But Sam," you may be tempted to reply, "with what ultimate goal in view do you ascribe glory and honor and praise to God?" None! For no goal is more ultimate than that.

"But Sam, what do you hope to accomplish by means of enjoying the majesty and perfections and goodness of God?" Nothing! Worship is not a means to the accomplishment of an end. *Worship is itself the end accomplished by all other means.*

Worship is not simply one part of your existence. It is *the point* of your existence.

PART 2

SCENES OF WORSHIP IN THE OLD TESTAMENT

CHAPTER 3

The What, Who, When, Where, and How of Biblical Worship

I've lost count of the number of weddings I've performed over the past fifty years of ministry, but I do remember one in particular. It was the wedding of an American man and a British young lady. She happened to be living with Ann and me at the time. When we sat down to discuss the details of the ceremony, she asked if I would be willing to use the vows that are frequently employed in older Anglican wedding ceremonies. "Sure," I said. Among the things that both the bride and groom would recite were these words of commitment: "My body will adore you, and your body alone will I cherish. I will, with my body, declare your worth." A bit later in the vows are these words: "With my body, I thee honor."

As I thought about these vows, I began to see how appropriate such words are not only for a husband and wife but also for the Christian and God. We worship God with our minds, hearts, and wills. But did you know that the Bible also calls us to adore, honor, and cherish God with our bodies? Numerous texts describe this, some of which we'll see in a moment. But for now, consider Romans 12:1, where Paul wrote, "I appeal to you therefore, brothers, by the mercies of God, to present your *bodies* as a living sacrifice, holy and acceptable to God, which is your spiritual worship." This really shouldn't surprise us given what Paul said elsewhere about our bodies: "Or do you not know that your body is a temple of the Holy Spirit within you, whom you have from God? You are not your own, for you were bought with a price. So glorify God in your body" (1 Cor. 6:19–20).

Our physical bodies are the temple, the dwelling place, of the Spirit of God himself. We tend to overlook that *spirituality is physical*. Five times in Genesis 1 we read of how God took stock of the physical creation and then said, "It is good." Although God is spirit, he created the entire physical realm and pronounced it good. We are not like the angels, who are spirit beings; we are also physical beings. And when God chose to enter this world in the person of Jesus to redeem us from sin, he took to himself a literal physical body. Here is how C. S. Lewis put it:

> There is no use trying to be more spiritual than God. God never meant man to be a purely spiritual creature. That is why He uses material things like bread and wine to put the new life into us. We may think this rather crude and unspiritual. God does not: He invented eating. He likes matter. He invented it. . . .
>
> I know some muddle-headed Christians have talked as if Christianity thought that sex, or the body, or pleasure, were bad in themselves. But they were wrong. Christianity is almost the only one of the great religions which thoroughly approves of the body—which believes that matter is good, that God Himself once took on a human body, and that some kind of body is going to be given to us even in Heaven and is going to be an essential part of our happiness, our beauty, and our energy.[1]

What would you say to a physically healthy married man who refused ever to embrace or kiss his wife? What would you think if he were to say, "Ah, my love for my wife is an affection of the heart. I don't need to love her physically, only emotionally"? I suspect that such a marriage would be headed for serious problems!

So, I want to talk about what it means to worship God with our bodies. But that is only one part of what I want us to consider. It is the "How" question in this chapter's title. But we must also answer the what, who, when, and where of worship.

---

1. C. S. Lewis, *Mere Christianity*, in *A Mind Awake: An Anthology of C. S. Lewis*, ed. Clyde Kilby (New York: Harcourt, Brace and World, 1968), 210–11.

What?

Perhaps the best way to answer the question "What is worship?" is to look at the terms used to describe it. There are forty-five different words in Hebrew for worship and a dozen or so in Greek. We'll look only at a few of the more prominent terms in the Old Testament terminology.[2]

1. The Hebrew word *halal* is used more than a hundred times and means something like "to be boastful," "to brag," or "to shout with excitement and triumph." The word carries the thought of excitement, exuberance, and exultation. When we sing, say, or shout "Hallelujah," we are saying, "Praise be to the Lord" or "Boast in the Lord!" It is used in such texts as these:

> Blessed are those who dwell in your house,
>> ever singing your praise! (Ps. 84:4)

> Let this be recorded for a generation to come,
>> so that a people yet to be created may praise the LORD.
>> (Ps. 102:18)

As one author has said, "*Halal* is the Hebrew equivalent of whatever you say when you are watching a football game and your team has just scored the winning points. . . . This is the word of any experience calling for excited boasting or joyful expression."[3]

2. The verb *yadah* means "to acknowledge in public" and is often translated in the Psalms as "to give thanks."

> I will *give thanks* to the LORD with my whole heart;
>> I will recount all of your wonderful deeds. (Ps. 9:1)

I'll have more to say about this in a moment.

---

2. More extensive insights into the nature of worship during the time of the Old Testament can be found in Andrew E. Hill, *Enter His Courts with Praise: Old Testament Worship for the New Testament Church* (Grand Rapids: Baker, 1993). In addition to the words cited in this chapter, he points to *darash* (to seek or inquire), *yare* (to fear or feel awe), *sharat* (to attend or minister), and *shaha* (bow down or do homage). See also Yoshiaki Hattori, "Theology of Worship in the Old Testament," in *Worship: Adoration and Action*, ed. D. A. Carson (Grand Rapids: Baker, 1993), 21–50.

3. Ronald Barclay Allen, *Praise! A Matter of Life and Breath* (Nashville: Thomas Nelson, 1980), 64.

3. The verb *barak* means "to bless"—

> Sing to the LORD, *bless* his name. (Ps. 96:2)

> *Bless* the LORD, O my soul,
>> and all that is within me,
>> *bless* his holy name! (Ps. 103:1)

4. The word *tehillah* is a derivative of *halal* and means "to sing *halals* to God, to laud and to praise with song." This is the word we find in Psalm 22:3:

> Yet you are holy,
>> enthroned on the praises of Israel.

5. The word *zamar* means "to pluck the strings of an instrument" or in some other fashion to "praise with music." We find it in texts such as these:

> It is good to give thanks to the LORD,
>> to sing praises to your name, O Most High. (Ps. 92:1)

> Sing to him, sing praises to him;
>> tell of all his wondrous works! (1 Chron. 16:9)

There are other Hebrew verbs that carry much the same meaning, such as *shir* (Ps. 96:1) and *ranan* (Ps. 95:1).

6. The word *shabah* means "to laud", as in Psalm 117:1:

> Praise the LORD, all nations!
>> Extol him, all peoples!" (Here the word rendered "extol" in the
>>> ESV could as easily be translated "*Laud* him, all peoples!")

The word means to speak well of someone, to eulogize them. Consider how we speak of those graduating with a superb academic record: "magna cum *laude*" and "summa cum *laude*."

7. The verb *rua* describes *shouting* to the Lord in joy, praise, and thanksgiving.

> Oh come, let us sing to the LORD;
> > let us make a joyful noise [i.e., let us shout] to the rock of
> > > our salvation! (Ps. 95:1)

> Make a joyful noise [i.e., shout!] to the LORD, all the earth!
> > (Ps. 100:1)

Biblical praise or worship is not only rarely, if ever silent; it is loud and noisy! More on this below.

There are other important words such as *qara*—"to proclaim" (Ps. 116:17) and *rum*—"to extol" or "to lift high" (Ps. 145:1). They are all words of sound. Worship in the Old Testament is almost always vocal and public.

We see then what worship is. It is the joyful, loud response of all that we are in adoration, celebration, and enjoyment of all that God is. In worship, we do not contribute to or increase God's greatness and glory, but we announce it, declare it, make it known, and proclaim the worth and majesty that is already and always true of him.

Who?

Is worship the privilege of an elite group of supersaints? Is it only the worship team and band who properly praise God? No! *All of creation* is responsible to worship and has the indescribable privilege of making known the greatness and glory of God.

> Let the heavens be glad, and let the earth rejoice;
> > let the sea roar, and all that fills it;
> > let the field exult, and everything in it!
> Then shall all the trees of the forest sing for joy
> > before the LORD, for he comes,
> > for he comes to judge the earth. (Ps. 96:11–13)

> Let the sea roar, and all that fills it;
> > the world and those who dwell in it!

> Let the rivers clap their hands;
> > let the hills sing for joy together. (Ps. 98:7–8)

> Make a joyful noise to the LORD, all the earth! (Ps. 100:1)

> Praise the LORD, all nations!
> > Extol him, all peoples. (Ps. 117:1; see Isa. 42:10–12;
> > > Rev. 5:11–14)

Even the angels are responsible to praise God:

> Bless the LORD, O you his angels,
> > you mighty ones who do his word,
> > obeying the voice of his word!
> Bless the LORD, all his hosts,
> > his ministers, who do his will!
> Bless the LORD, all his works,
> > in all places of his dominion. (Ps. 103:20–22)

> Praise him, all his angels;
> > praise him, all his hosts! (Ps. 148:2; cf. Ps. 89:5–7; Rev. 4–5)

When?

When is it appropriate to worship the Lord? *Always*! Is there ever a time that is inappropriate? No. Praise is an eternal exercise. Praise is not something you do only on a Sunday morning!

> I will bless the LORD *at all times*;
> > his praise shall *continually* be in my mouth. (Ps. 34:1)

> Then my tongue shall tell of your righteousness
> > and of your praise *all the day long*. (Ps. 35:28)

> In God we have boasted *continually*,
>> and we will give thanks to your name *forever*. (Ps. 44:8)

> I will sing of the steadfast love of the LORD, *forever*. (Ps. 89:1)

> I will sing to the LORD *as long as I live*;
>> I will sing praise to my God *while I have being*. (Ps. 104:33)

> Blessed be the name of the LORD
>> *from this time forth and forevermore!*
> *From the rising of the sun to its setting*,
>> the name of the LORD is to be praised! (Ps. 113:2–3)

> Through him then let us *continually* offer up a sacrifice of praise to God,
> that is, the fruit of lips that acknowledge his name. (Heb. 13:15)

To these we could add Psalms 71:6–8, 14–18, 24; 146:1–2; and Revelation 4:8.

Where?

In his encounter with the Samaritan woman at the well in John 4, Jesus said this in response to her question about whether it was fitting to worship God on Mount Gerizim or in Jerusalem, "Woman, believe me, the hour is coming when neither on this mountain nor in Jerusalem will you worship the Father.... But the hour is coming, and is now here, when the true worshipers will worship the Father in spirit and truth" (vv. 21, 23).

True worship has nothing to do with geography! It has nothing to do with where you are but rather what you believe and feel about the one true God. God couldn't care less which mountaintop you choose or in what city you live. In fact, it matters nothing at all to him whether your worship is on a mountain, in the valley, in this country, or in another. Many mistakenly think that worship is fitting only for a church sanctuary or some especially spiritual location, perhaps in the Holy Land or at a theology conference. But Jesus is Lord over the whole earth, and every square inch belongs to him.

You can worship him in your car, on a plane, during a walk in the neighborhood, while standing on the sideline of your child's soccer match, or while swimming in the pool. What matters is that you worship in the power of the Spirit and in accordance with truth. Your worship must be both theologically informed and spiritually empowered, both an expression of your mind and your spirit, both true and passionate, both thoughtful and affectionate.

Having said that, we can't overlook the fact that God calls on us primarily to worship him in corporate assembly with all of God's people:

> Sing praises to the LORD, who sits enthroned in Zion!
> Tell *among the peoples* his deeds! (Ps. 9:11)

We see this emphasis on worship among the people of God yet again in Psalms 22:22–25; 34:2–3; 35:18; 40:9–10; 84:1–4, 10; 95:1–7; 105:1; 135:1–3; 149:1; Colossians 3:16; Hebrews 10:24–25; and 1 Peter 2:4–10. I especially love Psalm 109:30:

> With my mouth I will give great thanks to the LORD;
> I will praise him *in the midst of the throng.*

One reason why God called his old covenant people to public praise is because that was the primary way in which he could receive the honor due his name. In Hebrew there is no word that means "thank you" when you are addressing God. That's hard for us to understand because words like *gratitude, appreciation,* and *thank you* are so common to us. In the Old Testament, the word used in place of *thanks* was *praise*! Instead of saying thank you to God, the people of Israel would turn and tell others what God had done. I'll illustrate from a story I once read.

A veteran medical missionary in India had developed a remarkable procedure to overcome the progressive blindness endemic to the people of that particular region. He would often comment that people who left his clinic, knowing they would now be able to see, would not say "Thank you," for that vocabulary was not in their dialect. Instead, they would say, "I will tell your name!" That is precisely what we find in the Old Testament. People praised God for all that he had done by telling of his name. It was their only way of saying thank you.

How?

The Bible is full of descriptions of the many bodily or physical expressions and postures of praise. Here are a few.

1. There is, first of all, *the clapping of hands*. I'm amazed at how often I hear people say that clapping of the hands or applauding of God is irreverent or sacrilegious. Are you kidding me? Consider these texts:

> Clap your hands, all peoples!
>> Shout to God with loud songs of joy. (Ps. 47:1)

> Let the rivers clap their hands;
>> let the hills sing for joy together. (Ps. 98:8)

> "For you shall go out in joy
>> and be led forth in peace;
> the mountains and the hills before you
>> shall break forth into singing,
>> and all the trees of the field shall clap their hands."
>> (Isa. 55:12)

Clapping is an expression of joy, triumph, and jubilation. When the mood or timing is right for clapping, do it with gusto. Of course, in times of somber and serious meditation or prayer, clapping would be less fitting. We must be sensitive to every situation in our times of worship.

2. *Dancing* is also frequently mentioned in Scripture. Let's remember that biblical dancing never involved two people of the opposite sex pairing off to music. Biblical dancing was never for the purpose of entertainment, amusement, or the cultivation of deep romantic feelings but was always an expression of joy and triumph following God's activity and grace shown to his people.

> Then Miriam the prophetess, the sister of Aaron, took a tambourine in her hand, and all the women went out after her with tambourines and dancing. (Ex. 15:20)

> Let them praise his name with dancing,
>> making melody to him with tambourine and lyre! (Ps. 149:3)

> Praise him with tambourine and dance;
>> praise him with strings and pipe! (Ps. 150:4; see also 2 Sam.
>> 6:14–16; Jer. 31:4, 13)

Someone may argue that since dancing is never mentioned in the New Testament, we are not allowed to incorporate it into our worship. But we know that dancing was encouraged and regularly practiced in the Old Testament, a truth no one disputes. Dancing is clearly not abrogated or forbidden in the New Testament. My view is that in the absence of an explicit prohibition of dancing in the New Testament, we may assume that it is an appropriate way of expressing our delight in God and our gratitude for all he has done for us. My friend Andrew Wilson articulates the theological argument for continuity between the two testaments this way: "The theological argument: continuity involves the assumption that since the same God is God of both testaments, and since his word still stands and is intended to be read in Christian meetings, none of his commands to his people can be set aside unless Jesus or the apostles clearly say so."[4]

3. People would also *stand* when they worshiped, a sign of respect and honor in the presence of God (see Pss. 134:1; 135:2; 2 Chron. 20:18–19). Although it is perfectly permissible to sit during corporate worship, especially for those who physically cannot stand, I find it extremely difficult to remain seated when God is being extolled.

4. *Kneeling* was also an appropriate posture in praise of God. Numerous examples can be cited in both the Old and New Testaments. People would kneel to pray (Dan. 6:10; Luke 22:41; Acts 7:60; 9:40; 20:36; 21:5; Eph. 3:14) and to praise (Ps. 95:6; 2 Chron. 6:13).

5. Some would bow their heads low or fall prostrate on the ground. One of the principal Hebrew words (*hawah*), often translated simply as "worship," means "to make oneself prostrate." We see this in Genesis 24:26, 48; Exodus

---

4. As stated in personal email, "We Can Dance If We Want To: A Response to Jonathan Leeman," June 23, 2016.

4:31; 12:27; 34:8; 1 Chronicles 29:20; 2 Chronicles 7:1–3; 20:18–19; Nehemiah 8:6; and Psalm 5:7. We should also remember that the Greek verb most often translated "worship" (*proskuneō*) literally means "to fall down and pay homage" (see especially Rev. 4:9–10; 5:8, 14; 7:11; 11:16; 19:10; 22:8).

6. I realize that *shouting* in a church service strikes some as irreverent and disruptive, but we can't ignore the overwhelming testimony of God's Word concerning this expression of joy and jubilation. I'm not suggesting that shouting is always appropriate. In church? Yes. At a memorial service for a friend who has died? No. Two men in my church regularly respond aloud to something in the sermon with loud shouts of, "Amen! Bless you, Lord!" On other occasions, they simply shout, "Yes!" If you still question whether shouting is appropriate, consider these texts:

> I will offer in his tent
> sacrifices with shouts of joy;
> I will sing and make melody to the LORD. (Ps. 27:6)

> Be glad in the LORD, and rejoice, O righteous,
> and shout for joy, all you upright in heart! (Ps. 32:11)

> Sing to him a new song;
> play skillfully on the strings, with loud shouts. (Ps. 33:3)

> Clap your hands, all peoples!
> Shout to God with loud songs of joy! (Ps. 47:1)

> Shout for joy to God, all the earth;
> sing the glory of his name;
> give to him glorious praise! (Ps. 66:1–2)

> My lips will shout for joy,
> when I sing praises to you;
> my soul also, which you have redeemed. (Ps. 71:23)

Jon Bloom, of Desiring God Ministries, raises a probing and uncomfortable question about why we may be reluctant to shout:

Do we ever feel the realities of the mercies of God, our redemption, the spiritual conflict we're engaged in, the promise of our resurrection, and Christ's ultimate triumph strongly enough to inspire a shout?

I ask this question for a couple of reasons. One, it might reveal a personal affectional deficit in our souls that we need to address with our Lord—that we're not connecting deeply enough with the realities of what's happened, and been promised, to us. And, of course, that's all of us to greater or lesser degrees. What we may need is to repent of giving excessive attention to lesser things, and spend more extended time meditating on "the surpassing worth of knowing Christ Jesus" (Philippians 3:8) in order to stoke the embers of our passion for him.[5]

Jon is not ignoring the fact that shouting can be superficial and calls for a close monitoring of our heart's motivation. But we should not let the fear of insincerity or showmanship blind us to the clear commands of Scripture. "What we all want," says Jon, "is for the saints to experience as much blessing of delighting in God as possible. And the Scriptures tell us, 'Blessed are the people who know the festal shout, who walk, O LORD, in the light of your face' (Psalm 89:15)."

7. The presence and use of musical instruments is pervasive in the Old Testament to describe how we are to worship the Lord. Here are some of those mentioned:

harps (1 Chron. 16:5; Pss. 33:2; 71:22)
lyres (1 Chron. 16:5; Pss. 33:2; 71:22; strings were made of the intestines of sheep; similar to a guitar)
cymbals (1 Chron. 16:5; Ps. 150:5)
trumpets (1 Chron. 16:42; 2 Chron. 7:6; Pss. 98:6; 150:3)
ten-stringed lute (Ps. 92:3; this could be a "zither" = a rectangular instrument with ten parallel strings)
flute (1 Sam 10:5; Isa. 30:29)
timbrel (Ps. 81:2 NIV; probably a portable drum)
pipe (Ps. 150:4; possibly an oboe-like instrument)

5. Jon Bloom, "Why Don't We Shout in Worship?," Desiring God, March 29, 2019, https://www.desiringgod.org/articles/why-dont-we-shout-in-worship.

stringed instruments (Ps. 150:4)

tambourine (Ps. 68:24–25)

8. Finally, there is the practice of *the raising of one's hands*. Explicit biblical precedent for doing so is pervasive. I don't know if I've found all biblical instances of it, but consider this smattering of texts.

> To you, O LORD, I call;
>> my rock, be not deaf to me,
> lest, if you be silent to me,
>> I become like those who go down to the pit.
> Hear the voice of my pleas for mercy,
>> when I cry to you for help,
> when I lift up my hands
>> toward your most holy sanctuary. (Ps. 28:1–2)

> So I will bless you as long as I live;
>> in your name I will lift up my hands. (Ps. 63:4)

> Every day I call upon you, O LORD;
>> I spread out my hands to you. (Ps. 88:9)

> I will lift up my hands toward your commandments, which I love,
>> and I will meditate on your statutes. (Ps. 119:48)

> Lift up your hands to the holy place
>> and bless the LORD! (Ps. 134:2)

> O LORD, I call upon you; hasten to me!
>> Give ear to my voice when I call to you!
> Let my prayer be counted as incense before you,
>> and the lifting up of my hands as the evening sacrifice! (Ps. 141:1–2)

> I stretch out my hands to you;
>> my soul thirsts for you like a parched land. (Ps. 143:6)

Then Solomon stood before the altar of the LORD in the presence of all the assembly of Israel and spread out his hands. Solomon had made a bronze platform five cubits long, five cubits wide, and three cubits high, and had set it in the court, and he stood on it. Then he knelt on his knees in the presence of all the assembly of Israel, and spread out his hands toward heaven. (2 Chron. 6:12–13)

And at the evening sacrifice I rose from my fasting, with my garment and my cloak torn, and fell upon my knees and spread out my hands to the LORD my God. (Ezra 9:5)

And Ezra blessed the LORD, the great God, and all the people answered, "Amen, Amen," lifting up their hands. And they bowed their heads and worshiped the LORD with their faces to the ground. (Neh. 8:6)

Let us lift up our hearts and hands
    to God in heaven. (Lam. 3:41)

I desire then that in every place the men should pray, lifting holy hands without anger or quarreling. (1 Tim. 2:8)

If someone should object and say that few of these texts speak exclusively of worship (see Pss. 63:4; 134:2), but only of prayer (as if a rigid distinction can even be made between the two; indeed, I can't recall ever worshiping God without praying to him!), my question is simply this: Why do you assume that the appropriate place for your hands is at your side and you need an explicit biblical warrant for raising them? Wouldn't it be just as reasonable to assume that the appropriate place for one's hands is raised toward heaven, calling for an explicit biblical warrant (other than gravity or physical exhaustion) to keep them low?

When asked, "Sam, why do you lift your hands when you worship?" the answer is: "Because I'm not a gnostic!" Gnosticism, both in its ancient and modern forms, disparages the body. Among other things, it endorses a hyperspirituality that minimizes the goodness of physical reality. Gnostics focus almost exclusively on the nonmaterial or "spiritual" dimensions of human existence and experience. The body is evil and corrupt. The body must be controlled and suppressed and kept in check lest it defile the pure praise of one's spirit. The body, they say, is little more than a temporary prison for the soul that longs to escape into a pure, ethereal, altogether spiritual mode of being. Nonsense!

The human hand gives visible expression to so many of our beliefs, feelings, and intentions. When I taught homiletics (the art of preaching), one of the most difficult tasks was getting young preachers to use their hands properly. Either from embarrassment or fear, they would keep them stuffed in their pockets, hidden from sight behind their backs, or nervously twiddle them in a variety of annoying ways.

Our hands speak loudly. When angry, we clench our fists, threatening harm to others. When guilty, we hide our hands or hold incriminating evidence from view. When we're feeling uneasy or fidgety, we sit on them to obscure our inner selves. When worried, we wring them. When we're afraid, we use them to cover our faces or hold tightly to someone for protection. When desperate or frustrated, we throw them wildly in the air, perhaps also in resignation or dismay. When confused, we extend them in bewilderment as if asking for advice and direction. When hospitable, we use them to warmly receive those in our presence. When suspicious, we use them to keep someone at bay or perhaps point an accusing finger in their direction.

Does it not seem wholly appropriate therefore to raise them to God when we seek him in prayer or celebrate him with praise? So again, why do I worship with hands raised? Because, like one who surrenders to a higher authority, I yield to God's will and ways and submit to his guidance, power, and purpose in my life. It is my way of saying, "God, I am yours to do with as you please."

Because, like one who expresses utter vulnerability, I say to the Lord, "I have nothing to hide. I come to you openhanded, concealing nothing. My life is yours to search and sanctify. I'm holding nothing back. My heart, soul, spirit, body, and will are an open book to you."

Because, like one who needs help, I confess my utter dependency on God for everything. I cry out, "O God, I entrust my life to you. If you don't take hold and uplift me, I will surely sink into the abyss of sin and death. I rely on your strength alone. Preserve me. Sustain me. Deliver me."

Because, like one who happily and expectantly receives a gift from another, I declare to the Lord, "Father, I gratefully embrace all you want to give. I'm a spiritual beggar. I have nothing to offer other than my need of all that you are for me in Jesus. So glorify yourself by satisfying me wholly with you alone."

Because, like one who aspires to direct attention away from self to the Savior, I say, "O God, yours is the glory, yours is the power, yours is the majesty alone!"

Because, as the beloved of God, I say tenderly and intimately to the Lover of my soul, "Abba, hold me. Protect me. Reveal your heart to me. I am yours! You are mine! Draw near and enable me to know and feel the affection in your heart for this one sinful soul."

For those many years when I kept my hands rigidly at my side or safely tucked away in the pockets of my pants, I knew that none would take notice of my praise of God or my prayers of desperation. No one would dare mistake me for a fanatic! I felt in control, dignified, sophisticated, and, above all else, safe. These matter no more to me. So, no, you need not raise your hands to worship God. But why wouldn't you want to?

Conclusion

I began this chapter with the words from an Anglican marriage ceremony. It is there that I wish to conclude and to say to God in my praise and celebration and worship of him:

My body will adore you, and [you alone] will I cherish. I will, with my body, declare your worth. . . . With my body, I thee honor.

FURTHER REFLECTIONS ON FEASTING
I SAW JONI DANCE (HOW A QUADRIPLEGIC WORSHIPS GOD)

If worship is ideally to involve our bodies as well as our hearts and minds, can a quadriplegic, confined to a wheelchair, truly honor God?

My wife and I were in Minneapolis in 2005 for a conference where Joni Eareckson Tada was speaking. Joni, a quadriplegic, was paralyzed in a diving accident in 1967. She was only seventeen at the time and celebrated her seventy-fifth birthday in October 2024. Joni, together with her husband, Ken, and a team from Joni and Friends Ministries, were on their way to England and then to Africa, but arranged to stop over in Minneapolis at John Piper's request and address the conference on the theme of suffering and the sovereignty of God. It is doubtful that anyone present, whether those of us in the audience or any of the speakers, had suffered the way Joni has. Few understand suffering's relation to the sovereignty of God with the biblical clarity and wisdom she does.

She delivered a stunningly great message. That in itself isn't news, for Joni has been speaking on this theme for many years, and the clarity of her convictions remains strong and articulate. I first met Joni in 1991 when we were both speakers at a Ligonier Conference hosted by R. C. Sproul in Orlando, Florida. I felt honored to meet her and even more so when she agreed to write the foreword to my book *To Love Mercy: Becoming a Person of Love, Acceptance, and Forgiveness* (NavPress; now out of print).

On this Saturday night, I saw something that was as impressive, if not more so, than anything I heard. The worship that night began with the rousing cry that we should march in the light of God. It was great to hear so many Reformed folk singing and, yes, actually moving (ever so slightly!) while they sang! But nothing could compare with what was happening on the right-hand side of the stage.

Joni handles her wheelchair as deftly as any NASCAR driver on a racetrack. No sooner had the music begun than Joni began to "dance." As much as a quadriplegic can dance, she danced. Joni has just enough movement and strength in her hands and shoulders to grip the controls on her chair and maneuver herself without the aid of others. Suddenly the chair began to move with the music. She thrust forward, then backward, then forward again, then backward. Smoothly, and yet with obvious passion, she turned to the right, then the left, then the right again.

I can't prove it, but my guess is that 2,500 pairs of eyes in that auditorium were fixed on the dancing quadriplegic! The forward and backward and side-to-side movements soon gave way to spinning. Joni began to turn her chair in circles, first clockwise, then back again. If she ceased her movements, it was only so that she could lift her hands as high as her paralysis would allow.

How Joni moved and "danced" is secondary. What's amazing is *that* she did. I was struck by the fact that a woman who has suffered so painfully and persistently for so many years loves her God and finds him so utterly worthy of her trust and hope that she wants to dance.

Joni shared in her message how she struggled spiritually in the early days and months after her accident. She wrestled with bitterness, self-pity, and anger at God and longed to die rather than live in that condition. But here she was, thirty-eight years into her paralysis, celebrating God, enjoying God, honoring and glorifying God. Not simply in her mind or her spirit but with her body as best that body could worship.

I was standing, as were most of the others. All of us could choose when to sit down, were we to tire of being on our feet. We could easily clap or shove our hands into our pockets. Throughout the conference, up till that night, I had taken for granted that I could walk out of the auditorium under my own power, feed myself, tie my shoes, and bathe without anyone's help. Joni, and others like her, don't take that for granted because they can't do any of those things. Yet, there she was, "dancing" in joy and delight and singing, "We are Marching in the Light of God." Marching indeed!

I thought to myself, *What she wouldn't give to do what you and I can but won't*. I'm talking about worshiping God with her body. She longs to praise and celebrate her God, not simply in spirit, mind, and soul, but with her arms, legs, and hands. That comes easily for the rest of us, at least in the physical sense. Many Christians, however, are terrified of raising their hands or kneeling or clapping or, dare I say it, dancing?

I'm not saying that everyone has to worship in the same way. I'm not saying that you and I are obligated to any particular physical expression when we praise our glorious God. But perhaps we need to think a bit more than we do about how to worship as holistic beings, men and women whose bodies have been bought with a price and are now the temple of the Holy Spirit. I don't want to put thoughts in Joni's mind or words in her mouth. But I can't help but wonder if every once in a while she looks out on an audience and says to herself, *Do they have any idea what a glorious gift and privilege it is to be able to celebrate and thank God and honor him with their bodies? I don't understand why they stand there like vertical cadavers.*

Actually, I don't think Joni would ever say anything like that, even to herself. I think she's far too humble, mature, and obsessed with God to use energy to criticize the rest of us for how we do or don't worship the Lord. So, let me put those words in my mouth and speak them to myself (and to you, if you think they apply). "Sam, do you have any idea what a glorious gift and privilege it is to be able to celebrate and thank God and honor him with your body? There are many others who would give almost anything to be able to do what you can but often won't."

Yes, of course worship is first and fundamentally an issue of the heart. It is the attitude of our minds and the passion of our souls and the commitment of our wills that we bring to God as we declare his majesty and proclaim his mighty works. But as I said, we are more than minds. We are bodies. We will always be bodies. So let us honor God with them, however that may seem fitting to you as you consider the magnitude of divine grace, mercy, love, and beauty.

I know how self-conscious people can be in a crowd, especially a Christian crowd. *What will others think? What will they say? Will I look like a fool? A weakling? An overly emotional, theological lightweight?* I don't think Joni cared what any of us thought. Perhaps if the time comes when she is supposed to worship us, she'll give it some consideration. Until then (which is never, of course), she's only concerned with what God thinks.

Finally, the greatest thing in all this is what it tells us not about Joni but about her God. What kind of God is this who can inspire such freedom and joy in one who, from a human point of view, would appear to have every reason to hate him? What kind of God is this who can evoke such confidence and trust in a person who faces such physical challenges? What kind of God is this who has the qualities, attributes, beauty, and glory that he can be found worthy of the praise and gratitude and "dancing" of a woman who has spent the last half century in a wheelchair? Wow! Now that's some God!

CHAPTER 4

Celebrating the Unsearchable
Greatness of the God Who Is Able

You can't not worship. Ignore my use of the ungrammatical double negative and try to understand what I'm saying. You can't not worship. Or to put it yet another way, "we can't not love something ultimate."[1] You may choose not to sing. You may choose not to bow down. You may choose not to lift your hands. You may choose not to give any outward or physical expression to your devotion, but you can't not worship.

Your heart and mind will always love something. It may be that you are so self-absorbed that you worship your own existence, your soul, your earthly abilities, and your accomplishments. It may be that you worship nature. Perhaps you are among those who believe the physical realm is in some sense divine or imbued with glory, and you are drawn to elevate it to a place of adoration, a place higher even than human beings, trees, mountains, streams, fields of lilies, gently flowing meadows, and the ocean and all it contains.

You may worship money without even knowing it, devoted to the pleasure it can purchase. Everything else in life is subordinate to your endless pursuit of wealth and the joy you are convinced it will bring you.

Simply put, you can't not worship. When God fashioned you in his own

---

1. James K. A. Smith, *You Are What You Love: The Spiritual Power of Habit* (Grand Rapids: Brazos, 2016), 20.

image, he hardwired your heart and mind so that you invariably look for something or someone into which you can pour yourself, to which you can devote yourself, and for which you can make the ultimate sacrifice. It is in that something or someone that you look for meaning and value and a purpose for living. That is what I mean when I say you can't not worship.

Maybe it's the beauty of the human body, the ecstasy of sexual intimacy, the hallucinogenic high of a chemical stimulant, the thrill of a Super Bowl victory, or a championship in the World Series. It may be that you prize promotion at your place of employment, the praise of your peers, or the satisfaction of finishing a project perfectly and on time. But the fact remains unchanged: you can't not worship.

The loyalty, love, devotion, and adoration of your soul will fix itself on something or someone. *You have an ultimate and unrivaled treasure* even if you can't always identify it. Believe me, it's there. So, my question for you is a simple one. If you can't not worship, why wouldn't you worship the most worthy and glorious thing that exists? If you can't not worship, why wouldn't you devote yourself to the one thing in all the universe that is actually deserving of your ultimate allegiance? If you can't not worship, why wouldn't you pursue the one thing, the only thing that can bring eternal satisfaction and joy to your heart?

I'm sure you see where I'm going with this. What reason could you possibly give for *not* devoting every ounce of physical, mental, and spiritual energy to the God of the Bible, the God who has Genesis 1 on his résumé, who called everything into existence out of nothing, who is immeasurably great, unfathomably beautiful, limitless in power, knowledge, love, mercy, and majesty?

Psalm 145

That is what Psalm 145 is all about. In Psalm 145 David, king of Israel, did his best to explain why God and God alone is worthy of all praise. It is the perfect starting point in our exploration of what authentic biblical worship is all about. Simply put, we need to know who this God is whom we adore. This is but one small step in the *education* of the believer that will ignite a fire of *exultation*. So, let's read it:

I will extol you, my God and King,
     and bless your name forever and ever.
Every day I will bless you
     and praise your name forever and ever.
Great is the LORD, and greatly to be praised,
     and his greatness is unsearchable.

One generation shall commend your works to another,
     and shall declare your mighty acts.
On the glorious splendor of your majesty,
     and on your wondrous works, I will meditate.
They shall speak of the might of your awesome deeds,
     and I will declare your greatness.
They shall pour forth the fame of your abundant goodness
     and shall sing aloud of your righteousness.

The LORD is gracious and merciful,
     slow to anger and abounding in steadfast love.
The LORD is good to all,
     and his mercy is over all that he has made.

All your works shall give thanks to you, O LORD,
     and all your saints shall bless you!
They shall speak of the glory of your kingdom
     and tell of your power,
to make known to the children of man your mighty deeds,
     and the glorious splendor of your kingdom.
Your kingdom is an everlasting kingdom,
     and your dominion endures throughout all generations.

[The LORD is faithful in all his words
     and kind in all his works.]
The LORD upholds all who are falling
     and raises up all who are bowed down.

The eyes of all look to you,
　　and you give them their food in due season.
You open your hand;
　　you satisfy the desire of every living thing.
The LORD is righteous in all his ways
　　and kind in all his works.
The LORD is near to all who call on him,
　　to all who call on him in truth.
He fulfills the desire of those who fear him;
　　he also hears their cry and saves them.
The LORD preserves all who love him,
　　but all the wicked he will destroy.

My mouth will speak the praise of the LORD,
　　and let all flesh bless his holy name forever and ever.

I want to impress on your heart that the "Thing" you were created to worship, adore, and love is God. You weren't created to spend your time gazing at your own reflection in a mirror. You weren't created to exhaust your energy trying to squeeze meaning and joy out of material stuff. You weren't created to devote your mental, physical, spiritual, and financial resources in the pursuit of the countless "idols" in our world that cry out for your affection. You were created for God: to see him, know him, celebrate him, rest in him, be satisfied in him, be enthralled and captivated by all that he is for you in Jesus Christ.

And in Psalm 145 David just scratched the surface of an infinity of reasons why this God and this God only is worthy of your undivided and singular devotion of heart, soul, mind, and body.

How Great Is Our God![2]

The heading above is not a question. It is a passionate proclamation, as you will shortly see as we turn our attention to Psalm 145. But first, a word about the role of this psalm in the prayer life of Israel.

---

2. Some of what follows has been adapted from my book *More Precious Than Gold: 50 Daily Meditations in the Psalms* (Wheaton, IL: Crossway, 2009) and is used here with permission.

I suppose there are as many kinds of prayers spoken prior to eating a meal as there are families who pray. When our two daughters, Melanie and Joanna, were young, the greatest problem we faced wasn't in getting them to pray but in getting them to finish before the food got cold. Neither of them was able to pray for the meal collectively, but they insisted on giving thanks for each individual item on the table. They thanked God for the potatoes, the fork, the milk, the salt, the napkin, the dessert, and just about anything else in sight. As time passed, we finally succeeded in getting our point across and were able once again to enjoy a hot meal!

At least one thing hasn't changed with the passing of centuries: people in the ancient world also expressed their gratitude to God before sharing a meal together. In fact, when they prayed before the midday meal, it was customary for them to recite all or part of Psalm 145. This was largely due to the statement in verses 15–16: "The eyes of all look to you, and you give them their food in due season. You open your hand; you satisfy the desire of every living thing."

But this psalm is important for more than what it tells us about where our food comes from. It is one of the most vibrant and expressive hymns of praise to be found anywhere in the Old Testament. It provides a marvelous declaration of the majesty and incomparable greatness of God and instructs us on our responsibility to worship him as he deserves. This is the only psalm in the entire book that has the single word *Praise* for its title.

Our approach to this psalm won't be verse by verse or in recognition of some elaborate structure. I'd like simply to summarize what it says, first, about God's character and, second, about our privilege and joy in celebrating him.

God's Character

David began with God's *greatness* (vv. 3, 6), a word that is horribly overused in our day and applied to anything from deodorant to the most obnoxious professional athletes. Historically, many have taken the adjective *great* and made it part of their name: Alexander the Great, Peter the Great, Catherine the Great, and in more recent times the comedian Jackie Gleason simply went by the title The Great One. And who could possibly forget the claim of boxer Muhammad Ali, who declared himself to be the GOAT: the Greatest of All Time? After Tom Brady won his seventh Super Bowl title, virtually everyone who follows football labeled him the GOAT.

But I beg to differ. God alone is great! Furthermore, his greatness is *unsearchable* (v. 3). No one ever has or ever will fully fathom the depths of his greatness. Not all the minds of all the ages using the most advanced scientific equipment can capture all that God is. He is utterly beyond and immeasurably past finding out. Many have claimed to have spoken the last word on some event or experience. But there never will be a "last word" on God. For in proclaiming that God's greatness is "unsearchable," David was saying that it is infinite. There is no boundary within which God's greatness can be confined. You need never fear that a day is coming, now or in eternity, when human beings will have discovered the last thing that can be said about God's greatness.

This is one reason why the Bible is so precious. It isn't simply a record of the religion of an ancient people or a volume of fascinating stories. The Bible is the infinitely and incomparably great God making himself known to you and me. The fact that the God who is by nature "unsearchable" has condescended and made himself "searchable" and "knowable" to hell-deserving people like you and me is almost too much for words.

David also pointed to God's *majesty* (v. 5), or better still, the *glorious splendor of his majesty*. There is nothing mundane about the majesty of God. A great light, luster, or spiritual brilliance emanates from his majesty's magnificence. God's majesty is blinding and breathtaking and beyond comprehension or calculation. This is the sort of majesty that mesmerizes, thrills, and enthralls.

Ah, but he is also *good* (vv. 7, 9). Can you envision how horrific it would be if this great and powerful and awesome God were bad? Don't take his goodness for granted, but joyfully celebrate it and rest confidently in it. To say that God is good is to say something about both his nature and his activity. He is good in the core of his being, and therefore all he does is also good. That doesn't mean we will always understand how some of what he does is good. At times it looks bad. But I assure you that it is good. And that is one of the things I look forward to in the age to come, when God will demonstrate to us how everything he ever did or permitted was perfectly and altogether good.

Our God is also *righteous* (v. 7). To say that God is righteous is not to say that he conforms to human standards of right and wrong. Rather, he conforms perfectly to the standards of his *own* perfections. One of the reasons we struggle to embrace the righteousness of God is that we judge him by our standards instead of the standard of his own nature. But if he is wholly and altogether righteous, how can unholy and unrighteous people like you and me enter his presence? The answer follows.

According to verse 8, God is "gracious and merciful, slow to anger and abounding in steadfast love." Yes, God has a holy temper, but he has a very long fuse! Even those who deny and blaspheme his name are recipients of his patience and long-suffering. He permits his enemies to live, to spew forth their horrid sacrilege while blessing them with food, air, and earthly pleasures, affording them even more time and opportunity to repent (cf. Rom. 2:4–5).

"Steadfast love" is the translation of the Hebrew word *hesed*, which is also rendered by such terms as *mercy, goodness, loving-kindness, loyal love,* and occasionally the word *grace.* Its primary emphasis is on God's covenant love and his steadfast commitment to his people.[3]

But look closely at verse 8. God is not simply steadfast and unchanging in his love. He also *abounds* in it. You and I know what it feels like to run low on love. We love others, even the unlovely and those who don't love us back, and we eventually run out of emotion. We can find ourselves empty of affection. We lack the capacity to love beyond a certain limit. But God abounds in his steadfast love. His love never scrapes the bottom of the barrel or needs to be replenished. Every time you and I might be tempted to think that God's love has run its course and met its limit, he proves us wrong as his love abounds and overflows and surprises us with new expressions of affection. You're never going to wake up and discover your sin has drained God's love of its supply. His love is an infinitely deep well of refreshing water.

All these qualities of character inform his deeds and give shape to his providential oversight of creation. So, let's look briefly at what this great, majestic, good, righteous, gracious, merciful, and longsuffering God *does*. In other words, let's move now from what David said God is like to what David said God does.

For one thing, he *works* (vv. 4, 5, 6, 9, 12). David went even further and

---

3. Sam Storms, *The Steadfast Love of the Lord: Experiencing the Life-Changing Power of God's Unchanging Affection* (Wheaton, IL: Crossway, 2025).

spoke of God's "mighty acts," "wondrous works," and "awesome deeds"! God has never done anything mundane or boring or routine. All his works and acts partake of the magnificence of his nature and reflect the beauty and harmony and glory of who he is.

More specifically, he *rules* (vv. 11–13). Unlike every other ruler, God is in office for life (see Dan. 4:3, 34)! There is no transition team to move from one heavenly administration to another. There are no inaugural ceremonies (God has always been on the throne). There is no concern over the qualifications of a vice God should the Almighty be unable to serve out the full extent of his term. There are no tearful goodbyes to the staff, no waving "so long" from the steps of a helicopter, no cleaning out of the desk in the heavenly Oval Office to make way for his successor.

Among earthly kings, especially in British history, we hear of James I and James II and Charles I and Charles II. While I was writing this book, Queen Elizabeth's firstborn son, Charles, was crowned King Charles III of England. Nothing of the sort ever occurs in the heavenly kingdom. There is no Yahweh I and Yahweh II, for God is first and last and there is no other. None preceded him, and none shall succeed him.

The everlasting ruler *upholds or sustains* (v. 14) all who are weak and prone to falling. We should read this verse in connection with verse 13 and "admire the unexpected contrast: he reigns in glorious majesty, yet conde-scends to lift up and hold up those who are apt to fall."[4]

He also *supplies* (v. 15) food and life and *satisfies* the desires of his cre-ation (v. 16). This truth about God is unpacked with even greater detail in Psalm 104. How often have you thought about the fact that God causes "the grass to grow" (104:14)? We typically speak only of God when it comes to the big, demonstrable miraculous events in history, such as the parting of the Red Sea, virgin conception of Jesus, and Jesus' bodily resurrection. But our God's greatness is seen in the fact that he oversees and causes the growth and development of every single blade of grass on the earth! His power and meticulous providential orchestration of something seemingly as insignifi-cant as grass is grounds for great praise of a great God.

God is altogether *righteous* in his dealings with us (v. 17). That's easy to believe when things are going well. But God is righteous in *all* his ways,

---

4. Charles H. Spurgeon, *The Treasury of David* (Peabody, MA: Hendrickson, n.d.), 3:380.

not just in the circumstances that favor us. Nothing is more difficult to acknowledge when we are in trouble, when he afflicts us, or when we feel he has been unfair.

And we must never forget that he is not only righteous but also "*kind* in all his works" (v. 17). We don't typically put those two words together, for it's difficult to be both at the same time. We swing to one or the other extreme and are either rigid and demanding or excessively lenient and tolerant. All too often the people we perceive as "righteous" are downright "mean" and inflexible. But in God, righteousness and kindness find perfect harmony, as seen most readily in Jesus, who was simultaneously high and humble, both strong and tender, righteous yet gracious, powerful and merciful, authoritative yet tender, holy yet always forgiving, just yet compassionate, at times angry yet also gentle, and firm yet friendly.

Finally, God *answers prayer* (vv. 18–19), *preserves* the righteous (v. 20), and *destroys* the wicked (v. 20). Do you "call" on God in truth and sincerity? Do you "cry" out to him in prayer? If you do, you can be assured that he will be "near" to you. Your prayers may not always be answered in the way you think is best, but they are always answered in the way God thinks is best.

When David declared that God "preserves all who love him" (v. 20), he didn't mean that the wicked can't kill the righteous. We see all the time and throughout history instances where the "wicked" persecute, imprison, torture, and kill those "who love" God. But David's point was that such is the worst and most they can do. They may take our lives physically, but God preserves our lives spiritually. Nothing done to us by evil people can separate us from God's love.

Some might be tempted to question whether God is really righteous and kind if he "destroys" or judges eternally those he regards as "wicked." But would God be worthy of our praise and adoration if he ignored wickedness, refused to judge evil men, and turned a blind eye to unrighteousness and idolatry? Would a God devoid of holiness and justice be a God whom we could reverence? I think not. Why, then, does he not judge and destroy us as well? After all, we were once "wicked" and immersed in unbelief. Yes, and the only reason he does not visit the judgment of our sin upon us is because he has visited it upon his Son in our place! But those who despise and spurn the offer of eternal life, which Jesus died to obtain, will surely be judged. God will "destroy" them.

Our Celebration of Our Great God

How does one respond to such a God? Such splendor, majesty, mercy, and might call for the loudest and most passionate of praise.

We are to *extol* God (Ps. 145:1), which literally means "to be high." God *is* high, and we acknowledge and declare it so. We can't make him higher than he already and always is, but we can declare him to be infinitely high and worthy of praise. To extol is to *exalt* above all others, to set as preeminent over every other thing. We also *bless* (vv. 1, 2, 10) and *praise* (v. 2), and *commend* and *declare* (vv. 4, 6) and *meditate* (v. 5) and *speak* (v. 6) and *pour forth* praise of his abundant goodness (v. 7).

As if that weren't enough, we *sing aloud* (v. 7) and *give thanks* (v. 10) and *make known* (v. 12) his mighty deeds. What do each of these expressions of praise have in common? They are all vocalized declarations. Some of you might say, "I can't carry a tune in a bucket. I can't sing. I'm extremely introverted and not expressive." I hear you. And all I want to say in response is this: you will never fully worship God in proportion to his greatness and will never experience the depths of delight that comes from celebrating who he is and what he's done until you give vocal expression to your praise.

And let's be diligent to do it *every day* (v. 2), and not just on Sunday morning. Indeed, our praise and exaltation of God is to continue *forever and ever* (vv. 1, 2, 21):

> Through all eternity to thee,
> A joyful song I'll raise;
> But oh, eternity's too short
> To utter all thy praise.[5]

A heart flooded with thoughts of the splendor of God and what he does can no more conceive of an end of praise than it can conceive of an end of God himself!

Above all else, may our praise and honor and joyful celebration of this God be *great*, for "great is the LORD, and [therefore] *greatly to be praised*" (v. 3). True worship must always be proportionate to the object of adoration.

---

5. Adam Clarke, quoted in Spurgeon, *The Treasury of David*, 3:384.

Great praise for a great God. "No chorus is too loud, no orchestra too large, no Psalm too lofty for the lauding of the Lord of Hosts."[6]

You will notice that I said nothing about the kind of songs we sing. One can genuinely worship God with a medieval hymn, a contemporary chorus, or spoken prose. I have said nothing about physical posture. One can genuinely worship God sitting, standing, kneeling, lying prostrate on the ground, dancing, with hands raised, with hands in pockets, with hands clapping, with tears flowing, or with a wide smile. I said nothing about the presence or absence of musical instruments. One can genuinely worship God by singing a cappella or with musical accompaniment, by the human voice alone or with a symphony orchestra. I said nothing about the freedom, form, or style in which worship is expressed. One can genuinely worship God through centuries-old structured liturgy or Spirit-prompted spontaneity, through prewritten confessions of faith or impromptu shouts of praise.

10,000 Reasons to Worship Our Great and Glorious God

> Now to him who is able to strengthen you according to my gospel and the preaching of Jesus Christ . . . to the only wise God be glory forevermore through Jesus Christ! Amen. (Rom. 16:25, 27)

As I said earlier, the ultimate goal of theology is not knowledge but worship. If our learning and knowledge of God do not lead to the joyful praise of God, we have failed. We learn only that we might laud. Theology without doxology is idolatry. The only theology worth studying is a theology that can be sung. As noted before, worship is an end in itself. It is not pursued with a view to anything higher or more important. It is not a means or instrument or stepping stone to something loftier; rather, it is the ultimate end for which all other activities are means or instruments.

With that in mind, you can see that I have used in the subheading Matt Redman's song "10,000 Reasons" to make an important point. Let me explain. From Psalm 145 we turn to Paul's concluding doxology in the book

---

6. Spurgeon, *The Treasury of David*, 3:376.

of Romans. When he referred to God in verse 27 as "the only wise God" (cf. 1 Tim. 1:17), he didn't mean that there are a bunch of other gods that are foolish and only our God is wise. No. There is only one God, and he is infinitely wise. He knows precisely what to do in every situation. He is never caught scratching his head, trying to decipher which of multiple options is the most effective way to achieve some goal he has in mind.

When you think back over the book of Romans and the many things God has done to achieve our salvation, you can rest assured that the process he chose was the wisest and best way to secure our forgiveness and exalt his own glory. There was no better way to save us than how he has saved us through Jesus.

So, then, what do Paul's words "to the only wise God be glory forevermore" mean? The interesting thing is that there is no verb here in the original text. Literally Paul was saying, "To him, glory!" Of course Paul was appealing to us to ascribe all glory to God alone. But let's be careful here. When we glorify God or when we give him glory, we are not adding to his majesty or making him more beautiful and honorable than he was before we decided to glorify him. We glorify God by *declaring* that he is glorious. We *acknowledge* it. We *prize* it. We *treasure* his glory. God's glory cannot increase or decrease. It is eternally infinite, and our task is to *make this known* to the world by means of the person and work of Jesus Christ whom we preach.

Why is God worthy of our praise? Psalm 145 gave us numerous reasons, and Paul's letter to the Romans also contains countless answers to that question. Even then, it is only a scratching of the surface of the many things about who God is and what he does that ought to elicit our adoration and exultation. Consider these:

- Jesus is the Christ who came in human flesh and was raised from the dead (Rom. 1:1–4).
- God calls us into relationship with Jesus such that we truly belong to him (Rom. 1:6).
- God loves us and has called us to be saints (1:7).
- The gospel is the power of God for salvation. No other power, no other means, no education or earthly accomplishment can save, only God's power in Christ (1:16).

- God has revealed himself in nature, thereby rendering all without excuse (1:19–21). In this way, we see that he is eminently fair and just in holding all accountable.
- Any and all may be saved, without regard for ethnicity, by faith in Jesus (3:21–24).
- God has provided Jesus as the propitiation for our sins, thereby satisfying the demands of his own justice and appeasing his wrath against sin (3:25).
- God declares us righteous by grace alone, through faith alone, in Christ alone (3:23–24).
- God justifies the ungodly (4:5).
- We now have peace with God by faith in Christ (5:1).
- We rejoice in hope of the glory of God (5:2).
- We can now rejoice in our suffering because God has assured us that it will ultimately produce in us a transformed character that endures (5:3–4).
- Our hope in God will never put us to shame (5:5).
- God has poured out his love into our hearts through the Holy Spirit (5:5).
- Christ died for ungodly people (5:6).
- God's love for us is seen preeminently in the gift of Jesus to die for us (5:7–8).
- The fact that Jesus died for us when we were his enemies is the guarantee that he will live for us now that we are his friends (5:8–11).
- Jesus, the last Adam, has overcome and triumphed through righteousness the first Adam, who plunged the race into sin and corruption (5:12–21).
- God has united us with Jesus, as seen and testified to in baptism (6:1–4).
- Because we died with Jesus, we now live with him and are no longer slaves to sin (6:5–11).
- We are no longer under law but under grace (6:14).
- We have been given the free gift of eternal life in Christ (6:23).
- God has enabled us to bear fruit for him (7:4).
- God is in the process and will ultimately bring to consummation our deliverance from the body of death in which we now live (7:24–25).

- There is therefore now no condemnation for those who are in Christ (8:1).
- The Holy Spirit now indwells us (8:11).
- We are the adopted sons and daughters of God (8:12–17).
- The Spirit bears witness to us that we belong to God as our Father (8:16).
- God has promised us that we will be fully redeemed and glorified in our bodies (8:18–25).
- The Spirit helps us when we don't know what to pray for (8:26–27).
- God assures us that he is orchestrating all events to make us look more like Jesus (8:28).
- God loved and foreknew us before the foundation of the world (8:29).
- God predestined us to be conformed to the image of Jesus (8:29).
- God called us and justified us and is so certain to glorify us that he speaks of it as an accomplished fact (8:30).
- God did not spare his own Son but delivered him up for us to guarantee that he will gladly provide us with all lesser blessings (8:32).
- Jesus intercedes for us with God and overcomes every accusation or objection (8:33–34).
- Nothing can separate us from God's love (8:35–39).
- God elected us to inherit eternal life based on nothing other than his sovereign and gracious good pleasure (9:6–22).
- God has assured us and all mankind that if we confess Jesus as Lord and believe God raised him from the dead, we will be saved (10:9–11).
- God has determined to save both believing Jews and believing Gentiles, uniting them as one people who will inherit all the promises (11:1–32).
- No matter what may come our way, we can rest assured that all things are from the Lord and through him and to him (11:33–36).
- God has given us guidance on what it means to walk in obedience to him, how to live righteously in a fallen and corrupt world (12:1–13).
- God has assured us that we need not seek vengeance on those who mistreat us for he will bring justice to bear on all (12:14–21).
- God has provided human government as a deterrent to human wickedness and a source of reward and praise for human obedience (13:1–7).

- God has granted us freedom on secondary matters and has urged us not to judge or condemn those who may differ with us on such issues (14:1–23).
- God supplies us with endurance and encouragement through the power of the Scriptures (15:1–7).
- God promises to fill us with all joy and peace and hope as we trust what he has revealed in the Scriptures (15:13).
- God has invited us to join him in changing history through prayer (15:30–33).
- God has assured us that we have the authority to resist Satan now and will one day be God's instruments by which the devil is fully and finally crushed (16:20).
- God has promised to strengthen us through the gospel (16:25–27).

Our God Is Able!

There is one more reason why God is worthy of our worship, and we find it in the opening words of Romans 16:25, where Paul declared that God is able! I trust you have noticed in Scripture how often the ability or power of God is emphasized and extolled. I often think of the question Jesus asked the two blind men in Matthew 9. "Do you believe that I am *able* to do this?" When they responded in the affirmative, Jesus said, "According to your faith be it done to you" (vv. 28–29). In other words, because you believe I have the power to heal the blind, I will do precisely that.

When a leper approached Jesus he said, "If you will, you *can* make me clean" (Mark 1:40). The leper had no doubts about the ability of Jesus to heal him. He just didn't know if Jesus wanted to. Jesus proceeded to heal the man. Later the father of a boy who was demonized and couldn't speak said to Jesus, "If you *can* do anything, have compassion on us and help us." Jesus responded by saying, "If you *can*! All things are possible for one who believes" (Mark 9:22–23). Believes what? Well, evidently he meant that if you believe I *can* do this, it will be done for you. Once again we see that Jesus places great emphasis on whether a person believes he has the ability and can do what is asked of him.

In Romans 4 we read about Abraham who, along with his wife, Sarah, was well beyond the age when they could have a child. But Abraham "grew strong in his faith as he gave glory to God, fully convinced that God was *able* to do what he had promised" (vv. 20–21). In Hebrews 11 we read yet again about Abraham, who was willing to offer up Isaac as a sacrifice because "he considered that God was *able* even to raise him from the dead" (v. 19). Paul told Timothy, his spiritual son, that his confidence in God had not wavered for he was convinced that God was "*able* to guard until that day what has been entrusted to me" (2 Tim. 1:12).

We see this emphasis on the power of God to do great things repeated in several doxologies. For example, one that you likely know well is found in Ephesians 3:20 where Paul declared, "Now to him who is *able* to do far more abundantly than all that we ask or think, according to the power at work within us." Jude closed his short letter by declaring, "Now to him who is *able* to keep you from stumbling and to present you blameless before the presence of his glory with great joy" (v. 24).

And then, of course, we have the doxology before us in Romans 16:25–27, the final paragraph in Paul's magnificent epistle to the Romans. Once again, Paul broke out in praise of him "who is *able* to strengthen you according" to the gospel of Jesus Christ (v. 25). Clearly, Paul intended for his concluding words to be a hymn or song of praise of the God who is *able* to do the incredibly glorious and majestic things that Paul described in Romans.

Do you believe this? May I suggest that before you pray, you begin by confessing and declaring, "God, I know without any doubt that you *can* do this for me. I don't presume to know whether you will, as I submit to your sovereign good pleasure. But I know and am confident that you are *able* and that no power in heaven or on the earth can thwart your sovereign purpose."

I didn't cite 10,000 reasons for our worship, but if given enough time and space, I think I could! All glory and praise be to him who loved us and saved us from our sins!

Praise be to the God who is always able!

CHAPTER 5

Sing to Him a New Song![1]

When we stand and sing praise to God, we should probably pause and express our gratitude to the sixteenth-century Protestant Reformer Martin Luther (1483–1546). Luther was largely responsible for introducing the practice of congregational singing into the life of the church. From the Council of Laodicea in the fourth century until Luther in the early years of the sixteenth century, virtually no one sang in church except for the ordained clergy.

Luther was convinced that if God's people were to worship God as the Bible commands, they must sing. He would often put Christian lyrics to the melodies sung in German beer taverns and introduce these songs in Protestant churches. Luther had an extremely high view of the life-changing power of music. In fact, one of Luther's enemies is reported to have said that he "had damned more souls with his hymns than with all his sermons!"

Luther was committed to the primacy of song for spreading the gospel and worshiping God. "I have no use for cranks who despise music," said Luther, "because it is a gift of God. Music drives away the Devil and makes people happy; they forget thereby all wrath, unchastity, arrogance, and the like. Next after theology I give to music the highest place and the greatest honor."[2]

That a man with such indomitable courage and intellectual brilliance should place such a high premium on singing is unexpected, to say the

---

1. Some of this chapter is an adaptation of what I wrote in *The Singing God: Feel the Passion God Has for You ... Just the Way You Are* (Lake Mary, FL: Passio, 2013), 21–23, and is used with permission.
2. Quoted in Roland Bainton, *Here I Stand: A Life of Martin Luther* (Nashville: Abingdon, 1950), 341.

least. "Experience proves," wrote Luther, "that next to the Word of God only music deserves to be extolled as the mistress and governess of the feelings of the human heart. We know that to the devils [i.e., demons] music is distasteful and insufferable. My heart bubbles up and overflows in response to music, which has so often refreshed me and delivered me from dire plagues."[3]

Luther had little patience for those who dismissed the power and primacy of singing. "He who does not find this [singing] an inexpressible miracle of the Lord is truly a clod and is not worthy to be considered a man."[4] Tell us what you really think, Martin! Luther insisted that "the gift of language combined with the gift of song was only given to man to let him know that he should praise God with both word and music, namely by proclaiming [the Word of God] through music."[5] Whether you wish "to comfort the sad, to terrify the happy, to encourage the despairing, to humble the proud, to calm the passionate, or to appease those full of hate, name the emotions, inclinations, and affections that impel men to evil or good—what more effective means than music could you find?"[6]

There are few things in God's creation that have the power that music has. What else in the world has such universal influence? Music is present in every human culture. Wherever it is found, it can unite or divide people. It stirs people to patriotic fervor, and it arouses them to unbridled fury. It can soothe the spirit, or it can bring disquiet and fear. Music can create comfort and inflict discomfort. Virtually everything we do in life is done to musical accompaniment: riding in elevators, shopping, eating in restaurants, driving to and from work, watching a movie, cheering on a sports team, and, of course, worshiping God!

I believe that God created tone, melody, and rhythm, together with our capacity to recognize them, because he wants to be worshiped and adored and magnified musically! Among the many functions of music, consider these two: its role in spiritual warfare and its capacity to intensify and channel our deepest and most heartfelt affection.

---

3. Bainton, *Here I Stand*, 341.

4. Bainton, *Here I Stand*, 343.

5. Quoted by Richard D. Dinwiddie, "When You Sing Next Sunday, Thank Luther," *Christianity Today*, October 21, 1983, 19–20.

6. Dinwiddie, "When You Sing Next Sunday, Thank Luther," 21.

Spiritual Warfare

Now the Spirit of the LORD departed from Saul, and a harmful spirit from the LORD tormented him. And Saul's servants said to him, "Behold now, a harmful spirit from God is tormenting you. Let our lord now command your servants who are before you to seek out a man who is skillful in playing the lyre, and when the harmful spirit from God is upon you, he will play it, and you will be well." So Saul said to his servants, "Provide for me a man who can play well and bring him to me." One of the young men answered, "Behold, I have seen a son of Jesse the Bethlehemite, who is skillful in playing, a man of valor, a man of war, prudent in speech, and a man of good presence, and the LORD is with him." Therefore Saul sent messengers to Jesse and said, "Send me David your son, who is with the sheep." And Jesse took a donkey laden with bread and a skin of wine and a young goat and sent them by David his son to Saul. And David came to Saul and entered his service. And Saul loved him greatly, and he became his armor-bearer. And Saul sent to Jesse, saying, "Let David remain in my service, for he has found favor in my sight." And whenever the harmful spirit from God was upon Saul, David took the lyre and played it with his hand. So Saul was refreshed and was well, and the harmful spirit departed from him. (1 Sam. 16:14–23)

Music has more than simply a psychological or emotional effect on people; it can drive away, frustrate, and defeat demonic forces. Look again at 1 Samuel 16:23—"And whenever the harmful spirit from God was upon Saul, David took the lyre and played it with his hand. So Saul was refreshed and was well, and the harmful spirit departed from him."

Let's remember the story. We are told in 1 Samuel 15:11 that God said, "I regret that I have made Saul king, for he has turned back from following me and has not performed my commandments." The result of Saul's sin was that the Spirit of God "departed" from him (1 Sam. 16:14). In the Old Testament, the people of God were not permanently indwelt by the Spirit. God would temporarily anoint kings, prophets, and others with the Holy Spirit so they might be equipped and empowered to fulfill their calling.

Here we are told that not only did the Holy Spirit depart from Saul but also that "a harmful spirit from the LORD tormented him" (1 Sam. 16:14).

In case you are wondering, yes, this is a demonic spirit. God is sovereign over all of creation and can use or employ anything and anyone to discipline his people. The apostle Paul's "thorn in the flesh" was inflicted upon him by a "messenger from Satan," but just as surely, this messenger was doing God's will.

The question for us is this: "Why or how did David's music have this effect? Why did the demonic spirit depart from Saul such that he was refreshed and made well every time David played the lyre?" There's no indication that David sang. He played instrumentally. Others might also have played, but nothing would happen. Why? What was so special about David? Why did *his* music carry such power?

The answer is in verse 18: "and the LORD is with him." There may well have been other musicians in Saul's court who were more skilled than David. Something about David empowered his music to soothe Saul's soul. The Holy Spirit infused the melodies and harmonies of David's music with supernatural power. "The pleasing sounds rising from his instrument transformed his harp [or lyre] into a strategic weapon of war which drove the enemies of God into agitation and retreat."[7]

Why? Because the Lord was "with" David! If God had not been with David, his music might have been entertaining and sweet and enjoyable to hear, but it would not have carried the power to drive a demon from Saul's soul and bring spiritual refreshment to him. There were probably others who were as skilled on the lyre as David, but in the absence of God their music would have left any demonic spirit firmly entrenched.

Music played or sung by those who love God, are filled with God's Spirit, and devote their talents to the glory of God irritates and agitates the enemy! This is why I often recommend to people who are under spiritual attack or are suffering from depression to play instrumental or vocal worship music at all times, wherever they are. Music devoted to God's glory played or sung by a person in whom the Spirit dwells creates a spiritual atmosphere that is repellent and offensive to Satan and his hosts. There's nothing magical in this. Demons don't dislike music. It isn't that they are offended by someone playing or singing off-key. It is the presence of God in and with the one playing/singing that accounts for this powerful impact.

---

7. John G. Elliott, "David's Harp and the Demons," *TMS* 2, no. 2 (2012): 71.

Even music written, played, or sung by an unbeliever can be used in this way if it is in the hands of a Spirit-filled, Christ-exalting believer. You don't have to be the one playing or singing. You don't have to be musically gifted in the least. The issue is whether God is "with" you.

Let's look at one more example, found in 2 Kings 3:15. The king of Israel was desperate to hear the word of the Lord regarding what would happen if he were to engage the Moabites in battle, so he sent for Elisha. Elisha then said, "'But now bring me a musician.' And when the musician played, the hand of the LORD came upon him." The result was that Elisha prophesied.

Why did Elisha want someone to play music? It would appear that music clears away interference between heaven and earth, similar to the way a rainstorm can clear the air of dust particles and make your radio more receptive to a distant station. Anointed and godly music creates a spiritual atmosphere in which God's voice can more readily be heard. It eliminates distractions and enables the heart to focus on God.

Elisha wanted to be quiet and calm before the Lord. He wanted to become emotionally, spiritually, and mentally in tune with and sensitive to what God would say. Sometimes it's important to put oneself in a mood that is more conducive to receiving and understanding divine revelation.

We see something like this in a couple of other texts. In 1 Samuel 10:5–13, we see that people would often prophesy while playing instruments. We also read in 1 Chronicles 25:1 that "David and the chiefs of the service also set apart for the service the sons of Asaph, and of Heman, and of Jeduthun, who prophesied with lyres, with harps, and with cymbals." Others are said to have "prophesied with the lyre in thanksgiving and praise to the LORD" (25:3). The instruments themselves didn't prophesy, but the music opened lines of communication and enabled the prophets to accurately hear the word of the Lord.

I've often been asked why we play background instrumental music when we pray for people. Are we just trying to create a mood and manipulate someone's emotions? Yes, we are trying to create a mood or atmosphere conducive to engaging with God and hearing his voice, and I make no apology for that. But no, we are not trying to manipulate anyone. We are simply seeking to minister effectively to people by acknowledging that the Holy Spirit uses music to soothe their hearts, put them at ease emotionally, and open their souls to God.

Singing versus Speaking

Some of you are afraid to sing. You'd never admit it, but singing is incompatible with your sense of dignity and decorum. It requires an emotional involvement that threatens the image of strength and self-sufficiency you are determined to project. Singing demands an overt display of private devotion. Some of you aren't comfortable with your feelings, and the thought of giving vent to them in sacred song is terrifying. This is why many men are less inclined to sing.

You probably wouldn't struggle as much if asked to speak about your Christian convictions. But singing is another matter. Why? Because singing makes you feel vulnerable. It brings to the surface passions that you feel more comfortable keeping tucked away, out of sight. You are determined at all costs to stay in control. Singing is a threat to your resolve to keep a grip on your feelings.

There is a vast difference between speaking and singing. It goes beyond the mere fact that some people are embarrassed to sing because they lack a melodious voice. Music has a peculiar power. Music infuses words with a dynamic energy that merely speaking them could never achieve. Warren Wiersbe put it this way:

> I am convinced that congregations learn more theology (good and bad) from the songs they sing than from the sermons they hear. Many sermons are doctrinally sound and contain a fair amount of biblical information, but they lack that necessary emotional content that gets ahold of the listener's heart. Music, however, reaches the mind and the heart at the same time. It has power to touch and move the emotions, and for that reason can become a wonderful tool in the hands of the Spirit or a terrible weapon in the hands of the Adversary.[8]

Listen again to the words of Martin Luther: "We want the beautiful art of music to be properly used to serve her dear Creator and his Christians. He is thereby praised and honored and we are made better and stronger

---

8. Warren Wiersbe, *Real Worship: Playground, Battleground, or Holy Ground?* (Nashville: Nelson, 1990), 137.

in faith when his holy Word is impressed on our hearts by sweet music."[9] There is no escaping the fact that the truth of God's "holy Word is impressed on our hearts by sweet music." Singing enables the soul to express deeply felt emotions that mere speaking cannot. Singing channels our spiritual energy. Singing evokes an intensity of mind and spirit. It opens the door to ideas, feelings, and affections that otherwise might have remained forever imprisoned in the depths of one's heart. Singing gives focus and clarity to what words alone often only make fuzzy. It lifts our hearts to new heights of contemplation. It stirs our hope to unprecedented levels of expectancy and delight. *Singing sensitizes.* It softens the soul to hear God's voice and quickens the will to obey.

When I'm happy, I sing. When my joy increases, it cries for an outlet. So, I sing. When I'm touched with a renewed sense of forgiveness, I sing. When God's grace shines yet again on my darkened path, I sing. When I'm lonely and long for the intimacy of God's presence, I sing. When I need respite from the chaos of a world run amok, I sing.

Nothing else can do for me what music does. It bathes otherwise arid ideas in refreshing waters. It empowers my wandering mind to concentrate with energetic intensity. It stirs my heart to tell the Lord just how much I love him, again and again and again, without the slightest tinge of repetitive boredom.

Singing in Scripture

So, let's now turn our attention to the Bible itself and its emphasis on singing in worship. Consider this brief survey.

> Then Moses and the people of Israel sang this song to the LORD, saying,

> "I will sing to the LORD, for he has triumphed gloriously." (Ex. 15:1)

> Hear, O kings; give ear, O princes;
>   to the LORD I will sing;
>   I will make melody to the LORD, the God of Israel. (Judg. 5:3)

---

9. Martin Luther, referenced in Mark Noll, "Singing the Word of God," *Christian History* 95 (2007).

Oh give thanks to the LORD; call upon his name;
    make known his deeds among the peoples!
Sing to him, sing praises to him;
    tell of all his wondrous works! (1 Chron. 16:8–9)

"Where were you when I laid the foundation of the earth . . .
when the morning stars sang together
    and all the sons of God shouted for joy?" (Job 38:4, 7)

Shout for joy in the LORD, O you righteous!
    Praise befits the upright.
Give thanks to the LORD with the lyre;
    make melody to him with the harp of ten strings!
Sing to him a new song;
    play skillfully on the strings, with loud shouts. (Ps. 33:1–3)

Sing praises to God, sing praises!
    Sing praises to our King, sing praises!
For God is the King of all the earth;
    sing praises with a psalm! (Ps. 47:6–7)

Shout for joy to God, all the earth;
    sing the glory of his name;
    give to him glorious praise! . . .
All the earth worships you
    and sings praises to you;
    they sing praises to your name. (Ps. 66:1–2, 4)

I will praise the name of God with a song;
    I will magnify him with thanksgiving. (Ps. 69:30)

Oh sing to the LORD a new song;
    sing to the LORD, all the earth!
Sing to the LORD, bless his name. (Ps. 96:1–2)

> Make a joyful noise to the LORD, all the earth;
>> break forth into joyous song and sing praises!
> Sing praises to the LORD with the lyre,
>> with the lyre and the sound of melody!
> With trumpets and the sound of the horn
>> make a joyful noise before the King, the LORD!
>> (Ps. 98:4–6)

> Sing to him, sing praises to him;
>> tell of all his wondrous works! (Ps. 105:2)

> And at the dedication of the wall of Jerusalem they sought the Levites in all their places, to bring them to Jerusalem to celebrate the dedication with gladness, with thanksgivings and with singing, with cymbals, harps, and lyres. (Neh. 12:27; see 12:28, 31, 38, 45–47)

In sum, more than 170 times in the Old Testament alone we either read of people singing praises to God or we are commanded to do so. Singing is also emphasized in the New Testament:

> I will pray with my spirit, but I will pray with my mind also; I will sing praise with my spirit, but I will sing with my mind also. (1 Cor. 14:15)

> Be filled with the Spirit, addressing one another in psalms and hymns and spiritual songs, singing and making melody to the Lord with your heart. (Eph. 5:18–19; cf. Col. 3:16)

> Is anyone cheerful? Let him sing praise. (James 5:13)

Undistracting Excellence

The psalmist exhorts us to worship "skillfully" (Ps. 33:3). This is a call for excellence in our praise of God. Here is how John Piper describes "undistracting excellence" in worship.

We will try to sing and play and pray and preach in such a way that people's attention will not be diverted from the substance by shoddy ministry nor by excessive finesse, elegance, or refinement. Natural, undistracting excellence will let the truth and beauty of God shine through. We will invest in equipment good enough to be undistracting in transmitting heartfelt truth.[10]

In other words, we strive to provide the highest quality sound equipment and lighting and the most aesthetically pleasing surroundings without worshipers ever being distracted by them from their focus on God and the truth about who he is. We shouldn't want anyone walking out of a Sunday morning service saying, "Wow! The sound was just right today—not too loud, not too low. And the lighting was so pleasant, neither too bright nor too dim. And that guy could really play the guitar, and that gal is amazing on the violin."

Of course, that is precisely what we strive to do in terms of sight and sound and musical instrumentation: we pursue excellence in all we do, but not so that worshipers would be distracted from God to focus on it. That is the difference between excellence and performance. Performance is designed to draw your attention to the singer, the sound technician, or the instrumentalist. Excellence is designed to direct your attention to God. Performance is man-centered. Excellence is God-centered. To quote Piper, "We do not pursue the atmosphere of artistic or oratorical performance, but the atmosphere of a radically personal encounter with God and truth."[11]

So what are the elements of spiritual excellence when it comes to music, singing, and our enjoyment of God in worship? Worship that honors God must be tethered to and reflect the revealed truth of Scripture. It must be Bible-based and Bible-saturated. The fundamental test to determine if our worship pleases God is the degree to which it conforms to Scripture. Don't ever sing anything that you do not believe is true. You wouldn't tolerate your pastor preaching heresy or theological error, so why would you tolerate it in yourself or in anyone else when it comes to singing?

---

10. John Piper, "What Unites Us in Worship," October 1, 2003, https://www.desiringgod.org/articles/what-unites-us-in-worship.

11. Piper, "What Unites Us in Worship."

The psalmist insists that we "play skillfully" (Ps. 33:3) on whatever instrument we employ in our praise. Worship that reflects the exquisite beauty of God must itself be technically and aesthetically pleasing. The excellence of God calls for excellence in our celebration of him. Certain rhythms and melodies make it hard to think about God. They are, by their very nature, distracting. They make it difficult to focus our thoughts on the lyrics and often feel inappropriate to the message contained in them. I'm not going to get into the argument about whether there are certain rhythms and melodies that are either intrinsically demonic or intrinsically divine. But we must strive to make our music fitting and appropriately expressive to the majesty and glory of the God whom we love and adore.

We must aim for all our worship, however expressed, to be joyful, free, and expressive without being flippant, silly, or beneath the dignity of God and the people worshiping him. This means some songs will be conducive to dancing in celebration, and other songs will be conducive to kneeling and awestruck reverence. Again, to quote Piper, "We will try to avoid being trite, flippant, superficial, or frivolous, but instead will aim to set an example of reverence and passion and wonder and broken-hearted joy."[12]

There is always a place for both simplicity and complexity in our worship. We need not always sing high church traditional hymns or low-church choruses. Sometimes we'll sing the simple song "I Love You, Lord," and at other times, the richly complex and deeply theological "Be Thou My Vision." They both have their place in our singing.

We must always strive to be intellectually engaged with the greatness of God at the same time our hearts are warmly touched and our emotions and affections are awakened and stirred. Some are afraid that this might degenerate into manipulation. Should we avoid anything that tends to arouse and awaken our affections and feelings? No. Precisely the opposite is true. Intensified affections and deepened emotions are to be celebrated as long as what awakens, intensifies, and arouses them is biblical truth! Sinful manipulation occurs only when music is employed to stir someone's emotions simply for the sake of the emotion itself. But if one's emotions are stirred by truth, by grace, by divine love, by the beauty of Christ, then praise God![13]

---

12. Piper, "What Unites Us in Worship."
13. W. Robert Godfrey points out that Reformed and cessationist churches "believe that the emotions themselves must not be trusted as an accurate guide to the truth, virtue, or the presence of

We must aim for all our worship, in whatever form, to be crafted, energized, and sustained by the Holy Spirit, whether that be through strategic planning days in advance or through Spirit-prompted, unprepared spontaneity in the very moment of our singing. I'll have much more to say about this in chapters 15–17, which are devoted to charismatic worship.

And let us be diligent to orchestrate our worship in a manner that is profoundly theocentric and Spirit-led.

> Shout for joy to God, all the earth;
>> sing the glory of *his* name;
>> give to *him* glorious praise!
> Say to God, "How awesome are *your* deeds!" (Ps. 66:1–3)

Note well: we are to "shout" in worship but always "to God" in praise. Shouting for shouting's sake, to give vent to your emotions, or as a way of seeking psychological relief is not fitting in church. But shouting to God in gratitude and joy and celebration of who he is and what he has done is most appropriate. Again, note well: we are not merely to "sing" but to "sing the glory of his name," not our own. Our focus is on the "deeds" of God: "your deeds," Lord, are what fill our hearts and direct our praise.

Why Must We Sing?

Worship encompasses the whole of life, from what we say to what we do and desire, as well as the numerous activities that occur in the corporate gathering of God's people. Here I want us to think primarily about worship as the verbal proclamation in song of the greatness and glory of God's name. This is what the author of Hebrews had in mind when he spoke of the "sacrifice of praise" as expressed in "the fruit of lips that acknowledge his name" (Heb. 13:15).

The reference to the "fruit of lips" in verse 15 must be contrasted with

---

the Holy Spirit. Rather the emotions must be properly channeled and directed. They must be governed by the sanctified intellect and will of the Christian. They must be the effect of true faith." "Worship and the Emotions," in *Give Praise to God: A Vision for Reforming Worship: Celebrating the Legacy of James Montgomery Boice*, ed. Philip Graham Ryken, Derek W. H. Thomas, and J. Ligon Duncan III (Phillipsburg, NJ: P&R, 2003), 368. Of course, most biblically grounded charismatic churches would agree with this and would never appeal to the emotions as a criterion for determining what is and is not biblically true.

what Jesus said when he denounced the hypocritical and vain worship of the Pharisees: "This people honors me with their lips, but their heart is far from me" (Matt. 15:8). That is not what the author meant when he spoke of praising God with our "lips." There is a world of difference between the labor of your lips and the "fruit" of your lips. The "fruit" of lips is what we say or sing that flows from a heart mesmerized by the mercy of God.

Just think of it: according to Jesus, you can "worship" God by singing, shouting, dancing, and loudly declaring loyalty and love, and have it all be vanity. If the "heart" is not engaged, worship is a sham. You can be orthodox and honored among men, fervent in your vocalized praise, quite "pious" by all outward indications; yet at the same time, your "heart" is distant, cold, and lifeless.

It's important to note that Jesus did refer to the "lips" and not just to our hearts or affections. In other words, God wants us to "sing" and "speak" and "shout" his praises. This is what Paul had in mind in Colossians 3:16: "Let the word of Christ dwell in you richly, teaching and admonishing one another in all wisdom, singing psalms and hymns and spiritual songs, with thankfulness in your hearts to God." Although one can surely worship without singing, we can't ignore the emphasis in Scripture on this expression of praise and joy in God. The singing of our praise is everywhere in Scripture.

But why singing? Why not just speak our praise to God? If we did, there would be no fear of excess emotion or the visible display of intense affections that might lead others to think we are unstable or lacking self-control. And no one would accuse us of being too fanatical about Jesus. I will only speak for myself here, but I can't envision expressing my devotion to God and my passionate feasting on all that he is for me in Jesus apart from singing.

Singing gives expression to deeply felt emotions that mere speaking is unable to communicate. When I sing, the intensely concentrated spiritual energy of my soul explodes in glorious praise of the God who is immeasurably more worthy than the most sophisticated speech can articulate. Often ideas, desires, and affections would otherwise remain imprisoned in the depths of my soul were I unable to sing them aloud. There is a unique power in song that brings clarity and conviction to what my heart often struggles to grasp. When I sing Charity Gayle's deeply moving tribute to the power of the blood of Christ, "Thank You, Jesus, for the Blood," I discover new levels of gratitude and wonder at what the death of my Savior has accomplished for me. Her song "I Speak Jesus" motivates me to declare aloud to all who can hear the majesty of what Jesus can do for my broken body and soul.

Singing stirs me to unprecedented levels of expectancy and drives the lingering presence of doubt from my heart. When I find my spirit cold and dry, singing sensitizes me to the realities of who God is and what he has done.

And my singing is always "to God" (Heb. 13:15). It is never random nor aimless. He is the focus of my faith, the object of my praise, the audience of One to whom I lift my heart. I suspect this is one reason certain people are uncomfortable with singing. It requires of them vulnerability, openness, and honesty as they direct their most heartfelt adoration, hopes, and desires "to God." They are fearful of the depth of commitment and devotion that singing "to God" entails. But sing "to God" we must.

> My heart and flesh sing for joy
> to the living God. (Ps. 84:2)

CHAPTER 6

The Life-Transforming, Demon-Defeating, Heart-Healing Power of Praise

We who live in the United States are witnesses and participants in a power struggle that occurs every four years. Whatever you think about US presidential races, be assured of one thing: they are all about the pursuit of power. Yes, there are certain individuals who run for office based on principle, but they are few and far between. Most do so because they have an insatiable passion for power.

Much of what we do in life is either from the fear of the power others possess or in our own pursuit of it. We talk about political power, nuclear power, purchasing power, power in the home, power in the office, power on the playing field. We are a power-hungry people. And one of the more dangerous things about power is that it is intoxicating and addictive. A small taste of real power invariably fuels a desire for even more. Charles Colson, former special counsel for President Richard Nixon during the Watergate scandal, once said that "power is like saltwater; the more you drink the thirstier you get."[1]

But Christians know there is no power on earth that can compare with the power of God. The gospel of Jesus Christ, said Paul, "is the power of God for salvation" (Rom. 1:16). When Paul prayed for the Christians in Ephesus, he asked that they might come to know "the immeasurable greatness of [God's]

---

1. Charles Colson, *Kingdoms in Conflict* (Grand Rapids: Zondervan, 1989), 272.

power toward us who believe" (Eph. 1:19). Paul prayed for himself and said that he wanted to know Christ and "the power of his resurrection" (Phil. 3:10).

Where might God's power be found? In what ways does God make it available to us? Paul spoke in Ephesians 3:20 of "the power [of God] at work within us." So, how do we tap into this power? We can certainly pray. We can study and memorize God's Word. We can regularly participate in the Lord's Supper. In all these ways, God's power is made available to us. But I want to talk about the power of God that is unleashed when God's people praise him. When the people of God unite in the adoration and exaltation of God, things happen. God moves. The Spirit goes to work in us and on our behalf to do things that we might otherwise never see happen.

Jehoshaphat and the Power of Praise

Let's begin by reading 2 Chronicles 20:1–23, a story with which I'm confident you are quite familiar.

> After this the Moabites and Ammonites, and with them some of the Meunites, came against Jehoshaphat for battle. Some men came and told Jehoshaphat, "A great multitude is coming against you from Edom, from beyond the sea; and, behold, they are in Hazazon-tamar" (that is, Engedi). Then Jehoshaphat was afraid and set his face to seek the LORD, and proclaimed a fast throughout all Judah. And Judah assembled to seek help from the LORD; from all the cities of Judah they came to seek the LORD.
>
> And Jehoshaphat stood in the assembly of Judah and Jerusalem, in the house of the LORD, before the new court, and said, "O LORD, God of our fathers, are you not God in heaven? You rule over all the kingdoms of the nations. In your hand are power and might, so that none is able to withstand you. Did you not, our God, drive out the inhabitants of this land before your people Israel, and give it forever to the descendants of Abraham your friend? And they have lived in it and have built for you in it a sanctuary for your name, saying, 'If disaster comes upon us, the sword, judgment, or pestilence, or famine, we will stand before this house and before you—for your name is in this house—and cry out to you in our affliction, and you will hear and save.' And now behold, the men of

Ammon and Moab and Mount Seir, whom you would not let Israel invade when they came from the land of Egypt, and whom they avoided and did not destroy—behold, they reward us by coming to drive us out of your possession, which you have given us to inherit. O our God, will you not execute judgment on them? For we are powerless against this great horde that is coming against us. We do not know what to do, but our eyes are on you."

Meanwhile all Judah stood before the LORD, with their little ones, their wives, and their children. And the Spirit of the LORD came upon Jahaziel the son of Zechariah, son of Benaiah, son of Jeiel, son of Mattaniah, a Levite of the sons of Asaph, in the midst of the assembly. And he said, "Listen, all Judah and inhabitants of Jerusalem and King Jehoshaphat: Thus says the LORD to you, 'Do not be afraid and do not be dismayed at this great horde, for the battle is not yours but God's. Tomorrow go down against them. Behold, they will come up by the ascent of Ziz. You will find them at the end of the valley, east of the wilderness of Jeruel. You will not need to fight in this battle. Stand firm, hold your position, and see the salvation of the LORD on your behalf, O Judah and Jerusalem.' Do not be afraid and do not be dismayed. Tomorrow go out against them, and the LORD will be with you."

Then Jehoshaphat bowed his head with his face to the ground, and all Judah and the inhabitants of Jerusalem fell down before the LORD, worshiping the LORD. And the Levites, of the Kohathites and the Korahites, stood up to praise the LORD, the God of Israel, with a very loud voice.

And they rose early in the morning and went out into the wilderness of Tekoa. And when they went out, Jehoshaphat stood and said, "Hear me, Judah and inhabitants of Jerusalem! Believe in the LORD your God, and you will be established; believe his prophets, and you will succeed." And when he had taken counsel with the people, he appointed those who were to sing to the LORD and praise him in holy attire, as they went before the army, and say,

"Give thanks to the LORD,
    for his steadfast love endures forever."

> And when they began to sing and praise, the LORD set an ambush against the men of Ammon, Moab, and Mount Seir, who had come against Judah, so that they were routed. For the men of Ammon and Moab rose against the inhabitants of Mount Seir, devoting them to destruction, and when they had made an end of the inhabitants of Seir, they all helped to destroy one another.

Jehoshaphat ascended to the throne of Judah (the southern kingdom) at the age of thirty-five and reigned for twenty-five years (873–848 BC). He was generally a good and righteous king who walked in the ways of the Lord (see 2 Chron. 17:3–5). The peace in Jerusalem, however, was being threatened (2 Chron. 20:1–4). Jehoshaphat's immediate response was to pray (vv. 5–13).

Notice three things in his prayer. First, he began with a *recognition of God's position* as God of heaven who rules "over all the kingdoms of the nations" (v. 6). God's absolute and unchallenged sovereignty was the basis for Jehoshaphat's confidence in prayer. Second, we read of his *remembrance of God's performance* (vv. 7–8). God had driven out the people from the land of promise and had given it to the descendants of Abraham. Third, he demonstrated humble *reliance on God's power*. He told God, "We are powerless" (v. 12) in ourselves. We have no hope apart from you stepping into this situation.

God responded to the people's prayer and praise by sending Jehoshaphat a prophet, a man named Jahaziel, who, through the Holy Spirit, told them to prepare themselves to witness a display of God's power:

> Do not be afraid and do not be dismayed at this great horde, for the battle is not yours but God's. (v. 15)

> You will not need to fight in this battle. Stand firm, hold your position, and see the salvation of the LORD on your behalf. (v. 17)

The response of Jehoshaphat and the people was crucial. We read in verses 18–19 that he and all the people worshiped the Lord. Note the variety of postures: Jehoshaphat himself "bowed his head with his face to the ground" (v. 18); all Judah and the people of Jerusalem "fell down before the LORD" (v. 18), while the Levites "stood up to praise the LORD" (v. 19). And all of them together worshiped "with a very loud voice" (v. 19). Nobody remained seated!

The strategy employed by Jehoshaphat as they prepared to engage in battle was incredibly strange and, from a purely human point of view, stupid. He first called on the people to "believe in the LORD your God" and to "believe his prophets" and "you will succeed" (v. 20). He then ordered the choir, the worship team, "those who were to sing to the LORD and praise him in holy attire" (v. 21), to go and stand in front of the opposing armies. The only weapon they were to take with them was their worship! There was nothing overly complex in what they were to sing. They were simply to say,

> "Give thanks to the LORD,
>   for his steadfast love endures forever." (v. 21)

Strange! If they were to sing, why not with words such as, "The LORD is great and mighty, and he will slay all our enemies"? Or, "God is omnipotent, and his will cannot be resisted"? But no. They simply sang a song in which they first gave thanks to God for all he had done and then declared that his "steadfast love endures forever!"

No arrows filled the sky. No swords were wielded against the enemy. No stones were thrown. No spears were needed. All they did was sing! And note what happened when they did. God was poised and ready to engage the enemy on their behalf. What happened to trigger the release of divine power? Look at verse 22: "And *when* they began to sing and praise. . . ." Might there be a cause-and-effect relationship between God's people praising and celebrating the steadfast love of the Lord and God moving on their behalf, unleashing his power to defeat their enemies and fulfill his promises? Yes!

In fact, when God's people began to sing and praise, God "set an ambush" against the Ammonites, Moabites, and people of Mount Seir. So "they were routed" (v. 22)! Look at the final line of verse 23: "They all helped to destroy one another." God sent confusion and chaos into the enemy camp so that instead of fighting against Judah, they turned on one another! Or as Andrew Hill puts it, God stirred the armies "into a spirit of self-destruction."[2] If you want to hear of the battle's aftermath, read verses 24–30.

Consider the influence of praise and worship on the enemies of God as described in Psalm 149:5–9:

---

2. Andrew E. Hill, *1 and 2 Chronicles*, NIV Application Commentary (Grand Rapids: Zondervan, 2003), 492.

> Let the godly exult in glory;
>> let them sing for joy on their beds.
> Let the high praises of God be in their throats
>> and two-edged swords in their hands,
> to execute vengeance on the nations
>> and punishments on the peoples,
> to bind their kings with chains
>> and their nobles with fetters of iron,
> to execute on them the judgment written!
>> This is honor for all his godly ones.
> Praise the LORD!

Today, in the era of the new covenant, our "enemies" are not physical armies of literal nations that surround and threaten us with bullets and bombs. Our enemies are demonic forces, principalities, and powers of spiritual darkness. But the principle hasn't changed: we defeat our enemies through the power of praise! Here is how Charles Spurgeon put it: "Praise and power go ever hand in hand. The two things act and react upon each other. An era of spiritual force in the Church is always one of praise; and when there comes some grand outburst of sacred song, we may expect that the people of God are entering upon some new crusade for Christ."[3]

Or consider what happened when Paul and Silas were beaten and imprisoned in Philippi: "About midnight Paul and Silas were praying and singing hymns to God, and the prisoners were listening to them, and suddenly there was a great earthquake, so that the foundations of the prison were shaken. And immediately all the doors were opened, and everyone's bonds were unfastened" (Acts 16:25–26). This earthquake was not the result of fracking or wastewater disposal! It was the release of divine power that occurred when Paul and Silas prayed and sang hymns to God!

Something similar happened earlier in Acts 13. Paul and Barnabas were in Antioch, gathered with the people of God there. And we read, "While they were worshiping the Lord and fasting, the Holy Spirit said . . ." (v. 2). It is no mere coincidence that the Spirit spoke prophetically *"while"* they

---

3. Charles H. Spurgeon, *The Treasury of David* (Peabody, MA: Hendrickson, n.d.), 3:459.

were worshiping the Lord! God intervenes and changes history when his people worship him! Why? What accounts for this connection between God's people worshiping and God releasing his power? The answer may be found in Psalm 22:3: "Yet you are holy, enthroned on the praises of Israel." Some translate this as: "dwelling in the praises of Israel" or "inhabiting" the praises of Israel. It has even been suggested that we should read this as a description that God is "sitting" upon the praise and worship of his people.

Praise creates a dwelling place for God in our situation. Praise does not make God more powerful. Neither does it compel him to act. But God is pleased by praise. He loves to act on behalf of his people when his people exult in him and exalt him in worship. Praise is where God lives! It is his home! That is why when we worship, things happen: the spirits of the discouraged are lifted and refreshed, sick bodies are healed, unsaved souls come to faith, the Spirit's voice is heard, relationships are healed, hope is restored, the Word of God is heard and obeyed, unforgiveness is overcome, bitterness disappears, demons are routed, stingy people become generous, and joy fills the hearts of God's people!

Consider what happened when the ark of the covenant was finally brought into the temple Solomon had built:

> And when the priests came out of the Holy Place (for all the priests who were present had consecrated themselves, without regard to their divisions, and all the Levitical singers, Asaph, Heman, and Jeduthun, their sons and kinsmen, arrayed in fine linen, with cymbals, harps, and lyres, stood east of the altar with 120 priests who were trumpeters; and it was the duty of the trumpeters and singers to make themselves heard in unison in praise and thanksgiving to the LORD), and *when the song was raised*, with trumpets and cymbals and other musical instruments, in praise to the LORD,
>
> > "For he is good,
> > for his steadfast love endures forever,"
>
> the house, the house of the LORD, was filled with a cloud, so that the priests could not stand to minister because of the cloud, for the glory of the LORD filled the house of God. (2 Chron. 5:11–14)

Once again, we see that when God's people proclaim his goodness and the glory of his love, God shows up in powerful ways. *When* they began to sing and praise, "the glory of the Lord filled the house of God," and the priests were knocked to the ground! This same principle is seen again in Psalm 68:1–4:

> God shall arise, his enemies shall be scattered;
>> and those who hate him shall flee before him!
> As smoke is driven away, so you shall drive them away;
>> as wax melts before fire,
>> so the wicked shall perish before God!
> But the righteous shall be glad;
>> they shall exult before God;
>> they shall be jubilant with joy!
>
> Sing to God, sing praises to his name;
>> lift up a song to him who rides through the deserts;
> his name is the Lord;
>> exult before him!

A more accurate translation of verse 4 would be, "cast up a highway for him who rides through the deserts." The imagery is drawn from the ancient custom among Eastern monarchs who would send heralds and pioneers before them to make all the necessary preparations for their arrival. Our praise prepares the way for God to act in power!

The Power of Praise in Defeating the Devil

In the previous chapter, we read in 1 Samuel 16 that a demonic spirit that tormented Saul was sent packing, as it were, every time David played on the lyre. Saul was refreshed and healed by David's instrumental praise of God. Our worship of God infuriates the devil. One of Satan's temptations of Jesus in the wilderness was the offer of all the kingdoms of the world and their glory. All Jesus had to do, said Satan, was "fall down and worship me" (Matt. 4:9). Satan's number one goal is to thwart God's number one goal. God's goal is to be enjoyed and glorified by his people. This is why Satan will do everything he can to confuse us, divide us, and set us against one another, all with a view to distracting us from our focus on God and disrupting our corporate praise of him.

Consider Satan's underlying motivation in attacking Job. Job was a devout and faithful worshiper of God, and Satan couldn't bring himself to believe that Job did it freely. It's as if Satan said to God, "Don't flatter yourself. Job doesn't worship you for nothing. You purchased his praise with gifts and good health and a wonderful family and great wealth. Let me at him, and we'll see if he still clings to you and sings to you." So God said, "Go for it." After Satan's assault, in which he destroyed all of Job's property and possessions and slaughtered his children, we read this in Job 1:20–22:

> Then Job arose and tore his robe and shaved his head and fell on the ground and worshiped. And he said, "Naked I came from my mother's womb, and naked shall I return. The LORD gave, and the LORD has taken away; blessed be the name of the LORD."
> In all this Job did not sin or charge God with wrong.

Satan wasn't satisfied. He told God that the only reason Job continued to worship was because he had his physical health. So God gave Satan permission to afflict Job with boils and sores from head to toe. But Job continued to worship God, and Satan didn't stand a chance.

We may never suffer as Job did, but you can rest assured that Satan will do everything he can to you individually and to us corporately to persuade us that God doesn't deserve our praise. Nothing infuriates and enrages him more than when, in spite of hardship, loss, and suffering, we exult in God and exalt him as altogether lovely, righteous, and great.

This is a warning to us all. Anytime there is an escalation of praise in a church, there is a corresponding escalation in spiritual warfare. I once heard J. I. Packer put it this way: "Whenever God moves, Satan keeps pace."

The Power of Praise in Blessing God's People

Have you noticed how difficult it is to hold a resentful, unforgiving, or angry thought in your head at the same time you raise your voice to worship the Lord? It's simply not possible to exult in God and extol his name while harboring bitterness and jealousy in your heart. I dare you to try it! Try holding in one dimension of your soul hateful and bitter thoughts about another Christian while you simultaneously hold joy, gratitude, and adoration of God. It can't be done. Or at least it can't be done for long. Eventually, one passion will crowd out and conquer the other.

Worship is the antidote to depression, despondency, fear, doubt, and disdain for others. Consider this prophecy from Isaiah:

> The Spirit of the Lord GOD is upon me,
>> because the LORD has anointed me
> to bring good news to the poor;
>> he has sent me to bind up the brokenhearted,
> to proclaim liberty to the captives,
>> and the opening of the prison to those who are bound;
> to proclaim the year of the LORD's favor,
>> and the day of vengeance of our God;
>> to comfort all who mourn;
> to grant to those who mourn in Zion—
>> to give them a beautiful headdress instead of ashes,
> the oil of gladness instead of mourning,
>> the garment of praise instead of a faint spirit;
> that they may be called oaks of righteousness,
>> the planting of the LORD, that he may be glorified. (61:1–3)

God's remedy for a "faint spirit" and for those who "mourn" is to show himself so great and gracious and glorious that they find themselves anointed with "the oil of gladness" instead of mourning and clothed with a "garment of praise" instead of a faint or weak spirit.

This is nowhere more in evidence than in the so-called psalms of lament. These are the psalms in which the author unashamedly and passionately pours out his heart to the Lord, crying aloud of his anguish, despair, and his sense of having been abandoned by God. I once heard someone explain that there are three elements in virtually every psalm of lament: "I'm hurting. They're winning. You don't care!" I encourage you to turn to each of these psalms and listen as the psalmists cry out in pain, distress, and loneliness and then resolve in their hearts to once again praise God: Psalms 7:1–2, 17; 13:1–2, 5–6; 31:9–10, 21–24; 35:17–18; 42:5, 9–11; 43; 57:4–11; 69:29–30.

When we worship God during our troubles and trials, he releases a supernatural power into our hearts that enables us to persevere and live through adversity. Sometimes he will even deliver us from the pain and heartache, but if not, he will always give us the strength to endure as long as it lasts.

Praise has the potential to hasten and quicken the process of spiritual healing in our hearts. It awakens us to remember all of God's marvelous blessings and the countless ways he has shown himself faithful in the past. It empowers us to trust him for the fulfillment of his promises in the future.

Worship, whether in private or in the corporate gathering of God's people, energizes the soul to conquer the lusts of the flesh. I can only speak for myself, but I find it almost impossible to sin when I sing. By focusing my mind on the truth of what I sing, together with affections elevated by the beauty of music, yielding to fleshly passions becomes increasingly difficult. It isn't so much that my fallen nature is diverted from pursuing its pleasures as it is that when I'm captivated by the pleasure that is found in Christ there is simply no room left in my soul to entertain sinful thoughts. Singing so rivets my heart on the exceedingly great glory of the truth in the lyrics that I struggle to get the consent of my will to turn away from the Lord.

Even on those occasions when I feel almost nothing of a holy and sacred nature, singing ignites the fire of faith and the longing for more of God. And once those affections for God are burning, singing functions like a bellows that blows on the flames of delight and joy and intensifies their presence in my heart. It is more than a little difficult to remain ungrateful when you are singing of the plethora of undeserved blessings God has showered on your life.

It isn't unusual for God to respond to our worship by supplying us with power for physical healing. But even if he doesn't, he will always enable us to respond as Job did: "The LORD gave, and the LORD has taken away; blessed be the name of the LORD" (Job 1:21).

Praise accelerates the process of sanctification. When we are absorbed and obsessed with God and his greatness, the power of sin loses its grip on our hearts. This doesn't mean that we can guarantee for ourselves a utopian, pain-free life if only we will worship more. But it does mean that when we are consumed with God, earthly problems and pain become increasingly more tolerable.

Gordon MacDonald's Testimony

Gordon MacDonald was at one time president of InterVarsity Christian Fellowship. But he yielded to temptation and was caught up in a compromising situation. He stepped down from all ministry and spent a couple of years in counseling and prayerful repentance. His marriage was saved, and he was eventually restored to ministry. He wrote about his experience in a book titled *Rebuilding Your Broken World*. In it he describes one occasion when worship accelerated the healing of his heart:

> In one of the darkest hours of my broken-world condition, I found myself one day in the front row of a Dallas church where I had been asked to give a talk. I had made a long-term commitment to be there, but had it not been for my hosts' hard work of preparation, I would have tried to cancel my participation. Frankly, I was in no mood to speak to anyone. But I felt constrained not to cancel, and so there I was.
>
> When the service began, a group of young men and women took places at the front of the congregation and began to lead with instruments and voices in a chain of songs and hymns: some contemporary, others centuries old. As we moved freely from melody to melody, I became aware of a transformation in my inner world. I was being strangely lifted by the music and its content of thankfulness and celebration. If my heart had been heavy, the hearts of others about me were apparently light because, together, we seemed to rise in spirit, the music acting much like the thermal air currents that lift an eagle or a hawk high above the earth.
>
> I not only felt myself rising out of the darkness of my spirit, but I felt as if I were being bathed, washed clean. And as the gloom melted away, a quiet joy and a sense of cleansing swept in and took its place. I felt free to express my turbulent emotions with tears. The congregation's praise was a therapy of the spirit: indescribable in its power. It was a day I shall never forget. No one in that sanctuary knew how high they had lifted one troubled man far above his broken-world anguish. Were there others there that day feeling as I did? Perhaps they would have affirmed as I did: *God was there.*[4]

Such is the life-transforming, demon-defeating, heart-healing power of praise!

---

4. Gordon MacDonald, *Rebuilding Your Broken World* (Nashville: Thomas Nelson, 1988), 178.

CHAPTER 7

The Pleasures of Praise

Nothing stirs the emotions of Christians like a discussion of the role of emotions in Christian men and women. Is it bad for a Christian to feel good? Or is it good to feel bad? Or are feelings irrelevant to the one who believes in Jesus? Are our emotions as Christians something to enjoy or avoid? Are they a source of delight, a sign of danger, or in some sense both?

These are important questions, but our focus is on emotions in worship and the degree to which they are expressed in our corporate praise of God. Sadly, too many Christians tend to gravitate to one end of the spectrum or the other. Some focus on feelings and judge the success of a Sunday service based on how high their emotions were elevated. Other believers focus on facts and consider feelings to be irrelevant. Some hanker after the mountain-top experience of emotional ecstasy, while others simply want to be informed of some new and insightful theological truth. They usually end up attending either the First United Church of Christian Feeling or the Orthodox Assembly of Christian Fact.

All too often the result is that one church resembles a Ringling Bros and Barnum & Bailey Circus while another is more like a visit to the county morgue! It seems that we are confronted with a choice between the frenzy of unbridled chaos on the one hand and the rigidity of immovable concrete on the other.

So what does the Bible have to say about our affections, our deepest and most intense desires, and the feelings that characterize and accompany them?

The Engagement of the Heart

We've already had occasion to note what Jesus said in his rebuke of the religious leaders of his day. But let's dive into it yet again.

> You hypocrites! Well did Isaiah prophesy of you, when he said:
>
> "This people honors me with their lips,
>   but their heart is far from me;
>   in vain do they worship me,
>   teaching as doctrines the commandments of men."
>   (Matt. 15:7–9)

Genuine, God-honoring worship includes as an essential element the coming alive of feelings and affections for God. When affections or feelings for God are absent, worship is dead. But what kind of affections? I would include here such things as joy, gladness, fear, awe, reverence, trembling, gratitude, love, exultation, delight, humility, brokenness, contrition over sin, heartwarming satisfaction, and a fervent, white-hot passion or zeal for God. Consider these biblical texts:

> But let all who take refuge in you rejoice;
>   let them ever sing for joy,
>   and spread your protection over them,
>   that those who love your name may exult in you. (Ps. 5:11)

> I will give thanks to the LORD with my whole heart;
>   I will recount all of your wonderful deeds.
>   I will be glad and exult in you. (Ps. 9:1–2)

> Be glad in the LORD, and rejoice, O righteous,
>   and shout for joy, all you upright in heart! (Ps. 32:11)

> My soul will be satisfied as with fat and rich food,
>   and my mouth will praise you with joyful lips ...

> for you have been my help,
>> and in the shadow of your wings I will sing for joy. (Ps. 63:5, 7)

> But the righteous shall be glad;
>> they shall exult before God;
>> they shall be jubilant with joy!
>
> Sing to God, sing praises to his name. (Ps. 68:3–4)

These are but a handful of dozens of similar texts where the engagement of the whole soul in joyful, glad-hearted enjoyment of God is described. Texts such as Psalm 5:7 speak of reverential fear in our worship:

> But I, through the abundance of your steadfast love,
>> will enter your house.
> I will bow down toward your holy temple
>> in the fear of you. (The psalmist clearly felt no inconsistency in
>>> speaking of his "fear" of the God whose "love" for him was
>>> "steadfast.")

There is a consistent emphasis on gratitude in the Psalms:

> Enter his gates with thanksgiving,
>> and his courts with praise!
>> Give thanks to him; bless his name! (Ps. 100:4; see Ps. 103:1–5)

Love is also often the focus in worship:

> Love the LORD, all you his saints! (Ps. 31:23)

Passion and hunger for God are essential in worship:

> O God, you are my God; earnestly I seek you;
>> my soul thirsts for you;

> my flesh faints for you,
>> as in a dry and weary land where there is no water. (Ps. 63:1)

If God's saving grace for us in Jesus Christ is displayed, explained, and understood, and we do not feel in our hearts things such as gratitude, joy, love, hunger for more, longing, hope, and fear of offending this great and gracious God, then we can go through all the motions of which the body is capable and sing to the heights of musical excellence and still not worship God in a way that truly honors him.

I realize that some people are terrified of emotionalism. But let's be clear: emotionalism is the artificial manipulation of heightened feelings for the sake of the feelings themselves. What I'm advocating is the awakening and intensification of heartfelt affections by means of biblical truth for the sake of God's glory. Here is how John Piper explains the significance of our Lord's statement that we worship God "in spirit and truth" (John 4:23):

> Worshiping in spirit is the opposite of worshiping in merely external ways. It is the opposite of empty formalism and traditionalism. Worshiping in truth is the opposite of worship based on an inadequate view of God. Worship must have head and heart. Worship must engage emotions and thought. Truth without emotion produces dead orthodoxy and a church full (or half full) of artificial admirers (like people who write generic anniversary cards for a living). On the other hand, emotion without truth produces empty frenzy and cultivates shallow people who refuse the discipline of rigorous thought. But true worship comes from people who are deeply emotional and who love deep and sound doctrine. Strong affections for God rooted in truth are the bone and marrow of biblical worship.[1]

We must be careful neither to manufacture feelings when they aren't really there nor suppress them when they are awakened. So let me go on record once again about the relationship between biblical truth and heartfelt affections:

---

1. John Piper, *Desiring God: Meditations of a Christian Hedonist* (Colorado Springs, CO: Multnomah, 2011), 81–82.

- For emotional heat to be holy, it must be the product of theological light.
- Spiritual feelings must arise as the fruit of our perception of spiritual realities.
- High and noble thoughts about God are inseparably linked to deep and pleasurable feelings for God.
- Worship is neither a mind trip nor an emotional binge. It is a biblical blend of our highest and noblest thoughts about God and our deepest and most passionate desires for God.

So we must never be afraid to enjoy God! The primary problem today is that far too many professing Christians enjoy everything in life except God. But listen to the psalmists once again:

> You make known to me the path of life;
>> in your presence there is fullness of joy;
>> at your right hand are pleasures forevermore. (Ps. 16:11)

> How precious is your steadfast love, O God!
>> The children of mankind take refuge in the shadow of your wings.
> They feast on the abundance of your house,
>> and you give them drink from the river of your delights.
>> (Ps. 36:7–8)

> Delight yourself in the LORD,
>> and he will give you the desires of your heart. (Ps. 37:4)

> Praise the LORD!
> For it is good to sing praises to our God;
>> for it is pleasant, and a song of praise is fitting. (Ps. 147:1)

Two Biblical Examples of Unashamed Extravagant Affection for God

Let's turn our attention away from principles and look more closely at two very personal examples of actual people whose affection for God was so unashamed and extravagant that they risked incurring the ridicule and disdain of others who thought they had crossed over the boundaries of what was proper and sophisticated and reasonable. One is from the Old Testament, and the other from the New.

David

The first is David, king of Israel. His story is found in 2 Samuel 6 and also in 1 Chronicles 13–15.

> As the ark of the LORD came into the city of David, Michal the daughter of Saul looked out of the window and saw King David leaping and dancing before the LORD, and she despised him in her heart. And they brought in the ark of the LORD and set it in its place, inside the tent that David had pitched for it. And David offered burnt offerings and peace offerings before the LORD. And when David had finished offering the burnt offerings and the peace offerings, he blessed the people in the name of the LORD of hosts and distributed among all the people, the whole multitude of Israel, both men and women, a cake of bread, a portion of meat, and a cake of raisins to each one. Then all the people departed, each to his house.
>
> And David returned to bless his household. But Michal the daughter of Saul came out to meet David and said [with extreme, biting sarcasm], "How the king of Israel honored himself today, uncovering himself today before the eyes of his servants' female servants, as one of the vulgar fellows shamelessly uncovers himself!" And David said to Michal, "It was before the LORD, who chose me above your father and above all his house, to appoint me as prince over Israel, the people of the LORD—and I will celebrate before the LORD. I will make myself yet more contemptible than this, and I will be abased in your eyes. But by the female servants of whom you have spoken, by them I shall be held in honor." And Michal the daughter of Saul had no child to the day of her death. (2 Sam. 6:16–23)

Both Saul and Jonathan had died, and David had been installed as king. One of the first things he did was to take steps to bring the ark of the covenant, the place where God's glorious presence was manifested, back to its rightful place in Jerusalem. The first attempt to bring it to Jerusalem was a disaster. God had given very specific instructions that no one was to touch the ark, or he would die. But as Uzzah and Ahio, the sons of Abinadab, were leading the cart on which the ark had been placed, the oxen pulling the cart stumbled and it teetered. Uzzah instinctively put out his hand to steady the ark and was instantly struck down by God and died.

David was terrified by this and decided it would be unwise to continue the journey: "How can the ark of the LORD come to me?" he asked (2 Sam. 6:9). So, he diverted the ark to the house of Obed-edom, where the ark remained for three months. David later returned and brought the ark to Jerusalem. He ordered every available musician to make use of every imaginable instrument, together with singers, to celebrate the return of the ark to Jerusalem. David himself put on a linen ephod and was dancing and leaping wildly and joyfully as the ark came into the city. Then we read this: "Michal the daughter of Saul came out to meet David and said [with extreme, biting sarcasm], 'How the king of Israel honored himself today, uncovering himself today before the eyes of his servants' female servants, as one of the vulgar fellows shamelessly uncovers himself!'" (2 Sam. 6:20)

Why was Michal so upset at her husband's behavior? Two reasons appear obvious. For one thing, he had violated her sense of regal dignity. It is one thing for a common man or common woman to dance in public, but a "king" has no business making a scene of that sort. The image Michal wanted to project as the wife of the king had been undermined. As far as she was concerned, *social sophistication was far more important than honoring God with passionate praise.* The custom of the day said that dignitaries like David didn't do things like that. "For heaven's sake, David, you have an image to uphold. Get ahold of yourself!"

The second reason is found in Michal's mention of the "female servants" (v. 20). David couldn't have cared less about who was there to see him. All he cared about was God. But Michal couldn't have cared less about God. All she cared about were the people present and what they thought about her husband. David was oblivious to his surroundings. He had no regard for his reputation, especially should it get in the way of his expressing his love, joy, and gratitude to God. Look at David's response to Michal: "And David said to Michal, 'It was before the LORD, who chose me above your father and above all his house, to appoint me as prince over Israel, the people of the LORD—and I will celebrate before the LORD'" (2 Sam. 6:21). And then, as if to make his point even more forceful, he effectively said to Michal: "Woman, you haven't seen anything yet! You think I acted in a disgraceful and socially inappropriate manner. Well, watch this!" Or perhaps we should let David speak for himself: "I will make myself yet more contemptible than this, and I will be abased in your eyes. But by the female servants of whom you have spoken, by them I shall be held in honor" (2 Sam. 6:22).

It's as if David said, "Michal, do you actually think I give a hoot what other people think? I couldn't care less. I care about what God thinks. I care about honoring him not only with my heart, soul, and mind but with my body as well. And if people are offended by that, that's their problem. But I would argue that, in fact, the servant girls were blessed to see their king so much in love with God that he threw caution to the wind and rejoiced unashamedly and extravagantly!"

I love Charles Spurgeon's comment on David's display of joy and affection:

> It is to be feared that the church of the present day, through a craving for excessive propriety, is growing too artificial; so that enquirers' cries and believers' shouts would be silenced if they were heard in our assemblies. This may be better than boisterous fanaticism, but there is as much danger in the one direction as the other. For our part, we are touched to the heart by a little sacred excess, and when godly men in their joy overleap the narrow bounds of decorum, we do not, like Michal, Saul's daughter, eye them with a sneering heart.[2]

A Personal Example

When I first came to believe in the gifts of the Holy Spirit and our church began to embrace new expressions of charismatic worship, I was extremely concerned with how people might perceive my own overt displays of passion and affection for the Lord. So I intentionally restrained myself lest I come under unwanted criticism. But that was soon to change. It started out as a Sunday morning like all others, except for the fact that I was being greatly stirred in my heart with loving affection for the Lord in a way that I had not experienced before. I was standing, as was my custom, in the front row as worship began.

---

2. C. H. Spurgeon, *The Treasury of David* (Peabody, MA: Hendrickson, n.d.), 1:85.

I felt welling up within me a joy and gratitude and adoration of the Lord that I had never known before. I so desperately wanted to raise my hands in worship, but the thought kept racing through my head: *Sam, there are two hundred pairs of eyes glued to your back right now. They are wondering, somewhat fearfully, what might be next in this journey of joy.* Fear gripped my heart. *What would happen,* I wondered, *if I were to raise my hands?* After all, no one in the church dared do so up until now. I know it sounds strange today, but in the late 1980s, lifted hands were more than a means of worship. They signaled charismatic beliefs and behavior. As I stood there, ever more overcome with delight in the Lord, worried about what others might think, there suddenly erupted in my mind these words: *Ah, the hell with them!* Excuse my language. I instantly repented but just as instantly lifted my hands in praise and honor of the Lord. And I've never looked back.

I don't know if anyone responded to me the way Michal did to David, but I had reached a point where I simply no longer cared. Although I would never compare myself to David, I understand his reaction to his wife. I also understand how Mary must have felt when she came under the critical eye of the apostles of Jesus.

Mary

Now let's turn to the New Testament and look at another expression of heartfelt praise, this time from a female. Jesus and the disciples found themselves in Bethany, a village two miles east of Jerusalem, in the home of Simon, a man whom Jesus had healed of leprosy. There were no fewer than fifteen men present—the twelve disciples, Jesus, Simon, and Lazarus—together with two women, Mary and her sister Martha. We are told in Mark 14 that Mary

came with an alabaster flask of ointment of pure nard, very costly, and she broke the flask and poured it over his head. There were some who said to themselves indignantly, "Why was the ointment wasted like that? For this ointment could have been sold for more than three hundred denarii and given to the poor." And they scolded her. But Jesus said, "Leave her alone. Why do you trouble her? She has done a beautiful thing to me. For you always have the poor with you, and whenever you want, you can do good for them. But you will not always have me. She has done what she could;

she has anointed my body beforehand for burial. And truly, I say to you, wherever the gospel is proclaimed in the whole world, what she has done will be told in memory of her." (vv. 3–9)

Mary's action, as described in verse 3, wasn't unusual or unexpected. Anointing people was a common thing in those days. Jesus himself was incredulous, and perhaps a bit offended, when Simon the Pharisee failed to anoint him (Luke 7:46; cf. Pss. 23:5; 141:5). What was unusual about Mary, indeed scandalous, was the sheer financial extravagance of her devotion and love. The alabaster flask was a vial made of fine-grained gypsum from which the perfume was extracted by snapping off the long, thin neck. John identified the flask's content as "very expensive ointment," nard to be specific (John 12). Her gift amounted to 300 denarii, the equivalent of a year's wage for a working man. *A full year's salary!*

The reaction of the disciples was predictable. For a moment, everyone must have sat in stunned silence, in utter disbelief of what they had just witnessed. *Did I just see what I think I saw?* they no doubt queried in their minds. Then they spoke out in angry denunciation (see Mark 14:4–5). In the first place, the perfume didn't belong to them! It was Mary's, and she was perfectly free to do with it whatever she pleased. So where do they get off taking her to task? There's no reason to think the disciples were motivated by greed or materialism. Nothing in their behavior indicated they wanted the money for themselves. They simply failed to realize the redemptive significance of what was taking place and the fact that the cross was just around the corner.

Their concern for the poor was sincere. In any other context, it may have been perfectly appropriate. In fact, it was customary on the evening of Passover to take up an offering for the poor of one's community. This may well be what prompted their anger over what Mary had done.

We must ask ourselves, "Is there a lid on the perfume of our passion? Or are we willing, like Mary, to break the bottle of our pride, of our very lives, and pour out our love and adoration and praise?" Most of us have been accused, often falsely, of many things. But rarely, and sadly, have I met someone who is consistently charged with being an extravagant lover of Jesus. I'm grieved by this, but no one has ever accused me, at least to my face, of "wasting" my time, money, and energy on Jesus.

The objection is quick in coming: "But if I do, what will others think? What will they say?" When we give ourselves wholly to Jesus, people will always misunderstand. *Spiritual extravagance almost always leads to criticism.* Even your friends will misjudge you, and your family will take offense. Worst of all, churchgoers may ask you to leave! We expect the world to mock us. The values of our society are so warped that we should never be surprised by its disdain. But all too often, even Christians and church leaders will deem as wasteful and excessive our worship of Jesus.

Let's not forget that those who took issue with Mary included Peter, John, Matthew, Andrew, and James, among others. I suspect that even Simon and Lazarus doubted what she did. People who "like" Jesus and "respect" him, who even sing songs about him, will often be the first to scold you for the uninhibited and extravagant display of your deep delight in the Friend of Sinners.

For many in the church, anything more than the minimum is too much. To exceed the traditional, to cross the boundaries of what they consider socially appropriate and proper, will be deemed as waste. Jesus called it beautiful (v. 6).

True love never calculates. Genuine worship is never measured. Authentic affection never asks, "How little can I give and still meet the accepted standards of decency?" True, heartfelt adoration never asks, "What is the minimum I can get by with and not be thought of by others as holding back?" The heart of true worship is unfamiliar with the word "enough" and utterly oblivious to what others deem fitting. The disciples thought Mary had gone way overboard and had wasted this precious perfume. "Mary, be reasonable," they said to themselves. "Where is your sense of proportion?"

I'm convinced that if Mary felt anything at this moment, it was that she had given too little. Perhaps she felt tempted to apologize for the perfume, not because it was so expensive but because it was so cheap compared to the infinite value of the one she anointed. Imagine a conversation that could easily have passed between Mary and Peter:

P: "Three hundred denarii! Mary, are you sure you want to do this? I mean, really!"

M: "Oh my, Peter. You're right. I can't believe I was so stupid and calloused and unthinking. What's the matter with me? I hope you and the others will find the grace to forgive me."

P: "That's okay, Mary. Don't be too hard on yourself. Surely you haven't forgotten how many times I messed up in the last three years. If I only had a denarius for every time I stuck my foot in my mouth!"

M: "Thanks, Peter."

P: "Think nothing of it! We all make mistakes. Remember, it's all part of growing up spiritually. Maturity comes with time. Every once in a while we all miscalculate and tend to go overboard."

M: "*Overboard?* What do you mean?"

P: "What do you mean 'what do I mean'? I mean overboard. After all, 300 denarii is a staggering sum of money."

M: "*Staggering?* You mean pathetic and paltry, don't you?"

P: "No, Mary. I mean staggering, as in way, way, way too much."

M: "Peter, I don't know how to say this without offending you, but we're on different planets! Yes, I'm embarrassed by what I did, but not because 300 denarii is so much but because it's such a small sum of money in comparison with the incomparable worth of Jesus."

Christians have often been accused of lacking common sense, and rightly so. But there is at least one occasion when so-called common sense is "nonsense," and that is when a Christian expresses his or her love for Jesus. There is a vast difference between the economics of common sense and the economics of love, and each has its place. Common sense follows the dictates of wisdom. Love is energized by the passions of the heart.

I can hear the protests of those whose common sense told them that Mary had violated what was proper and prudent: "She's out of control! She has no sense of proportion. She's so undignified! Mary, what's the matter with you? We have a reputation to uphold. An image to protect. A position to maintain." Such is their judgment because all they see is Mary. All they see is the wasted perfume. All they see is disorder. *All Mary sees is Jesus.*

What do you see when you worship? Other worshipers? Words projected on a screen? A worship leader? A hymnbook? An orchestra or guitar player or drummer? A dancer? Someone raising their hands or lying prostrate on the ground? You watch as you wonder how much longer this can possibly last. If you remain a spectator of people rather than a participant, extravagant worship will never make sense. Common sense will always prevail over passion. It will always strike you as such a waste: of time, of energy, of your reputation. Those who found fault with Mary stood aloof to watch rather than to worship and thus mistook her beautiful act of adoration for waste. Mary didn't stand aloof but drew near. All she saw was Jesus. And what she did felt so inadequate, so paltry, so minimal.

Even after getting a proper grip on what Mary had done, misunderstanding persists. You can hear it in the typical response: "Wow, Mary sacrificed a lot to worship Jesus." No! Think carefully about this: Mary saw Jesus as one whose beauty and worth were so infinitely more satisfying than all rival pleasures that nothing she gave up to gain him felt like a sacrifice.

A sacrifice is some price we pay, some hardship we endure to gain something else. For example, I may sacrifice the joy of ice cream for the benefit of losing weight. Or I may give up nine dollars to see a good movie. I hope the weight loss and the movie make worthwhile the sacrifice I made to get them. My point is that in every sacrifice there is a sense of loss, of something paid or forfeited or given up.

But not for Mary! *What she gained in knowing and enjoying and loving Jesus transformed into a great joy what might otherwise be thought of as a painful sacrifice.* She gladly endured the rebuke of the disciples. She joyfully humbled herself in public. She happily gave away a year's wage. Why? Because in doing so, she gained the joy of enjoying God and, in this way, exalted him above all earthly treasure!

Once you see Jesus as Mary saw him, you will never ask, "How much money will it cost me?"

Once you have tasted the sweetness of the Savior, as Mary did, you will never ask, "What will people think?"

Once you have experienced and known and enjoyed Jesus, as Mary did, you will never ask, "Will I die as a martyr? Will I lose the respect of others? What physical comforts will I forfeit?"

Ask yourself this: "If I were to describe the depth and intensity of my devotion to Jesus, what words would I use?" Would you employ words like *exuberant, demonstrative, passionate, extravagant*? Or would your devotion to the Son of God be more accurately described as *measured, calculated, restrained,* and *guarded*?

I think I know the answer to that question when it comes to David in the Old Testament and Mary in the New Testament. But what about you and me?

Delight Yourself in the Lord!

Before we leave this topic of the pleasures of praise, we need to look closely at a genuinely remarkable but easily misunderstood exhortation in the Old Testament. It is the one we find on the lips of David in Psalm 37. Let's look at it in its broader context.

> Fret not yourself because of evildoers;
>> be not envious of wrongdoers!
> For they will soon fade like the grass
>> and wither like the green herb.
>
> Trust in the Lord, and do good;
>> dwell in the land and befriend faithfulness.
> *Delight yourself in the Lord,*
>> *and he will give you the desires of your heart.*
>
> Commit your way to the Lord;
>> trust in him, and he will act.
> He will bring forth your righteousness as the light,
>> and your justice as the noonday.
>
> Be still before the Lord and wait patiently for him;
>> fret not yourself over the one who prospers in his way,
>> over the man who carries out evil devices!
>
> Refrain from anger, and forsake wrath!
>> Fret not yourself; it tends only to evil.
> For the evildoers shall be cut off,
>> but those who wait for the Lord shall inherit the land. (vv. 1–9)

To "delight" in the Lord is closely related both to what precedes in verse 3, where David calls on us to "trust" in the Lord, and to what follows in verse 5, where we are called on to "commit" our "way" to the Lord. Likewise, the same God-centered focus continues as we are told again in verse 5 to "trust in him" and in verse 7 to "be still before the LORD and wait patiently for him."

All these exhortations that have God as their focus are set over against the tendency to "fret" yourself over evildoers and to be "envious" of them. Instead of fretting over the prosperity of sinners, we are to trust in God, delight in God, and commit our way to God. And that only makes sense if there is more gladness, peace, joy, comfort, and delight in God than there is in all the riches amassed by human effort.[3]

If your delight is wholly in God, then your desires will not be for anything that diminishes his centrality in your soul. You won't want anything that has the potential of turning your heart to trust in anyone but him. If your "desires" are for the stuff of this world that would detract from your complete satisfaction in God, then you aren't truly delighting yourself in him.

But why joy? Why do the biblical authors, such as David, make delight or joy in God so central to our relationship with him? Is it not enough simply to obey God or fear God or worship God or believe in God? Why joy? Why delight? Why does it matter so much?

Not long ago a blogger criticized Christian hedonism for insisting that we come to God and praise God for the joy to be found in him. He said that we should worship God simply because God deserves to be worshiped. Well, of course, he does. No one disputes that point. But Christian hedonism directs our attention to the *how* of worship. How is God most glorified in his people? And I would insist that *God is most glorified in his people when they experience in themselves, by God's saving and sanctifying grace, the affections*

3. I once asked John Piper how we avoid reading this text as an endorsement of the prosperity gospel or a gospel that uses God to get goodies, so to speak. In other words, what prevents us from seeking our joy and satisfaction in God as a pathway to laying hold of other desires of the heart? In other words, how do we avoid making God a tool or instrument or means for the pursuit of joy in something other than him? He responded in a private email by saying that the "desires" of the heart must be desires that are satisfied in *more of God* in more and more ways. If that were not the case, we would not truly be delighting in God as an end in itself but only using God to get what we enjoy more than what may be found in him alone. Piper wrote to me, "I often say that the desire of the heart that we get is God himself. True. But the text implies plurality, and so I am willing to say that we get more of God in more ways when we delight in him. It does not promise that all we can conceive of enjoying will come to us, but that our desires to taste more of God in many ways will be arranged according to God's wise and loving plan."

of joy, delight, and satisfaction that God himself experiences in God himself. So, there is obviously something special about joy.

Therefore, let's resist any temptation to relegate joy and delight to a place of secondary importance. We must also resist the tendency among many to describe joy as little more than the unintended effect or result or inadvertent fruit of some other Christian duty. Instead, let joy in God, delight in God, not in his gifts but in God himself, be the focus of our efforts through the power of the Holy Spirit. For in our delight and joy in God is God most gloriously glorified in us.

Rejoice in the Lord! Are You Kidding?

One of the more famous statements Paul made is found in Philippians 4:4–7. You may know it by heart:

> Rejoice in the Lord always; again I will say, rejoice. Let your reasonableness be known to everyone. The Lord is at hand; do not be anxious about anything, but in everything by prayer and supplication with thanksgiving let your requests be made known to God. And the peace of God, which surpasses all understanding, will guard your hearts and your minds in Christ Jesus.

But wait a minute! Rejoice in the Lord? Are you kidding? Is Paul kidding? Does he have any idea what he's saying? Is he so out of touch with the harsh realities of life that he can be this flippant and happy-go-lucky?

Rejoice in the Lord? Are you suggesting that Christian men and women whose lives were turned inside out by an earthquake, a flood, a tornado, or a forest fire are to "rejoice in the Lord"? Seriously?

Or how am I supposed to rejoice in the Lord when the memory of past sins weighs so heavily on my heart? How can I obey this command when people I love are being persecuted and are suffering unjustly? I just lost my job. My mother died last week. My children won't even talk to me. The car won't start, and I don't have the money to get it fixed. I'm supposed to see the doctor next week, but I'm too scared of what he'll say. Rejoice in the Lord? Yeah, right.

I understand this reaction. Truly, I do. But before you dismiss Paul as some sort of first-century Pollyanna, remember this: he wrote those words while in prison. He wrote those words, not knowing if he might be beheaded for nothing more than declaring his allegiance to Jesus Christ. The man who wrote those words knew more about suffering and deprivation than all of us combined. So, if you still want to dismiss his counsel as unhelpful, go ahead. But don't do so on the assumption that he was naive or unacquainted with grief or was insulated from the kind of pain and heartache that you're facing right now.

Is it not obvious that Paul is calling us to an experience that is unrelated to our external circumstances and in some way transcends them? Charlie Brown once said, "Happiness is a warm puppy." But what happens when the puppy runs away? What happens when the puppy dies? No, the kind of "happiness" that Paul has in view is not tied to a warm puppy, money in the bank, a clean bill of health, or peaceful family relationships. It's tied to Jesus Christ.

So let's begin there, with Jesus Christ. After all, it is there, in him, in relation to our Lord, in the context of all we know that he has so graciously done for us, that we are to rejoice: "Rejoice *in the Lord*!"

Joy is expressed in a variety of styles and circumstances. Paul couldn't have cared less whether it is with hands raised or one's face pressed against the ground. It matters not whether it is to the rhythm of a fast-paced worship song or in solemn silence with tears streaming down one's face. What concerned Paul, and must concern us, is the ground or reason for our joy. There is a sense in which Paul was declaring, "Jesus is our joy," and he is ours and we are his regardless of whether the sky is clear and sunny or threatens us with an approaching funnel cloud. That is why we can rejoice "always," at all times, in every circumstance, no matter the pain or pleasure. Our joy is constant not because our circumstances are but because Jesus is.

PART 3

SCENES OF WORSHIP IN THE NEW TESTAMENT

CHAPTER 8

How to Worship Without Insulting God

In the first two chapters of this book, I briefly addressed the question of how to worship a God who has no needs. To say it yet again: How do you honor a God whose honor is already and always has been infinite? What do you bring to a God who owns everything? What do you give a God who lacks nothing?

When you worship, do you think God is weak and bring him strength?

When you worship, do you think God is ignorant and bring him knowledge?

When you worship, do you think God is helpless and bring him service?

When you worship, do you think God is confused and bring him wisdom?

What mental picture do you have of God when you worship? Frazzled, frustrated, desperate, and dependent, holding up his hands, hoping that some of the people he made will recognize his plight and fill up his depleted resources? Listen to what the Bible says on this:

> The God who made the world and everything in it, being Lord of heaven and earth, does not live in temples made by man, nor is he served by human hands, as though he needed anything, since he himself gives to all mankind life and breath and everything. (Acts 17:24–25)

> Oh, the depth of the riches and wisdom and knowledge of God! How unsearchable are his judgments and how inscrutable his ways!

> "For who has known the mind of the Lord,
>   or who has been his counselor?"
> "Or who has given a gift to him
>   that he might be repaid?"
>
> For from him and through him and to him are all things. To him be glory forever. Amen. (Rom. 11:33–36)

How do we worship God without insulting him? That may sound like a strange question. After all, how can worship insult God? Worship, by definition, glorifies and honors him. Yes. But there is a way of "worshiping" God that actually is an insult and an offense to him as God. To understand this, we must begin by noting what these two passages say about God. It is foundational to our understanding of God and our worship of him as God.

Acts 17:24–25

Look carefully at Paul's statement in Acts 17. He mentioned three things about God, all of which should be familiar. But I want us to think of these truths in terms of how they affect how we worship God. The three things Paul said pertain to creation (God is the source of all things), providence (God is sovereign over all things), and preservation (God sustains all things).

We begin with creation. God made the world. Everything in the world owes its origin and existence to God. "Everything in it" (v. 24) means not just the world in general but everything in particular in that world. God didn't create some vague and undefined entity called the world and then that world somehow itself produced or generated all the varied manifestations of life and form and mind. No. God made every single item in it. Nothing is exempt; nothing is self-sustaining; nothing is self-existent. Nothing can lay claim to being the cause of its own existence, nor can we attribute its existence to any cause other than God. This includes all of humanity and whatever we can produce or conceive. This includes angels and the natural creation: animals, bugs, plants, bacteria, fungi, planets, dirt, neutron stars, rainbows, hail, fire, clouds, hair, and kidneys.

Paul then turned to the truth of divine providence and declared that this God who made all things is also "Lord of heaven and earth" (v. 24). He rules all that he has made. He directs it and oversees its development and direction. Nothing escapes his oversight or control. God didn't create the world only to have it slip through his fingers and spin out of control. He is Lord! Lord over hurricanes and humans, over winds and waves, over nations and kings and princes, over war and peace, poverty and prosperity.

Finally, Paul mentioned God's preservation of all he has made. He declared that God "gives to all mankind life and breath and everything" (v. 25). Notice that the truth of divine preservation is expressed in the present tense. God's preservation and upholding of all things is ongoing, unceasing, and everlasting. He never rests, he never sleeps, he never takes a sabbatical; there is never so much as a nanosecond in which God is not exerting his infinite energy to uphold, sustain, watch over, think about, and love you. If God withdrew his preserving power, we would immediately cease to exist, not by slow decay or neglect; we would vaporize, and not a single atom of our being would continue.

This work of preservation applies to all humanity (v. 25). There are no exceptions. Even those who hate and reject him continue to exist as an expression of his longsuffering and mercy, giving them opportunity to repent. Those of all races, colors, and nationalities; those of all levels of social, economic, and financial attainment; the weak and the strong, the beautiful and the ugly, the popular and the unknown receive life and breath from their Creator.

He gives to all life, that is, existence (Isa. 42:5). If it is God who gives life and sustains life, it is also God who chooses when, where, and why to withdraw that life; the one who is Lord over life is for that reason also Lord over death.

He gives to all breath—ongoing existence—preserving and sustaining every living thing (Col. 1:17). If all breath comes from God, that includes the breath with which you worship; God says, "Here is breath with which to praise me. Be sure you don't presume you could praise me apart from my sustaining presence and the gift of breath."

Paul wrapped up with a universal, all-encompassing declaration. Whatever is not included in the words "life" and "breath" is encompassed by the word "everything"! Whatever else one may say of anything, it comes from God; not just life and breath, but success, food, power, good intentions, and all else.

Paul then drew two conclusions based on this understanding of who God is and what he does. Since all this is true of God, he doesn't dwell in what humans make (cf. 1 Kings 8:27; Isa. 57:15). The creation cannot contain or envelop the Creator. God cannot and will not be confined by anything we make or build, no matter how elegant or exquisite it may be. God is not like some of you who make your living in home construction. God does not build a home and then live in it. He transcends all homes. He exceeds all dimensions, specifications, and measurements, and he utterly and infinitely fills the universe.

Second, God is not served or cared for by humans as if needy or dependent. The word in Acts 17:25 translated "to serve" is *therapeuzō* (from which we derive our term *therapy*) and means to heal, to take care of, to nurse. It is often used of men serving other men, especially in the healing of disease. God has no wounds that you can heal. God has no deformities that you can rectify.

This, then, is why worship is primarily about our receiving from God out of the abundance of his infinite reservoir of resources and then extolling his goodness and generosity in meeting every conceivable need of our hearts. We must resist with all the strength we can muster any thought that by worshiping we are serving him as though he were needy.

Romans 11:33–36

Now look at how Paul in Romans 11:33–36 reinforced this truth. We can't worship God without grasping what Paul was saying in this paragraph. Note, first of all, the three declarations he made about the nature of God.

First, God's riches, wisdom, and knowledge are infinitely deep. Therefore, you cannot supply God with something he lacks. You can never study the extent of God's riches, wisdom, and knowledge and say, "I've reached the bottom. I've gone as far as can be gone. I've seen the extent. I've counted the final dollar that God owns. I've grasped the last bit of information God knows." No. Never.

God's riches cannot be recorded on a financial ledger. No calculator has enough space on its display to register all that God owns. "The earth is the LORD's and the fullness thereof, the world and those who dwell therein" (Ps. 24:1). "Behold, to the LORD your God belong heaven and the heaven of heavens, the earth with all that is in it" (Deut. 10:14). "Yours, O Lord, is the greatness and the power and the glory and the victory and the majesty, for all that is in the heavens and in the earth is yours. Yours is the kingdom, O Lord, and you are exalted as head above all" (1 Chron. 29:11). Every molecule in the far reaches of the galaxy belongs to him.

Not only is God's wealth infinite and unending, so, too, is his wisdom. God is never at a loss for how to accomplish a purpose, a means to achieve an end, a pathway to reach a destination, an instrument to fulfill a goal. God never scratches his head, pondering which of two ways is most efficient to fulfill his desires. God never ponders diverse paths as if he doesn't know instantly and exhaustively the best thing to do for his glory and our good.

Moreover, God's knowledge is infinitely deep. Paul wasn't speaking about our knowledge of God, as if to say that we will never exhaust all there is to know about God. The knowledge of God here is the extent, depth, and dimensions of what he, as God, knows. "Great is our Lord, and abundant in power; his understanding is beyond measure" (Ps. 147:5).

Second, God's judgments are infinitely unsearchable. His ways and means of carrying out his eternal purpose are ultimately inscrutable, infinitely beyond the capacity of human minds to decipher or comprehend. Therefore, how dare we then judge him or call him to account or question his activities? The word "judgments" (krima) refers to his determination of guilt and innocence and whether, when, and how to respond. With immediate judgment? With longsuffering and patience? With saving mercy? All these determinations are beyond our ability to decipher or ultimately comprehend.

Third, God's ways are infinitely inscrutable. The word "ways" (hodos) refers to conduct, a way of life, and decisions a person makes. This encompasses why a person thinks the way he or she does, feels, reasons, discriminates, decides, acts, chooses, and determines what means are best to achieve the greatest ends. Why does God prevent one storm system from producing a killer tornado but permit it with another? Why does God spare one city but decimate another? Why does a righteous man die while a wicked one lives? Why does God prosper one person's efforts in starting up a new business and permit another to fall into bankruptcy? Why does God elevate one world leader to a position of great prominence and humble another in defeat and disgrace? Why does one die of cancer while another is healed? God's ways are simply beyond our feeble, finite, and fallible capacity to understand.

But of this we may be sure: God never does wrong. He never errs. He never regrets a decision he makes.

You and I can't sneak a peek behind the curtain, look between the lines, peer into the darkness, gaze around the corner, or explore underneath the carpet and expect to fully comprehend what God is doing. Give it up! You will only experience frustration. The only reasonable response to God's unsearchable and inscrutable way of running the universe is faith and humble submission.

Paul then asked three rhetorical questions. First, who has ever figured out God's mind? God himself made this point in Isaiah 55: "For my thoughts are not your thoughts, neither are your ways my ways, declares the LORD. For as the heavens are higher than the earth, so are my ways higher than your ways and my thoughts than your thoughts" (vv. 8–9). This should serve to bridle our tongues when we arrogantly think that we can figure out God's means and motives. We often say to one another, "I know what you're thinking." That is never possible with God, unless he has explicitly revealed his thoughts in Scripture.

Paul then asked, who has ever told God what to do? God does not need advice on how to behave or counsel to extricate himself from difficult and ticklish situations. God never faces a conundrum without a perfect solution. With God, there are no enigmas, puzzles, or mysteries. God never lacks sufficient wisdom to know how best to govern his universe.

Whatever we know about God and his ways is because he has graciously chosen to reveal it to us in Scripture (cf. Rom. 1–11). But no one knows the mind of God in a way that he can become his counselor. The one thing you and I want to do more than anything else we can't: *we can never give God advice.* We can never instruct him in the best way to run the universe. He doesn't need our help. He doesn't need our insights. How pompous and prideful of us to think that we are in a position to counsel God and provide him with guidance (see Isa. 40:13–14).

Finally, who has ever made God his debtor? If he is infinitely rich and owns everything, having made it all, what can humans possibly give him that they didn't first receive from him? No one gives to God as if we originate or create things he otherwise does not or would not have. Our "giving" does not increase his inventory of goods and services (cf. 1 Chron. 29:11). God owns it all. No matter how much Bill Gates or Elon Musk own, they are penniless paupers compared with God. You can still enrich Gates or add to Musk's bank account, if only by a few dollars. Why? Because, as much as they own, they don't own it all. But God does! Whatever you give to him, he already gave to you (see 1 Chron. 29:12, 14, 16). You can't put God in your debt since God owns it all and therefore can't be given anything that isn't already his. You can't do anything that would result in God owing you anything!

The apostle then closed with three stunning doxological assertions (v. 36).

1. All things are from God: he is the source.
2. All things are through God: he is the means.
3. All things are to God: he is the goal.

Everything that exists came "from him" and continues to exist "through him" as he exerts the power to sustain and preserve it in existence, and everything ultimately is designed "for him," that is, to bring him honor and praise and majesty (11:36).

What all this means is that God doesn't need you and me. He lacks nothing. There isn't anything we can give him or do for him that he doesn't already have, for he is God. We cannot serve him as if he were needy, give to him as if he were lacking, supply to him as if he were depleted, support him as if he were dependent, empower him as if he were weak, inform him as if he were ignorant, or heal him as if he were wounded. To worship him as if this were not true is to insult and dishonor God.

To "Serve" God (as If He Were Needy) Is to Insult Him

As I briefly noted above, if you come to God in worship to serve him, as if he were needful of you and what you have to offer, you insult him to the core, and you dishonor him with every breath and word and physical gesture.

What comes to mind when you think about "serving" another person? Clearly, it is their need, whether that requires your physical performance of some task for which they lack either the strength or time, emotional support during a season of distress, monetary aid during a time of financial crisis, or encouragement during a time of despair. Service comes in many forms, but in every instance the one being served is lacking in some capacity or handicapped in some way or is needy, whether physically, emotionally, financially, or spiritually. Invariably, the person who serves is put on display as being generous, kind, strong, or resourceful. The person who is served is revealed as weak, deficient, depleted, or in distress.

We see this illustrated every time there is a natural disaster somewhere in the world. I was on a plane not long after Hurricane Katrina struck our southern coast, especially the city of New Orleans. There were at least twenty young people on the flight who had taken time out of their education and jobs to assist those in need. When the announcement was made over the intercom who they were and where they were headed, all the other passengers broke out in spontaneous applause. The reason is obvious. These were the givers, the servers, who were prepared to sacrifice time, effort, and money to assist those in need. No one applauded the people of New Orleans. They were the needy ones who were being helped and aided by the young people on that plane. My point is simply that we must be diligently careful that in our efforts to serve and worship God, we do not envision him as needy and dependent on what we can bring or provide. God gets the applause for serving us. We are the ones who are depleted and weak and hurting. God is the one who sacrifices to bring us the aid we so desperately need, so he gets the praise.

Do you not see, then, that anytime you propose to "serve" God as if he were in any way lacking, you dishonor him? To come to God in a time of worship as if he were needy and your service supplies what he lacks draws attention to yourself. Serving God in this way dishonors and detracts from his glory.

I can hear you saying right now, "Wait a minute, Sam! Doesn't the Bible describe us as being the 'servants' of God? Are we not commanded repeatedly in Scripture to 'serve' him? So, how can you say that 'serving' God is evil and dishonoring to God?"

Yes, it is true that Paul often called himself a "servant" of Christ Jesus (Rom. 1:1) and exhorted the church in Rome to "serve the Lord" (Rom. 12:11; see also 16:18). So, we must begin by defining what it means to be God's "servants" without belittling him as needful of us.

First, we are rightly called God's servants or bondslaves because he owns us. We have been "bought with a price" (1 Cor. 6:20), the blood of Christ. We belong to him. Jonathan Edwards gave expression to this truth in an entry in his personal diary, dated Saturday, January 12, 1723:

> I have this day solemnly renewed my baptismal covenant and self-dedication, which I renewed when I was received into the communion of the church. I have been before God; and have given myself, all that I am and have to God, so that I am not in any respect my own: I can challenge no right in myself, I can challenge no right in this understanding, this will, these affections that are in me; neither have I any right to this body, or any of its members: no right to this tongue, these hands, nor feet: no right to these senses, these eyes, these ears, this smell or taste. I have given myself clear away, and have not retained any thing as my own. I have been to God this morning, and told Him that I gave myself *wholly* to Him. I have given every power to Him; so that for the future I will challenge no right in myself, in any respect.[1]

By "giving" himself in this way to God, Edwards recognized God's absolute ownership of all he was and willingly submitted to God's prior claim on the whole of his life.

Second, we are rightly called God's "servants" insofar as we submit to his authority and acknowledge his right to tell us to do whatever he pleases. We have mistakenly interpreted God's commands as directives for how we are to serve him when, in fact, they are God's way of defining how he wants to serve us. He commands my obedience and then amazingly offers his help. That is why obedience is not hard (see Deut. 30:11; Matt. 11:28–30 [contrast Matt. 23:4]; 1 John 5:3). Christ's "yoke" is easy, and his "burden" is light because *whatever God requires, he provides*! The God who commands is the God who mobilizes all his inexhaustible resources and divine energy on behalf of those who wait on him.

Our response to God's call to radical commitment and obedience to everything commanded in Scripture is not something we do for him, but something he enables us to do for others. We can confidently sacrifice ourselves for others because Jesus sacrifices himself in serving us. He has promised to serve me by sustaining my will as I risk loving those who may not love back. There is nothing to which he calls me that he does not gladly and with unwavering consistency promise to provide for so that I may fulfill it.

---

1. Jonathan Edwards, *Letters and Personal Writings*, ed. George S. Claghorn (New Haven, CT: Yale University Press, 1998), 762.

Try to envision God as a doctor and ourselves as patients. The patient doesn't go to the doctor with a prescription in hand or a diagnosis in mind. He goes to the doctor because the doctor alone knows the problem and can prescribe a remedy. The patient magnifies the doctor when he goes for relief from pain. The patient does not elevate himself above the doctor by seeking his aid. The doctor's glory is revealed in serving his patient and using all his knowledge and resources to relieve his discomfort or cure his disease.

Likewise, God is most honored when we seek from him the healing, restoration, joy, and fulfillment he delights to provide for us. We are the patients in need of help. God is the physician who provides a cure. "Patients do not serve their physicians," says Piper. "They trust them for good prescriptions. The Sermon on the Mount and the Ten Commandments are the Doctor's prescribed health regimen, not the Employer's job description."[2] Thus, we honor God most when we trust him to serve us as a physician serves his patients.

So, yes, serve God, but not because you believe your service supplies God with what he otherwise lacks. Or, to use Paul's words, "God is not served as though he needed anything," or "God is served, but not because he needs anything." If the motivation for your service is your belief that God is needy and dependent, then you dishonor him. But if your service is grounded in your confidence that whatever you do or offer him is simply returning what he has already given you or done in and through you, you honor him.

God has no deficiencies that need to be replenished. Instead, we have the deficiencies, and he is infinite in wisdom and power and readiness to serve us. He has the resources. We have the needs, not vice versa. So, how do we serve God without belittling him? Peter tells us in 1 Peter 4:10–11:

> As each has received a gift, use it to serve one another... whoever serves, as one who serves by the strength that God supplies [not in the strength that you think you supply or muster up or produce]—in order that in everything God may be glorified through Jesus Christ, to whom belong glory and power forever and ever. Amen.

---

2. John Piper, *Desiring God: Meditations of a Christian Hedonist* (Colorado Springs, CO: Multnomah, 2011), 171.

By all means serve God, but always as the one who receives, not as the one who gives. His purpose in the earth is not sustained by our energy. Rather, we are sustained and strengthened by his. We have nothing of value that is not already his by right. Jesus himself said, "For even the Son of Man came not to be served but to serve, and to give his life as a ransom for many" (Mark 10:45; Matt. 20:28).

Here Jesus made a claim that is, as best I can tell, unprecedented in the annals of human religion. When one closely examines the countless moral philosophers and religious leaders in history, in virtually every case they labor to drum up a following of devoted disciples who serve their every need and cater to their every whim. But Jesus was altogether different. His purpose in coming to earth and calling people to follow him wasn't to build up his personal wealth or increase his physical comforts. His aim from beginning to end was to serve others, to give himself on their behalf, to expend his energy and efforts to bring them into the joy of salvation and knowing God.

John Piper is to be commended for having captured the essence of our Lord's purpose during his earthly ministry. Jesus, he explains, did not come looking for people to work for him. He came to work for us. He came to serve us. Jesus didn't come to recruit you to meet God's needs. God has no needs. Jesus came to bring you the resources of God to meet your needs. He lived a sinless life that you should have lived, but couldn't, precisely to meet your need for acceptance with the Father. He died a death you should have died, but now you don't have to, again to meet your needs. He rose from the dead and supplies us with the Holy Spirit to meet our needs. He was exalted to the right hand of God and reigns in supremacy over all principalities and powers precisely to meet our needs and to make us joyful and satisfied in him forever.[3]

The most urgent question you can ask each day is whether you know what your most pressing needs are and whether you will let the risen Christ come into your life to meet those needs—whether you will let him be your servant.

If you still think God needs what you can bring him, recall the psalmist's words in a passage that virtually drips with divine sarcasm. God slaps our arrogance in the face when he says,

---

3. See Piper, *Desiring God*, 168–74.

> If I were hungry, I would not tell you,
>   for the world and its fullness are mine . . .
> call upon me in the day of trouble;
>   I will deliver you, and you shall glorify me. (Ps. 50:12, 15)

When we come to God for rescue and deliverance and help in our time of need, everyone wins. We get rescued, and God gets honored! We must remember that "the gospel is not a help-wanted ad. Neither is the call to Christian service. On the contrary, the gospel commands *us* to give up and hang out a help-wanted sign."[4]

This all struck me as profoundly odd the first time I heard it. God is our servant because he uses all his divine resources to help, strengthen, support, and provide our needs as we obey his command to serve others. In one of his parables, Jesus said,

> Stay dressed for action and keep your lamps burning, and be like men who are waiting for their master to come home from the wedding feast, so that they may open the door to him at once when he comes and knocks. Blessed are those servants whom the master finds awake when he comes. Truly, I say to you, *he will dress himself for service and have them recline at table, and he will come and serve them.* (Luke 12:35–37)

Here we see that the "master" insists on serving even in the age to come when he will gloriously appear "with his mighty angels in flaming fire" (2 Thess. 1:7–8). Why? Because it is the very nature of God not to be served, as if he were dependent on what we can supply him, but to overflow in abundant goodness to bless needy people like us.

Not yet convinced? Consider this stunning declaration from the prophecy of Isaiah: "From of old no one has heard or perceived by the ear, no eye has seen a God besides you, who acts for those who wait for him" (64:4). The good news is that this God who acts and works on our behalf never tires, becomes weary, or sleeps! God never says, "Whoa, give me a break. I've been up for days, and I'm tuckered out. I need a rest." According to Psalm 121:3,

---

4. Piper, *Desiring God*, 171.

God never sleeps: "He who keeps you will not slumber." Why? Because "the everlasting God, the Creator of the ends of the earth . . . does not faint or grow weary" (Isa. 40:28). He never sleeps because he's never tired. After all, how could a being whose power is limitless suffer exhaustion?

The fact that God isn't tired isn't because he doesn't work. On the contrary, God works all the time. He governs the nations (Rev. 15:3) and upholds the universe in existence each moment (Heb. 1:3), and continually feeds the animals of the earth (Ps. 104:21; Matt. 6:26). As 2 Chronicles 16:9 tells us, God is constantly on the prowl, looking for ways to work for those who put their hope in him. He wants more work because it means more opportunities for him to demonstrate his power, wisdom, love, and mercy. To think that we might have resources to relieve him or resupply his depleted energy is to besmirch his character as infinitely self-sufficient. If God needs something to do anything, he simply speaks it into existence out of nothing!

In our misguided zeal, we say, "Oh, God, how can I serve you? What can I do for you?" To which God replies, "No, no. You've got it backward. The question is, 'What can *I* do for *you*? I am here to serve you! *You* don't strongly support me. I'm God! *I* strongly support you.'" We must never forget that God is always the giver, and we are always the recipients.

Again, we read, "Behold as the eyes of servants look to the hand of their master, as the eyes of a maidservant to the hand of her mistress, so our eyes look to the LORD our God, till he has mercy upon us" (Ps. 123:2). And Jesus declared, "I am the vine; you are the branches. Whoever abides in me and I in him, he it is that bears much fruit, for apart from me you can do nothing" (John 15:5).

Nothing that I've said in this chapter should be interpreted to mean that we can simply sit back and do nothing, as if our philosophy of life is governed by the principle "Let go and let God." We are to work hard, but in the same way that the apostle Paul did, by means of and through our constant dependence on the grace of God (1 Cor. 15:10). It is, after all, God who works in us to will and to do for his good pleasure (Phil. 2:13). When Paul turned to describe his success in taking the gospel to the Gentiles, he would only speak of "what Christ has accomplished through" him (Rom. 15:18; cf. 2 Tim. 4:17; Heb. 13:20–21).

Now, how does all this relate to worship? This relates directly to our motivation in worship. As I explained in an earlier chapter, for years I used to view worship as a time during which I would give of myself to God. But worship is primarily a craving for God. Worship is me declaring to the world that God is my all in all, that he alone can quench the thirst of my soul and satisfy my hunger.

Recall again how David compared his yearning for God with the imagery of a deer in a desert land, panting for life-giving water. "As a deer pants for flowing streams, so my soul pants for you, O God. My soul thirsts for God, for the living God" (Ps. 42:1–2). The focus in this word picture is not the deer but the water. It is on the cool, refreshing, sustaining properties of the desert stream that all eyes are fixed. The deer brings nothing to the brook but its desperation and its thirst. This is how we must come to God when we worship: desperate, thirsty, hungry, yearning, and dependent.

If you know you need God's help, you are postured to honor him and not yourself. It is God's very nature as immeasurably strong and resourceful to serve those who acknowledge they are weak and empty. The bottom line is that you and I must come to worship *spiritually famished* and desperate for what God alone can supply. The one thing we bring to God in worship that truly honors him is our need, a need that only he can meet.

So, when you worship, you come confessing your inability to do anything or to offer anything that will empower God or enrich God or enhance God or expand God. You come with heartfelt gratitude to God for the fact that whatever you own, whatever you are, whatever you have accomplished or hope to accomplish is all from him, a gift of grace. You come declaring in your heart and aloud that if you serve, it is in the strength that God supplies; if you give money, it is from the wealth God has enabled you to earn; if it is praise of who he is, it is from the salvation and knowledge of God that God has provided in Christ Jesus. You declare and celebrate the all-sufficiency of God in meeting your every need. You praise his love because if he were not loving, you would be justly and eternally condemned. You praise his power because if he were weak, you would have no hope that what he has promised he will fulfill. You praise his forgiving mercy because apart from his gracious determination to wash you clean in the blood of Christ, you would still be in your sin and hopelessly lost.

When you worship you come with an empty cup and say, "God, glorify yourself by filling it to overflowing." You come with a weak and wandering heart and say, "God, glorify yourself by strengthening me to do your will and remain faithful to your ways." You come helpless and say, "God, glorify yourself by delivering me from my enemies and troubles." You come with your sin and say, "God, glorify yourself by setting me free from bondage to my flesh and breaking the grip of lust and envy and greed in my life." You come with your hunger for pleasure and joy and say, "God, glorify yourself by filling me with the fullness of joy. God glorify yourself by granting me pleasures that never end. God, glorify yourself by satisfying my heart with yourself. God, glorify yourself by enthralling me with your beauty, by overwhelming me with your majesty, by taking my breath away with fresh insights into your incomparable and infinite grandeur. God, glorify yourself by shining into my mind the light of the knowledge of God in the face of Jesus Christ."

Come to Worship "for" God

I will wrap up this chapter by appealing to one word in one of my favorite worship songs. If you misunderstand this short, three-letter word, your worship of God will turn into a slanderous insult. Let me explain.

At my church, we often sing a Matt Redman song titled "Here for You." I often tell our people that little words can mean a lot. They can make the difference between good and evil, between heaven and hell. In this case, a single, short word is the only thing that prevents an act of worship from degenerating into a colossal insult to God. It's the word *for*. How so, you ask? Resist the urge to disregard my concern. Don't make the mistake of thinking that a preposition couldn't possibly matter that much. It does.

Imagine for a moment that a person in your church has fallen ill and is bedridden. While helplessly laid up, their house suffers from disrepair. The yard is overgrown and desperately in need of care. You and a small group from the church show up unexpectedly at his home, prepared to do for him what he simply cannot do for himself.

"Why are you here?" he asks. "What's this all about?"

"We are here *for* you," everyone responds in unison.

Think about the meaning of *for* in that sentence. You are telling your friend that you are present to provide a service *for* him, to act on his behalf. He is weak and sickly and in great need, and you and your friends are there to do for him what he lacks the strength and ability to do on his own.

Once the house has been cleaned and the yard has been mowed, the hedges trimmed, and the trash hauled off, the sick man says, "I can't believe you are so kind to me. That you would provide this service *for* me is amazing. I've been so weak and exhausted, I simply didn't have the energy to do for myself what you've done *for* me. Thanks so much."

What are you doing when you gather corporately on a Sunday or at any other time and sing praise to God? What is your intent? What is it that you believe you are achieving? When you sing, "We are here for you," in what sense do you use the word *for*? If you are singing and praying and praising and preaching in order to do *for* God what you and your friends did *for* that sick and needy man, you have insulted God. Now, why do I say that? Remember what the apostle Paul said in his speech on Mars Hill: "The God who made the world and everything in it, being Lord of heaven and earth, does not live in temples made by man, nor is he served by human hands, as though he needed anything, since he himself gives to all mankind life and breath and everything" (Acts 17:24–25). Simply put, God does not need you or me. He is altogether self-sufficient, dependent on no one. He is in fact the one who is responsible for the existence and preservation of all life, yours and mine. Therefore, he cannot be "served" as if he were needy or exhausted or weak or lacking something that only you and I and the people of your church can supply. To arrive on a Sunday morning and declare to God, "We are here *for* you," in the sense that you believe there is something you can give to God that he doesn't already have or that you can fill a gap or overcome a deficiency, is to insult God to the very core of his being.

That is why we must be extremely careful that we are never there *for* God in the sense in which we might be there *for* an invalid or someone who is destitute of the resources to care for himself.

But let's go back to your gracious and loving service *for* your friend who is bedridden. Let's assume that after your hard day at work in his yard in 100-degree heat, you are desperately thirsty. Suddenly there appears a truck at the curb, offering ice-cold, refreshing water. You run up to the driver and say, "We are here *for* you." Your obvious intent is that you are there *for* what the driver can supply. You don't pretend to bring him anything other than your thirst. You are desperate for refreshment. Without it you will faint. You are there humbly asking him *for* what he alone can provide: life-giving, thirst-quenching, soul-refreshing water.

Here's another illustration that makes the same point. Once you hear the music in your street, you know the ice cream truck is approaching. So you run out to meet it, only to hear the ice cream man ask, "What are you here for?" You wouldn't interpret the word *for* to suggest that you are there to help him, to bring him something he lacked. Far less are you there to do something on behalf of the ice cream he sells.

You are there *for* the ice cream in the sense that you want it, you need it, you've been desperate for the joy it brings when you eat it. You don't serve the ice cream, as if it were needy. It serves you!

That is how we are here *for* God. We cannot add to his resources as if he were in lack. He is infinite and immeasurably abundant and needs nothing from us. Rather, we are here *for* God in the sense that we need him as a thirsty man needs water, as a hungry traveler needs food, as a bankrupt beggar needs money, as a guilty soul needs forgiveness, as a broken heart needs healing, as a lost sinner needs salvation. That is why we are here *for* God. Only he can supply what we lack. Only he can give us what we need. If we gather *for* God, thinking that he stands in need of us, we insult him. But if we gather *for* God to drink deeply and feast upon all that he is for us in Jesus, we honor him.

The worshiper comes not to infuse God with breath but to receive it from him. The worshiper makes no pretense of filling up what is lacking in God but cries out for God to fill his or her heart with divine and supernatural life. That is how a simple, short, three-letter word can be used either to denigrate and dishonor God on the one hand or to honor and extol him on the other. May it always be the latter when we come together and say, "We are here *for* you!"

CHAPTER 9

The Freedom of Worship in the New Covenant

Is there all that much difference between how saints worshiped God during the time of the old covenant and how we do today, under the new covenant? Oh my, yes! Look with me at one text, Hebrews 12:18–24:

> For you have not come to what may be touched, a blazing fire and darkness and gloom and a tempest and the sound of a trumpet and a voice whose words made the hearers beg that no further messages be spoken to them. For they could not endure the order that was given, "If even a beast touches the mountain, it shall be stoned." Indeed, so terrifying was the sight that Moses said, "I tremble with fear." But you have come to Mount Zion and to the city of the living God, the heavenly Jerusalem, and to innumerable angels in festal gathering, and to the assembly of the firstborn who are enrolled in heaven, and to God, the judge of all, and to the spirits of the righteous made perfect, and to Jesus, the mediator of a new covenant, and to the sprinkled blood that speaks a better word than the blood of Abel.

Numerous lessons can be learned from this passage, but my focus here is on only one. It concerns the unmistakable contrast between the old covenant, represented by Mount Sinai, and the new covenant, represented by Mount Zion.

This contrast runs throughout the book of Hebrews. In each of the first ten chapters, Jesus is shown to be superior to someone or something: in chapter 1, it's the prophets of the old covenant; in chapters 1 and 2, the angels; in chapters 3 and 4, Moses; in chapter 4, Joshua; in chapters 5–9,

Aaron; in chapter 8, the old covenant itself; in chapter 9, the tabernacle; and in chapter 10, the sacrifice of Jesus is demonstrated to be in every way superior to the sacrifices offered during the time of the old covenant. Thus, we see that Jesus is a better mediator who has provided us with a better covenant enacted upon better promises. As a better high priest, he has offered a better sacrifice that assures us of a better hope, a better possession, and a better country, namely, the new heavens and new earth.

Here in Hebrews 12:18–24, the author did it again. Although his aim was the same, his approach was somewhat unusual. He contrasted the old covenant under Moses with the new covenant under Christ by comparing the two mountains that are symbolic or representative of each. But more important for our purposes, he vividly contrasted the people's experience as they drew near to God. Consider the remarkable differences that exist between the subjective experience of worshipers in the old covenant, under Moses, and that which is our privilege today in the new covenant, under Christ.

I'd like to ask you two questions. First, what do you typically bring with you to church on Sunday? And second, what do you expect to happen? Let's start with the first. I've often scanned the people assembled in my church, and I have never seen anyone arrive with a goat in tow. No one has brought a lamb to the service prepared to cut its throat and offer its blood on the platform. And I'm very grateful for that! Neither has anyone entered the auditorium with a turtledove or a grain offering. And why is that the case? Because no such sacrifice or blood offering can do anything to bring us to God in confidence that our sins have been fully and finally forgiven and our consciences wiped clean and set free from the condemning power of sin and guilt.

You come on a Sunday carrying with you a Bible, I hope, but not an animal sacrifice. You come knowing that the only sacrifice that could ever atone for your sins has already been offered once and for all time. You come confident that the obedience to the law required of you has already been provided in the sinless life of Jesus. You come confident and assured that the penalty required because of your sin has already been paid by the death of Jesus on the cross. And you come confident that God wants you to come boldly to his throne of grace to find mercy and help in time of need. You come knowing that Jesus, as Hebrews 7:25 tells us, stands joyfully at the Father's right hand to intercede on behalf of all those who come to God through faith in him.

I want to move beyond the objective differences between the old covenant under Moses and the new covenant under Christ. Consider how those objective differences affect our subjective state of mind and heart; how the differences between the old covenant and new covenant are expressed in our experience, in our affections and feelings, in the mood and atmosphere of a worship service. In thinking about that, we will find an answer to our second question, namely, what do you expect to experience on any particular Sunday?

Under the old covenant, the blood of bulls, goats, and lambs could never take away the guilt of sin. Those sacrifices only reminded people that sin remained because they knew they had to come back year after year to offer the same blood offerings over and over again. But in the new covenant, Christ has offered a single sacrifice of himself and of his own blood, once for all, that has forever removed our guilt, shame, and condemnation.

Now my question is this: What difference should this make in your heart when you draw near to God? What difference should there be in your affections, feelings, emotions, thoughts, and hopes? Does it make any difference? Is your experience any different from that of an old covenant believer approaching God in worship? Absolutely yes, or at least I hope you answered in your heart with a resounding yes!

I want us to think about what happens when we gather to pray, sing, celebrate, say thank you, partake of the Lord's Supper, and study God's Word. My concern is that far too many Christians come somber, sad, fearful, and tearful, almost as if they were attending a funeral service rather than the celebration of a resurrection from the dead!

The Israelites' Experience at Mount Sinai
(Hebrews 12:18–21)

The author of Hebrews vividly contrasts the experience of the people of Israel at Mount Sinai (vv. 18–21) with the experience of Christians at Mount Zion (vv. 19–24). Seven features describe the encounter of Israel with God at Sinai, which are then contrasted with seven characteristics of what we experience under the new covenant. These two mountains, Sinai and Zion, are designed to represent two covenants: the old covenant under Moses and the new covenant under Jesus. As we see repeatedly in Hebrews, the author wants us to understand that this new covenant and its blessings are better than what Israel experienced under the old.

The seven things the Israelites encountered at Mount Sinai are found in verses 18–19. Here the author draws upon Exodus 19:16–19 and 20:18–21; and Deuteronomy 4:11–14; 5:23–27. Let's look at the first two of these texts:

> On the morning of the third day there were thunders and lightnings and a thick cloud on the mountain and a very loud trumpet blast, so that all the people in the camp trembled. Then Moses brought the people out of the camp to meet God, and they took their stand at the foot of the mountain. Now Mount Sinai was wrapped in smoke because the LORD had descended on it in fire. The smoke of it went up like the smoke of a kiln, and the whole mountain trembled greatly. And as the sound of the trumpet grew louder and louder, Moses spoke, and God answered him in thunder. (Ex. 19:16–19)

> Now when all the people saw the thunder and the flashes of lightning and the sound of the trumpet and the mountain smoking, the people were afraid and trembled, and they stood far off and said to Moses, "You speak to us, and we will listen; but do not let God speak to us, lest we die." Moses said to the people, "Do not fear, for God has come to test you, that the fear of him may be before you, that you may not sin." The people stood far off, while Moses drew near to the thick darkness where God was. (Ex. 20:18–21)

As you can see, worship during the old covenant under Moses was not always a pleasant, uplifting, or emotionally exhilarating experience. It was terrifying, foreboding, and intimidating.

So, the author here in Hebrews 12 mentioned seven features of what the Israelites encountered: (1) a tangible or touchable mountain, (2) a blazing fire, (3) darkness, (4) gloom, (5) a tempest, (6) the sound of a trumpet, and (7) a voice that so utterly terrified them that they begged God to shut up!

The terms in verses 18–19 are designed to evoke an image of the awesome majesty of God who made his presence known at Sinai. And yet, somewhat ironically, God remained hidden to Israel. Notwithstanding all the noise and fearsome sights they encountered at Sinai, God was distant, obscured, and remote. The voice of God was of such a nature that instead of asking him to continue speaking, the people begged that he be silent.

This wasn't because God is evil. It was because the people were! It was their sin that provoked God's anger. It was God's holiness that kept them at bay. All these visual and auditory phenomena were simply another way of saying, "Your sin and guilt remain; and God is infinitely holy and righteous and cannot be approached unless a perfect sacrifice to cover that sin and guilt is offered."

Look again at verse 20. To reinforce and teach with unmistakable clarity the truth of God's holiness and the corruption that sin has brought on all of creation, God issued a decree that not only could no human being approach the mountain, not even a cow or goat, dog or cat could come near. If it did, it died! In fact, the sight of that mountain engulfed in fire, smoke, gloom, and doom was so foreboding that even Moses declared that he was trembling with fear (see Deut. 9:19).

I said earlier that these two mountains, Sinai and Zion, represent two covenants. Better still, they speak of two ways of viewing our relationship with God. At Sinai there is gloom and doom. Everything says, "Stay away! Do not draw near! You are not worthy to be close to God." At Zion there is joy and freedom. Everything says, "Come close! Draw near. Christ, by his blood and the forgiveness he has brought to you, has made you worthy to enter God's presence."

Our Experience at Mount Zion (Hebrews 12:22–24)

Beginning with verse 22, the author turns his attention to the liberating and joyful experience of those who draw near to God under the terms of the new covenant. But let's first take note of the statement in verse 18, "You have not come," and contrast it with the way verse 22 opens, "But you have come." To "come" or "draw near" to God is a recurrent theme in Hebrews. We see this same verb in Hebrews 4:16 where we are invited to "draw near" to the throne of grace in prayer. In 7:25 we are encouraged to "draw near" to God through faith in Christ because he lives to make intercession for us. In 10:22 we are exhorted to "draw near with a true heart in full assurance of faith," and in 11:6 we are described as those who "draw near to God."

I direct your attention to this recurring emphasis in Hebrews because I want you to understand your extraordinary privilege as a believer in Jesus. You can now draw near to God, come to God, and do so without the slightest tinge of fear or hesitation that you might be rejected. That's what Christianity is all about: drawing near to God even as he draws near to us. It's about relationship, about "nearness" and "dearness" and the unparalleled joy and peace that come from experiencing *relational intimacy* with our Creator and Redeemer! So, if you ever find yourself in a religious setting or a church service or in any other context that sends the message "Stay away, go back, don't come any closer," my advice is that you run away! That isn't Christianity. That isn't a New Testament church. New covenant Christianity invites you to draw near to God, to experience his love, acceptance, and forgiveness.

So, let's look now at that to which or those to whom we "have come." Notice the past tense. It's already a reality, an accomplished truth. This is an experience of the present, not just a future hope. The writer was describing what is true of us as the church now. This is a reality we encounter from the day of our conversion and throughout our Christian lives, all the way to the end.

Rather than experiencing fear, dread, and a sense of being distant from God, Christians have come into an experience of unparalleled joy and festive celebration! The reason is simple: through the blood of Jesus Christ and the establishment of the new covenant, we now live in God's presence fearlessly, boldly, and confidently.

Notice the seven features of our experience:

1. We "have come to Mount Zion and to the city of the living God, the heavenly Jerusalem" (v. 22). These three designations are synonymous and all refer to one thing. Mount Zion was the site of the Jebusite stronghold that David captured and made his royal residence some seven years after he became king. Zion eventually became the standard way of referring to the site of the temple and the city of Jerusalem as a whole.

Of course, the writer was not talking about the literal or physical mountain of Zion or the earthly city of Jerusalem, for he was contrasting it with the literal, physical Mount Sinai. Unlike Sinai, the mountain to which we "have come" cannot "be touched." The mountain to which we have come is the *heavenly* Jerusalem. Our identity as citizens of the kingdom of God is not tied to any earthly city, whether Oklahoma City, Jerusalem, or Washington, DC. We are citizens of the heavenly Jerusalem. Although the heavenly Jerusalem in its fullness has not yet been revealed to us, as it will come only when the new earth is established as our eternal dwelling, we are already its citizens and may even now enjoy its blessings.

Describing the heavenly Jerusalem as the city of the "living" God points to the fact that God is alive and active and very much present there. You and I don't draw near to an idea or an image of God or to some statue but to the God who is life.

2. We have come "to innumerable angels in festal gathering" (v. 22). Literally, these are "myriads" of angels, thousands upon thousands of them. The fervent joy implied by this gathering is in stark contrast to the doom and gloom experienced by the Israelites at Sinai. This multitude of angels is assembled in "festal gathering" (a word found only here in the New Testament but used in extrabiblical literature of parties and celebratory festivities). This word connotes excitement, revelry, and well-being.

God is often described in Scripture as being surrounded by tens of thousands of angels. Take this one example from Deuteronomy 33:2:

> The LORD came from Sinai
>   and dawned from Seir upon us;
>   he shone forth from Mount Paran;
>   he came from the ten thousands of holy ones,
>   with flaming fire at his right hand.

Or consider what we see in Revelation 5:11–12:

> Then I looked, and I heard around the throne and the living creatures and the elders the voice of many angels, numbering myriads of myriads and thousands of thousands, saying with a loud voice,
>
> "Worthy is the lamb who was slain,
>   to receive power and wealth and wisdom and might
>   and honor and glory and blessing!"

Do you realize what is happening in the countless plain auditoriums across the land every time we lift our hearts and voices in song and in praise of God? Do you realize that we are quite literally joining in with the myriads of angels surrounding the throne of the Lamb in heaven? We do not draw near to worship the angels but to join them in worshiping God!

I can't help but wonder what the angels must be thinking as they observe us make such feeble efforts to join them in praising God: *Look at those humans. Don't they realize their sins have been forgiven? Don't they realize they have been freely given eternal life when they deserved only eternal death? Don't they realize they are praising the God of heaven and earth? Can't they see the beauty and majesty and glory of this great God of ours? Don't they know what joy, exuberance, and festive celebration is called for? What's the matter with those people, anyway?*

3. We have come "to the assembly of the firstborn who are enrolled in heaven" (v. 23). These are people redeemed by the blood of the Lamb, as they are the only ones described in Scripture as having their names written down or enrolled in a book in heaven (Luke 10:20; Phil. 4:3; Rev. 13:8; 17:8; 21:27).

The point is that none of us worship merely as members of our local church. We join together with the universal church in heaven to adore and exalt God and his Christ! This, then, is the entire communion of saints, believers from both Israel and the church, the one people of God. Think about it: those who are described in verses 18–21 as fearing the presence of God are now celebrating in his very presence in heaven with all the other redeemed of every age! And we are one with them in this exalted worship of God!

4. We have come "to God, the judge of all" (v. 23). The reason for referring to God as "judge" is to reassure us that the judgment passed on us is one of acceptance, reconciliation, and forgiveness. That is why Paul so loudly declared that there is now no condemnation for those in Christ Jesus (Rom. 8:1). But this reference to God as the "judge" also reminds us that the one we adore, honor, and praise will ultimately bring evildoers and unbelievers to account at his throne.

5. We have come "to the spirits of the righteous made perfect" (v. 23). That they are "spirits" means these are the saved of all ages who, after physical death, entered the presence of God in a disembodied state. It isn't their final condition, as they will be physically raised and glorified at the time of Christ's second coming. But here we have explicit evidence for the intermediate state, that time between one's physical death and the time

of one's bodily resurrection. All the redeemed of every age are at this very moment together with angels celebrating the Lamb of God. And we "have come" to them in the sense that every time we worship or gather as the body of Christ on earth, we are one body, one people with them. Our voices and hearts are united with theirs in the praise of God.

So don't ever think that when a Christian man or woman dies, he or she falls into some sort of soul sleep or condition of perpetual unconsciousness. This passage (Heb. 12:23) clearly reminds us that when a Christian dies, he or she enters a state of conscious joy and celebration of the Lord Jesus Christ! Your friends and family members who knew Jesus Christ as Lord and Savior and have died physically are among those described here. They are very much alive, thinking, feeling, shouting, dancing, and celebrating in the presence of God, and we join with them in this worship each time we gather as the people of God on earth.

6. We "have come to Jesus, the mediator of a new covenant" (v. 24). We do not come to any mere mortal or to yet another fallen and corrupt human whose own sin must be atoned for. We do not come to Moses, Mary, Aaron, Sarah, Joshua, Daniel, Isaiah, Paul, or Peter, as great as such men and women were. We come to Jesus because he has established a new covenant in his blood by which we may draw near to God by faith.

7. We "have come to the sprinkled blood that speaks a better word than the blood of Abel" (v. 24). Why is the shed blood of Abel mentioned here, and why is it contrasted with the blood of Christ? Abel was the first man to have his blood shed. His brother Cain killed him. And his shed blood cries out for vengeance and justice. But when Jesus shed his blood, it spoke a word or delivered a message far better than that which Abel's blood made known. Whereas the blood of Abel spoke of vengeance and judgment, Christ's blood speaks of forgiveness and pardon. Christ's blood speaks of grace, mercy, and freedom.

What Difference Does All This Make in How We Worship?

We've seen that in the descriptions of the old covenant and Sinai there is an overwhelming portrait of God's unapproachability, as opposed to the experience of full and unhindered access to God and Christ in the new covenant.

The portrayal of the gathered assembly at Zion speaks of joy and exultation, warmth, openness, and acceptance, as opposed to the dismal portrayal of Sinai and its unmistakable message: "Stay away!"

I'm asking you to embrace a new way of thinking about what we, the church of Jesus Christ, are called upon to provide for those we invite to join us. I'm calling on every local church to change its way of thinking about what happens when they gather corporately to sing, pray, and speak God's Word. When we read this passage, there is no escaping the fact that the celebration of the new covenant resembles the revelry of a national holiday.

So, to what are you calling and inviting people when you ask them to come to your local church? Is it a place of dread where God is remote, distant, and unapproachable? Or are you calling people to join you in the experience of unparalleled joy? We are not to be unduly raucous or rowdy, but Christians, of all the people on the earth, have reason to celebrate with joy and exultation.

I'm not saying that there isn't a time for quiet reflection. I'm not saying that we shouldn't tremble in awe of God's majesty and holiness. I'm not saying we should never talk about God's wrath or the reality of judgment. What I'm saying, instead, is that even when we spend time reflecting on such truths and feeling the weight of God's holiness, we should very soon thereafter rejoice in gratitude and glad celebration that his holiness does not keep us at arm's length and that his wrath has been poured out upon and absorbed by Jesus. Yes, we must talk about the reality of sin, but never in such a way that we fail to speak of forgiveness. Yes, we must sing about God's infinite righteousness, but never without reminding ourselves that he has drawn near to us in saving grace and mercy through Jesus Christ.

I long for the atmosphere at my church to be unmistakably relational and personal, not dry and imposing. Everything about the church's life in the new covenant says, "Come! Find acceptance here. Be a part of this community, this family." May we never create an atmosphere or send a message that says, "Be afraid, be hesitant, perform in this way and act in that way so that you will prove acceptable to God."

When God spoke from Sinai, the people trembled in fear and begged him to be silent. But when God speaks to us through his Word, we hear grace, redemption, and freedom, and we should long to hear more. God's Word need not frighten us as it did them, because our sin has been forgiven,

God's wrath has been satisfied, and the breach between heaven and earth has been healed.

Do our sermons, songs, prayers, and rituals flash with the doom and gloom of Sinai, or do they reverberate with the light, love, and forgiveness of Zion? I pray that it would always and forever be the latter.

Freedom of Expression in New Covenant Worship

In his excellent book *Let the Nations Be Glad! The Supremacy of God in Missions*,[1] John Piper draws attention to yet another way in which new covenant worship differs from that in the old covenant.

He reminds us that worship in the Old Testament was rooted in and governed by the culture of a theocratic nation operating under the very precise dictates of the Mosaic code of law. One need only peruse the book of Leviticus to see the meticulous instructions given by God to which the people of Israel were bound in their worship. But when we come to the New Testament and the principles of the new covenant, we find very little in the way of precise instruction for how worship is to occur. This is largely because, with the coming of Christ and the covenant he instituted by his blood, the worship of God is to take place among numerous diverse ethnicities in various cultural contexts. To apply the principles of Jewish worship from within one historical time frame, as practiced by one ethnicity, to Gentiles around the world is simply not possible.

"What marks this true future worship," says Piper, "which has broken into the present from the glorious age to come, is that it is not bound by localized place or outward form. Instead of being on this mountain or in Jerusalem, it is 'in spirit and truth'" (John 4:23–24).[2] He reminds us that "in the New Testament, worship is significantly de-institutionalized, de-localized, de-externalized. The entire thrust is taken off ceremony and seasons and places and forms and is shifted to what is happening in the heart—not just on Sunday but on every day, and all the time in all of life."[3] In the New Testament "there is a stunning indifference to the outward forms

---

1. John Piper, *Let the Nations be Glad! The Supremacy of God in Missions*, 2nd ed. (Grand Rapids: Baker Academic, 2007).
2. Piper, *Let the Nations be Glad!*, 218.
3. Piper, *Let the Nations be Glad!*, 221.

and places of worship. At the same time, there is a radical intensification of worship as an inward, spiritual experience that has no bounds and pervades all of life."[4] One of the reasons for this, notes Piper, "is that the New Testament is not a manual for worship services. Rather, it is a vision for missions in thousands of diverse people groups around the world. In such groups, outward forms of worship will vary drastically, but the inner reality of treasuring Christ in spirit and truth is common ground."[5]

Piper contends that the reason why the worship and focus of the New Testament is so radically spiritual, rather than ritualistic and traditionalistic, is that Christianity is a missionary faith. The gospel of Jesus Christ is to be proclaimed to all nations, and the radical, internal, profoundly spiritual nature of true worship will assume differing external expressions depending on the particular culture in which it is embedded. In the Old Testament, all worship was regulated by the dictates of the Mosaic code. With the abolishing of the Mosaic covenant, virtually all formal, external expressions of worship are gone. That isn't to say the New Testament has nothing to say about what is essential to Christ-exalting worship. We are called on to read the Scripture in public, preach the Word, pray, sing (Eph. 5:19; Col. 3:16), and present our bodies in heartfelt devotion to the Lord (Rom. 12:1–2). But the essence of worship in the New Testament is unrelated to form or ritual and consists primarily in the joy of being satisfied with God.

None of this suggests that anything goes when it comes to public worship. Whatever is approved must be demonstrably illustrative or expressive of the truths revealed in Scripture and always theologically consistent with them. Admittedly, this is not an empirical science, as differing people from diverse traditions have conflicting ways of judging what is edifying to the body of Christ. At one service I attended, a young girl suddenly traversed the front of the auditorium doing cartwheels! To her way of thinking, this was a physically expressive way of giving vent to her freedom in Christ and the joy of being saved from hell. How is this any different from a woman (or man) dancing in an unprovocative, nonsexual manner at the side of the auditorium? Perhaps the young lady doing cartwheels would argue that God has gifted her physically in this way, which is one way she expresses

---

4. Piper, *Let the Nations be Glad!*, 222.
5. Piper, *Let the Nations be Glad!*, 222.

gratitude for his blessings. I'm quite sure that many will insist that such a physically demonstrative expression does little to draw attention to God and only serves to platform her personal gymnastic ability.

The "principle" by which I believe we should evaluate what is and is not acceptable to God in worship is neither only that which is explicitly prescribed in Scripture (known as the regulative principle) nor everything that is not explicitly forbidden in Scripture (known as the normative principle). Rather, depending on the culture, place, time, and participants, we are free to worship God in whatever way we find to be consistent with the truths of God's Word and suitable expressions of what is expressly asserted in Scripture. Much more can be said about what is acceptable to God in worship, and I've included further thoughts in appendix C, so be sure to check that out.

In the final analysis, the questions that must always be asked are these: Does this particular way of worshiping exalt and extol the greatness of God and his saving work in Christ Jesus? Does this particular expression in our corporate gathering serve to intensify in our hearts a satisfaction with all that God is for us in Jesus? Does our chosen form of worship edify the saints and make the gospel clearly known (see 1 Cor. 14:26)?

CHAPTER 10

The Sacraments as Worship

The Lord's Supper and Baptism

The Lord's Supper, or the Eucharist

In chapter 1, I cited C. S. Lewis's comment that part of his problem with praise was his failure to see that "it is in the process of being worshipped that God communicates His presence to men." I agree. And nothing bears this out more clearly than what we experience of God during observance of the Lord's Supper. If the notion of *Communion as worship* strikes you as odd, I suggest that you, like countless others, have lost sight of the role of the sacraments in the life of the local church. Whereas *singing* may well be the most obvious way to worship, it is by no means the only way. Here's what I mean.

When, on the night of his betrayal, Jesus uttered the awesome words "This is my body.... This is my blood" (Matt. 26:26, 28), he was providing a pledge of his abiding presence with his people that is to be recalled and experienced whenever they break bread together. Despite his impending death and exaltation to the Father's right hand, Jesus would yet be truly and powerfully "there" whenever his followers gathered to celebrate the sacrament. The implication is that in spite of Christ's physical departure from the earth, the bread and wine of the Lord's Supper, in some sense, serve to mediate his spiritual presence with those who know and love him. The elements not only point to and recall his death, but they also awaken us to the fact that Christ in his saving and sanctifying power is forever in our midst.

Paul's statement in 1 Corinthians 10:16 is especially important in this regard. We read, "The cup of blessing that we bless, is it not a participation in the blood of Christ? The bread that we break, is it not a participation in the body of Christ?" To partake of the elements of the Lord's table is to come under his influence and power; it is to commune and share with his abiding presence; it is to experience in a special way all those saving benefits and blessings that Christ's body and blood obtained for us.

This is simply another way of saying that the Lord's Supper is a *means of grace*. Don't be misled by this phrase. I am *thoroughly* Protestant. What I'm advocating here has nothing to do with the doctrine of transubstantiation or other related Roman Catholic concepts. The Roman Catholic Church contends that the sacrament contains the grace it signifies. That is to say, the elements of bread and wine inherently possess the power of rendering holy those to whom they are administered. This alleged inherent power of the sacraments to confer grace is analogous to that of *fire* to *burn*. Fire burns because it is ordained by God and imbued with power to that end. So, too, the Roman Catholic Church contends, the sacrament confers grace because it contains God-ordained, grace-imparting efficacy. Therefore, the sacrament conveys grace *ex opere operato*, which, being interpreted, means "by the working of the thing worked." That is to say, it is the nature of the sacrament that, when properly administered, it produces a given effect irrespective of either the recipient or the person officiating.

The Catholic doctrine of transubstantiation contends that a physical conversion of ordinary bread and wine into the literal body and blood of Jesus occurs at the moment the words of consecration or blessing are pronounced by the priest. The fact that after this transformation the elements still look, taste, smell, and feel like bread and wine is due to a distinction the Roman Catholic Church makes between the *substance* of a thing and its *accidents* (i.e., its external features). The bread and wine continue to *appear* as such but are *essentially* and *truly* the literal body and blood of Jesus.

When I refer to the Lord's Supper as a *means of grace*, I most certainly do not mean that the bread and wine in any way cease to be bread and wine or that they become something other than the simple physical realities we know them to be. Furthermore, we are not saved by partaking of this or any other ordinance. We do not receive forgiveness of sins, nor are we regenerated in the waters of baptism. The Lord's Supper does not atone for sin in any sense of the word. The ordinances do not impart eternal life to the believer, but they do confirm, strengthen, and heighten our awareness and enjoyment of that life. The bread and wine are *means* or *instruments* by which God quickens us to apprehend, understand, visualize, and experience the sanctifying influence of the Holy Spirit and his unique ministry of shining the light of illumination and glory on Jesus.

The reception and experience of spiritual blessing is often described in Scripture in terms of eating and drinking (see especially Ezek. 47:12 in conjunction with Matt. 4:4; 5:6; 8:11; Luke 14:15; John 4:13; 6:33, 35, 41, 48, 50, 51; Rev. 2:17; 19:9; 21:6; 22:1, 2, 17). Might we not infer, then, that "as our natural food imparts life and strength to our bodies, so this sacrament is one of the divinely appointed means to strengthen the principle of life in the soul of the believer, and to confirm his faith in the promises of the gospel"?[1]

This can happen in other ways, to be sure, but they are not for that reason "means of grace" in the way that I am using that phrase here. For example, I am often deeply stirred and edified by gazing on the majesty of God's creation, by watching a young child pray, or by reading of the courage of a dying saint. All such experiences may bring me closer to Christ and motivate me to service, gratitude, and sacrifice. But they are not, strictly speaking, "means of grace." I might not be able to specify precisely in what way(s) the influence of the Spirit through the Lord's Supper differs from his influence through other "natural" phenomena. I'm not even sure I need to. The point is simply that, unlike a multitude of other activities and experiences that may well edify, the Lord's Supper is ordained by God and required by Scripture to function as a means for mediating the spiritual presence of Jesus in the hearts of God's people.

I don't think my experience is unique when I say that I invariably find participation at the table of the Lord to be a profound moment of increased spiritual blessing. It is a means, through prayerful reflection, by which the Lord manifests his glory, love, mercy, and kindness to my religious consciousness. The Spirit works profoundly at the time of Communion to awaken in my mind and to impress upon my heart the eternal significance of Christ's finished work at Calvary and his love, not merely for people in general, but *for me* in particular.

---

1. Charles Hodge, *Systematic Theology* (Grand Rapids: Eerdmans, 1970), 3:647.

Protestantism and the Presence of Christ

The sacrament or ordinance of the Eucharist, also known as the Lord's Supper or Communion, is a crucial element in all true worship. This makes it especially important to differentiate between what I believe is the biblical perspective and that of the Roman Catholic Church.

At the Fourth Lateran Council in 1215 (also known as the Twelfth Ecumenical Council), the doctrine of transubstantiation became an official dogma of the Roman Catholic Church, largely through the influence of Pope Innocent III (1161–1216). The more comprehensive articulation of the Roman Catholic view is found in the documents of the Council of Trent. Consider the following excerpts:[2]

> First of all, the holy council [of Trent] teaches and openly and plainly professes that after the consecration of bread and wine, our Lord Jesus Christ, true God and true man, is truly, really and substantially contained in the august sacrament of the Holy Eucharist under the appearance of those sensible things.[3]
>
> But since Christ our Redeemer declared that to be truly His own body which He offered under the form of bread, it has, therefore, always been a firm belief in the Church of God, and this holy council now declares it anew, that by the consecration of the bread and wine a change is brought about of the whole substance of the bread into the substance of the body of Christ our Lord, and of the whole substance of the wine into the substance of His blood. This change the holy Catholic Church properly and appropriately calls transubstantiation.[4]

In chapter 8, canons 1 and 2, we read the following:

> If anyone denies that in the sacrament of the most Holy Eucharist are contained truly, really and substantially the body and blood together with the soul and divinity of our Lord Jesus Christ, and consequently the whole

---

2. All the citations below are taken from *The Canons and Decrees of the Council of Trent*, trans. H. J. Schroeder, OP (Rockford, IL: Tan, 1978).

3. *Council of Trent*, 13.1, p. 73.

4. *Council of Trent*, 13.4, p. 75.

Christ, but says that He is in it only as in a sign, or figure or force, let him be anathema. If anyone says that in the sacred and holy sacrament of the Eucharist the substance of the bread and wine remains conjointly with the body and blood of our Lord Jesus Christ, and denies that wonderful and singular change of the whole substance of the bread into the body and the whole substance of the wine into the blood, the appearances only of bread and wine remaining, which change the Catholic Church most aptly calls transubstantiation, let him be anathema.[5]

And in another place:

And inasmuch as in this divine sacrifice which is celebrated in the mass is contained and immolated in an unbloody manner the same Christ who once offered Himself in a bloody manner on the altar of the cross, the holy council teaches that this is truly propitiatory and has this effect, that if we, contrite and penitent, with sincere heart and upright faith, with fear and reverence, draw near to God, *we obtain mercy and find grace in seasonable aid.*[6]

The following declarations of anathema (often rendered by the word *accursed*) should be carefully noted.

If anyone says that in the mass a true and real sacrifice is not offered to God; or that to be offered is nothing else than that Christ is given to us to eat, let him be anathema.[7]

If anyone says that the sacrifice of the mass is one only of praise and thanksgiving; or that it is a mere commemoration of the sacrifice consummated on the cross but not a propitiatory one; or that it profits him only who receives, and ought not to be offered for the living and the dead, for sins, punishments, satisfactions, and other necessities, let him be anathema.[8]

---

5. *Council of Trent*, 13.8, p. 79.
6. *Council of Trent*, 22.2, pp. 145–46.
7. *Council of Trent*, 22.1, p. 149.
8. *Council of Trent*, 22.3, p. 149.

As one who, in the opinion of the Roman Catholic Church, stands "accursed," let me simply reaffirm what I wrote earlier in this chapter about the "presence" of Christ in the Lord's Supper. It should be noted, however, that there has never been complete agreement among Protestants on this subject. During the early years of the Protestant Reformation, a bitter split between two of its principal leaders concerned this very point.

Luther versus Zwingli

Huldrych Zwingli (1484–1531), leader of Protestant reform in Switzerland, and the German Reformer Martin Luther (1483–1546) could not come to theological terms on this issue of the presence of Christ in the Lord's Supper. Whereas both Zwingli and Luther repudiated transubstantiation as well as the belief that in the Eucharist was a repetition (or even a re-presentation) of the sacrifice of Christ for both the living and dead, they could not agree on the nature of Christ's *presence* in the elements.

Fearing the political consequences if the German and Swiss reformations did not unite, Philip of Hesse, leader of the German princes, issued an invitation to both Zwingli and Luther to meet at his castle in Marburg in 1529 to reconcile their differences on the Lord's Supper. Luther and his associate Philip Melancthon represented the German wing of the Reformation, while Zwingli and Oecolampadius represented the Swiss.

Luther argued vigorously for the doctrine of consubstantiation (although, as best I can tell, he never used that precise term), according to which the literal body and blood of Jesus were present in, through, under, and around the physical elements of bread and wine, without the latter undergoing any substantive change. Zwingli, on the other hand, insisted that the elements of bread and wine *symbolized* the body and blood of Jesus.

The debate proved fruitless. Luther stubbornly insisted on the literal force of the words: "This is my body," while Zwingli, no less stubbornly, pointed to the words of Jesus: "It is the spirit that quickeneth; the flesh profiteth nothing; the words that I have spoken unto you are spirit and life" (John 6:63). The dialogue was often bitter and is reported to have been along these lines:

Zwingli: "I remain firm at this text, 'the flesh profiteth nothing.'
   I shall oblige you to return to it. You will have to sing a
   different tune with me."

Luther: "You speak in hatred."

Zwingli: "Then declare at least whether or not you will allow John 6
   to stand?"

Luther: "You are trying to overwork it."

Zwingli: "No, no, it is just that text that will break your neck."

Luther: "Don't be too sure of yourself. Our necks don't break as
   easily as that."

Although they jointly affirmed fourteen articles of faith (such as the Trinity and justification by faith alone), they could not agree on the nature of Christ's presence in the elements. One final meeting was arranged. With tears in his eyes, Zwingli approached Luther and held out the hand of brotherhood, but Luther declined it, saying, "Yours is a different spirit from ours." To which Zwingli responded, "Let us confess our union in all things in which we agree; and, as for the rest, let us remember that we are brethren. There will never be peace in the churches if we cannot bear differences on secondary points." Luther replied, "I am astonished that you wish to consider me as your brother. It shows clearly that you do not attach much importance to your doctrine."

Unmistakably, these were men of deep conviction who believed that much was at stake in this issue. You can see that I have argued for a somewhat mediating position between the two. Whereas I reject any notion of a literal, physical presence of the body and blood of Jesus in the elements of bread and wine, I do affirm a *spiritual presence*, for lack of a better expression, that serves as a *means of grace* for the upbuilding and encouragement and internal strengthening of the believing soul.

FURTHER REFLECTIONS ON FEASTING
THE EXTINCTION OF INTINCTION

I want to include in this chapter a few thoughts about why I so strongly dislike intinction and why I believe it is detrimental to the message communicated in the Eucharist and to the fullness of what I believe the believer should experience in partaking of the elements.

For those of you not familiar with the word *intinction*, it refers to a particular way in which the elements of the Lord's Supper are served and ingested. With intinction, the believer dips the bread into the cup and ingests it in one act. There is no eating of the bread as a separate act or drinking of the cup as a separate act. Here is a more formal dictionary definition: "the action of dipping the bread in the wine at the Eucharist so that a communicant receives both together."[9]

At Bridgeway Church, where I formerly served as lead pastor, we observed the Eucharist by intinction for several years, much to my displeasure. We have recently enacted what I call the "extinction of intinction." Here is why. First, with intinction something quite profound is lost in terms of what both the bread and the wine signify. When I partake of the bread, I want to meditate on the reality of Christ's body, broken for me. His human frailty and the reality of his body being nailed to a tree for me are so important that I want the opportunity to meditate on and pray and worship over that profound reality. The action of physically ingesting the bread is a beautiful picture of my spiritually ingesting what that bodily sacrifice achieved for me.

It is much the same with the cup. The shedding of blood for the forgiveness of sins is unique and worthy of special focus. Yes, the body and blood are together the grounds for our hope. It was the holistic offering of Christ on the cross that saved. But when Jesus instituted the Eucharist, he spoke distinctly of the breaking of the body and the pouring out of the blood, and he ordained that each should be received for what it signifies.

What I'm saying is that when I ingest a soggy piece of bread (sorry for putting it so crudely; I don't want to be irreverent), I lose sight of the body that is broken that I am to eat, and I lose sight of the blood that is poured out that I am to drink. Maybe it's just my weakness, but there is

---

9. *Concise Oxford English Dictionary*, 12th ed., ed. Angus Stevenson and Maurice Waite (Oxford: Oxford University Press, 2011), 744.

something special about pausing and reflecting on each element as it is individually ingested. I think this is why Jesus instituted them separately and explained them separately and distributed them to the disciples separately. When I don't have the opportunity to drink the cup, but only ingest the wine as part of the bread, something is missing, something is lost in what I think our Lord wanted us to know and celebrate and to trust and thank him for.

Second, I don't want this to sound legalistic or overly rigid, but Jesus didn't institute the Eucharist by way of intinction. The very clear example he established in the Gospels that appears to be reflected in 1 Corinthians 11 is two separate elements, each of which is to be individually explained and individually distributed and individually blessed and individually received by the believer. I'm not comfortable with deviating from the clear biblical precedent unless we have very good reasons to do so, reasons that are unavoidable and clearly override whatever inconvenience or extra work is required of us to serve the two separately.

As you may know, in Catholicism there was a long tradition of withholding the cup from the laity when the Eucharist was served. This was due to two primary factors. First, they feared the spilling of the literal blood of Christ in the serving of it individually to each person. Obviously, this was based on the false concept of transubstantiation. Second, it was also done to elevate the priest to a level of spirituality unattainable by the average believer. Only the priest was privileged enough to drink the cup as well as eat the bread. The Catholic Church argued that if a believer ingested the bread, it was "as if" he or she had ingested the cup as well. The whole sacrament was contained in each part.

I think they were greatly mistaken in this. Those true believers who received only the bread were deprived of the joy of fixing their hearts and minds on the cup, which represented the blood that secured their redemption.

I'm not suggesting there is a perfect parallel between what the Catholic Church did and the practice of intinction. However, there is the danger that intinction will, over time, undermine or diminish the capacity of the believer to fully embrace, understand, and enjoy the reality of the bread that is broken and the blood that is poured out.

Please understand that I'm not saying that if you continue to utilize intinction, you are in sin or that the celebration of the Eucharist in this manner is sub-spiritual. I realize that in some churches and other settings, there are logistical demands that call for the use of intinction. In churches of considerable size, it may be impractical to provide individual cups for each participant. And in the era of COVID and other communicable diseases, the use of a single cup has become impractical. I'm simply saying that intinction is less than ideal and that you stand to lose much in terms of your appreciation for what the Eucharist is designed to signify and accomplish.

If you attend a church or happen to visit one this week where intinction is practiced, continue to celebrate the Eucharist with joy and thanksgiving (while praying that a more biblical manner of serving the elements will soon be implemented).

Water Baptism

I can still vividly remember the day in April 1960 when I was baptized at the First Baptist Church in Shawnee, Oklahoma. I don't remember a time when I didn't believe in Jesus, but I do recall that my faith seemed to come alive in an incredibly powerful way during a week of evangelistic meetings at the church. As was expected of Southern Baptists, I walked down the aisle and publicly confessed my trust in Christ. I was baptized two nights later, along with several others who had come to saving faith.

It's incredibly strange that among all the controversies that have plagued the Christian church in its now two-thousand-year history, none have been as vitriolic and divisive as those surrounding the two ordinances of the church: baptism and the Lord's Supper.

Here I want to address five questions regarding baptism. (1) What is the meaning of baptism? (2) What is the biblical mode of baptism? (3) What are the qualifications for baptism? How might one know if he or she is ready to be baptized? (4) Why is it that we who identify as credobaptists will baptize only believers in Jesus? Why do we oppose so-called infant baptism? (5) Should people who were baptized as infants be baptized again, or is phrasing the question in that way misleading?

What Is the Meaning of Baptism?

What does baptism mean? Why does it play such a prominent role in the life of the Christian and the church? And how does it contribute to our worship of God? Baptism is a sign, which is to say it signifies something beyond itself. It is a pointer that directs our attention to several important truths.

First, baptism is designed to direct our attention to the source and cause of our salvation: the death, burial, and resurrection of Jesus. We are not saved because of or through baptism but because of and through Christ and what he did for us. When people witness a person being baptized, they should immediately think about the way salvation has been obtained for us and passionately praise God for his grace.

The living Christ was crucified for our sins. He was then buried in the tomb of Joseph of Arimathea. He was finally raised from the dead and entered into a new and glorious phase of life. In other words, *baptism in water is a visual enactment of the gospel itself.* The gospel is the good news of what God did in and through his Son, Jesus Christ, to obtain for us redemption and forgiveness of sins. The Jesus who lived a sinless and perfect life on our behalf was crucified, suffering the judgment and wrath of God we deserved. The sufficiency and adequacy of his atoning death were confirmed when God raised him from the dead to a new life.

So, when you watch someone who is alive be immersed or buried beneath the waters of baptism, only then to be raised up out of the water, you are witnessing the gospel. You are seeing with your eyes and hearing with your ears what God did for sinners in Jesus. And for this he is to be extolled.

Second, baptism is a visible picture of the believer's death in Christ's death as well as his or her resurrection in Christ's resurrection. In other words, baptism is a picture of the believer's identification or union with Christ. It's more than simply a statement that I belong to Christ. It is a statement that I am "in" Christ. I am united with Christ. My life has no meaning or purpose apart from Christ. We are one—I in him and he in me. This is Paul's point in Romans 6:3–4: "Do you not know that all of us who have been baptized *into* Christ Jesus were baptized *into* his death? We were buried therefore with him by baptism *into* death, in order that, just as Christ was raised from the dead by the glory of the Father, we too might walk in newness of life."

When Christ died, he died our death. Baptism declares and signifies our identification with him in it. Look again at the threefold use of the word *into*. The word is designed to highlight our union with Christ so that what happened to him is reckoned by God as having happened to us. We are united to him spiritually so that his death becomes our death. But when we are baptized, we don't stay buried beneath the water. We are raised up out of the water as new people, pointing to the glorious truth that his resurrection life has become ours as well.

Paul said much the same thing in Colossians 2:11–12: "In him also you were circumcised with a circumcision made without hands, by putting off the body of the flesh, by the circumcision of Christ, having been *buried with him* in baptism, in which you were also *raised with him* through faith in the powerful working of God, who raised him from the dead."

Third, baptism is also the way in which a Christian says, "I am a new creation. The person you saw step into the waters no longer exists. He or she has been created anew by the power of the Holy Spirit. The person who emerges from the waters is governed by new affections and a new power." In other words, the person who is baptized is making it known that he or she has, by God's grace, taken on a new identity. "I am not the person you once knew. That person has died to the world and its ways. That person is now alive to God and his kingdom." In other words, in baptism we say, signify, and symbolize our faith in Christ. Faith unites us to him, and baptism symbolizes that union.

Fourth, baptism is a physical representation of what happens spiritually in the life of one who trusts Christ. In the waters of baptism, literal dirt is washed from the physical body. This symbolizes or illustrates the washing of spiritual dirt from the soul. Just as water cleanses a garment of a dark stain or blemish, so the Holy Spirit, through the blood of Christ, cleanses our hearts and minds and spirits from the stain of sin and guilt. Several texts make this clear. Here are two:

> And now why do you wait? Rise and be baptized and wash away your sins, calling on his name. (Acts 22:16)

> But when the goodness and loving kindness of God our Savior appeared, he saved us, not because of works done by us in righteousness, but according

> to his own mercy, by the washing of regeneration and renewal of the Holy
> Spirit, whom he poured out on us richly through Jesus Christ our Savior, so
> that being justified by his grace we might become heirs according to the
> hope of eternal life. (Titus 3:4–7)

Fifth, baptism is the Christian's *public pledge of allegiance* to Jesus
(1 Peter 3.21). To be baptized "in the name" of the Father, Son, and Holy Spirit
points to a change of ownership. It is a visible and vocal declaration that the
person now belongs to Christ. It is an individual's statement for all to see and
hear that from this point on they are devoted to Jesus and are determined
by his grace to follow Christ in all of life. Water baptism is the way in which
a follower of Jesus makes it known that they are not of this world, that they
are governed by a new system of values and beliefs. Although the Christian
is a citizen of an earthly state, their ultimate allegiance and dedication are
to Christ and his kingdom.

What Is the Biblical Mode of Baptism?

At Bridgeway Church, where I served as lead pastor for fourteen years,
and at Convergency Church OKC, where I now attend, we immerse new
believers in water. They are submerged under the water and then brought up
out of it. We do not sprinkle or pour water over the heads of these believers.
Why? We have three reasons.

First, most now agree that the Greek word for *baptism* means to dip,
plunge, or immerse. The practice of sprinkling or pouring emerged later in the
first few centuries after Christ as infant baptism became more widespread.

Second, the several accounts of baptism in the New Testament speak of
people going down into water to be immersed. We see this in Acts 8:36–39:

> And as they were going along the road they came to some water, and the
> eunuch said, "See, here is water! What prevents me from being baptized?"
> And he commanded the chariot to stop, and they both went down into the
> water, Philip and the eunuch, and he baptized him. And when they came
> up out of the water, the Spirit of the Lord carried Philip away, and the
> eunuch saw him no more, and went on his way rejoicing.

This passage makes more sense if they were going "down into the water" to immerse or submerge the eunuch, not sprinkle him. We also read in John 3:23 that John the Baptist "was baptizing at Aenon near Salim, because water was plentiful there, and people were coming and being baptized." If all you need is enough water to sprinkle, what's the point of saying that "water was plentiful there"?

Third, baptism by immersion more clearly portrays our identification with Christ in his death, *burial*, and resurrection.

What Are the Qualifications for Baptism?

People have often said to me, "Sam, I'm just not ready for baptism." The obvious implication in their words is that they believe they must do something to prepare themselves for baptism. They must rid their lives of some bad habit or recurring sin. They must seek the forgiveness of those they've sinned against. They think that before they can be baptized, they have to make considerably more progress in the Christian life. They have the idea that God intended it only for people who would stand up under the most rigorous scrutiny. In other words, they consider baptism an ordinance designed for people who have it all together, or at least sufficiently together that they are now qualified. The qualification, so they reason, is their responsibility.

It's a bit like a minor league baseball player who is told by the team manager that he's not "ready" for the big leagues. He still needs to work on his hitting. And his defensive skills could use some work. Once he gets those things functioning at a higher and more effective level, he still has to grow up emotionally and be certain that he's mentally prepared for the pressure of playing in the major leagues. Such is how many think of baptism. But it is bad thinking, unbiblical thinking, and we need to rid ourselves of it once and for all.

I'm not saying that anyone, regardless of their spiritual loyalties, should be baptized. What I am saying is that when it comes to the person who is born again and believes in Jesus as Savior, only God can make you "ready" for baptism. And he's already done it! The moment you trusted Christ as Savior, God "readied" you or "qualified" you to signify your union with Christ in water baptism. Whatever moral preparation you think is needed before you get baptized has already been achieved by Jesus. Whatever obedience to God's law you think must be achieved before you get baptized has already been accomplished by Jesus on your behalf.

The apostle Paul put it this way in his prayer for the Colossian church: May you be "strengthened with all power, according to his glorious might, for all endurance and patience with joy, giving thanks to the Father, who has qualified you to share in the inheritance of the saints in light" (Col. 1:11–12).

The point is this: you can't do anything to get yourself "ready" for baptism; you can't do anything to "qualify" for baptism. Jesus Christ has already done it all. Your "readiness" is not your righteousness; Christ's righteousness is imputed to you by God through faith in Jesus. Your "qualification" to be baptized in water is that you are trusting Jesus as the only truly "qualified" person who ever lived.

So, if you are holding back or delaying your baptism because you think you have to improve your life first or do something to make God proud of you, or at least stop doing the things that make God ashamed of you, you have failed to understand the gospel. The gospel is the good news that God has already done everything to qualify you and prepare you through the life, death, and resurrection of Jesus Christ. When you were united to Jesus by faith, you were instantly and fully qualified and made ready for baptism.

I am not suggesting, however, that you are to do nothing in preparation for baptism. It's important that you understand what baptism means. It's important that you aren't trusting in baptism but in Jesus' death and resurrection on your behalf. So, yes, it's crucial that you are instructed sufficiently in the meaning of baptism that it becomes a significant event both for you and everyone who bears witness to it.

But if you are trusting Jesus as Lord and Savior, you are as ready and qualified as you will ever be. Waiting five years or ten years will do nothing to improve your readiness or increase your qualifications. Christ has already done that for you, and nothing you do can improve upon it.

A Defense of Believer's Baptism

Why do I believe that only believers should be baptized in water? Why am I a credobaptist rather than a paedobaptist (*credo* comes from the Latin and means "I believe," hence baptism is for believers only; *paedo* comes from the Greek word for infant).

Before I answer that question, I will briefly explain why some Christians baptize their infants. The primary reason comes from their understanding of the relationship between Old Testament circumcision and New

Testament baptism. In the Old Testament, male infants were circumcised as the outward sign of entrance into the covenant community of Israel. This did not guarantee their salvation but marked them as recipients of the external blessings of a national covenant into which they were introduced by physical birth.

Christian baptism, so goes the paedobaptist argument, is the New Testament counterpart to Old Testament circumcision. It does not guarantee the salvation of infants but sets them apart as children of covenant parents who are thus included in the external blessings and responsibilities of the people of God. Baptized infants are thus "under the umbrella," so to speak, of God's new covenant blessings. Parents pray that their infant will personally receive the blessings of salvation in Christ, which baptism signifies. They hope and trust that baptism is the foreshadowing of what will take place when their child personally embraces Jesus as Savior. This is closely related to the idea that God deals not merely with individuals based on personal faith but with corporate entities based on covenant promise.

Paedobaptists also appeal to what they call "household" baptisms in the New Testament (see Acts 16:15, 33; 1 Cor. 1:16). Surely, they contend, there must have been infants in these households. Infants of Christian parents were therefore made recipients of water baptism.

Why am I not convinced by this? For the following reasons. First, the narrative examples in the New Testament portray baptism as being administered only to believers (see Acts 2:41; 8:12; 10:44–48; et al).

Second, baptism is portrayed in the New Testament as a symbol of the beginning of spiritual life (Rom. 6:3–4; Gal. 3:27; Col. 2:12 as well as "an appeal to God for a good conscience" (1 Peter 3:21). Unless one is prepared to predicate salvation and spiritual life to unbelieving infants or suggest that they are capable of making a conscious appeal to God for a good conscience, it would appear that baptism is restricted to those who consciously trust Christ.

Third, baptism is consistently portrayed as inextricably tied up with (conscious) faith and repentance (e.g., Acts 2:38, 41; 8:12–13, 36; 10:47–48). This is especially the case with Colossians 2:12 (see below).

Fourth, in all examples of so-called household baptisms the broader contexts make clear that only "believers" were baptized. Look at the story of the conversion of the Philippian jailer:

> And they spoke the word of the Lord to him and to all who were in his house. And he took them the same hour of the night and washed their wounds; and he was baptized at once, he and all his family. Then he brought them up into his house and set food before them. And he rejoiced along with his entire household that he had believed in God. (Acts 16:32–34)

It's quite clear that members of the "household" were old enough to hear and understand "the word of the Lord" spoken to them (Acts 16:32; thereby excluding infants) and old enough to understand what it meant for a person to believe in God and thus have reason to rejoice because of it (Acts 16:34; thereby again excluding infants; see also John 4:53).

Paul claims that he baptized "the household of Stephanas" (1 Cor. 1:16). But we see in 1 Corinthians 16:15 that the "household" of Stephanas, whom Paul baptized, "were the first converts in Achaia" who "devoted themselves to the service of the saints." Some have also appealed to Peter's sermon on the day of Pentecost. There we read,

> Repent and be baptized every one of you in the name of Jesus Christ for the forgiveness of your sins, and you will receive the gift of the Holy Spirit. For the promise is for you and for your children and for all who are far off, everyone whom the Lord our God calls to himself.... So those who received his word were baptized, and there were added that day about three thousand souls. (Acts 2:38–41)

As for the children in verse 39, they were at least old enough to be "called" by the Lord. And then, as if to confirm it, Luke recorded that "those who *received his word* were baptized" (Acts 2:41). There is no indication that those who were too young to respond to the "call" of God and too young to "receive" God's word were baptized.

Fifth, we must consider the nature of the new covenant inaugurated by the death and resurrection of Jesus and one way (although there are many) in which it differs from the covenant God made with Abraham. We read in Hebrews 8:11 of one of the chief characteristics of the new covenant and those who are members of it: "And they shall not teach, each one his neighbor and each one his brother, saying, 'Know the Lord,' for they shall all know me, from the least of them to the greatest."

During the time of the Old Testament, the people of God were a mixed community. Israel was composed of both believers and nonbelievers. Not everyone who was circumcised in his flesh was circumcised in his heart. Again, this simply means that not everyone who received the physical sign of the old covenant was born again or regenerate. This is why members of the nation of Israel had to be exhorted to "know" the Lord. But under the new covenant, we encounter an entirely different situation. Every member of the new covenant is a believer. Every member of the new covenant has been born again. Notice what the author said: *They shall all know me, from the least of them to the greatest*" (Heb. 8:11). This promise that every member of the new covenant will experience personal and firsthand intimate saving knowledge of God is one of the main reasons I don't baptize infants.

We must remember that God's covenant with Israel was *theocratic* in nature. Israel was not only the people of God; it was also a political entity. Therefore, all those who were physically circumcised were members of the covenant community, whether they ever came to saving faith or not. That's not true in the new covenant. Only those who come to saving faith are members of the new covenant community.

To say that every member of the new covenant knows the Lord doesn't mean that there aren't in our midst people who claim to know Christ but don't. But those who are genuinely saved and genuinely members of the new covenant are all born again and justified by faith in Jesus.

As noted above, paedobaptists say that since in Old Testament times circumcision, as the sign of the covenant, was applied to all, even though many never came to saving faith, baptism, as the sign of the new covenant, should be applied to all, even though many who are baptized will never come to saving faith.

But the new covenant differs significantly from every biblical covenant that preceded it, and thus, the analogy breaks down. Unlike in the Old Testament, everywhere in the New Testament, we read that members of the new covenant are born-again, justified believers in Jesus. Therefore, it is only to them that the ordinance of baptism is applied. Members of the new covenant are those who have the law of God written on their hearts, who belong to God in a relationship of personal intimacy, who know God, and whose sins have been forgiven. That is why I do not baptize infants. Infants who have not yet trusted Christ for salvation are not members of the new covenant.

Sixth, I can't help but notice the absence in the New Testament of any explicit portrayal of an infant ever being baptized.

Seventh, and finally, let's look again more closely at Colossians 2:11–12: "In him also you were circumcised with a circumcision made without hands, by putting off the body of the flesh, by the circumcision of Christ, having been buried with him in baptism, in which you were also raised with him through faith in the powerful working of God, who raised him from the dead."

Contrary to the paedobaptist argument, the New Testament counterpart to Old Testament circumcision isn't baptism; it's regeneration, the new birth. Or again, it is spiritual circumcision of the heart, not water baptism, that corresponds in the new covenant to old covenant physical circumcision of the flesh. By the way, even if one were to concede that water baptism is the new covenant counterpart to old covenant circumcision, the former is consistently predicated on the faith of the individual, unlike the latter. Indeed, this is the very point of Colossians 2:12.

Water baptism is a sign of the circumcision of the heart and the new life and cleansing from sin that it brings. The sign of the new covenant isn't baptism but spiritual circumcision, the "cutting away" of the heart of flesh, of which water baptism is an outward, symbolic expression. But more important still is Paul's reference to "faith" in Colossians 2:12. This personal, experiential trust in Christ is what differentiates entrance into the new covenant from entrance into the old covenant. During the time of the old covenant, infants obviously did not receive circumcision "through faith." Personal faith was not necessary for membership in the old covenant. But Paul said that only "through faith" is an individual united with Christ in his death, burial, and resurrection. It is only "through faith" that an individual enters into the new covenant and experiences its blessings, and that is something an infant cannot do. Simply put, if baptism is "through faith" it must be a personal, conscious act, an act of which infants are incapable.

Should Those Who Were "Baptized" as Infants Be "Baptized" Again?

One of the questions I'm often asked comes from Christians who were raised in a Presbyterian church or perhaps a Methodist or Anglican church where infant baptism was practiced. The question they ask is this: "I was baptized as an infant many years ago. Isn't that good enough? Should I be baptized again now that I am a believer in Jesus?"

I hope this doesn't offend those of you who fall into this group, but infant "baptism" is not biblical baptism. In other words, the religious ritual to which you were subjected in which water was sprinkled on your head is not biblical, Christian baptism. Baptism is what happens in water when a Christian, a believer in Jesus, declares publicly his or her faith in him as Lord and Savior. Therefore, if you were "baptized" as an infant, you were not truly "baptized." To be baptized as a believer in Jesus is not to be baptized "again"; it is to be baptized for the first time.

Please don't think that I'm being critical of your parents, who had you sprinkled as an infant. I'm quite sure they meant well. They did it as an expression of love for you and in faithfulness to what they believed was biblical. But their love and sincerity do not transform the act into genuine biblical baptism. For there to be a biblical baptism, there must be conscious, personal, saving faith in Jesus. So my strong word of encouragement to those of you who were sprinkled as an infant but have not been baptized since you became a believer in Jesus is that you obey God's Word and be baptized.

FURTHER REFLECTIONS ON FEASTING
THE QUESTION OF SPONTANEOUS BAPTISMS

Is it permissible or even preferable that local churches make available water baptism immediately upon someone's profession of faith in Jesus Christ? Permissible, yes. Preferable, no.

First, Acts 2:41 is the first instance of so-called spontaneous baptisms. But the gospel had been clearly presented to the crowd that day (vv. 22–36), and we might well assume that more was said to the people that isn't found in Acts 2. After all, most of the speeches in Acts are compressed summaries, and scholars tend to agree that they only represent a fraction of what was actually said or preached. We must also remember that the people on that day in Acts 2 ("men of Israel," v. 22) were adult, educated Jewish men and women who likely had substantial familiarity with Scripture. Their response to Peter's presentation of the gospel was not truly spontaneous, as they understood the nature and purposes of God from the Old Testament. That is rarely the case with someone who might get saved after visiting a church for the first time. My point is simply that the people of Acts 2 had a prior foundation in biblical truths even if it wasn't a fully formed new covenant perspective.

Second, in Acts 8 Philip provided the Ethiopian eunuch with a thorough gospel presentation (v. 35). Again, it should be assumed that their dialogue was long and involved and that the eunuch fully understood the gospel. The fact that in verse 36 the eunuch is the one who brought up the possibility of baptism indicates that Philip would have already explained to him what it was and wasn't and how it related to the gospel. We must also remember that the eunuch had no local church to which he could return and be baptized. He was the first convert in his country. If he was to be baptized, it had to be on the spot, overseen by Philip.

Thus, in both Acts 2 and 8, it appears that the people who were baptized were well informed about the gospel. Unless the message preached on the day of baptisms at your local church is likewise entirely gospel-focused, I wonder if those who respond wanting to be baptized can be expected to have been sufficiently informed as to its nature and purpose.

Third, we don't know if Cornelius and his household were baptized the same day that Peter led them to Christ (they probably were), but again, Cornelius would have heard an extensive explanation of the gospel (Acts 10:34–43). He was also a man who apparently, for some time, had a knowledge of the God of Israel (10:1–2).

Fourth, the case in Acts 19:1–7 is an unusual one. The disciples of John the Baptist had evidently been instructed well on the coming of the Messiah but were ignorant of the Spirit's descent on Pentecost.

Fifth, what would happen at a local church if some people responded to the invitation to immediately be baptized and then found themselves uncertain or unable to answer the question asked of them: "Have you trusted in Jesus alone for the forgiveness of your sins?" If they should hesitate or appear to have little knowledge about what it even means to trust Jesus, would we pull them back out of the water? That would be horribly awkward and confusing for many. It seems to me that if we expect someone to answer that question in a sincere and informed manner, some measure of instruction should precede it. Also, we ask them if they are committed to following Jesus in the power of the Spirit all the days of their life. I think it is unwise to presume that many of them would know what that entails.

Sixth, most people at my church in Oklahoma City have said that the best part of our baptism service is listening to the testimonies of each candidate being read from the platform. They usually respond with celebration and applause. If we do spontaneous baptisms, not only would most people in the assembly not know the person being baptized, but they would be deprived of hearing their testimony of how they came to saving faith.

Seventh, I've had many people come to me asking to be baptized a second time because they were either too young or too uninformed about the gospel to appreciate and understand their "first" baptism. Spontaneity is exciting and alerts us to the power of the gospel, but I fear that many will later realize they didn't understand what was happening. And that deprives them of the joy of reflecting on what they have done in response to what Jesus has done.

Eighth, I fear that some (many?) who respond on the spot and get baptized may not understand much (if anything) about what is and is not happening. Do they think that the water saves them? Do they connect baptism with the forgiveness of sins? Only a prior time of instruction can ensure they don't have unbiblical concepts of what baptism does and does not entail.

Finally, from a purely logistical point of view, spontaneity could likely prevent the candidate's parents, grandparents, and extended family from witnessing and participating in the ordinance. Most who are baptized at Bridgeway have a father, mother, or grandparent officiate and pray. If we baptize people on the spot, that is unlikely to happen.

All that being said, there may be circumstances in which baptism immediately following a profession of faith in Christ is appropriate. I am not prepared to argue that spontaneous baptisms are always unbiblical or sinful. But they strike me as pastorally unwise and face too many logistical barriers that serve only to undermine the ability of the candidate to fully understand and appreciate this incredibly important experience in their relationship with Christ.

CHAPTER 11

Sacrificial Giving Smells Good to God!

How We Worship God with Our Money

Hold on! Why include a chapter on money in a book on worship? What does the former have to do with the latter? Does our attitude toward money and the use of it have the potential to worship and honor God? Yes, it does!

I want to come straight to the point and justify from Scripture why sacrificial giving is an act of worship and is profoundly pleasing to God. After I do so, we'll dig deeply into what Scripture says about how we should view money and how we use it. But first, look with me at what Paul wrote in Philippians 4:18. After we do so I'll provide some background information on how Paul arrived at his conclusion. The following is his interpretation of what the Philippians did when they sent a substantial financial gift to support him in life and ministry: "I have received full payment, and more. I am well supplied, having received from Epaphroditus the gifts you sent, a fragrant offering, a sacrifice acceptable and pleasing to God."

Look closely at Paul's language. He referred to this financial gift as "a fragrant offering" or perhaps "an aroma of fragrance" that is "pleasing to God." The picture, said Gordon Fee, "is that of the 'aroma' of the sacrificial fire wafting heavenward—into God's 'nostrils,' as it were."[1] We see this same imagery following the devastation of the great flood. After the water had

---

1. Gordon D. Fee, *Paul's Letter to the Philippians*, New International Commentary on the New Testament (Grand Rapids: Eerdmans, 1995), 451.

subsided, "Noah built an altar to the LORD and took some of every clean animal and some of every clean bird and offered burnt offerings on the altar. And when the LORD smelled the pleasing aroma, the LORD said in his heart, 'I will never again curse the ground because of man, for the intention of man's heart is evil from his youth'" (Gen. 8:20–21). Aaron was instructed to offer up a ram as a "burnt offering" to the Lord. "It is a pleasing aroma, a food offering to the LORD" (Ex. 29:18). Three times in Leviticus 1 the food offerings are said to be "a pleasing aroma to the LORD" (Lev. 1:9, 13, 17).

Of course, we today no longer offer up a sacrifice of food or a ram or any other animal. The final and all-sufficient sacrifice offered up on our behalf is Jesus himself. And yet Paul used identical terminology to describe the death of Christ on the cross. In Ephesians 5:2 Paul spoke of Christ's death as "a fragrant offering and sacrifice to God."

Perhaps the most well-known use of this language is found in Romans 12:1, where Paul appealed to all Christians "to present your bodies as a living sacrifice, holy and acceptable to God, which is your spiritual worship." The word translated "present" (cf. Rom. 6:13, 16, 19) is an echo of the language we saw in Leviticus 1. The point is that when we offer up our "bodies" to God, we are engaging in authentic and God-exalting "worship." Paul undoubtedly was using the word *bodies* here in a comprehensive, holistic way. It includes the totality of who we are. It was Paul's way of saying, "God wants *you*! He doesn't merely want a gift. He wants the *giver*!" Sadly, some believers think of the Christian life as exclusively spiritual or immaterial in nature. But our bodies (and our possessions) are just as important. Our bodies have been redeemed by the blood of Christ and are the temple, or dwelling place, of the Spirit. Our bodies will be fully redeemed, glorified, and raised to life in the new heavens and new earth. So never forget that your body belongs to God no less so than your spirit. Thus, to "present" your "bodies" unto God means that you consecrate and dedicate everything you are and own in such a way that God is seen to be glorious and great.

This presentation or offering to God is a "living" sacrifice, one that does not die or have a temporary shelf life. Presenting ourselves to God is holistic and perpetual. There is no time limit. It also must be a "holy" sacrifice, by which Paul meant that you and I are set apart for God, consecrated exclusively for him and his glory. This must be a sacrifice that is "acceptable" to God. Perhaps a better rendering of this word is "well-pleasing" to God.

Of note is the fact that the same Greek word is used here that we find in Philippians 4:18 (*euareston*). The devotion and dedication to God of ourselves and our possessions brings him pleasure!

That our giving or presentation of this sort is truly worship is confirmed by Paul saying it is our "spiritual worship" (Rom. 12:1). The word translated "worship" is the same one used in Romans 9:4, where Paul said one of the blessings experienced by Israel was "the worship," likely referring to all the activities and sacrifices offered up in the temple. When we present ourselves to God, we are worshiping him! But what kind of worship did Paul mean?

The word translated "spiritual" is the Greek word from which we get our English term *logical*. It may be that Paul was saying our worship is reasonable, wholehearted. Some have suggested it means appropriate, rational, perhaps even fitting the circumstances, worship that makes sense in view of the way God has treated us so mercifully in Christ Jesus. But I think the word *spiritual* better captures the idea Paul had in mind. Our worship is never to be mechanical, merely external, automatic, or simply a ritual. It is genuine and flows from within our hearts and spirits.

We mistakenly think worship is only singing. It is everything we are, do, and offer up to God to bring honor to his name. Simply put, we are to make use of our bodies, which is to say, the totality of who we are, to display the worth of God and all that he is for us in Christ.

We find similar language again in Hebrews 13:15–16: "Through him [Christ Jesus] then let us continually offer up a sacrifice of praise to God, that is, the fruit of lips that acknowledge his name. Do not neglect to do good and to share what you have, for such sacrifices are pleasing to God." The author of Hebrews spoke extensively about "sacrifices": the blood of bulls and goats and lambs offered up as a sacrifice on the altar of the old covenant, first in the tabernacle and later in the temple. But we've also heard that Jesus came as the fulfillment of all such sacrifices and that by his offering up of himself to suffer for our sins, he fully and finally satisfied the wrath of God against us and secured our eternal forgiveness. Thus, with the coming of Jesus, the meaning of "sacrifice" changed. Our sacrifice is no longer a goat or a turtledove or a grain offering, but an entire life devoted to the glory and praise of God. We give our all that God might be seen as beautiful and worthy. Our praise of him is designed to awaken the world to him as the preeminent treasure in the universe.

So, we must remember that the fact that the sacrifices of the Mosaic covenant are no longer required of Christians under the new covenant does not mean we have nothing to bring as a sacrifice to God. The important difference between our sacrifices under the new covenant and those of the old covenant is that we do not come to God to obtain forgiveness of sins but because they have already been fully and finally forgiven through Christ. Furthermore, our sacrifices are not bloody, but spiritual. And they are not to be limited to specified days of the year in accordance with feasts and other rituals, but are to be continual and daily, to be offered always.

Don't overlook that God-pleasing praise is not merely one of singing but also of serving. The sacrifice of praise is more than a song. It's also rigorous work, heartfelt generosity, and true compassion for those who are hurting and in need. God loves to see that as much as he loves to hear the other. We see this clearly in verse 16, where the doing of good and the sharing of our possessions is also referred to as a "sacrifice" of praise to God. The point is that you can't worship God in a way that pleases him if you continue to greedily clutch your money and time and turn your back on the needs that exist in the body of Christ.

But how is it that doing "good" and being generous with our money is an act of worship? Worship is obviously all about making God look good. The sacrifice of praise is designed to make known the preeminent value of God. We worship to magnify him as our greatest and most highly prized treasure. So, how does financial generosity do that?

Is it not obvious? When you make generous and sacrificial use of your wealth to help others, you declare that your treasure is in heaven, not on earth. To do good to those in need and to give abundantly to the work of Christ in and through the church shows that you are living not for this world or this city but for the city and the world that are to come. It is your way of saying that your greatest joy isn't in what your money can purchase for you in this present "city" but in what it can do to promote the glory of God in that "city" that is to come.

When we live and give sacrificially for Christ's sake, we make him look more valuable than things. In Hebrews 13:14 the author declared that "here we have no lasting city, but we seek the city that is to come." This is not just a statement of theological truth. It is a revelation of the orientation of your heart. If your heart is set on seeking the city that is to come, you are set free from bondage to material wealth, and you will gladly give generously as another act of praise to God. To be stingy with your time, energy, or money is definitive proof that you have no idea what verse 14 is all about!

When our hearts are supremely satisfied in God, they won't look for satisfaction in the stuff of the cities of this present world. When we set our hearts on the Creator rather than the creation, when we trust in all that God is for us in Jesus rather than in what worldly comfort and opulence can supply, we honor him, magnify him, and declare that he alone is of supreme worth and value. When our hearts are abundantly full of the presence of Christ and the pleasures he imparts, they will overflow in the sacrifice of praise, lips that proclaim his superiority to anything we might own or enjoy in this city. And that verbal praise will stir our hands to work for the good of others and give to alleviate their suffering.

Ask yourself this question: "Does the way I live show that Jesus is more precious to me than possessions? Does the use of my time, energy, and money show that my heart is set not on this present city but the one that is to come?"

And all of this, the writer said, is eminently "pleasing to God" (Heb. 13:16). Why? Because it magnifies the worth of his Son, Jesus Christ, and is a blessing to the very people for whom he suffered reproach, shame, and death outside the camp. There's another reason it's pleasing to God. In Hebrews 13:5 we were exhorted to keep our lives free from the love of money and to be content with what we have because God has promised always to be with us and never to leave or forsake us. If you love yourself and your money inordinately, you will find every excuse possible not to obey verse 16. If you love money, you will trust *it*, rather than the presence of God, to bring you happiness. If you love money, you will cherish it and strive to obtain all this present "city" can provide instead of seeking the spiritual treasures of the city that is to come.

The way you keep your life free from the love of money is by trusting God's promise that he will never leave you nor forsake you. Therefore, every time you offer up the sacrifice of doing good and sharing your wealth, you make it clear to all concerned that you aren't dependent on money for your happiness but on God and all that he is for you in Jesus and all that he has promised to provide for you in the city that is to come.

So, when we come to Philippians 4:18, we see that Paul transformed the significance of the believers' monetary support by reformulating it in terms of a sacred and sacrificial offering to God. Their financial support of Paul was a distinctively religious or spiritual act of worship. Walter Hansen sums it up best:

> These gifts can no longer be measured simply in terms of financial value or social value. God's pleasure in the gifts reframes them with spiritual, divine significance.... The meaning of the gifts is derived not so much from the way they benefit Paul, the one who received these gifts, but from the way that the Philippians, those who gave these gifts, fulfilled the will of God and pleased God by their gifts.[2]

I trust that all will now agree that the sacrificial use of our money is as much an act of biblical worship as is singing, dancing, or any other expression of heartfelt adoration of God. We are now ready to look more closely at what the Scriptures say about our attitude toward money in general.

Why Is Talking about Money So Controversial?

Scripture has more than 2,300 references to finances and money. Many would prefer that the Bible say nothing at all on the subject because any mention of it makes them feel uncomfortable. Some feel guilty for not being generous and for having fallen far short in financial stewardship. Others feel uncomfortable because they think the only time a preacher would ever bring it up is when he wants to elevate his own personal standard of living.

Then there are those who are uncomfortable because they believe that among the topics one should never talk about in public, money and how we spend it is right up there at the top of the list. For these people, it's a violation of personal boundaries to talk about finances.

There's another sort of Christian who gets uncomfortable when money is mentioned. They aren't necessarily derelict in their stewardship of money. They aren't necessarily stingy or suspicious of leadership in the church. Their discomfort comes from a conviction that to speak of money is evidence of a

---

2. G. Walter Hansen, *The Letter to the Philippians*, The Pillar New Testament Commentary (Grand Rapids: Eerdmans, 2009), 324.

lack of faith. If we simply had enough trust in God to provide, we wouldn't need to consider those hundreds and hundreds of Bible verses that talk about money. Whatever the church needs to thrive would simply flow in effortlessly and without fanfare.

Then, of course, a few people in the local church aren't bothered at all or for any reason when money is mentioned. Their response is, "Bring it, brother! Preach it! Why have you waited so long and been so reluctant to speak on something so essential to Christian living?" And that raises a crucial question we need to address: Is the subject of financial stewardship an essential element of Christian worship? Not optional, but essential. I can't imagine anyone who takes the Bible seriously saying, "No, it isn't." Let's pursue this point a bit further.

If you discovered that a close friend of yours, who professed to be a Christian, rarely if ever read the Bible, you would be concerned for them and would at the right time call them to account. Or perhaps they simply refused to share their faith with a non-Christian when given the opportunity. My hope is that you would challenge them regarding their overt disobedience to God's Word.

Would you not do the same thing if you discovered they were habitually lying and deceiving people? Would you not be concerned if it came to light that they were developing an emotional affair with a coworker or if you heard them use profanity on a regular basis? What would be your response if it became evident that they had largely stagnated in their relationship with Christ and had simply stopped growing, perhaps even reverting to their old ways of sin and selfishness? Or maybe they've fallen prey to false doctrine and are espousing some novel idea that has no basis in the Bible.

I trust that all of us agree that these are matters of great concern and that they should be addressed. So why do we put financial stewardship in a separate category and treat it as if it were an unmentionable topic? Why does one's use of material resources get a free pass when these other issues, which are collectively referred to far less in Scripture than is money, are so openly talked about?

I suppose some may argue that there's something uniquely and intimately personal about money that puts it in a category unto itself. Really? More intimately personal than one's sex life or the way someone speaks about their spouse, or more personal and intimate than their prayer life or any other aspect of Christian experience?

The intriguing fact is that most men will more readily talk with other men about their struggles with sex than they will their battle with materialism. My goodness! If that doesn't shed some light on the nature of what we're dealing with, nothing will.

Now, if I were going to address this subject in another context, perhaps in a third world country, a church in downtown Manhattan, or an Eastern European socialist setting, I might say things a bit differently. But here in America in 2025, I'm convinced we approach the subject of financial stewardship in the Christian life the way we do for two primary reasons.

First, our understanding of "tithing" has a major impact on whether and how much we give and whether we believe giving is a biblical responsibility of every Christian. I was raised as a Southern Baptist, and in the SBC few things are more sacred than the concept of the "tithe," the giving of 10 percent of one's income. I was taught this from my childhood, and my parents were faithful tithers, as were my sister and I.

But as I studied the Scriptures, I concluded that with the coming of Christ and the establishment of the new covenant, under which Christians live, no specific percentage is mandated as the minimum or maximum of giving.[3] The problem is that many conclude that if no specific percentage is mandated, then giving itself isn't mandated. In other words, many—and I mean many—Christians have taken this truth and greatly, though quietly, rejoiced, using it as an excuse to give very little or nothing at all. You can almost hear them say, "Whew! That's a relief. God doesn't require a specific amount of my income. I guess that means we can buy that new house and go on that expensive vacation, and I can finally purchase that new set of golf clubs." Or they say, "Well, I guess this means giving isn't that important in our worship of God. If it were, God would have told us precisely how much to give. So, if I choose to give very little or perhaps even nothing at all, that's part of my freedom as a Christian who is no longer bound by Old Testament law." That is precisely how people think. That is precisely how they rationalize their stinginess.

---

3. I address this issue at length in the chapter titled "Are Christians Obligated to Tithe?" in my book *Tough Topics: Biblical Answers to 25 Challenging Questions* (Wheaton, IL: Crossway, 2013), 319–40.

People often ask me, "Okay, Sam, then how much *should* I give?" My response is twofold. I first ask, how much do you *want* to give? Considering what you know about the cross of Christ, about saving grace, heaven, the Holy Spirit, forgiveness, the beauty of Christ, the reality of hell, and the fact that people without Jesus Christ are going there, how much do you *want* to give?

If my first answer isn't adequate, I say, "Why don't you *start* with 10 percent and see where it might lead?" There's nothing especially sacred about 10 percent, but I think it's a great place to begin. "But Sam, I thought you said we don't have to give 10 percent." That's right, you don't. You have the tremendous privilege of giving more!

Second, our approach to financial stewardship has been warped and badly shaped by the flourishing of the prosperity gospel in our churches. The excessive self-indulgent lifestyle of certain so-called Christian leaders has put a sour taste in our souls when it comes to the subject of money and ministry in the local church. Many are so offended by the shameless appeals for more, the endless round of offerings, and the opulent lifestyle of those to whom the money is given that they find it almost impossible to think about the subject, much less speak about it. And thus, they are upset when someone actually tries to present a biblical perspective on the issue of financial stewardship.

I'll share one more thing before we see what the Scriptures have to say about giving. My dad was a banker for the first thirty-five years of his working life. He often said to me, "Give me five minutes in a man's checkbook, and I'll tell you everything you need to know about him. I'll tell you whether he loves God, his wife, and his children. I'll tell you whether he really believes the Bible. I'll tell you what he values and what he hates, what he believes, and how he spends his time. I'll tell you whether he can be trusted or whether he lies. I'll tell you how he'll respond in a crisis and in times of ease." I used to think my dad was exaggerating, but no more.

When I asked him how he could be so certain of all this, he quoted to me Matthew 6:21: "Where your treasure is, there your heart will be also." His point was spot on target. Jesus is telling us that how one uses one's money and material resources will tell you everything you need to know about the character and conduct of the person, be they male or female, young or old.

1 Chronicles 29:6–20

The first text we'll examine is found in 1 Chronicles 29:6–20, where we read of the wealth raised for the temple's construction.[4] On reading this, one might think that we should congratulate David and the people of Israel for their generosity. But a closer look reveals that God was responsible for their giving.

Early in chapter 29, David declared that he made provision for the temple "so far as I was able" (v. 2). The people likewise "made their freewill offerings" (v. 6). They "rejoiced because they had given willingly" and "with a whole heart they had offered freely to the LORD" (v. 9). David said that it was "in the uprightness" of his "heart" that he had "freely offered all these things" (v. 17). The people joined him in his generosity, "offering freely and joyously" to God (v. 17). This is precisely the attitude and mindset that should be true of all of us when we give to the work of the kingdom.

If you are wondering what prompted these acts of financial generosity, the answer is found in David's words as he "blessed the LORD in the presence of all the assembly" (29:10). This blessing takes the form of a dozen affirmations concerning who God is and what he does, all of which undoubtedly stimulated God's people to give so much to the building of the temple.

David pointed to God's "greatness ... power ... glory ... victory and ... majesty" and to the fact that "all that is in the heavens and in the earth" belong to God (29:11). In other words, all the wealth the people of Israel amassed and gave back to God was already in God's possession. He owns everything! "Both riches and honor come from you," said David (v. 12). From a purely human point of view, the money and wealth given for the building of the temple seemed to have come from the work, savings, and investments of the people. Perhaps some of them had profited from shrewd business transactions. Perhaps a few had turned an extraordinary profit on the sale of some land. But no matter, David said *all riches* come from God!

The energy and whatever the people employed to build their wealth were also gifts from God, for it is in his "hand" to "make great and to give strength to all" (29:12). Power, influence, ingenuity, success, commitment, whatever

---

4. Some of what follows concerning 1 Chronicles 29:6–20 is adapted from my book *Pleasures Evermore* (Colorado Springs, CO: NavPress, 2000), 61–64, and is used here with permission.

it might be, are the result of the gracious and kind operation of a giving God working in and through his people for their welfare and his glory.

Perhaps the most instructive thing David said comes next in 29:14: "For all things come from you, and of your own have we given you." David didn't say "*to* your own," as if everything originated with the people and ended with God. Rather, it was "*of* [or *from*] your [God's] own" that they had given to God. In other words, whatever they gave they first received from God. David said much the same thing in 29:16: "O LORD our God, all this abundance that we have provided for building you a house for your holy name comes from your hand and is all your own." We do not offer to God what he lacks. In giving we do not add to his resources or increase the balance of his bank account. How can you increase the wealth of someone who already owns it all?

Finally, David was concerned for his son Solomon and prayed that God would "keep forever" this mentality and desire to give in his heart and "in the hearts of" the people of Israel (29:18). God's enabling in this matter is not simply that he makes it possible for us to work hard, not simply that he bestows riches on whomever he pleases, but that he actually *gives us the willingness to give*! Yes, the people did the giving (v. 9). They gave willingly, of their own accord, and with joy. This was genuine giving, freely chosen, joyfully engaged. They made decisions. Real decisions. Sacrificial decisions. Decisions that made a difference. Decisions without which the temple would not have been built. But mysteriously, in ways that you and I will never fully understand, beneath and behind these choices was the gracious, enabling work of God.

What all this means is that our God is a God of infinite, immeasurable wealth. He owns everything that is. He does not stand in need of gifts or offerings or contributions as if he were poor, helpless, and dependent. We are the poor, helpless, dependent ones. God is always the giver. We are always the getters! We must understand this if we are to progress in growth in our Christian lives and in our pursuit of holiness, and especially in our efforts to honor and extol God in worship.

Philippians 4:10–20

One might expect that my second text would be drawn from 2 Corinthians 8–9, where we find Paul's most extended teaching on money and stewardship.

But I have chosen instead to look at Philippians 4:10–20. My conviction is that we learn more about money from this chapter and its role in worshiping God than in any other place in the Bible.

I rejoiced in the Lord greatly that now at length you have revived your concern for me. You were indeed concerned for me, but you had no opportunity. Not that I am speaking of being in need, for I have learned in whatever situation I am to be content. I know how to be brought low, and I know how to abound. In any and every circumstance, I have learned the secret of facing plenty and hunger, abundance and need. I can do all things through him who strengthens me.

Yet it was kind of you to share my trouble. And you Philippians yourselves know that in the beginning of the gospel, when I left Macedonia, no church entered into partnership with me in giving and receiving, except you only. Even in Thessalonica you sent me help for my needs once and again. Not that I seek the gift, but I seek the fruit that increases to your credit. I have received full payment, and more. I am well supplied, having received from Epaphroditus the gifts you sent, a fragrant offering, a sacrifice acceptable and pleasing to God. And my God will supply every need of yours according to his riches in glory in Christ Jesus.

To our God and Father be glory forever and ever. Amen.

I should point out that, as was his custom, Paul probably dictated this letter to a secretary, most likely Epaphroditus. But as was also his custom, now that he had reached the end, he probably reached out and took the pen from Epaphroditus and wrote this concluding paragraph not only as a formal thanksgiving to the believers in Philippi but also to express his deep affection for them as his fellow believers in Jesus.

FURTHER REFLECTIONS ON FEASTING
CHARGING FOR SERVICE?

Some have wondered why Paul would have alluded to the church's financial support in Philippians 1:5 only then to drop the subject and then bring it up again here at the conclusion of his letter. We don't know, but part of the answer may be in Paul's personal perspective and policies concerning money. In a day when talking about money in church is either expected or avoided, we need to take a minute and consider Paul's financial policy (see especially 2 Cor. 11:7–12). A quick summary will suffice.

Paul clearly believed he had a right to be supported by those to whom he ministered (see 1 Cor. 9:1–19; Gal. 6:6; 2 Thess. 3:8; 1 Tim. 5:17–18; cf. Matt. 10:10; Luke 9:3–4; 10:4, 7; 3 John 5–8), even though he consistently chose not to avail himself of it. We know that he actively solicited financial assistance for *other* Christians in need (1 Cor. 16:1–4; 2 Cor. 8–9), but only rarely did he actively solicit financial assistance for himself (Rom. 15:24). While serving in a city like Corinth, he was not opposed to accepting financial assistance from other churches where he had ministered in the past (cf. 2 Cor. 11:8–9; Phil. 4:10–20). Thus, as a general rule, he would not accept support from a church while he was living in their midst and ministering to them (1 Thess. 2:9; 2 Thess. 3:6–12), but only after he had departed.

Since teachers, philosophers, and orators in ancient times were expected to charge for their services in proportion to their skill and gifting, Paul's refusal to accept financial support from the churches exposed him to the accusation of being a fraud. The false teachers had put Paul in a no-win situation: if he refused remuneration, he betrayed his own awareness of inauthenticity, incompetence, and lack of authority, but if he received remuneration, it was because he was greedy and thus was guilty of peddling the gospel. Add to this the fact that manual labor, such as tent-making (Paul's chosen trade), was viewed by the Greeks with disdain.

Paul clearly knew that the reputation of the gospel was, to a degree, dependent on his own integrity. Paul's stature and position in the first century was not unlike that of Billy Graham in the twentieth. Evidently, he didn't want to take any chances that someone might think he was in the ministry for the money. He knew the allure of wealth and chose to take extreme measures to guard himself from any possibility of temptation or grounds for slander. He wanted to be absolutely free to preach the truth without exposing himself to the pressure of those with money. In this way, he could not be charged with fashioning his message according to the whims of the wealthy.

Paul also wanted to set an example of the virtue of self-support and the inherent value of manual labor. If any were inclined to think that physical work was beneath the dignity of a Christian, Paul was determined to set them straight (cf. 2 Thess. 3:6–12). In this way, he could avoid being a financial parasite or economic burden on others. This was undoubtedly an expression of his deep affection for his converts (see 2 Cor. 11:9–11). As Murray Harris points out, "By offering the 'price-less' good news totally free of charge, [Paul] was dramatizing in his own conduct the very appeal of the gospel as the good news of God's free grace [in Christ] (cf. 11:7; 1 Cor. 9:12, 18)."[5] What a remarkably effective object lesson of the nature of redemptive mercy!

So Paul waited to speak of the Philippians' financial support because of his reluctance to make a big deal of it lest people think he was in the ministry for the money.

Now we'll look closely at Paul's perspective on money and material prosperity.

The Philippians' Monetary Gift and Paul's Gratitude

"I rejoiced in the Lord greatly" (Phil. 4:10), said Paul, probably when Epaphroditus arrived from Philippi with the gift they had sent to him. But the *reason* he gave for his joy is surprising: "that now at length you have revived your concern for me" (v. 10). Paul clearly did not intend for these words to be taken negatively or as a criticism of the Philippians, but he knew there were some who would probably twist them in that way. So he explained both what he didn't mean and what he did mean.

The adverb translated "now at length" or "at last" in some versions implies that there was a considerable gap in time since the Philippian church had last supported him financially. He didn't mean to say that he had been

---

5. Murray J. Harris, *The Second Epistle to the Corinthians: A Commentary on the Greek Text* (Grand Rapids: Eerdmans, 2005), 765.

expecting something sooner and "*It's about time you thought about me and my needs.*" This was simply Paul's acknowledgment that communication between him and the Philippians had finally been revived after a lengthy period of no contact.

In giving thanks for their gift, Paul was careful to point out that he knew the delay in receiving help was because of a lack of opportunity, not a lack of affection or love. They hadn't ceased to care for Paul, nor were they reconsidering whether to continue financial support of his work. His point, then, was that circumstances evidently beyond their control prevented their commitment from blossoming forth.

I've never been much of a gardener or given to horticulture. My philosophy has typically been that if something ain't growing, cut it down and start over! In the late winter of 1983, we were living in Dallas when the city was struck with a long-lasting ice storm. It killed pretty much everything. We had a sweet gum tree in our front yard that took a hard hit from the storm. I can recall that as spring approached, most everything else in our yard started to recover and show signs of life. But not the sweet gum tree. I wanted to cut it down. It was ugly and useless. My wife, Ann, wouldn't have it. She insisted that I be patient. Sure enough, after several more months, what once appeared dead came to life and blossomed.

That is precisely the imagery Paul used here in verse 10. The verb *revived* is a botanical metaphor that means to blossom or bloom again. There is a sense, then, that this is Paul's way of marveling at the Philippians' generosity rather than complaining at the absence of it. Just as in springtime a tree puts forth fresh shoots, thereby proving that it is alive, so also the Philippians' interest in Paul had at last found a way to express and demonstrate itself concretely and lovingly.

We don't know what hindered the Philippians from helping Paul. Perhaps no one was able to make the long journey from Philippi to Rome until Epaphroditus stepped forward and volunteered to go. There may have been an economic downturn in Philippi, and they simply didn't have the money. Perhaps it was bad weather. Who knows? But clearly it was not for lack of desire, and Paul was careful to tell them he knew this to be the case.

Paul also wanted to make certain that no one thought his joy was over the gift itself, as if to suggest that he loved the Philippians only because of their generosity. He was aware that some might interpret his joy in receiving the gift as a sign of immaturity and weakness, as if he were like a child who had just received a new toy. Or possibly he had succumbed to materialism and was consumed by the size of the gift. Or maybe some would take the expression of joy as a veiled request for more.

Consider how some people articulate their gratitude. When they purportedly say "thanks," what they are actually doing is rebuking the giver for having given so little so late. Or they voice it in a way that makes you think they are expecting another gift, bigger and better the next time. Not Paul.

In any case, the apostle quickly proceeded in Philippians 4:11–13 to declare that his joy over the reception of the gift was not because his happiness depended on material prosperity. Some have suggested that when Paul said in verse 11, "not that I am speaking of being in need," he meant that when their gift arrived, he actually didn't need it because through some other means, perhaps inheritance, he had obtained sufficient funds to support himself.

No, I don't think so. Paul said what he did not because he was, in fact, prosperous but because the issue of personal prosperity or poverty had absolutely no bearing on his joy in life. We will see in verses 14–23 that his joy was primarily because of the spiritual fruit the Philippians themselves would enjoy because of their generosity.

The key statement for us is found in verse 11. It's the word translated "content." On hearing this, the Philippians would have immediately thought of the Stoic philosophers of their day who were committed to eliminating all external dependence; they would strive to detach themselves from any physical needs so they could live without anyone else's help. For the Stoics, the self-sufficient, self-contained man was the one who had rendered himself independent of external circumstances and sources of support. All resources necessary for coping in life were to be found within one's own heart and mind. The Stoic was dependent on neither people nor possessions.

So, what separated Paul from them? He gave the answer in 2 Corinthians 3:5: "Not that we are sufficient in ourselves to claim anything as coming from us, but our sufficiency is from God." This is the grand paradox: the independence from the world and wealth that we as Christians strive to obtain comes through dependence on all that God is for us in Christ! The "sufficiency" or "contentment" pursued by the Stoic philosophers of Paul's day came from within oneself. Paul's came from without. Paul was not an independent man. He was *wholly dependent on Christ* and thus independent of the support and resources of anyone else.

Don't misunderstand what Paul was saying. This is not laziness, fatalism, or yielding passively to whatever comes our way. Rather, it is a detachment from anxious concern by having learned to live immune from the poison of circumstances. Paul didn't mean by this that we shouldn't try to improve our lot in life, nor did he mean that we shouldn't enjoy the material blessings God has given us. He simply meant that whether he had a lot of stuff or nothing at all, his confidence in God and his joy in life were unchanged!

Notice how Paul expanded on this and unpacked it for us in verse 12. He said in verse 11 that he had "learned" to be content, and again in verse 12, "I have learned the secret." The point is that contentment is not natural to human nature. This isn't something we are born with. In fact, we are born discontented and dissatisfied. Contentment must be learned. And there is only one way this happens. You can learn contentment only by finding Jesus Christ to be enough. You must grow and deepen in your knowledge of him before you will experience any degree of independence from the stuff of this world. You learn contentment in the school of human experience only as you face hard times and discover how, in the midst of them, Christ is sufficient for everything you need.

If you and I always lived without need, if everything was given to us in abundance, if we never felt stretched or challenged, Christ would have little opportunity to be glorified in our lives. Thus, to "learn" this all-important lesson, one must progress through life, facing, embracing, and enduring hardship along the way. Like a child who starts out in the first grade learning her ABCs, and then moves on to reading and writing and eventually the ability to research difficult topics and write persuasive position papers, so, too, we have to grow and mature from one stage to the next until we find Jesus sufficiently beautiful, sufficiently powerful, and sufficiently sweet that the loss of everything else hardly registers in our hearts.

Paul then said he knew how "to be brought low" (Phil. 4:12) and how to endure "hunger" and "need" (v. 12). When Paul said he knew "how to be brought low" he wasn't referring merely to financial poverty but to a way of life that was like the one Jesus embraced (see Phil. 2:8 for the same verb). To know what Paul had in mind, we should consider 1 Corinthians 4:11–13 and 2 Corinthians 6:4–5; 11:23–29.

He also had in view the dejection and oppression that comes from material lack. When you endure hunger, thirst, cold, physical suffering, persecution, and opposition from your enemies but remain constant and joyful through it all, rather than becoming bitter and angry, you have "learned" the secret of being content in Christ.

Paul also knew how to live in prosperity. You might say, "That's no big deal; so do I! Living in prosperity is no problem!" Well, actually it is. It may well be easier to be a Christian when life is hard than when everything is going our way. Paul was saying, "I know how to be abased and yet not crushed by it. I know what it's like to thrive in abundance and yet not be unduly exalted." Most people experience something altogether different. For them, when times are good, God is good and they're happy. But when times are bad, God is bad and they're sad.

Paul said something entirely different: "I know how to be deprived of a lot of material things and how to face adversity without thinking that life has lost its purpose, and I know how to possess wealth and health without being deceived into thinking that such is really what makes life worth living. I suffer no excessive depression when I lack the essentials of life, far less the luxuries, but neither do I allow myself to be puffed up and negligent of spiritual zeal in the midst of prosperity."

Happiness or contentment or a deep sense of joy and satisfaction transcend bodily conditions and material possessions; genuine joy thrives independently of both turbulence and tranquility. Paul was saying, "I can go to bed poor and hungry and maintain my spiritual and emotional equilibrium, and I can go to bed filled and prosperous and remain unaffected by it all." Paul did not choose lack, loss, or deprivation as a way of life. He simply said that he had learned to accept whatever came his way because the source and strength of his joy and contentment were not tied to stuff or physical comfort. His relationship with Jesus Christ made both lack and prosperity irrelevant to his daily existence.

You may have grown up with wealth and prosperity. There's nothing wrong with that. Praise God for his abundant blessings. But would you be content and joyful in Jesus if you were suddenly forced to live in poverty? Have you become so dependent on the ever-present stuff of life, the luxuries and gadgets and the knowledge that you'll never go without a meal when you're hungry, that you assume you deserve it all, that God owes it to you, that he's not worthy of your trust if he doesn't continue to supply you with all good things?

Or maybe you grew up suffering from lack, perhaps in virtual poverty. Perhaps you learned along the way how to cope with loss and deprivation in a way that honors Christ. What would happen if you suddenly became wealthy? Would abundance and prosperity corrupt you? Or would you struggle with guilt at having so many possessions? The issue for us all is resting and rejoicing in Jesus to such an extent that neither poverty nor prosperity affects us, whether for good or ill.

Paul said in 4:12 that he had "learned" to be content in all circumstances. He had "learned" the secret of how to thrive "in any and every circumstance." So, what specifically had he "learned" and what was his "secret"? The answer is in verse 13: it was through the intimacy of his relationship with Jesus, or more literally, "in union with the one who infuses me with strength." When he said it was "through" Christ, he didn't mean merely that Christ was the instrumental cause. Paul was referring to his life "in" Christ, his daily existence in loving and trusting intimacy with Jesus, who enabled him.

Paul had in mind the beauty and glory of Christ's person, his saving work on the cross, his resurrection life, his intercession on our behalf, and the hope of his second coming. Paul had learned that when a person becomes consumed with Christ, the otherwise painful sharp edge of deprivation and loss doesn't carry the painful punch it otherwise would. The more majestic Christ appears the less glamorous and appealing will be the things of this earth.

We must not wrench this text from its context and make it apply to everything in life. Paul was talking about his ability to remain humble and not grow arrogant, prideful, or self-reliant based on circumstances. In other words, the "all things" in verse 13 is not universal in scope. It is a reference back to the "in any and every circumstance" of verse 12.

Neither should this verse be used to manipulate people. I would be badly twisting this verse if I used it this way: "Hey, folks, we need your help in youth ministry. We need some mature adults to help lead the small groups. And you can't say no to this appeal simply because you've never worked with youth before, because you don't speak well, or because you are convinced you don't have the spiritual gifts needed for this sort of thing. After all, you can do all things through Christ who strengthens you!"

The "all things" refers to the variety of circumstances in which Paul found himself, be they an overabundance of food, physical comforts, safety, money for ministry, and large crowds who listened to and followed him, spending undeserved time in a prison in Rome, being vilified by his enemies, or going without adequate food and clothing and being exposed daily to the possibility of execution.

Five Crucial Observations

First, Paul wanted the Philippians to know that because of their financial gift, they had come to "share" in his "trouble" (Phil. 4:14). The fact that they gave so much so often proves that when Paul hurt, they hurt. When he grieved, they grieved. Paul interpreted their financial commitment as a deep and personal identification with him in his labors. This is like what we see in 3 John 8, where those who support others in ministry become "fellow workers for the truth." It didn't matter that the Philippians were separated from Paul by more than eight hundred miles.

The second thing to consider is the fact that the Philippian church was only a few months old! These were brand-new, baby Christians! Yet Paul said they had already embraced the responsibility of generous financial steward-ship and had on several occasions sent a monetary gift to him (vv. 15–16). This ought to forever put to rest the objection I often hear: "Well, we can't expect new Christians to give. They aren't mature enough. They don't under-stand enough of the Bible." Nonsense!

And we must never forget that when Paul referred to the extraordinary generosity of the Macedonians in 2 Corinthians 8–9, he was talking primar-ily about the church and Christians in Philippi (the churches in Thessalonica and Berea would also have been included). Listen again to what he said about them as a way of encouraging the Corinthian Christians to give generously to the poverty-stricken saints in Jerusalem.

> We want you to know, brothers, about the grace of God that has been given among the churches of Macedonia, for in a severe test of affliction, their abundance of joy and their extreme poverty have overflowed in a wealth of generosity on their part. For they gave according to their means, as I can

testify, and beyond their means, of their own accord, begging us earnestly for the favor of taking part in the relief of the saints—and this, not as we expected, but they gave themselves first to the Lord and then by the will of God to us. (8:1–5)

My third observation relates to what Paul said in Philippians 4:17. He was clearly concerned that his eager acknowledgment of their generosity might be mistaken for a veiled request for more. So, he explained his true motivation in expressing his gratitude. Paul's point here is that what really got his spiritual juices flowing was not what he received from their giving but what they gained! He said, "I seek the fruit that increases to your credit" (v. 17). Paul regarded their gift to him as a spiritual investment entered as a credit to their account, an investment that he envisioned would pay them rich dividends.

But what precisely was the "fruit" that increased to their credit? If Paul was not saying that when Christians give, God promises to make them rich, what was he saying? What was the fruit that would come to them? I think he had several things in mind.

We are in fact told in Scripture that if we give, we will get, but not in the sense promoted by advocates of the prosperity or health and wealth gospel. Paul said in 2 Corinthians 9:6–8; 10–11,

The point is this: whoever sows sparingly will also reap sparingly, and whoever sows bountifully will also reap bountifully. Each one must give as he has decided in his heart, not reluctantly or under compulsion, for God loves a cheerful giver. And God is able to make all grace abound to you, so that having all sufficiency in all things at all times, you may abound in every good work. . . . He who supplies seed to the sower and bread for food will supply and multiply your seed for sowing and increase the harvest of your righteousness. You will be enriched in every way to be generous in every way, which through us will produce thanksgiving to God.

God gives to those who give but not in order that they may become personally wealthy and hoard their money or squander it on excessive luxuries. God gives to those who give so that those who give might be able to give even more! We are channels and conduits of God's generosity, not reservoirs!

There is also the approval and affirmation from God when he sees our sacrifice and generosity. God is *pleased* with gracious giving! This was Paul's point in Philippians 4:18 ("pleasing to God"). The fruit of increased joy comes to the giver when he or she experiences partnership in spreading the gospel. I should also mention the assurance that God will give them greater responsibilities and even more productive opportunities. In other words, God says, "Demonstrate to me that you are faithful in the small things, and I will entrust more to you in even greater things."

Part of the "fruit" is increased reward in heaven. If you think it is sinful to give with a view to gaining a heavenly reward, you haven't listened closely to Jesus (see Matt. 6:3–4) or Paul (1 Tim. 6:18–19). There is also the fruit of enriched fellowship and intimacy with the ones to whom you give. Finally, indescribable fruit comes from knowing that God is glorified when people give him thanks for your generosity.

I'll now return to my five observations, the fourth of which comes from Paul shifting his metaphors in Philippians 4:18. Before this he had used the terminology of banking and business, but here he employed the language of Old Testament ritual sacrifice and the priesthood. And what he said in doing so is nothing short of shocking. Most of us probably think of money as just that, money. It's nothing more than a medium of exchange, a way of purchasing what we want. It hardly suggests anything spiritual in nature. But Paul begged to differ. When Christians give generously and sacrificially to the work of ministry, their gift is nothing less than "a fragrant offering, a sacrifice acceptable and pleasing to God" (v. 18).

My favorite smells growing up were those of fried pork chops on Saturday night, the fragrance of freshly cut grass on a baseball field, and the mint from our backyard. Paul wanted you to picture God looking upon the offering box as you walk by, dropping in your contribution, or each time you sign up to give through automatic debit: "Sniff, sniff. Mmm. I caught a whiff of that! Whew! Sweet!" Generous, sacrificial giving by Christians smells good to God! It honors him. It reflects greatly on his abundant provision. Reluctance to give, or even outright refusal to do so, also smells to God, but I won't explain precisely how. I'll leave it to your imagination.

How else can it be said? There is nothing mundane or merely material in sacrificial giving to the cause of Christ. It may not feel special to you (although it should). It may not smell good to you. But as we see in 3 John,

God says it is a "faithful" thing, a "beautiful" thing, an expression of "love," as he also now here in Philippians 4 says it is a sweet-smelling aroma that makes God happy.

Dear friend, if knowing the effect on God of your generosity, not to mention knowing the immeasurable sacrifice Christ made to save you from eternal damnation, does not stir you to regular and sacrificial giving, nothing else I can say will make a difference. You are the one who stands to lose the "fruit" that would otherwise abound to your account.

"But Sam, I'm so *afraid of poverty*. I'm terrified that if I give, I won't have enough to get by." I know the fear you're describing. Almost everyone does. And Paul knew it too. That's why he said what he did in Philippians 4:19, which leads me to my final point.

Paul deliberately repeated in verse 19 two words used in the previous verses. In verse 18, he said, "I am well *supplied*." Now, in verse 19, he declared that God shall "*supply*" every need. Same word. In verse 16, he referred to his "*needs*" being met by their gift. Now, in verse 19, it is God who will supply every "*need*" of the Philippians, and every need of yours and mine.

I think Paul was telling us two things by this. He first wanted us to understand that if we find the desire to give in our hearts, he will more than amply supply the resources to do it. You've heard the old saying, "You can't out-give God." That's Paul's point. You can't give beyond God's ability to provide you with what is needed. Paul also wanted us to know that the "every need" you and I have is also spiritual and emotional in nature. He was talking not only about financial supply but also the strength, endurance, and hope necessary to persevere in the face of hardship.

"But Sam, are you sure God really has enough to go around?" Well, let's listen to what Paul said. He declared that God will supply us "according to his riches" in Christ Jesus. If I may be allowed to render this as I think Paul intended: "God will gloriously supply every need of yours in proportion to his eternal and infinite riches in Jesus Christ." He doesn't give "out of" his riches, as when a millionaire donates a hundred dollars to a local charity. No, he gives "according to" his wealth, which is to say, on a scale befitting his wealth, in a manner that reflects how infinitely wealthy God is.

Simply put, all our needs combined cannot even begin to plumb the depths of God's infinite resources to meet them. This assurance of God's faithful supply is no justification for being lazy or disregarding God's commands to be generous. Yes, God was taking care of Paul's every need, and he will take care of ours. But how did he do it? He supplied Paul's every need through the obedient, diligent, responsible, active, worshipful, and loving financial generosity provided by the Philippians! God uses people. He employs means. He doesn't drop cash or coin from heaven. He uses us. Consider the privilege. And extol God in your giving!

CHAPTER 12

Enthroned! Encircled! Extolled!

Revelation 4

After this I looked, and behold, a door standing open in heaven! And the first voice, which I had heard speaking to me like a trumpet, said, "Come up here, and I will show you what must take place after this." At once I was in the Spirit, and behold, a throne stood in heaven, with one seated on the throne. And he who sat there had the appearance of jasper and carnelian, and around the throne was a rainbow that had the appearance of an emerald. Around the throne were twenty-four thrones, and seated on the thrones were twenty-four elders, clothed in white garments, with golden crowns on their heads. From the throne came flashes of lightning, and rumblings and peals of thunder, and before the throne were burning seven torches of fire, which are the seven spirits of God, and before the throne there was as it were a sea of glass, like crystal.

And around the throne, on each side of the throne, are four living creatures, full of eyes in front and behind: the first living creature like a lion, the second living creature like an ox, the third living creature with the face of a man, and the fourth living creature like an eagle in flight. And the four living creatures, each of them with six wings, are full of eyes all around and within, and day and night they never cease to say,

"Holy, holy, holy, is the Lord God Almighty,
who was and is and is to come!"

And whenever the living creatures give glory and honor and thanks to him who is seated on the throne, who lives forever and ever, the twenty-four elders fall down before him who is seated on the throne and worship him who lives forever and ever. They cast their crowns before the throne, saying,

> "Worthy are you, our Lord and God,
>> to receive glory and honor and power,
> for you created all things,
>> and by your will they existed and were created." (Rev. 4:1–11)[1]

In his treatise *Religious Affections*, Puritan pastor and theologian Jonathan Edwards (1703–58) contended that "the way to learn the true nature of anything, is to go where that thing is to be found in its purity and perfection."[2] Therefore, to demonstrate the nature of religious experience, Edwards would direct our attention to the affections of those who have died in Christ Jesus and are now in heaven. I think this applies equally well to the question of the nature of true worship. If we hope to understand what worship is in its purest and most pristine form, we need to focus our attention on heaven. So, what is happening in heaven right now? And by "right now" I mean right now! Literally. John was given a vision that answers this question, and the portrait it provides is undoubtedly as true today as it was nearly two thousand years ago.

Revelation 4–5 is a vision of the majesty of a sovereign God in complete control of his creation. From an earthly perspective, it might seem that the enemies of God's kingdom are winning. Christians are being persecuted, imprisoned, and martyred. Tragedy, trial, and turmoil are rampant, and the Dragon (Satan), the Beast, and the False Prophet appear to have the upper hand. All hope of light at the end of the tunnel grows dim because the tunnel has no end. The tunnel is all there is. History simply has no purpose. Dreams of finally emerging out the other side are shattered. There is no other side!

---

1. For an extended commentary on these many texts in Revelation, see my commentary, *Our God Reigns: An Amillennial Commentary on Revelation* (Fearn, Ross-shire, UK: Mentor, 2024). Much of what follows in the next three chapters is adapted from that commentary and is used here with permission. Parts of chapters 12 and 13 have been adapted from my book *One Thing: Developing a Passion for the Beauty of God* (Fearn, Ross-shire, UK: Christian Focus, 2004), 65–82, and are used here with permission.

2. Jonathan Edwards, *Religious Affections*, ed. John E. Smith (New Haven, CT: Yale University Press, 1969), 114.

But John's vision reveals that appearances can be deceiving! The course of history isn't determined by political intrigue or military might but by God. What John discovered is that there are two worlds or two dimensions of reality. One is earthly and visible, the other is heavenly and invisible. Remarkably, it is the latter that controls and determines the former. Or better still, it is God who is sovereign over both!

It's as if the Holy Spirit says to John (and to us), "Listen to me. Things are not as they appear. I'm about to show you things as they really are. I'm about to take you into the throne room of God himself. Things aren't running amok. The devil hasn't won. Evil hasn't triumphed. Neither fate nor cruel chance governs the universe. He who was and is and is to come has everything well in hand." Here in Revelation 4 and 5, we are given a biblical worldview: not a Hollywood worldview, a Wall Street worldview, or a Washington, DC, worldview. This is the worldview of the Bible that comes from seeing God as he truly is.

As John looked, he saw a vision of the triune God, enthroned, encircled, and extolled. In Exodus 33:18, Moses made a simple request of God: "Please show me your glory." God placed him in the "cleft of a rock" and caused his glory to pass by. Here in Revelation 4–5, we are granted access to the sight of God's glory that Moses saw only in passing, in part.

The first two words in Revelation 4:1, "After this," do not mean that the events of chapters 4–5 occur after the events of chapters 1–3, as if this were a description of their chronological sequence. Rather, these words indicate that the *vision* of Revelation 4–5 came to John after the *vision* of Revelation 1–3. In other words, we are given the sequence in which John experienced his visions, not the historical order in which they actually occurred (see also 7:1, 9; 15:5; 18:1; 19:1).

Enthroned!

The voice John heard was that of Jesus Christ (cf. 1:10–11). As John looked, he was confronted with a breathtaking, knee-knocking, heart-pounding, eye-popping vision of the triune God. He saw the Lord enthroned, encircled, and extolled. What follows in chapters 4 and 5 of the Apocalypse stretches the imagination and tests our capacity to grasp the beauty of God. Resist the temptation to read these verses as you would a newspaper, novel, or even the book of Romans. In fact, it is precisely here that we are confronted with the limitations of human language. Nothing in our vocabulary is fully adequate to explain, account for, or illustrate the ineffable majesty of God and the worship of angels and saints.

In Revelation 4:3 we see God in a resplendent blaze of unapproachable light, the jewels refracting the glory and majesty of his luminous beauty. Here is where all worship begins: in the throne room of heaven where God reigns supreme! When we see God as he is, incomparably sublime and incontestably sovereign, we will praise him as we should in unison with the heavenly hosts. This is not a pathetic deity wringing his hands over a world catapulting into oblivion. He does not pace the floor of heaven with furrowed brow, riddled with anxiety over the outcome of human history. God reigns!

If asked to describe God, what terms would you employ? I fear that many Christians are so deficient in their knowledge and experience of God that they'd portray him as a formless, passionless, gray blob of abstract power. John's vision, on the other hand, is a virtual kaleidoscope of color, sound, sight, and smell! John sees all the colors of the rainbow magnified!

The one on the throne appears to be jasper, an opaque stone that tends to be red but is also found in yellow, green, and grayish blue. Jasper suggests the qualities of majesty and holiness and is used later in Revelation as an image for the overall appearance of the new Jerusalem, which manifests the glory of God (21:11). It is also the material from which its walls are constructed (21:18) and the first of its twelve foundations (21:19).

The sardius (or carnelian) was a red stone similar in appearance to a ruby. It evokes the image of both divine jealousy and righteous wrath, both the burning zeal of God for the fame of his name and his just and resolute response to those who would bring reproach upon it.

The rainbow reminds us of the faithfulness of God when he first set this sign in the heavens as a pledge to Noah following the great flood. Also found in Ezekiel 1:28, the rainbow reminds us that God's wrath and judgment, perhaps symbolized by the sardius as well, as described in the subsequent visions, are tempered by his mercy and his promise to Noah never again to totally destroy the earth. In Ezekiel the rainbow is explicitly said to portray the radiant appearance of God's glory. Here it emanates like an emerald, reminding us that our God is filled not only with jealous zeal but tender-hearted affection.

Of course, John was not saying that God *is* a jasper or a sardius, but that his appearance was *like* such precious stones. This is not photographic reproduction but symbolic imagery. John wanted to stir our imaginations and inflame our hearts, not fill our minds with endless facts.

The atmosphere of this scene is bathed in mystery and awash in wonder. Worship without wonder is lifeless and boring. Many have lost their sense of awe and amazement when it comes to God. Having begun with the arrogant presumption of knowing about God all that one can, they reduce him to manageable terms and confine him to a tidy theological box, the dimensions of which conform to their predilections of what a god ought to be and do. That they've lost the capacity to marvel at the majesty of God comes as little surprise. Warren Wiersbe explained:

> We must recognize the fact that true wonder is not a passing emotion or some kind of shallow excitement. It has depth to it. True wonder reaches right into your heart and mind and shakes you up. It not only has depth, it has value; it enriches your life. Wonder is not cheap amusement that brings a smile to your face. It is an encounter with reality—with God—that brings awe to your heart. You are overwhelmed with an emotion that is a mixture of gratitude, adoration, reverence, fear,—and love. You are not looking for explanations; you are lost in the wonder of God.[3]

Our wonder in God's presence, however, is not born of ignorance but of knowledge. We know something about the majesty of God and, for that reason, are lost in wonder, love, and praise. We can't stand in awe of someone of whom we're ignorant. Our wonder deepens with each degree of understanding.

But is it practical to worship when the world is falling apart? John's life was at risk. Of all the apostles, he alone had survived. Who knew how much longer he had? In such a crisis, why would the Spirit escort John into heaven and point to the adoring and passionate praise of angels and odd creatures and saints? Because it's the only thing that made sense! Worship is no flight from reality. Nothing is more real than what John saw, heard, and sensed around the throne of God.

3. Warren Wiersbe, *Real Worship: Playground, Battleground, or Holy Ground?* (Nashville: Nelson, 1986), 44–45.

Some will read Revelation 4–5 and say, "Ah, this is all well and good. But of what practical benefit is it to me at work? How does this help me respond to an abusive and overbearing boss? How does it help me fight the temptation to lust after one of my coworkers? How does it help me love my spouse and my kids? How does it strengthen me to endure times of financial strain and physical pain?"

This vision of God enthroned, encircled, and extolled is eminently practical because praise restores our sense of ultimate value. It exposes the temporary and tawdry stuff of this world. Worship energizes the heart to seek satisfaction in Jesus alone. In worship we are reminded that this world is fleeting and unworthy of our heart's devotion. Worship connects our souls with God's transcendent power and awakens us to true beauty. It pulls back the veil of deception and exposes the ugliness of sin and Satan. Worship is a joyful rebuke of the world. When our hearts are riveted on Jesus, everything else in life becomes so utterly unnecessary, and we become far less demanding.

Encircled!

In John's vision, the throne of God is the center of all heavenly activity. The throne is the focus of a series of concentric circles made up first of a rainbow, then the four living creatures, then the twenty-four enthroned elders. According to Revelation 5:11 (and again in 7:11), a great host of angels also encircle the throne. Eventually, all creation joins the worshiping throng (see 5:13).

We read in Revelation 4:3 that "around the throne" is a "rainbow" and now in verse 4 "around the throne" are twenty-four thrones on which sit twenty-four elders. They are wearing white garments and golden crowns (4:4), prostrating themselves before God in worship (4:10; 5:14; 11:16; 19:4), and casting before him their crowns (4:10). They are singing hymns of praise to God (4:11; 5:9–10; 11:17–18) while holding harps and bowls full of incense said to represent the prayers of Christians (5:8).

Who are they? What are they? Some see in them an exalted angelic order, like the cherubim and seraphim. Several factors point to them being a species of angels. Later, in Revelation 5:8, they are described as bringing the prayers of the saints to God. In Revelation 5:5 and 7:13–14 they interpret for

John the meaning of his visions, a typical angelic function in Scripture. And in 4:9–10; 5:8, 14; 7:11; and 19:4 they join with the four living creatures and the rest of the angels in worshiping God.

On the other hand, nowhere else in Scripture are angels called "elders." In Revelation it is the people of God who wear crowns, are clothed in white, and sit on thrones (2:10; 3:4–5; 3:21; 7:13–15; 19:7–8, 14; 20:4). But this may be because these are angels who symbolize or represent the saints.

Others think they are exalted Old Testament believers. King David organized the temple servants into twenty-four orders of priests (1 Chron. 24:3–19), twenty-four Levitical gatekeepers (26:17–19), and twenty-four orders of Levites commissioned to prophesy, give thanks, praise God, and sing to the accompaniment of harps and lyres and cymbals (25:6–31).

Another possibility is that they are exalted New Testament saints, particularly individual Christians who have sealed their faith through martyrdom and are now glorified and participating in an exalted heavenly life. Thrones are sometimes used as a metaphor for the heavenly reward of the righteous. But if they are only New Testament saints, why the number twenty-four? Could this be a symbol for their continuous, twenty-four-hour worship, day and night?

I find it difficult not to see in the number twenty-four a reference to the twelve tribes of Israel and the twelve apostles of the New Testament church (they are associated again in Rev. 21:12–14). If so, the elders may be representatives of the redeemed community from both testaments. But are they human or angelic representatives? Probably the latter, insofar as they bring the prayers of the saints before God (5:8) and sing of the redeemed in the third person (5:9–10). Also, the fact that these twenty-four elders are distinguished from the redeemed multitude in Revelation 7:9–17 indicates they are angelic representatives of all the people of God.

If they are angels, I doubt they look like the fat little cherubs with dimpled cheeks that hang playfully suspended above a baby's crib. These are powerful and majestic creatures whose radiance reflects the glory of the one they so adoringly worship and serve.

What's important, however, isn't who they are but what they do. They are mesmerized by God's majesty, obsessed with his glory, and committed to unending and adoring praise.

The lightning and thunder, undoubtedly quite literal, are also symbolic of God's awesome power and infinite might and remind us of the revelation of God at Mount Sinai (Ex. 19:16–18; 20:18–20). They may well be emanations of the endless energy of God's own being, pointing to the limitless depths of divine power. The number seven in Revelation often symbolizes divine perfection and completeness. Thus, the seven spirits are the one Holy Spirit represented under the symbolism of a sevenfold or complete manifestation of his being.

The four living creatures remind us of the seraphim of Isaiah 6 and the cherubim of Ezekiel 1:5–25 and 10:1–22. Could they be symbolic of the created world itself, all of which is responsible to render praise to God? This is suggested by the number four, which points to the totality of the natural order: the four points of the compass, the four corners of the earth, and the four winds of heaven. Are they angels, or perhaps another "species" of created, supernatural beings?

These creatures are standing on something that looks like a sea of glass resembling crystal (Rev. 4:6). Its surface stretches out before the throne to reflect the flashing light that proceeds from the character of God. They appear to stand in front, behind, and on either side of the throne (they are "before" and "around" the throne in 4:6, and "before" the throne in 5:8). Some suggest they are supporting the throne itself. Their focus is entirely on God, not on one another or anything or anyone else in heaven.

The description of these creatures in 4:7 may be designed to suggest qualities in the God they serve: the lion pointing to royal power; the calf/ox, a symbol of strength; the man, an expression of intelligence and spirituality; and the eagle, an embodiment of swiftness of action.

Extolled!

Their worship (Rev. 4:8) is *unending*: "Day and night they never cease to say" (cf. Rev. 14:11). As there is constant and perpetual punishment in hell, so there is constant and perpetual praise in heaven. Some of you may struggle to remain focused and engaged during the twenty to thirty minutes of praise that happens each Sunday at your local church. But is thirty minutes a week really that much of a burden? Isn't the God portrayed for us in Revelation 4–5 worth at least thirty minutes of our undivided attention and adoration?

The focus there is on three of God's attributes: his holiness, his sovereignty, and his eternality.

First, the emphasis on God's *holiness* here in Revelation 4:8 is an echo of Isaiah 6. When Isaiah saw God for who he was, he also saw himself. Knowledge of God always awakens a knowledge of oneself. God's holiness always exposes our sinfulness. But the holy God is also the gracious Redeemer, for the hot coal applied to Isaiah's lips spoke of forgiveness and cleansing.

The God who captivates these heavenly worshipers is also *sovereign.* He is "the Almighty," for he sits on the divine "throne"—mentioned fourteen times in this chapter, a symbol of divine authority, dominion, and power.

He is also the *eternal* God "who was and is and is to come" (cf. Ex. 3:14). Although timeless in his essential being, the phrase "who is to come" points more to God's impending return in the person of Jesus to consummate his kingdom than to the idea of eternal existence.

The praise that comes from the four living creatures gives way to that of the twenty-four elders (4:9–11). The word *worship* means to fall prostrate at someone's feet. What gloriously appropriate repetition: they fall down before him to fall down before him! This is the first occurrence in Revelation of the paired verbs "to fall down" and "to worship," which are used to describe two stages of a single act of adoration and thus appear to be synonymous (they are also paired in 5:14; 7:11; 11:16; 19:10; and 22:8; this combination is also found in Matt. 2:11; 4:9; 18:26; Acts 10:25; 1 Cor. 14:25).

Why do the elders fall face down? Over and over again, they hit the dirt, prostrate in God's presence (Rev. 4:10; 5:8, 14). Is it simply mechanical obedience to some heavenly liturgy? What do they see, hear, feel, believe, or think that could induce such an extravagant response? What possesses them to fall over and over and over again?

No sooner do they stand than they fall! It isn't that they fall, come to their senses, and then stand, dusting themselves off, a little embarrassed for having momentarily lost their composure. They can't bear the thought of standing in the presence of such beauty and glory. The only reasonable, rational, sensible thing to do is to fall down! Nothing would be more inappropriate or out of order than to remain upright. They don't fall because they are wounded, weak, or fearful. They fall because they are overwhelmed!

Why do the four living creatures not cease day or night from praising?

Is it an expression of mere "duty"? Is their adoration coerced or perhaps the fruit of bribery? Undoubtedly not! Consider every alternative. What else could possibly compare with the joy of unending adoration and delight in the splendor of God? No one put a gun to their heads or threatened them with hell should they decline to worship. Why should they cease? For whom should they give up their praise? To do what? To go where? What can compare, rival, or compete in its capacity to fascinate, fulfill, satisfy, and enhance? Is there another being more splendid? Is there another god more beautiful?

True worship, such as we see in Revelation 4–5, is not simply unending; it is *uninhibited*. The atmosphere around the throne is charged with an *unashamed exuberance*. Physical expressions of delight, fear, joy, and awe are commonplace. Unlike heaven, unfortunately, worship wars continue to rage in churches on every continent on earth. Whereas some enjoy the atmosphere of a religious carnival, Sunday morning in other churches bears a striking resemblance to the county morgue! Your choice these days is often between the frenzy of unbridled chaos or the rigidity of immovable concrete. Our personal preferences notwithstanding, in heaven affections are ablaze for God. Bodies are prostrate in his presence. Praise is passionate. Enjoyment is extravagant. There is little, if any, fear of feelings.

I'm surprised by how unsettling this is to some people. Could it possibly be due to their lack of familiarity with the central figures in Scripture? Consider, for example, King David. Do you know why people love the Psalms and always seem to return to them in times of need? Look no further than the passion of their author, a man who virtually breathed holy desperation for God. A man whose heart beat with a chronic longing for God's presence. A man who thirsted and hungered for God and rejoiced and exulted and reveled in God. A man who was as exuberant in his celebration of righteousness as he was broken when injustice prevailed.

Or consider the apostle Paul. Although you may not think of him as an emotional or passionate person, his epistles are full of earnest longings of soul and spirit. His heart was ablaze with love for God and his mind flooded with high and exalted thoughts of his Savior. He happily spurned the comforts of this life, counting all things as rubbish (Phil. 3:8) that he might experience the unparalleled thrill of knowing Jesus. He was constrained by love, often moved to tears of sympathy, and roused to holy anger by those who would bring harm to the church of Jesus Christ.

Paul's letters are filled with references to his overflowing affection for the people of God (2 Cor. 12:19; Phil. 4:1; 2 Tim. 1:2; and especially 1 Thess. 2:7–8). He spoke of his "very heart" (Philem. 12, 20) for them, of his affection and sympathy (Phil. 2:1), of his anguish of heart and the tears he shed for their welfare (2 Cor. 2:4), of his continual grief for the lost (Rom. 9:2), and of his wide-open heart (2 Cor. 6:11).

Surely Jesus himself during his earthly ministry was a passionate man greatly moved in heart and spirit with holy affection. He was not ashamed or hesitant to pray with "loud cries and tears" (Heb. 5:7). The gospel writers spoke of him as experiencing amazement, sorrow, and grief (Mark 3:5), zeal (John 2:17), weeping (Luke 19:41), earnest desire (Luke 22:15), pity and compassion (Matt. 15:32), anger (John 2:13–19), love (John 15:9), and joy (John 15:11). In Luke 10:21 he is said to have "rejoiced in the Holy Spirit" as he was praying to the Father. He declared in John 15:11 and 17:13 that one of the principal aims of his earthly mission was to perfect the joy of his followers. Thus, our joy is the joy of Jesus in us!

I don't believe it's possible to truly understand and appreciate God's great things without being stirred with passion, zeal, joy, delight, and fervor. Only unyielding spiritual blindness prevents the human soul from being greatly impressed and powerfully moved by the revelation of such eternal splendor.

The inhabitants of heaven feel compelled to cast down their crowns to acknowledge that any personal honor or power or authority is ultimately God's. They proclaim the Creator worthy of glory and honor and power because by his will "they existed and were created" (literally, "they were and they were created"; Rev. 4:11).

But why the apparent illogical order of the verbs? How can the "existence" of everything precede creation? In one sense, all things "first" existed in God's mind and then came into being by God's will. Or perhaps the preservation of all things is mentioned before creation to encourage the persecuted people of God with the assurance that whatever befalls them is encompassed within their Creator's ultimate purpose.

Conclusion

What is the practical takeaway of our time in Revelation 4? I'll give you one short answer regarding our battle with temptation. Again, the question is this: What does this vision of God's worship in Revelation 4 have to do with my holiness and my struggle with sin? How does meditating and prayerfully reflecting on this majestic description of God affect my battle with temptation? Why spend so much time and energy on God's character and beauty?

The answer is simple. It is so that you will walk out of your local church Sunday service and, throughout the course of every day, be spiritually dazed with a deeper grasp of God's grandeur and a heart filled with adoration and awe. I want you to finish reading this chapter with your mouth wide open in wonder and your eyes bulging from your head in stunned incredulity. And here is why.

Spiritually stunned people are not easily seduced by sin. People in awe of God will always find sin less appealing. When you are dazzled by God, it is difficult to be duped by sin. When you are enthralled by his beauty, it is hard to become enslaved by unrighteousness. People whose attention has been captured by the beauty of Christ find little appeal in the glamour of this world. People whose hearts are enthralled with the revelation of God's greatness turn a deaf ear to the otherwise alluring sounds of sin, the flesh, and the devil. Here is how professor and author James Hamilton put it:

> What will it take to set you free from the world's idolatries—what will it take to keep you from trusting in things that are no gods at all? What will make you free from the world's immoralities—what will it take to make you untouched by the lust for smut that the world peddles and with which worldlings ruin their lives? What will it take to liberate you from the world's false perspective on the way things are—the perspective that assumes there is no god, there is no revelation of truth in the Bible, and there will be no judgment? I'll tell you what it will take: it will take seeing God as he is. Beholding God will break the chains of idolatry because when you see God, you see what Deity is, and that exposes the idols as worthless and unworthy of [your] trust. Beholding God will purify you from immorality because when you see God you see what beauty and faithfulness are, and that exposes the ugliness of adultery. Beholding God will give you new lenses through which to look at the world because God himself defines reality.[4]

---

4. James M. Hamilton Jr., *Revelation: The Spirit Speaks to the Churches* (Wheaton, IL: Crossway, 2012), 130.

CHAPTER 13

"Weep No More!"

Revelation 5

Then I saw in the right hand of him who was seated on the throne a scroll written within and on the back, sealed with seven seals. And I saw a mighty angel proclaiming with a loud voice, "Who is worthy to open the scroll and break its seals?" And no one in heaven or on earth or under the earth was able to open the scroll or to look into it, and I began to weep loudly because no one was found worthy to open the scroll or to look into it. And one of the elders said to me, "Weep no more; behold, the Lion of the tribe of Judah, the Root of David, has conquered, so that he can open the scroll and its seven seals."

And between the throne and the four living creatures and among the elders I saw a Lamb standing, as though it had been slain, with seven horns and with seven eyes, which are the seven spirits of God sent out into all the earth. And he went and took the scroll from the right hand of him who was seated on the throne. And when he had taken the scroll, the four living creatures and the twenty-four elders fell down before the Lamb, each holding a harp, and golden bowls full of incense, which are the prayers of the saints. And they sang a new song, saying,

"Worthy are you to take the scroll
    and to open its seals,
for you were slain, and by your blood you ransomed people for God
    from every tribe and language and people and nation,

and you have made them a kingdom and priests to our God,
    and they shall reign on the earth."

Then I looked, and I heard around the throne and the living creatures
and the elders the voice of many angels, numbering myriads of myriads
and thousands of thousands, saying with a loud voice,

"Worthy is the Lamb who was slain,
to receive power and wealth and wisdom and might
and honor and glory and blessing!"

And I heard every creature in heaven and on earth and under the
earth and in the sea, and all that is in them, saying,

"To him who sits on the throne and to the Lamb
be blessing and honor and glory and might forever and ever!"

And the four living creatures said, "Amen!" and the elders fell down
and worshiped. (Rev. 5:1–14)

I sometimes feel the same way John did as he stood before the throne of
God—not that I've ever been in the presence of the throne of God. But
reading Revelation 5:3–4 resonates with my fears and anxieties about where
human history is going and whether we will ever emerge from this colossal
mess we've created for ourselves.

Things were bad in John's day in the late first century. John was the last
living apostle, exiled to the island of Patmos. Five of the seven churches to
which Jesus had written letters were struggling. John was keenly aware of
the persecution that had come upon the people of God. In Revelation 1, he
identified himself in verse 9 as "your brother and partner in the tribulation
and the kingdom and the patient endurance that are in Jesus."

I'm not in the least surprised that he reacted the way he did in Revelation
5. He saw "in the right hand of him who was seated on the throne a scroll
written within and on the back, sealed with seven seals" (v. 1). This "scroll," in
all likelihood, had written within it the content of God's purpose in human
history. In other words, the scroll contained history's content, course, and

consummation. It recorded how things would end for both Christians and non-Christians. This scroll revealed who wins and how. The fact that "no one in heaven or on earth or under the earth was able to open the scroll or to look into it" (v. 3) understandably stirred John's fears and stoked his anxiety.

Scholars disagree on whether the book was a rolled-up scroll or a codex (the forerunner of the modern book form). Those who believe it was a scroll contend that its contents could not be revealed until all seven seals were broken. However, others have pointed out that there is evidence that seals on a legal document would have written upon them a summary of the scroll's contents. Thus, with the breaking of each seal, an element of the more complete contents of the scroll would be revealed. If that is the case, the book's contents would consist of what transpired immediately in chapter 6 and the remainder of Revelation.

It's quite amazing, is it not, that none of the four living creatures could break the seals on the scroll and discover its content? Nor could any of the twenty-four elders or any among the millions of angels surrounding the throne. "No one," said John—literally no one—"was found worthy" or qualified or powerful enough "to open the scroll or to look into it" (v. 4).

Notice that in verse 2 a "mighty angel" is the one who proclaimed that no one in heaven or on earth was able to open the scroll or reveal its contents. This wasn't an ordinary angel but a "mighty" or "strong" angel. Furthermore, this angel had never sinned. This angel had refused to join Satan in his rebellion against God. Yet not even a strong and sinless angel could open the book.

And so all creation in heaven and earth stood motionless and speechless as a search was undertaken for someone worthy to open this book. Was no one capable of bringing history to its ordained end? *Call your congressman! Call your senator! Write letters of inquiry to the most brilliant of scientists and astrophysicists! If necessary, get in touch with the White House! Surely someone here on earth is worthy enough and strong enough to open the book of human history and tell us its contents and its consummation!* John's disappointment evoked a flood of tears as he contemplated the painful postponement of God's redemptive purposes. Was there *no one* who could take authority over history and ensure that God's enemies would be judged and his people vindicated?

Yes, there was. "Stop crying, John," said one of the elders. "Weep no more! There is one who is worthy." But when this person appeared, symbolically in the form of an animal, it wasn't what John expected. After first seeing a lion (in v. 5), John was amazed to see a lamb (in v. 6). And even more amazing, the lion and the lamb were the same person! The lamb was indicative of Jesus' atoning sacrifice (Isa. 53:7; perhaps also the Passover lamb was in view). This lamb was "standing, as though it had been slain," or more literally, "slaughtered," with its throat cut.

So, what is it that made Jesus, the Lion of Judah, worthy to do what a strong and sinless angel couldn't do? For one thing, the Lion of the tribe of Judah created this angel, together with the myriad other angelic beings. But that isn't the primary reason he alone was worthy to open the scroll. He was worthy because he had "conquered" (v. 5). But how did he conquer, and what did he conquer? Merely dying wouldn't make him worthy. The two thieves crucified on either side of Jesus also died, but they were hardly worthy. How, then, was his death a victory?

Jesus' death qualified him to break the seals and reveal the content of the scroll because, as verse 9 makes explicitly clear, by means of his "blood" alone, people from every tribe and language and people and nation were "ransomed," or redeemed, from sin and condemnation. He "conquered" because his death was not the end but was followed by resurrection. And he made those he ransomed into "a kingdom and priests" to God who will "reign on the earth" (v. 10).

The word "between," or "in the midst of" (v. 6), could suggest that the Lamb was actually on the throne, surrounded by the four creatures and the twenty-four elders. But it is more likely that the Lamb was standing near the throne, for in verse 7 he is portrayed as coming up to the throne and taking the book from the one who sits upon it. Thus, again, we see the consistent New Testament portrait of the Son at the right hand of his Father's throne.

The phrase "the slaughtered Lamb" is also found in 5:12 and 13:8. Here the fact that the word "slain" or "slaughtered" is introduced with the comparative particle "as though" or "like" does not mean that the Lamb only appeared to have been slaughtered, but rather that the Lamb had been slaughtered and was now alive, thus combining the two theological motifs of death and resurrection.

But if it was slain, how could it stand? Clearly, having once been slain, the Lamb had now been raised. Here we see again the glorious truth of resurrection! The Lamb wasn't slumped over in a lifeless heap or limping along as if on its last legs. The Lamb stood as a sign of its resurrected life! This is John's forthright way of saying in no uncertain terms: Jesus Christ is alive!

Until Jesus Christ returns to this earth in the Second Coming, victory is achieved not by the sword but by a sacrifice. Jesus conquers through the cross! The power to change lives and orchestrate history flows from the love of a crucified carpenter who then literally and physically rose from the dead. Our King, Jesus Christ, does not win converts by killing his enemies but by dying for them—and then rising again to eternal life. Make no mistake: when he returns it will be to destroy his enemies. At that time, mercy will give way to judgment.

We see here not just the key that unlocks the mystery of why the universe exists; we see the mystery itself: Jesus. He is why there is something rather than nothing. God created the universe not only through Jesus but *for* Jesus. By saying the universe exists for Jesus, I mean that everything that exists was brought into being to admire, adore, enjoy, celebrate, and relish the beauty and splendor of the Lamb of God in his victory over sin, death, and the devil! And in that admiration and celebration, we find our most satisfying joy and delight.

Prayers and Praise

At the sound of such gloriously great news, there is only one appropriate response: singing! But before we note the singing, don't miss the reference to praying. The "prayers of the saints" (Rev. 5:8) are more than simple requests or petitions for personal blessing. They are more than impassioned pleas of men and women on earth, in the church, for God to reveal his glory and his justice in bringing righteous retribution on his enemies and in vindicating truth and goodness (see 6:9–11; 8:3–4).

The term translated "bowl" or "vial" occurs twelve times in Revelation (5:8; 15:7; 16:1, 2, 3, 4, 8, 10, 12, 17; 17:1; 21:9). The meaning of "bowl" in 5:8, however, appears to be slightly different from the meaning in the other eleven references. Here the "bowls" are filled with incense and are used in a positive, beneficial way, while in the other references, they are said to contain the wrath of God and are used to inflict punishments on the earth and its inhabitants.

The four living creatures and the twenty-four elders sing a "new song" (cf. Ps. 98:1; Isa. 42:10–13) because the Lamb has defeated the powers of evil and has inaugurated a new creation. And why is the Lamb worthy of praise? Because he has died, and by dying has redeemed men and women from every corner of the earth, and by redeeming them has made them (i.e., you and me!) into a kingdom and into priests.

The best manuscript evidence for Revelation 5:10 leads to the translation: "And you have made *them* a kingdom and priests" rather than "made *us*." If the latter were correct, it would support the idea that the elders are human, but the far better attested "them" would seem to differentiate the elders from "those" who are redeemed by the Lamb and made a kingdom of priests.

There is also the question of the verb tense of "reign" in verse 10. Both the future ("they *shall* reign on the earth") and the present tense ("they *are*" or "*do* reign on the earth") are supported by substantial manuscript evidence. According to Revelation 1:5–6, we are already a kingdom and priests to God, as is also the case here in 5:10. This would support the idea that the redeemed currently reign on the earth. This is an example of the already / not yet tension in Scripture. We *already* reign as a kingdom and priests, but *not yet* have we entered the full dimensions of that reign (which will come only with the creation of the new earth).

God's Love of Ethnic Diversity

God loves ethnic diversity, as clearly evident from the purpose of Christ's sinless life, substitutionary death, and bodily resurrection. God's aim is to have a redeemed bride for his Son from more than one or two or ten ethnic groups, but from all ethnic groups, from "every tribe and language and people and nation" (Rev. 5:9). Ethnic diversity is at the very heart and core of God's saving purposes in Christ. And his purpose is that they will live and worship and serve in Christ-centered harmony. All of them are priests, none more so than others. All rule and reign, none more so than others. White Christians are not one kingdom of priests and black Christians another. Chinese Christians do not constitute their own kingdom of priests while Arab Christians comprise another. We are all, regardless of ethnicity, regardless of physiological differences, one kingdom of priests. A God-glorifying kingdom of priests cannot despise one another because of racial differences or live in suspicion of the worth and value of the other based on racial differences.

When you permit feelings in your heart of dislike, suspicion, and disdain toward a person of a different skin color, you are blaspheming the majesty of the Creator God. You are denouncing the redemptive work of Jesus Christ. You are despising the shed blood of the cross. You are slandering the power of God in shaping men and women of all ethnicities in his image. You are denigrating and denying the purpose of God in redeeming men and women of all ethnicities and colors to make them a kingdom of priests. Racism is blasphemy. You cannot worship and glorify the majesty of God or embrace his redemptive purposes in Christ while treating his supreme creation with contempt—whatever color, culture, or age that creation might be.

An Avalanche of Praise

Suddenly in John's vision there is a snowball effect that leads to an avalanche of praise. A holy turbulence engulfs the heavens. As the choir sings of God's majesty, the adoration of the Lamb moves out in ever-widening circles (see Rev. 5:11–13), almost a ripple effect as if a huge stone had been cast into the center of an otherwise calm lake. At first it is the four living creatures singing their song of praise. They are then joined by the twenty-four elders. In verse 11, thousands and thousands of angels follow suit. If that were insufficient, we read in verse 13 that "every creature in heaven and on earth and under the earth and in the sea, and all that is in them" begins to praise the risen Lamb. The sevenfold shout of worship in verse 12 rings out like the resounding chimes of a huge bell:

POWER! . . . WEALTH! . . . WISDOM! . . . MIGHT! . . . HONOR! . . . GLORY! . . . BLESSING!

Education–Exultation–Exaltation

In chapter 4, I argued that if we don't know who God is, how he thinks, what he feels, and why he does what he does, we have no grounds for joy, no reason to celebrate, and no basis for finding satisfaction in him. That is why our careful and meticulous study of the heavenly vision in Revelation 5 is so crucial to our lives as Christians.

Delight in God cannot occur in an intellectual vacuum. Our joy is the fruit of what we know and believe to be true of God. Emotional heat, such as joy, delight, and gladness of heart, apart from intellectual light (i.e., the knowledge of God), is useless. Worse still, it is dangerous, for it inevitably leads to fanaticism and idolatry. The experience of heaven's inhabitants confirms that our knowledge of God (education) is the cause or grounds for our delight in him (exultation), which blossoms in the fruit of his praise, honor, and glory (exaltation).

What this tells us, once again, is that *the ultimate goal of theology isn't knowledge, but worship.* If our learning and knowledge of God do not lead to the joyful praise of God, we have failed. We learn only that we might laud, which is to say that *theology without doxology is idolatry.* The only theology worth studying is a theology that can be sung!

Adoration of the Lion and the Lamb

What about Jesus makes him worthy of your adoration and praise? What about Jesus makes him irresistibly attractive? Why is he alone worthy of your wholehearted allegiance and love?

Consider once again the portrait of Jesus in symbolic language. In Revelation 5:5 he is called "the Lion of the tribe of Judah," but in Revelation 5:6 he is also portrayed as the "Lamb" who had been slain, though now standing, because alive. So, which is he? Both! Jesus is both Lion and Lamb. And it is in this glorious juxtaposition of what appear to be two contrasting images that we find the answer to our question. Think about this for a moment:

> The Lion in whom we find unimpeachable authority is also the Lamb who embodies humility and meekness in the highest degree.
> The Lion who wields power and strength that none can resist is also the Lamb who walked this earth in weakness and suffering, resisting none.
> The Lion who rules the world and governs its every move is also the Lamb who was meekly led to slaughter by his enemies.
> The Lion who is known for his uncompromising commitment to righteousness is also the Lamb who overflows in love to sinners like you and me.

The Lion whose majestic beauty captivates the human heart is also the Lamb who condescended to take upon himself the likeness of a man and was, in appearance, quite ordinary and unimpressive.

The Lion who commands total obedience from everyone is also the Lamb who, in his earthly life, submitted himself in obedience to the law of God.

The Lion, who is holy and pure beyond our wildest imagination, is also the Lamb who is gracious, kind, and tenderhearted to all.

The Lion who could silence a raging storm with a single word is also the Lamb who refused to revile those who nailed him to a cross.

The Lion, who is life itself, is also the Lamb who willingly died for his enemies.

The Lion who is exalted high above the heavens, immeasurably beyond all of creation and myriads of angels, before whom the most powerful kings and commanders on earth are but a speck of dust on the balance, is also the Lamb who condescended to become one of us and suffer the trials and challenges put upon him by weak and sinful men.

The Lion, who is in himself infinite holiness and righteousness and purity and power is also the Lamb who welcomes broken sinners into his presence and makes intimate friends with his enemies.

The Lion who in himself needs nothing, being altogether self-sufficient, is also the Lamb who gives and gives and then gives yet again generously and abundantly.

The Lion who is of such blinding glory and brilliance that adoring angels cover their faces is also the Lamb who humbled himself and identified with his creatures so that they might behold him and enjoy him forever.

The Lion who, as Paul said in Philippians 2, exists from all eternity in perfect equality with the Father and the Spirit, equal in all respects as to his divinity, is also the Lamb who in time and history humbled himself and took on the likeness of sinful men and women.

The Lion who is known for his majesty is also the Lamb who is known for his meekness.

The Lion who drove the robbers and thieves out of the temple is also the Lamb who only days later allowed those very robbers and thieves to nail him to a cross.

The Lion who commands absolute obedience from his creatures is also
the Lamb who in obedience honored every command of his Father.
The Lion who rightly burns with wrath against the rebellious and
unbelieving is also the Lamb who in the place of the rebellious and
unbelieving endured in his own body and soul that very wrath.

He is at one and the same time a lion-like lamb and a lamb-like lion
without any inconsistency or contradiction.

God of Love, God of Wrath

An important point that many would prefer I skip is that the God who is
adored for his beauty, holiness, and majesty in Revelation 4–5 is the same
God who pours forth wrath, destruction, and terror through the series of
seal, trumpet, and bowl judgments.

The four living creatures who worship God in Revelation 4–5 also call
forth the four horsemen of the first four seal judgments in 6:1–8. The seven
trumpets are blown by the seven angels who stand before God in heaven
(8:2, 6). The designation of God in 4:9–10 as he "who lives forever and ever"
is found in 15:7 in connection with the "bowls full of the wrath of God." As
Richard Bauckham observes, "It is the God whose awesome holiness the
living creatures sing unceasingly who manifests his glory and power in the
final series of judgments."[1]

Even more explicit is the literary link between the seventh of each series
of judgments and the statement in 4:5. In the latter, we read of "flashes of
lightning, and rumblings and peals of thunder" issuing from the throne. This
formula is then echoed at the opening of the seventh seal judgment (8:5), the
sounding of the seventh trumpet (11:19), and the pouring out of the seventh
bowl (16:18–21). In other words, the holiness of God described in Revelation
4–5 is most clearly manifested in the judgments on evil in the seals, trumpets, and bowls.

It is no wonder, then, that when George Frideric Handel read and

---

1. Richard Bauckham, *The Theology of the Book of Revelation* (Cambridge: Cambridge University
Press, 1993), 41.

reflected on the vision of the Lion-like Lamb and the Lamb-like Lion, Jesus Christ, he put to music these glorious words:

> Hallelujah! Hallelujah! Hallelujah! Hallelujah! Hallelujah!
> Hallelujah! Hallelujah! Hallelujah! Hallelujah! Hallelujah!
> For the Lord God Omnipotent reigneth!
> Hallelujah! Hallelujah! Hallelujah! Hallelujah!
> For the Lord God Omnipotent reigneth!
> Hallelujah! Hallelujah! Hallelujah! Hallelujah!
> For the Lord God Omnipotent reigneth!
> Hallelujah! Hallelujah! Hallelujah! Hallelujah!
> For the Lord God Omnipotent reigneth!
> Hallelujah!
>
> The kingdom of this world is become the kingdom of our Lord
> And of His Christ.
> And of His Christ.
>
> And He shall reign for ever and ever,
> And He shall reign for ever and ever,
> And He shall reign for ever and ever,
> And He shall reign for ever and ever,
>
> King of kings, forever and ever! Hallelujah! Hallelujah!
> And Lord of lords, forever and ever! Hallelujah! Hallelujah!
> King of kings, forever and ever! Hallelujah! Hallelujah!
> And Lord of lords, forever and ever! Hallelujah! Hallelujah!
> King of kings, forever and ever! Hallelujah! Hallelujah!
> And Lord of lords
> King of kings and Lord of lords
>
> And He shall reign
> And He shall reign
> And He shall reign

He shall reign
And he shall reign forever and ever.

King of kings, forever and ever,
And Lord of lords, Hallelujah! Hallelujah!
And He shall reign forever and ever,
King of kings! And Lord of lords!
King of kings! And Lord of lords!
And He shall reign forever and ever,
Forever and ever and ever and ever
Hallelujah! Hallelujah! Hallelujah! Hallelujah! Hallelujah!
Hallelujah!

Conclusion

We must resist any inclination to disregard John's vision as irrelevant, as if it were but a distant dream, an ethereal, far-off heavenly phenomenon of which we on earth can only wonder. This is not virtual reality. This is no computer-generated facsimile. It is far more real than anything this temporal world can offer.

The glory of the Holy Spirit is that he can take each syllable of this inspired portrait and set it ablaze so that the fire of its truth and life-changing power might forever burn within our hearts. Thus, may we be led to join the twenty-four elders and the four living creatures and the chorus of countless millions of angels, together with the redeemed even now in heaven, in the relishing and enjoyment of our great and glorious God!

Why, you ask? Because this is why you exist! This is the reason there is a "you" and a "me." This is the purpose for which Christ died and rose again. This is the goal of all history that is contained in the scroll, namely, that we might glorify, honor, and exalt our great triune God by finding in him and his love beauty, grace, power, and the deepest delight our hearts could ever hope to experience.

CHAPTER 14

Worshiping the God Who Wins

Revelation 11, 15, 19

One might reasonably say that the book of Revelation is primarily about the worship of the God who wins. We've already looked at Revelation 4–5 and the worship that transpires in heaven. But three additional texts call for some comment.

Revelation 11:15–19

Revelation is all about a conflict between good and evil, between the Christ and the Antichrist, between the Lamb of God and the Beast, between the kingdom of our Lord Jesus Christ and the kingdom of Satan and all his demons. And the good news is that God wins! One of the clearest statements to this effect is found in Revelation 11:15–19 and the description of the seventh trumpet judgment.

> Then the seventh angel blew his trumpet, and there were loud voices in heaven, saying, "The kingdom of the world has become the kingdom of our Lord and of his Christ, and he shall reign forever and ever." And the twenty-four elders who sit on their thrones before God fell on their faces and worshiped God, saying,
>
> "We give thanks to you, Lord God Almighty,
>   who is and who was,

for you have taken your great power
and begun to reign.
The nations raged,
but your wrath came,
and the time for the dead to be judged,
and for rewarding your servants, the prophets and saints,
and those who fear your name,
both small and great,
and for destroying the destroyers of the earth."

Then God's temple in heaven was opened, and the ark of his covenant was seen within his temple. There were flashes of lightning, rumblings, peals of thunder, an earthquake, and heavy hail.

In his commentary on Revelation, Joel Beeke rightly points out that this "passage in Revelation describing what will happen after the blowing of the last trumpet is *proleptic* or anticipatory. John is so certain of the fulfillment of what he prophesies that he speaks of it in the past tense, as though it were already an accomplished fact."[1]

How could John have heard these "loud voices" if they occurred "in heaven" (Rev. 11:15; see also 12:10; 19:1)? Elsewhere John spoke as if from an earthly perspective and used the phrase "*from* heaven" (Rev. 10:4, 8; 11:12; 14:2, 13; 18:4). It would seem that on a few occasions John was either in a visionary trance state or bodily/spiritually present in heaven when he received his revelations. The "loud voices" are either those of the angelic hosts worshiping God or perhaps of the saints in heaven (Rev. 7:9; 19:1, 6), or of the twenty-four elders who are then portrayed as falling down in worship and speaking their praises in 11:16–18.

We must not pass over without comment the fact that these voices are "loud"! In an earlier chapter, I addressed the fact that often in Scripture the worship of God is expressed with loud shouting. If there is shouting on earth in response to the greatness of our God, you can rest assured that the shouting in heaven is loud! No one in heaven, be they angel, saint, living creature,

---

1. Joel R. Beeke, *Revelation*, The Lectio Continua Expository Commentary of the New Testament (Grand Rapids: Reformation Heritage, 2016), 327, emphasis original.

or elder, has qualms about making their adoration and thanksgiving heard. None in heaven would dare turn to a shouting saint or a loud angel and ask them to tone it down. We have much to learn from them.

The declaration is that Satan's domain, as the "god of this world" (2 Cor. 4:4) and "the prince of the power of the air" (Eph. 2:2; cf. 6:12) and "the ruler of this world" (John 12:31; 14:30; 16:11), has now finally and wholly been taken by the Lord and his Christ! Note that in Revelation 11:15, we read of the "kingdom of the world" (singular) not "kingdoms" (plural). All the secular empires of this earth are actually one earthly kingdom ruled by Satan, but now under the sovereign sway of Jesus.

Whereas in 1 John 5:19 we are told that, in some sense, in this present age, "the whole world lies in the power of the evil one," a day is coming (this day, described in 11:15–19) when such shall no longer be! This is the consummate overthrow of all God's enemies and the manifestation of the universal and cosmic extent of his rightful rule! Whereas the "world" could refer to the totality of creation, it more likely refers to the world of humanity that stands opposed to God and labors to resist his purposes. Interestingly, the only other verbal parallel to this phrase is found in Matthew 4:8 where Satan offers dominion of "the kingdoms of the world" to Jesus if he will only bow before him. The implication is that such dominion was, at that time, Satan's to offer. But no longer! G. B. Caird explained:

> In one sense God's sovereignty is eternal: he entered on his reign when he established the rule of order in the midst of the primaeval chaos (Ps. xciii. 1–4); he has reigned throughout human history, turning even men's misdeeds into instruments of his mercy; and above all he reigned in the Cross of Christ (xii. 10). But always up to this point he has reigned over a rebellious world. A king may be king *de jure*, but he is not king *de facto* until the trumpet which announces his accession is answered by the acclamations of a loyal and obedient people.[2]

Four additional observations are called for. First, the past tense "has become" in verse 15 is used *proleptically*, that is to say, a future event is so

---

2. G. B. Caird, *A Commentary on the Revelation of St. John the Divine* (New York: Harper & Row, 1966), 141.

certain to occur that it is described as a reality of the past. Second, who is the "he" in verse 15 that "will reign forever and ever"? Is it God the Father, the "Lord" of verse 15, or God the Son, that is, "his Christ"? Or is it both, as John envisioned them as an inseparable unity? Third, a phrase parallel to "he shall reign forever and ever" is found in Revelation 22:5, where it refers to *us* in the new Jerusalem! God will reign forever and ever, but so will we—with him! Finally, this verse is not saying that political parties and positions of earthly power and authority will be taken over by Christians so that the world will finally be Christianized. Verse 15 does not refer to what will happen before Christ returns but what will happen when and after he returns. It describes not this present age in which we live but the future age of eternity.

The Declaration of the Twenty-Four Elders

The twenty-four elders once again resume their familiar posture: face down in the presence of God. With every occurrence of this in Revelation, it becomes evident that the most appropriate posture of worship is that of being face down on the ground! Their cry is one of gratitude. They address God as the "Lord our God, the Almighty" (cf. 19:6). The word "Almighty" (*pantokratōr*) means "sovereign ruler" or "ruler over all." The Roman Caesars presumptuously adopted this title for themselves. But this day will expose them as charlatans and usurpers as God exerts his rightful lordship over all.

But something is missing. Their declaration "who is and who was" (Rev. 11:17) lacks the third element found earlier, "who is to come" (1:4; 4:8). In all likelihood, this means that the final part of the threefold description of God ("him who is and who was and who is to come") is not merely a reference to his sovereignty over the future or of his timeless nature, but specifically speaks of the end time when God, by means of the return of Christ, will break into world history and overthrow once and for all every opposition. *The God who "is to come" has come!* The promise of ultimate victory is so utterly immutable that John spoke of it as if it had already arrived.

The rage of the nations is provoked by the inception of God's rule through his Christ (Rev. 11:18). This is a clear reference to Psalm 2:2—"The kings of the earth set themselves, and the rulers take counsel together, against the LORD and against his Anointed" (see also vv. 5, 10–12). The word translated "wrath" (*orgē*), which is said to have come, is always used in Revelation of the final outpouring at the end of history (6:16–17; 14:10–11; 16:19; 19:15). Note well: the nations were enraged (Gk. *ōrgisthēsan*) and God's wrath (Gk. *orgē*) came. This is an example of how the punishment fits the crime: their rage against God is met by God's rage against them!

The fact that this is the time "for the dead to be judged" (Rev. 11:18) and the faithful rewarded proves that John was envisioning the end of history. The parallel in Revelation 20:12–13, which all acknowledge speaks of the final judgment, makes this inescapable. Again in verse 18, we see that the punishment fits the crime (sin), for God "destroys" (Gk. *diaphtheirai*) those who have sought to "destroy" (*diaphtheirontas*) the earth (the "earth" here is probably a reference to God's people).

Believers, on the other hand, now receive their heavenly "reward," part of which, perhaps, is bearing witness to the judgment of those who have persecuted them (and thus this, too, is God's positive answer to the prayer of Revelation 6:9–11). For the response of God's people (described in almost identical terms) to judgment of the wicked, see Revelation 18:24–19:5. For other elements of this "reward," see Revelation 2:7 (22:14); 2:11; 2:17; 2:26–27; 3:5 (7:14); 3:12; 3:21; 7:15–17; 22:3–4; 22:14.

I mention all of this to make one vital point. Often our worship is restricted to giving thanks for God's redemptive love in Christ, his grace, his kindness, his power, or some other attribute or action of God taken on our behalf. And that is all well and good. But how often do you pause to give thanks for the display of God's wrath? How much time do you spend worshiping (Rev. 11:16) God and giving thanks to God (v. 17) for judging idolaters, unbelievers, and those who have attempted to destroy the earth (v. 18)? God's holy wrath, no less than his kindly saving mercy, is reason for praise and adoration. Would a God who merely winked at sin and evil be worthy of our devotion? We worship God for all he is and does, a truth that we will soon encounter again in Revelation 19.

A Concluding Vision of Heaven Opened

Was the ark of the covenant somehow translated into heaven before the fall of Jerusalem in 586 BC? There is no way to know. There is a tradition in Judaism that some expected the return of the ark of the covenant at the end of history when God would once again graciously dwell among his people. Indeed, one legend had it that Jeremiah removed the ark to safety in a cave or buried it on Mount Sinai, where it would remain hidden until the final restoration of Israel (see 2 Macc. 2:4–8; cf. 2 Bar. 6:5–10; 80:2). But no such expectation is found in the biblical literature.

People couldn't look upon the ark in the Old Testament. Those who transported it were given special instructions for how to cover the ark without looking upon it. The reason was because the ark represented or embodied God's holiness and the object lesson was to awaken and alert people to their sin. But the fact that the temple was now open and the ark was "seen" (v. 19) indicates that sin has been forgiven and the barrier to God's presence has been torn down. Thus, most likely "the ark is shown here as a symbol, representing God's covenant with his people."[3]

This, then, is the glorious achievement of God and the grounds for our worship. God the Father sent God the Son in the power of God the Holy Spirit to defeat and overthrow the works of the devil and, by doing so, to deliver his people from the guilt and condemnation of their sin. And this marvelous and majestic description of the seventh trumpet judgment is a reminder to us all that God wins! Not all the nuclear power on earth can thwart the full and final revelation of his kingdom authority. Not all the backroom shenanigans of conspiratorial politicians and power brokers can delay the ultimate judgment of all unbelievers. Not all the immoral chaos and vain philosophy of a world gone mad can prevent the ultimate rule and reign of King Jesus. And for this, God is deserving of our loud and heartfelt praise!

Revelation 15:2–4

Yet another portrayal of godly worship is found in Revelation 15:2–4. This intervening paragraph, beginning with verse 2, looks back to the theme of final judgment in 14:14–20 and portrays the consummated defeat of Satan, which the victorious and vindicated saints now celebrate in song. They "conquered the beast" and Satan himself, as 12:11 tells us, "by the blood of the Lamb and by the word of their testimony" and by loving Jesus and treasuring

3. Richard D. Phillips, *Revelation*, Reformed Expository Commentaries (Phillipsburg, NJ: P&R, 2017), 336.

him more than their own earthly lives. They are described as holding harps and standing on "a sea of glass mingled with fire" (15:2).

Given this chapter's "new/second exodus" motif, the "sea" probably alludes to the Red Sea through which the Israelites were delivered. Others have seen it as identical to the "sea of glass, like crystal" (Rev. 4:6), which stands before the throne in heaven. It may also be that the "sea" here connotes cosmic evil and the chaotic powers of the dragon resident within it, over which the saints have now emerged victorious.

The victorious saints now sing in praise of God for defeating the beast on their behalf. They sing "the song of Moses" and "the song of the Lamb." Are these two different songs or one and the same? There's no way to be certain.

Given the background for this in Exodus, perhaps we are to understand Moses as the source or author of a song he and the Israelites sang about God in praise for deliverance at the Red Sea during the time of the exodus. But the Lamb of God has secured for his people an even greater exodus, one that delivers not simply from physical slavery out of Egypt but from spiritual slavery out of sin. The song is thus about the Lamb. He is the content, focus, and principal theme of their singing.

The lyrics that follow in Revelation 15:3–4 do not appear to be drawn from the song of Moses in Exodus 15 but rather come from a variety of Old Testament texts. However, the themes in 15:3–4 most assuredly do derive from the song in Exodus 15. The lyrics here in verses 3–4 begin: "Great and amazing are your deeds." All God's works are stunning. There is nothing bland or boring about what God does. All his deeds are the sort that amaze and shock us because they exceed anything a human being might produce. They are awe-inspiring. None of his deeds are computer-generated facsimiles of reality. They *are* reality! The psalmist declared something similar:

> Great are the works of the LORD,
>   studied by all who delight in them.
> Full of splendor and majesty is his work,
>   and his righteousness endures forever.
> He has caused his wondrous works to be remembered:
>   the LORD is gracious and merciful. (Ps. 111:2–4)

The attribution, "O Lord God the Almighty," is found repeatedly in the prophets Haggai, Zechariah, and Malachi. "Just and true are your ways," echoes Deuteronomy 32:4. It would seem that this phrase parallels the first, "showing that God's sovereign acts are not demonstrations of raw power but moral expressions of his just character."[4] We may not immediately recognize the justice in all God does, but we can trust that he never violates what is morally proper. His judgments against an unbelieving world are both true and just. No one is treated unfairly. We find almost identical language in Revelation 16:7: "And I heard the altar saying, 'Yes, Lord God the Almighty, true and just are your judgments!" (see also Rev. 19:2). And clearly, this is said with regard to the final judgment poured out against those who oppose God and his kingdom (see 16:5–6).

Much that God either does or permits is confusing to us all. We wonder why he strikes down a godly man in his youth and allows the wicked to live a hundred years. You may wonder, as I do, why he tolerates one earthly tyrant who persecutes the church and, at the same time, brings another crashing down in humiliation and shame. But one day we will see all God's deeds, and we will marvel and declare that everything he has ever done is both just and true.

In particular, the saints are singing about the punishment of God's (and their) enemies, not only in terms of the seal, trumpet, and bowl judgments that they endure but also the everlasting torment inflicted upon them as described in Revelation 14:9–20.

We read in 15:3–4, "O King of the nations! Who will not fear, O Lord, and glorify your name?" This echoes Jeremiah 10:7. If the answer to this question is "No one," that is, everyone will fear and glorify God's name, does this imply universalism? No (see Phil. 2:8–11). Even unbelievers will be compelled to acknowledge that God is to be feared and is deserving of all glory and honor and praise.

"For you alone are holy. All nations will come and worship you, for your righteous acts have been revealed" (Rev. 15:4; from Pss. 86:8–10; 98:2). Again, those among the nations who do not respond voluntarily in saving faith will be divinely and justly compelled to acknowledge this truth. Others take a

4. G. K. Beale, *The Book of Revelation: A Commentary on the Greek Text* (Grand Rapids: Eerdmans, 1999), 795.

more positive approach, seeing in this text (v. 4) a reference to the conversion of the nations as they behold the vindication of God's people and the righteousness of God's ways.

Revelation 19:1–10

Why does your local church exist? Your church does many things. You preach Scripture. You pray. You evangelize and go on mission trips. You gather in small groups and sing. You serve, love, and sacrifice for one another. You strive for ethnic reconciliation and biblical justice. But *why* do you do these things? You do them because of the reason why you exist. You exist to make Christ known, to exalt his beauty and majesty, to act and speak and live in such a way that Christ is seen as preeminent and glorious and worthy of all your heart's affection, joy, and delight.

I have one goal when I write. Every subsidiary goal helps me to achieve my highest, singular goal. And that goal is to be an instrument in the hands of the Holy Spirit by which your heart's affections might be transformed, your mind's thoughts might be aligned with who God is, and your spirit's desires might be to praise and magnify Jesus.

My ultimate goal is that God, as revealed in Jesus Christ by the power of the Holy Spirit, might be treasured, prized, enjoyed, and extolled as supreme and altogether satisfying to your soul. Any church that exists for anything less is not aligned with Scripture. Many churches may do many different things, and that is fine. But if the many different things that these churches do don't serve the single ultimate aim of exalting God as revealed in Jesus Christ by the power of the Holy Spirit, these churches have failed to achieve what God had in mind when he called them out of sin and darkness into the light of the kingdom of Christ.

And why should any of us believe that the God of the Bible is the sort of God who deserves this sort of single-minded, wholehearted admiration and enjoyment? We are given numerous reasons here in Revelation 19:1–10. Our God is a

God of salvation and glory and power (v. 1),
God whose judgments are true and just (v. 2),
God who vindicates his servants and avenges their blood (v. 2),

God of small people and great people (v. 5),

an almighty God who reigns in sovereignty over all that he has made (v. 6), and

a God who ordained from eternity past that his Son, Jesus Christ, would have a bride, a people whom he redeemed from sin and death, with whom he will celebrate in the great marriage feast (v. 7).

Virtually everything we read in Revelation 17–18 is a description of the judgment that God will bring to bear against Babylon, that global network of human defiance, unbelief, and idolatry. The satanically energized conspiracy among the nations of the earth to cast aside and crush Jesus is finally and forever crushed and destroyed in these chapters.

Revelation 17 opens with these words: "Come, I will show you the judgment of the great prostitute who is seated on many waters" (Rev. 17:1). Then, in chapter 18, we read this: "Fallen, fallen, is Babylon the great!" (Rev. 18:2). In verse 8 we find that "she will be burned up with fire; for mighty is the Lord God who has judged her." And in verse 10, "Alas! Alas! You great city, you mighty city, Babylon! For in a single hour your judgment has come."

Then chapter 19 begins with the words, "After this," which is to say, after the portrayal of the certainty and finality of God's judgment against wicked Babylon, that world city and civilization that opposed him. What follows in Revelation 19:1–10 is the response of God's people and the angelic hosts to the judgment that God will bring on Babylon. "He has judged the great prostitute" (v. 2). *And for this reason, he is to be praised.*

Thus, what we have in Revelation 19 is John's hearing of the worship in heaven as God's creation and the church celebrate their Lord's triumph over wicked Babylon. In fact, worship of our great triune God is not only the purpose of the book of Revelation. It is the purpose for all existence. It is why we are here. Revelation 17–19 are saying to all, "Don't worship the wealth of Babylon. Worship God! Don't worship the power of Babylon! Worship God! Don't worship any of the sensual or worldly pleasures that Babylon offers you. Worship God!"

John recorded for us what he heard in heaven so that we on earth might join in the celebration and admiration and adoration of the God who not only judges Babylon but who also has redeemed men and women from every tongue and tribe, nation and people. John wrote this while sitting in exile on the island of Patmos. We listen to it while sitting in luxury, peace, and calm in a local church building or the living room of a friend's home. Surely we can join with him in the praise of who God is and what he has done.

Do you realize what is happening when we sing our praises to God? We are saying that we refuse to be seduced by Babylon's treasure and pleasure. We are saying that we refuse to buy into the satanic lie that there is more satisfaction to be found in the world than in Jesus. We are saying what David said in Psalm 16:11, that it is in God's presence that we find fullness of joy and at God's right hand that we experience pleasures that never end.

Worship is far more than singing songs. We sing to celebrate and proclaim the God of heaven and earth. We sing to enjoy him. We sing to savor all that he is for us in Jesus. We sing and pray to connect with God himself. Worship is all about engaging, encountering, and enjoying God.

Now that we all understand the ultimate purpose of this first paragraph of Revelation 19, let's pull it apart piece by piece.

Eavesdropping on the Worship of Heaven's Inhabitants (vv. 1–2)

I greatly envy John. Here, once again, he was allowed to eavesdrop on what was happening in heaven. He heard a "great multitude" shouting praise and crying out to God. Who is it that he heard? Were these angels, or perhaps the twenty-four elders we encountered back in Revelation 4–5, or were these the voices of the four living creatures? It could be the martyred saints, those who had been killed because of their allegiance to Jesus. My guess is that it was probably all of them, joining together as if they were a heavenly choir.

Note carefully that this declaration in verse 1 is more than a simple doxology. "Salvation" belongs to "our God" in the sense that he alone can provide redemption and forgiveness of sins. Whatever other so-called god you may seek, you may find much, but you won't find deliverance from divine judgment.

"Glory" belongs to "our God" in the sense that the weighty, priceless beauty and splendor for which our souls long and with which we will be captivated for all eternity are found only in the Christian God. For most in our society, God is inconsequential. If he is regarded at all, he is regarded as very lowly. When I once heard someone take the Lord's name in vain, cursing wildly with a string of "G-ds" I challenged him. He immediately apologized by saying, "Oh, I'm sorry. I didn't mean anything by it." My response was, "That's precisely the problem! God *doesn't* mean anything to you. He is inconsequential to your life and your language. He has value to you only to the degree that his name adds punch to your profanity."

And "power" belongs to "our God." Not weakness, not feebleness, not fragility, but omnipotent power to create and uphold the universe and to supply us with everything we need to thrive in a broken world.

The multitude's declaration of praise is no doubt in response to the judgment on Babylon described in chapters 17 and 18. This is confirmed by verse 2 (note the transitional word "for"). God is to be praised and all power and glory ascribed to him precisely because "he has judged the great prostitute" (v. 2). Far from the outpouring of wrath and the destruction of his enemies being a blight on God's character or a reason to question his love and kindness (as unbelievers so often suggest), they are the very reason for worship!

Revelation 15:3–4 and 16:5–7 show that God's judgments against the unbelieving world system and its followers are "true and just." They are true and just because the great prostitute "corrupted [cf. 17:1–5; 18:3, 7–9] the earth with her immorality," thereby meriting divine vengeance. Of all the questions I am asked by people, the one that rings most loudly and consistently is this: "How can God do this and be just? How can God permit that and be just? If God were just, he would do A and not B and most certainly would never permit Y or Z." I cannot explain how or why or for what purpose God does all that he does, but this I know with absolute certainty: whatever he does, be that saving a soul or judging another, granting access to heaven or casting into hell, he is always and ever wholly just and true!

You might think that the word translated "Hallelujah" (lit., "Praise Yahweh") would appear everywhere in the New Testament. It actually occurs only four times in the New Testament, all of which are found here in Revelation 19:1, 3, 4, 6. The ESV translates the final phrase in verse 2, "on her," when it literally should read, "from her hand." This may simply be a figure of speech in which a part ("hand") represents the whole (all of Babylon). Or it may be that God has avenged the blood of his bondservants, which was shed by her hand (cf. 2 Kings 9:7).

Praising God for the Eternal Duration of Babylon's Destruction (vv. 3–4)[5]

As if once were not enough, now "once more" the cry of Hallelujah! is sounded. The wording here comes from the Old Testament description of God's judgment against Edom (Isa. 34:9–10) and is similar to Revelation 14:11, all of which points to the never-ending nature (or effect?) of Babylon's judgment. Beale suggests that "the portrayal of the city's *eternal* judgment may be a partial polemic against the mythical name *Roma aeterna* ('eternal Rome'), which was one of the names for the Roman Empire."[6] This verdict is then echoed (note their "Amen," a formal expression of ratification and endorsement) by the twenty-four elders and four living creatures (cf. Ps. 106:48 for this combination of "Amen" and "Hallelujah").

Praising God from Both Small and Great (v. 5)

Whose "voice" is this that John hears in Revelation 19:5? Is it Jesus? Could it be Michael or one of the other angels, or perhaps one of the four living creatures? The fact that it came "from the throne" has led some to say this is Jesus calling everyone to worship the Father. If so, would he say, "Praise *our* God," "Give praise to *your* God," or even "Give praise to *my* God"? In any case, those called on to praise God (again, given the context, for the judgment of Babylon and all God's enemies) include all God-fearing bondservants, both great (powerful and important) and small (weak and unnoticed). Worship is incumbent on us all, regardless of our earthly status, socioeconomic achievement, reputation, or accomplishments.

Praising God for His Sovereign Reign (v. 6)

Again, a "great multitude" shouts forth its praise (Rev. 19:6). Surely this is the same group, whoever they may be, that began this worship service in verse 1. Only here, their voice is even louder (like the "roar of many waters" and "mighty peals of thunder"), gradually increasing as they reflect more deeply on the reasons why God is worthy of praise (as stated in verse 2 and all of chapter 18).

When we lived in Kansas City, I had the privilege on several occasions of attending Kansas City Chiefs football games. Arrowhead Stadium, where the

---

5. See "Further Reflections on Feasting" at the end of this chapter.
6. Beale, *Revelation*, 929.

Chiefs play, is famous for being one of the country's loudest, if not the loudest, outdoor sports arena. And I can testify to it. During a typical moment in the game, I could turn to my wife, Ann, with my lips pressed against her ear and loudly say something, and yet she couldn't hear a thing. Such was the level of excitement among the fans. But that pales in comparison with the roars that are incessantly heard around the throne of God! Would that the worship at our local churches be comparable to "the roar of many waters" and "the sound of mighty peals of thunder"!

The judgments of God against Babylon are indicative of God's "reign" (v. 6). This is important because the wickedness and rebellion of all earthly, nonbelieving people and nations might appear to call into question whether God is actually in control. We tend to think that the rampant evil in our world is a sign that God has lost his grip on creation and the affairs of men.

But no! God is to be worshiped precisely because he and he alone reigns through it all. His will is done in both heaven and earth. Nothing in Revelation has caught him by surprise. The one thing that will keep you singing praises and extolling our God is your assurance that he is almighty and sovereign and in control even if the evil plans of Babylon on earth end up costing you your livelihood or even your life.

Praising God for the Salvation and Sanctification of the Bride of Christ (vv. 7–8)

Do you realize that the way in which God brings glory to himself and gladness to us is by graciously and lovingly securing a bride for his Son, our Savior, Jesus Christ? The totality of the biblical story, from Genesis to Revelation, is concerned with God's redemptive pursuit of a people for Jesus. All of history consummates here, in the spiritual union and joy and ecstasy of God's people with God's Son.

The image of Jesus as the Bridegroom and his people as the bride reaches back into the Old Testament. But it was Jesus himself who spoke of this more than any other. Jesus replied to the religious leaders that his disciples were not fasting because he, the Bridegroom, was present with them (Matt. 9:14–15). When he would depart, then they would fast. He described heaven as being like a wedding feast: "And again Jesus spoke to them in parables, saying, 'The kingdom of heaven may be compared to a king who gave a wedding feast for his son'" (Matt. 22:1; see 1–14). He portrayed his second coming as the coming of a bridegroom (Matt. 25:1–13). When John the Baptist described himself in relation to Jesus, he basically said, "I am the best man, but Jesus is the bridegroom" (see John 3:29).

Let's begin by noting the bride's clothing, or as David Aune has put it, "the bridal trousseau."[7] The "fine linen, bright and pure" is an obvious and intentional contrast with the clothing of Babylon (where it functions as "a symbol of decadence and opulence,"[8] and the clothing of the bride (where it functions as a symbol of righteousness and purity; see especially the Old Testament background for this imagery in Isa. 61:10). The "fine linen" is then said to symbolize "the righteous deeds of the saints" (Rev. 19:8). Some believe this points to the idea repeated throughout Revelation of the saints holding to the testimony of Jesus (cf. 19:10), that is, bearing witness to Jesus in both word and deed (see Rev. 1:9; 6:9; 11:7; 12:11, 17; 20:4). Others emphasize the idea of purity that results from persevering faith amid trials and suffering (cf. Rev. 3:5–6).

Another suggestion is that the phrase "righteous deeds of the saints" points instead to God's act of vindication on behalf of the saints. In other words, God's act of judgment against Babylon and the Beast, persecutors of the saints, is a declaration of acquittal—that is, God has vindicated them. He has passed judgment *on their behalf*. If so, the "fine linen" points to the final reward for having lived righteously rather than the righteous living itself.

Finally, note the classic theological tension between divine sovereignty and human responsibility. On the one hand, the bride "has made herself ready" (19:7). There is something we must do. We must be prepared for that day. We are responsible to obey what God has called us to do in Scripture. I tremble at the thought of how much time and money were required so my daughters could be "ready" to meet their respective bridegrooms as they walked down the aisle! They exercised to lose weight, purchased cosmetics, hired hairdressers—and their wedding dresses, well, you can only imagine the painstaking process of selecting just the right one and the monetary price I had to pay. But it was worth every dollar!

Yet, on the other hand, "it was granted to her [by God] to clothe herself" (19:8). In this tension, see Philippians 2:12–13. Yes, the bride must actively

---

7. David E. Aune, *Revelation 17–22*, Word Biblical Commentary (Nashville: Thomas Nelson, 1998), 3:1030.

8. Aune, *Revelation 17–22*, 3:1030.

and willingly pursue purity of life ("work out your own salvation with fear and trembling"), yet all the while acknowledging that it is God's grace that makes it possible ("for it is God who is works in you, both to will and to work for his good pleasure"). The good deeds, the righteous deeds with which we are clothed, are a gift from God. Paul said in Ephesians 2:10 that they have been prepared for us before the foundation of the world that we might walk in them. And this makes it all the more fitting and appropriate that we should give God the glory, as we saw in Revelation 19:7.

Praising God for the Marriage Supper of the Lamb (vv. 9–10)

There is a slight change in perspective from Revelation 19:7–8 to verse 9. In the former verses, the bride is viewed corporately, on the verge of marrying the Lamb. But in verse 9 the focus is on individual believers who are portrayed as invited guests at the marriage supper. Both pictures describe the intimacy of communion between Jesus and his people. But this is an invitation to which you and I must personally respond. Many, sad to say, ignore the requested RSVP upon having received a wedding invitation. But to be a part of this wedding, each person must respond in repentance and faith and embrace the Bridegroom as their own!

Of all possible scenarios or spiritual metaphors that could have been used to portray the relationship between the Lamb, Jesus Christ, and his people, why was that of marriage and a wedding feast (cf. Isa. 25:6) chosen? What is it in this imagery that John finds particularly appropriate when describing the nature of how we feel about and relate to Jesus? Joy? Celebration? The beginning of a new life together? Intimacy? Trust? Oneness? Commitment? Delight in one another? Yes!

As the father of two daughters, I know what it costs to pay for and host a wedding reception and dinner. I did the best I could for my two girls, given the money available to me then. But nothing will ever compare with the feast that the heavenly Father plans on hosting for his Son, the bridegroom, together with his bride, the church. Not all the exquisite foods and luscious desserts you've enjoyed at the most lavish wedding feasts can compare with what the Father has planned for his Son!

The angel speaking to John has anticipated our objection that surely this is all too good to be true. It must be a spectacular exaggeration. "Ah," says the angel in Revelation 19:9, "These are the true words of God." So, when you hear him say that those who are invited to this wedding feast are "blessed," you had better believe it!

There is an obvious contrast between, on the one hand, the marriage "supper" of the Lamb, to which the bride is invited, and, on the other, the "great supper" of God (Rev. 19:17–18), to which the birds are invited that they might eat the flesh of his enemies! At the end of history, there will be two great suppers, one of which all people will attend. Either you will eat or be eaten! Either you are a guest who dines or you are the dinner! One is a reward for faith and righteousness, the other a punishment for unbelief and wickedness.

People have often wondered why John would be so naive as to fall at the feet of an angel and worship. Some have tried to dismiss the problem by saying that the word "worship" (*proskunēsis*) refers to a normal gesture of respect, far short of genuine worship. Whereas the word can often have this meaning in the Bible, the angel's response in 19:10 and his advice to John indicate otherwise. There are at least two answers to this problem, both of which bear a measure of truth.

First, this is only the first of two such occurrences, the other in Revelation 22:8–9. It may be that John, much like Daniel in chapter 10 of his prophecy, was overwhelmed with the brilliance and power of this angelic being. Let us remember that in 18:1, an angel is described as "having great authority" and so completely reflecting the glory of God that "the earth was made bright with his glory."

Second, the angel has just pronounced an awesome beatitude or blessing on John and others who are invited to the marriage supper, immediately followed by a powerful declaration that authenticates its reality: "These are the true words of God" (v. 9). The impact of this statement may have been more than he could fathom. He may have thought that any spiritual being commissioned from the throne of God with such profound news deserved special reverence. But is there any other reason why the Spirit, through John, would include this story? Yes.

First, note that it is the angel as the giver of prophetic revelation (esp. seen in 22:8–9) that explains why John prostrates himself in this way. But "in rejecting worship the angel disclaims this status: he is not the transcendent giver of prophetic revelation, but a creaturely instrument through whom the revelation is given, and therefore a fellow-servant with John and the Christian prophets, who are similarly only instruments to pass on the revelation. Instead of worshiping the angel, John is directed to 'worship God' (19:10; 22:9) as the true transcendent source of revelation."[9] As 22:16 makes clear, "the angel is a mere intermediary, Jesus is the source of the revelation."[10] The angel wants to make clear that when it comes to revelation, he belongs on the side of the creatures who receive it, while Jesus belongs on the side of God who gives it.

Second, it may be that John is reinforcing in this story one of the principal themes of the entire book, namely, the difference between true worship and idolatry. Everyone in Revelation either worships God or the dragon/Beast/Babylon. There is no third way or middle ground.

Third, and related to the above, is the fact that this scenario presents both an example and a warning of how easy it is to be deceived and seduced into idolatry. If someone like John, who had received such marvelous revelatory experiences as found in Revelation, can fall prey to this temptation, how much more should we be on the alert!

You and I, together with John and all those who have been invited and made fit to attend the marriage supper of the Lamb, have one ultimate responsibility and privilege: "Worship God" (v. 10). Why? Because "the testimony of Jesus is the spirit of prophecy" (cf. 1:2, 9; 12:17; 19:10; 20:4). I want to help you understand the connection between the command to worship God and the declaration that the testimony of Jesus is the spirit of prophecy.

The Greek would allow us to render the first part either of two ways: (1) "the testimony *about* Jesus," or (2) "the testimony *which comes from* Jesus," that is, which Jesus himself bears or declares. The latter option points to the idea that all true prophecy originates in the words and acts of Jesus. But I think the former option is more likely. It highlights the idea that all true prophecy consists in testimony or witness to/about Jesus himself. Jesus is its content and focus (whether directly or indirectly). In other words, you should only worship God because the testimony of all prophecy is about Jesus, not about angels, not about mere human beings, but about and concerning the God-man, Jesus Christ.

The second half of this statement may mean that all true prophecy is inspired by the Holy Spirit (i.e., energized and sustained by him). Or it

9. Richard Bauckham, *The Climax of Prophecy: Studies on the Book of Revelation* (Edinburgh: T&T Clark, 1993), 134.

10. Bauckham, *The Climax of Prophecy,* 134.

may mean that the essence of prophecy, the purpose and principle of it all, is bearing witness to Jesus. Or again, it may mean that the (Holy) Spirit is chiefly characterized by prophetic manifestations. And since you who know Jesus have the Holy Spirit dwelling within you, you therefore potentially may prophesy concerning who Jesus is and what he has done.

Conclusion

The wedding day is near. The bridegroom is coming! Have you betrothed yourself to Christ? Have you made yourself "ready" by turning to him in faith and clinging to him above all others? The invitation has been extended. If you wish to attend the marriage feast of the Lamb, you must respond. RSVP in trust, adoration, and confident hope that Jesus alone can save your soul, forgive your sins, and clothe you in fine linen. For all this, let us honor, extol, and worship our great triune God!

FURTHER REFLECTIONS ON FEASTING
WORSHIPING GOD FOR HIS WRATH

In the May 1, 2013, issue of *The Christian Century*, an article by Mary Louise Bringle reported that the Presbyterian Committee on Congregational Song (PCOCS), operating under the authority of the Presbyterian Church, U.S.A. (PCUSA), evaluated the theological merits of the popular worship song *In Christ Alone* (written by Keith Getty and Stuart Townend). Evidently, they were preparing for the release of the denomination's new song collection, *Glory to God*.

The song's second stanza contains the line "Till on that cross as Jesus died, the wrath of God was satisfied." An earlier version of the denomination's hymnal had changed it to read, "Till on that cross as Jesus died, the love of God was magnified." Although no one would deny that God's love was magnified in the death of Christ for us, Getty and Townend, much to their credit, refused to approve the change. The committee, wrote Bringle, was faced "with a choice: to include the hymn with the authors' original language or to remove it from our list."

The final vote was six in favor of retaining the song with its original wording and nine against. The no votes prevailed, and the song was removed.

I must say that, although disappointed, I wasn't surprised by this event. It is simply one more stage in the gradual redefinition of God in which his wrath is no longer regarded as a personal attribute but, at best, an impersonal expression of the law of consequence (needless to say, without divine wrath, one wonders what that "consequence" could possibly be).

For many, the concept of *wrath* is thought to be beneath God. New Testament scholar C. H. Dodd (d. 1973), for example, spoke for many when he said that the notion of divine wrath is *archaic* and that the biblical terminology refers to no more than an inevitable process of cause and effect in a moral universe. In other words, for such as Dodd, divine wrath is an impersonal force operative in a moral universe, not a personal attribute or disposition in the character of God. Wrath may well be ordained and controlled by God but is clearly no part of him, as are love, mercy, kindness, and the like.

Clearly, Dodd and others misunderstand divine wrath. It is not the loss of self-control or the irrational and capricious outburst of anger. Wrath is not the expression of a celestial bad temper or God lashing out at those who "rub him the wrong way." Divine wrath is righteous antagonism toward all that is unholy. It is the revulsion of God's character to that which is a violation of God's will. Indeed, one may speak of divine wrath as a function of divine love! For God's wrath is his love for holiness, truth, and justice. It is because God passionately loves purity, peace, and perfection that he reacts angrily toward anything and anyone who defiles them. J. I. Packer asked this question: "Would a God who took as much pleasure in evil as He did in good be a good God? Would a God who did not react adversely to evil in His world be morally perfect? Surely not. But it is precisely this adverse reaction to evil, which is a necessary part of moral perfection, that the Bible has in view when it speaks of God's wrath."[11]

Leon Morris agreed:

---

11. J. I. Packer, *Knowing God* (1973; repr., Downers Grove: IVP, 1993), 151.

Then, too, unless we give a real content to the wrath of God, unless we hold that men really deserve to have God visit upon them the painful consequences of their wrongdoing, we empty God's forgiveness of its meaning. For if there is no ill desert, God ought to overlook sin. We can think of forgiveness as something real only when we hold that sin has betrayed us into a situation where we deserve to have God inflict upon us the most serious consequences, and that is upon such a situation that God's grace supervenes. When the logic of the situation demands that He should take action against the sinner, and He yet takes action for him, then and then alone can we speak of grace. But there is no room for grace if there is no suggestion of dire consequences merited by sin.[12]

But does the Bible actually speak of wrath as a characteristic feature of God's nature? Indeed it does. The terminology for wrath is itself instructive in this regard. The Greek word *thumos* is derived from *thuō*, which originally meant "a violent movement of air, water, the ground, animals, or men."[13] It came to signify the panting rage that wells up in a man's body and spirit. Thus, *thumos* came to mean passionate anger, arising and subsiding quickly. It occurs twice in Luke, five times in Paul, once in Hebrews, and ten times in Revelation. Outside of Revelation it is used for God's wrath only once (Rom. 2:8). In Revelation it refers to God's wrath seven times, six of which have the qualifying phrase "of God" (14:10, 19; 15:1, 7; 16:1; 19:15).

The word *orgē* is much more suited to a description of God's wrath in the New Testament. It is derived from *orgaō*, which speaks of "growing ripe" for something or "getting ready to bear." It thus gave *orgē* the meaning of a settled disposition or emotion arising out of God's nature. It is specifically said to be "of God" in John 3:36 (on the lips of Jesus, no less); Romans 1:18; Ephesians 5:6; Colossians 3:6; and Revelation 19:15. We read of the "wrath of the Lamb" (a shocking juxtaposition of terms, to say the least) in Revelation 6:16 (see also Rev. 6:17; 11:18; 14:10; 16:19).

---

12. Leon Morris, *The Apostolic Preaching of the Cross* (Grand Rapids: Eerdmans, 1965), 185.
13. *Theological Dictionary of the New Testament*, ed. Gerhard Kittel (Grand Rapids: Eerdmans, 1965), 3:167.

One should especially take note of Revelation 19:15, where John speaks of "the winepress of the fury of the wrath of God the Almighty," where "fury" is a translation of *thumos* and "wrath" is a translation of *orgē*.

Numerous texts could be cited, but I'll bring this to a close by mentioning only two. The apostle John was quite explicit when he declared that "whoever believes in the Son has eternal life; whoever does not obey the Son shall not see life, but the wrath of God remains on him" (John 3:36). Paul echoed John with this statement: "For the wrath of God is revealed from heaven against all ungodliness and unrighteousness of men, who by their unrighteousness suppress the truth" (Rom. 1:18; see also Eph. 5:6).

Here is why this was such a sad day for the PCUSA: if Jesus Christ did not himself suffer under and satisfy the wrath of God, we will. The only reason the wrath of God does not "remain" on sinners is because it fell on Christ. Our only hope that God's wrath is not "against" us is that it was against Christ. If Jesus did not propitiate the Father's wrath and satisfy in himself, on the cross, the holy and righteous demands of divine justice, we have no hope. Worse still, we have no gospel, no good news, nothing to offer a lost and dying world.

Praise God from whom all blessings flow! And one of the greatest and most precious of those countless blessings is the provision of a substitute, his Son, who lovingly and freely chose to endure our death and exhaust in himself the wrath we so richly deserved. I have one hope for eternal life, one foundation for the forgiveness of sins, and it is the glorious truth that "*on that cross as Jesus died, the wrath of God was satisfied!*"

PART 4

HOW CHARISMATICS WORSHIP

CHAPTER 15

How Charismatics Worship (1)

Music, Spontaneity, and the Affections of the Heart

There was a time when the difference between Pentecostal-charismatic worship and that which you might encounter in more Reformed and cessationist[1] churches was largely one of song selection. The former opted for contemporary compositions, while the latter preferred more traditional hymns. Those days are long gone, as both groups are now often heard singing a mixture of contemporary and traditional. The differences between the two, however, remain and are seen primarily in the expectations each brings to a Sunday service.

When it comes to corporate gatherings on Sunday, evangelical cessationists typically orchestrate their gatherings around the expository sermon, whereas charismatics view congregational singing as central. The former often treat worship[2] as little more than an unavoidable prelude to the exposition of Scripture, after which the service is considered over. Charismatics often put the sermon before worship as an entrance into praise. Whatever truth is learned is preparation for heartfelt celebration in singing, dancing, and even the exercise of revelatory and healing gifts.

---

1. A cessationist is a person who believes certain more overtly miraculous or supernatural gifts of the Holy Spirit "ceased" to be given by God to the church sometime toward the close of the first century or somehow in conjunction with the final recognition of the sixty-six books of the biblical canon (approximately AD 367).

2. My use of the term *worship* in this way is not meant to suggest that only corporate singing qualifies as such. Preaching and celebration of the sacraments and prayer are certainly all acts of worship.

One reason for this difference is found in these groups' respective beliefs concerning where God has pledged to meet his people. Cessationists define their experience of God primarily in terms of intellectual growth and what they learn of him in Scripture when it is preached and taught. They are driven by the conviction, and with this I would agree, that Scripture is God's primary means for making himself known to us. Throughout biblical history, God's standard way of first establishing and sustaining personal communication with the redeemed is through his commissioned messengers, whether prophets, apostles, pastors, or teachers (cf. Eph. 4:11).

Thus, cessationists would testify to having encountered God, assuming they would even use such language, when their knowledge of his character and ways expands and deepens. They feel confident that God has been honored and his presence affirmed when his truth has been expounded in preaching, sacrament, confession, and creed. They often will question the need to "experience" God if the revealed truth about him is accurately understood and proclaimed in sermon and song.

Little, if anything, more is to be expected by the believer in terms of "sensing" God's nearness, seeing his power, or feeling his love. In fact, excessive concern with these latter elements or time devoted to their pursuit is often viewed as, at best, secondary, and, at worst, dangerous. Cessationists often warn others that such desires for subjective engagement with God have the potential to distract the Christian from serious and rigorous intellectual grappling with the biblical text.

But, and all Christians need to listen closely, the written Word does more than merely communicate truth *about* God: it also *mediates the very person and power of God*. We would not be amiss in viewing preaching as sacramental in nature. That is to say, God draws near to his people *in preaching* to comfort, encourage, and strengthen them. As J. I. Packer said, "The proper aim of preaching is to mediate meetings with God."[3] The Bible is not a dead letter! It is living and active, sharper than any two-edged sword that convicts reveals, enlivens, rebukes, and awakens the heart and mind to both the ugliness of sin and the beauty and splendor of God (see Heb. 4:12–13).

---

3. J. I. Packer, *Truth and Power: The Place of Scripture in the Christian Life* (Wheaton, IL: Harold Shaw, 1996), 158.

As we will see below, whereas charismatics don't dismiss the authority of the written Word, they do sometimes minimize, if not in theory, at least in practice, its capacity to bring them into authentic experience of God. Worship, on the other hand, is viewed as an *unmediated closure* with God that is unencumbered by what they perceive to be potentially divisive and often complex dogmas. Each group has much to learn from the other.

Structure or Spontaneity?

Cessationists are generally reluctant to allow into a service what wasn't planned in advance or printed in the bulletin. Those accustomed to high church traditions or who embrace the regulative principle of worship often oppose any violation or disruption of prescribed liturgy. They find comfort and a measure of emotional security in predictability and procedures that strike a familiar chord. Anything less is typically viewed as violating the requirement that all be conducted "decently and in order" (1 Cor. 14:40). They tend to be suspicious of spontaneity and often view the latter as a way of justifying either laziness or emotionalism. The last thing they want on Sunday morning is to be surprised by something novel or unexpected. What charismatics view as freedom and sensitivity to the Spirit's leading are often viewed by cessationists as irreverence and an excuse to cover up a lack of studied preparation.

Charismatics tend to associate spirituality with flexibility or an openness to sovereign, impromptu interruptions by the Spirit. If cessationists fear spiritual surprises, charismatics are terrified of the boredom that so easily comes with repetition. They are reticent to impose a structure on their gatherings that might, in their words, "quench the Spirit." God must be allowed the freedom to shorten the service, extend it, or redirect its focus in ways unanticipated and unannounced by the pastoral leadership. This is not to endorse all efforts to manufacture a sense of God's presence. Some charismatics experience God's presence, love, and the freedom secured for us in Christ by dancing, others while singing in the vernacular of the people, still others by singing in the Spirit (tongues). Others connect with God through a prophetic word or word of knowledge, or perhaps a healing, while some sense God's affection in moments of complete silence and meditation on the cross. Most charismatics long for the Holy Spirit to lead or guide them in overtly expressive and joyful praise. The Spirit does more than merely motivate or stimulate God's people to worship. Insofar as the Spirit permanently indwells each believer, he elicits God-exalting praise from within them.

Yet another difference between the two is largely due to the expectation by charismatics of hearing what they call God's "present tense voice." What is God saying *now*? What is his Spirit leading us to do *today*? Is the "cloud" moving? Conversely, cessationists typically see their responsibility as providing a venue for the explanation of God's "past tense voice," that is, his written Word as it is found in the canonical text. For the charismatic, emphasis is often placed on the contemporaneity of God's presence and activity and less on the past display or the future hope of it.

My own experience has been that both approaches can be embraced without sacrificing the intent and integrity of either. I see no insurmountable obstacles, other than stubbornness and pride, to integrating structure and spontaneity. The Spirit can lead the advanced planning of a service as easily as he can break in, unannounced, during the course of liturgy. It's true that a rigid and inflexible commitment to "order" can breed lifeless ritual. But it's equally possible for an agenda lacking shape or direction to breed chaos and an absence of theological substance. A preacher can experience a powerful anointing on Thursday afternoon while prayerfully writing a sermon, no less than he can on Sunday morning as the Spirit imparts insights heretofore unseen.

Sadly, I must say, some expressions of charismatic worship operate on the false assumption that spontaneity reflects a greater openness to the Spirit's presence than does worship that is scripted or preplanned. The fact is that there is no reason why worship cannot embrace both. As just noted, the Spirit of God can exert his influence on the prayerful, advanced preparation of a particular sequence in the service no less so than he does when the worship leader is consciously open to revelatory interruptions during singing.

Noncharismatic or more traditional worship is often structured in such a way that the believer can arrive at church confident that a now familiar order of service will be followed: a call to worship (often with the reading of a selection from the Psalms), a confession of faith (perhaps with the Apostles' or Nicene Creed), a prayer of thanksgiving, a reading from the Old Testament followed by a reading from the Gospels and an epistle, and an expository sermon (not necessarily based on any of the texts just read). Often, hymns will be interspersed, although some will place congregational singing at the beginning of this liturgy or at its close. The Lord's Table then follows with an explanation of its significance, the consecration of the elements, a prayer of individual preparation and/or confession of sin, the words of institution, the epiclesis, the breaking of bread, the drinking of the cup, a prayer of thanksgiving, and the benediction.

There is no reason why one's experience of the Spirit and ever-deepening intimacy with God cannot occur at any time during this sort of liturgical sequence. Even charismatic worship has its own liturgical order in which the people are led along a path into an experience or sensation of the presence of God through the uninterrupted flow of music. There has never been a consensus among charismatics as to the proper sequence of songs, although many have insisted that the movement begins with the joyful and celebratory praise associated with the outer court of the temple, progressing from there, as it were, into the holy of holies. The service would then turn to thanksgiving, the extolling of God's grace, adoration, followed by a heightened sense of intimacy in the most holy place. The latter is often identified with true worship.

Although it would be overly simplistic to reduce either tradition to a one-word summation, it often appears that traditional, noncharismatic worship envisions the goal to be one of grateful *response* to God's revelation of himself in Scripture while contemporary, charismatic worship is viewed as consummating in one's personal *experience* of the Spirit's presence that is often physically felt and spiritually euphoric. Again, though, one wonders why our worship cannot be both. *Why do we simply assume that enlightenment and experience are antithetical?* Why do we automatically assume that if an element in the service is planned, the Spirit cannot make his presence known in the midst of it? Why is it that people believe we must choose between being intellectually informed by canonical revelation, on the one hand, and being spiritually transformed by the manifest presence of God, on the other?

The goal of worship can easily be both to *extol* God's greatness and to *enjoy* his presence, both to express gratitude for his gift of salvation and feel his affection for his children. The truth of revelation is not merely for *mental consumption* but also for *experiential delight*. Otherwise, the former can easily degenerate into a lifeless formalism while the latter yields chaotic emotionalism. There are certainly dangers on both sides of this unnecessary divide. The anticipated emotional high of a Sunday service can become as routine and repetitive as that which comes from reading preselected texts from a prayer book.

We must remind ourselves that the Holy Spirit is no more tied to an unchanging liturgy than he is to spontaneity and improvisation. I can personally sense God's love for me in the reading of a biblical text as much as when the Spirit bears felt witness to my spirit that I am a child of God (Rom. 8:16). I can be as easily brought to tears upon hearing Romans 5:6–11 unpacked in a sermon as I can upon the sensible awareness of the love of God poured out into my heart through the Holy Spirit who has been given to me (Rom. 5:5). And I can as easily sin by making an idol of my experience as I can by priding myself in understanding the theology of a biblical text.

As I've tried to make clear earlier in this book, to exult and exalt should never be placed in opposition to one another, as if to honor God we must choose one or the other. In fact, God is most greatly exalted in me when I exult in the wonders of his mercy and kindness in Christ. This is no less true in preparing and preaching an expository sermon. Finalizing one's message on a Wednesday is not necessarily a sign of pride, self-reliance, and independence from God, any more than the unprepared, spontaneous delivery on a Sunday morning is a sign of humility and trusting the Spirit to move as he wills. The latter can be as prideful as the former. And the former can be as fleshly as the latter.

As a charismatic, I've often been asked by younger pastors to describe my method for sermon preparation and the rhythm of life during a typical week. My response has always been a convergence of prayerful study and openness to Spirit-induced, revelatory interruptions. I would typically begin sermon preparation on Monday morning and conclude by sometime on Wednesday. I never sensed in this approach that I was not open to the prompting of the Spirit or that I was locked into an immovable habit governed solely by the mind. I have always taken this approach because it then afforded me the opportunity to prayerfully reflect on the meaning of the biblical text for several days in advance of Sunday. The Spirit often prompted me to see new truths in the passage I was planning on preaching. Fresh insights, helpful applications, and a heightened sense of God speaking to me through the text would occur in the days *after* finalizing the sermon, leading up to its proclamation on Sunday morning. In this way, I provided an opportunity for the Spirit to lead me in careful study of the text as well as providential intrusions into my heart of things that should be communicated that I had not thought of during preparation.

The Role of Music and the Affections of the Heart

Charismatic worship often views music as possessing something of a sacramental nature in that it becomes a channel for the tangible experience of the presence and power of the Holy Spirit. The worship set will be structured in such a way that the transition between songs is uninterrupted by the spoken word or even by the reading of Scripture. In this way, the individual is believed to be led into deeper communion with God. This is often called "flow," referring to the unbroken movement from one song or element of worship into another. If there is too long of a pause between songs, it feels like a lull, while too fast of a transition can be jolting. While some may argue that "flow" is potentially a way to manipulate the congregation into certain emotions, Steven Felix-Jager contends that it is rather "a means to unify and connect the elements of worship for a cohesive experience."[4]

There is yet another reason why this flow can serve a sanctifying purpose. Often the worshiping believer is drawn into an ever-increasing and deeper awareness of God's saving grace as the music continues. The sweetness of the worshiper's focus on the greatness of God's mercy in Christ and his steadfast love is accentuated and sustained by the uninterrupted flow from one song into another. It is not at all unusual for the believer's heartfelt concentration to be disrupted when one song abruptly ends and there is no immediate transition into another.

I often encounter intense debates over the potentially manipulative nature of worship music. No one denies that music can exert a transformative influence on the worshiper. The question is whether the latter is complicit in this effect or is being unwittingly impacted by a leader whose goal is to elevate the emotional euphoria of his/her audience as an end it itself. In a *Christianity Today* article, Kelsey Kramer McGinnis explains that

---

4. Steven Felix-Jager, *Renewal Worship: A Theology of Pentecostal Doxology* (Downers Grove, IL: InterVarsity, 2022), 141.

songwriters and worship leaders use tempo and dynamic changes, modulation, and varied instrumentation to make contemporary worship music engaging, immersive, and, yes, emotionally moving. . . . As worshipers, we can feel it. Songs with lengthy interludes slowly build anticipation toward a familiar hook. Or the band drops out so voices sing out when the chorus hits. Plus the lyrics themselves can cue our behavior ("I'll stand with arms high and heart abandoned").[5]

We should never forget that each of us is responsible for how we allow music to influence our thoughts and affections. McGinnis adds,

Worshipers have agency. They decide how much they open themselves to emotional direction. Even extreme examples of musical propaganda require receptivity on the part of the listener. Musical propaganda is most effective when the music is used to increase devotion—to build on our faith—not change or alter beliefs. But once there is trust and buy-in, a dangerous, exploitative emotional manipulation is possible.[6]

Although I'm not a musician, I understand how a particular chord structure or progression, together with modulation and tempo can affect the mind in such a way that there is a corresponding physiological response, be it tears or laughter, joy or lament. But as McGinnis points out, "Music does not simply act upon the listener; there is a dialectic between an individual and music in which each influences and responds to the other."[7]

For example, whenever I listen to a performance of Handel's *Messiah*, specifically the "Hallelujah Chorus," I can feel my affections being progressively intensified and the truth of its message heightened in my heart as the music swells in an ever-increasing crescendo. It is the difference between merely saying "Hallelujah," on the one hand, and hearing it repeatedly sung in this magnificent composition, on the other. I don't believe I'm being manipulated, as if the music is intentionally designed to override my conscious will.

5. Kelsey Kramer McGinnis, "Worship Music Is Emotionally Manipulative. Do You Trust the Leader Plucking the Strings?" *Christianity Today*, May 26, 2023, https://www.christianitytoday.com/ct/2023/may-web-only/worship-music-emotionally-manipulative-leader-hillsong.html.
6. McGinnis, "Worship Music Is Emotionally Manipulative."
7. McGinnis, "Worship Music Is Emotionally Manipulative."

I'm happy to feel the heightened joy, gratitude, and awe that comes from an awareness that Jesus is truly "King of kings and Lord of lords." Of course, if at any time during some intense celebration of the Lord worshipers begin to feel coerced or artificially led into an emotional high that is unrelated to the truth of what is being sung, they are responsible to rein in their affections and bring their experience into alignment with God's Word.

Editor-in-chief of G3 Ministries, Scott Aniol, among others, is highly critical of the music in contemporary charismatic worship. He contends that it "has been carefully designed to create a visceral experience of the feelings that then become evidence of God's manifest presence. This fits the sacramental theology of charismatics perfectly, but it does not fit the theology of non-charismatic evangelicals, especially those who consider themselves Reformed."[8] But could it be that this "visceral experience" of "feelings" is precisely what charismatics believe it to be, namely, the sanctifying power of the Spirit's manifest presence? I'm not suggesting that any "feeling" is itself evidence of God's presence, but there are certainly occasions when it might be. Is this not like what Paul described in Ephesians 3:14–21, a tangible—dare I say "visceral"?—sense of God's profound and passionate love for his children, a love that cannot be computed or fully comprehended? When the love of God is poured out into our hearts by the Spirit (Rom. 5:5), would this not elicit a "visceral" feeling that is due entirely to God's presence?

Felix-Jager suggests that "worship creates a charged space for God to bestow blessings upon people in the form of healings and miracles."[9] This "space" is simply another way of describing an avenue or means or, better still, an opportunity for God to impart his sanctifying grace that may bring healing, a prophetic revelation, or another miraculous activity. That this operation of God's supernatural presence may create so-called visceral feelings is actually to be expected. If such feelings are themselves the fruit of our Spirit-awakened understanding and delight in who God is for us in Jesus, they should be welcomed and encouraged.

---

8. See Scott Aniol, "Stop Singing Hillsong, Bethel, Jesus Culture, and Elevation," *By the Waters of Babylon* (blog), G3, February 21, 2022, https://g3min.org/stop-singing-hillsong-bethel-jesus-culture-and-elevation/.

9. Felix-Jager, *Renewal Worship*, 50.

Worship as the Enjoyment of God

It bears repeating that worship is successful not when worship itself is enjoyed but when God is! One critic of charismatic worship asked a series of either/or questions that can best be answered by "both/and": "Is the intensity of Pentecostal [or charismatic] worship a rational response of the heart, or is it a sensation? Is it evoked by consideration of truth, or charmed by a combination of chord progressions? Is the goal to rightly value and admire God, or to feel my feelings?"[10] My answer to this false dichotomy is that the intensity of worship is *both* a rational response to the truth of God's word *and* the sensations of joy, peace, and hope it produces. My heartfelt consideration of truth is itself justifiably intensified by an aesthetically pleasing chord progression. And why can't my valuation and admiration of God awaken in me feelings of gratitude and delight and soul satisfaction? This same author contends that "Christian worship has to first pass through the filter of a Spirit-filled understanding." Yes! For there to be legitimate, Christ-exalting heat in the heart, there must first be biblically faithful light in the mind. But to make worship entirely about the latter will eventually produce intellectual arrogance rather than reverential awe and joy.

Can't the thoughtful, precise reflection on the Word, when it is preached, live harmoniously with the effect of heightened affections that a well-constructed musical sequence facilitates? Must the latter always be viewed as manipulative, or might it be the Spirit's way of driving more deeply into our hearts and minds the glory of the truth we've just heard? It matters little, if at all, whether the worship leader is attired in jeans and a T-shirt, while strumming an acoustic guitar, or adorned in a freshly starched shirt and silk tie while playing a pipe organ. Undoubtedly, there are some songs that only an organ or orchestra can play, while others are more suitable for a keyboard and drums. But I know of nothing in Scripture that gives pride of place to one over the other.

If one wonders about the ascendancy of contemporary songs to the exclusion, or at least the subordination of more classic hymnody, the answer may, at least partially, be traceable to the latter's tendency to keep God at relational arm's length from the singer. This may be due both to the overly

---

10. David de Bruyn, in a series of articles on worship at www.religiousaffections.org.

structured nature of more traditional hymns and the high-minded lyrics that often intentionally (or unintentionally) suppress one's emotional engagement with God. A not unrelated factor is "a certain amount of aesthetic snobbery, idolatry of the intellect, romanticizing of past history, [and] denominational and theological chauvinism" that are occasionally found in some critics of contemporary worship.[11]

I must also respond to a particular choice of words from our critic. He refers to churchgoers being "charmed by a combination of chord progressions." Perhaps he intends something I am missing, but it sounds as if he's suggesting that the ever-increasing affections of joy and peace and love that music can easily evoke is like what an Indian guru does to a cobra with his rhythmic playing of a flute. The believer is mesmerized, or "charmed," by the carefully crafted sequence of chords and thus elevated into a mindless state of emotional euphoria. Although this critic doesn't use the word, I sense that he views charismatic worship as exerting a *hypnotic* effect on the Christian. Whereas this may apply to some expressions of charismatic worship, it is highly pejorative and misleading in that it suggests that a worship leader is intentionally deceptive and manipulative, seeking only to induce an altered state of consciousness in the people present.

So, what, then, is the proper relationship between music and the heightened emotions that it can so easily awaken and sustain? This question has sparked a controversy that is sweeping through the evangelical world today. I once thought that the so-called worship wars ended around the turn of the century, but I was wrong. They continue to rage. Hardly a day passes when I don't read of a denunciation of contemporary worship music and, in particular, the way in which so many more recently composed songs awaken, elevate, and intensify the affections of believers.

Studies have been conducted that reveal how certain chord structures and progressions influence the emotional mindset or experience of the Christian. Critics of contemporary music have jumped on this and concluded that such songs are dangerously manipulative and serve only to heighten

---

11. John M. Frame, *Contemporary Worship Music: A Biblical Defense* (Phillipsburg, NJ: P&R, 1997), 52. The best and most comprehensive treatments of the nature and influence of contemporary worship are found in two books by Lester Ruth and Lim Swee Hong: *Lovin' on Jesus: A Concise History of Contemporary Worship* (Nashville: Abingdon, 2017); and *A History of Contemporary Praise and Worship: Understanding the Ideas That Reshaped the Protestant Church* (Grand Rapids: Baker Academic, 2021).

spiritual feelings or affections. They are responsible, so we are told, for the spiritual euphoria that many in charismatic churches experience during a corporate worship gathering. These songs should therefore be avoided. On this view, it would appear that the primary (if not sole) purpose of all worship music is to inform the mind of the many reasons why God is worthy of our devotion.

We need to remember, however, that we are holistic beings, shaped and fashioned in the image of God. And no less a part of that image than the mind and body is the heart, the affections, the emotions of the soul. To suppress one's emotional response to the beauty and splendor of God is in effect to question God's wisdom in creating us the way he did. I'm certainly not suggesting that emotion is an end in itself, as if our primary goal in worship is to stir up the passions of the heart and to stimulate feelings of elation unrelated to biblical truth. But when the heart is moved by the greatness of God, when the emotions are awakened by the glory of Christ, when the Spirit ignites in the depths of our inner being a heightened awareness of the majesty of all that God is and does for us in Jesus, to resist and suppress the surge of spiritual euphoria in our souls is to quench the Spirit.

Some people are more affected by music than others. I am one who is easily susceptible to the intensified stirring in my inner being when God is praised and celebrated in song. I make no apology for this. When the inspired and inspiring revelation of God in Scripture is set to music, it works more powerfully in me than when it is merely spoken, read, or recited. Music is truly sacramental. When anointed by the Spirit's presence, it opens my eyes with greater clarity to the splendor of who Jesus is. I sense my Savior's love, mercy, and compassion more readily. I feel the transformative power of the Spirit more directly and with more impact than at virtually any other time or by means of any other instrumentality.

When theology is put to song, my objections to what I might previously have struggled to believe are put to rest. My doubts are subdued by the Spirit. My otherwise restrained affections are unleashed in exuberant celebration of the exalted Christ, and my joy in him is magnified. I sense his presence, his peace, and his promises become ever more precious. God has ordained music, song, and instrumental accompaniment to channel into the depths of my spirit a renewed and heightened sense of his presence and love.

If this is not the case, one wonders why God has ordained that we sing our praises instead of merely reciting them. What purpose is there in music, if not to awaken, arouse, and intensify those affections of the heart by which we experience ever-intensifying love, joy, peace, hope, godly fear, satisfaction, and zeal, just to mention a few?

No one has helped me more in understanding this than Jonathan Edwards (1703–58), who insisted, rightly so in my opinion, that "there never is any case whatsoever, any lively and vigorous exercise of the will or inclination of the soul, without some effect upon the body, in some alteration of the motion of its fluids, and especially of the animal spirits."[12] This language is probably unfamiliar to many, so a brief word of explanation is in order.

Edwards argued that because of the union between the soul and the body, that is, between the immaterial and material dimensions of how God made us, any substantial movement in the former will find a corresponding expression in the latter. In other words, when we Christians are awakened in our minds to the glory and beauty of God and all that he has done for us in Christ, we will necessarily experience some alteration in our affections and in our bodies. In fact, in the absence of these affections there can be no true spirituality. Affections such as love, fervency, heartfelt joy, peace, godly fear, hatred of sin, sorrow, hope, passionate desire, spiritual thirsting, gratitude, compassion, and zeal are the unavoidable fruit of the mind being enlightened and informed regarding the great things of God and his work for our salvation in Christ Jesus.

The point Edwards was making is that these are not fleeting, insubstantial or dangerous emotions unrelated to our relationship with God. They are the very essence of what he called "true religion." They are the desired fruit of the multiple truths that the Spirit has enlightened the mind to grasp. And how, you ask, does this relate to worship? Edwards gave the answer: "The duty of singing praises to God, seems to be appointed wholly to excite and express religious affections. No other reason can be assigned, why we should express ourselves to God in verse, rather than in prose, and do it with music, but only, that such is our nature and frame, that these things have a tendency to move our affections."[13]

---

12. Jonathan Edwards, *Religious Affections*, ed. John E. Smith (New Haven, CT: Yale University Press, 1969), 98.

13. Edwards, *Religious Affections*, 115.

Note carefully what Edwards was saying. We sing our praises in worship *precisely* to "excite and express religious affections." He wasn't saying that any and all affections or heightened emotions are necessarily good and godly; only those that are awakened and stirred by the mind's apprehension of the truth are to be embraced. Neither he nor I would ever endorse affections or feelings or emotions stirred up as an end in themselves, wholly unrelated to revealed biblical truth. It is the latter, and only the latter, that serves to kindle the fire of godly and Christ-exalting feelings and elevated affections.

It is certainly possible for a worship service to be conducted in such a way that the aim is solely to generate heightened bodily sensations that have little if anything to do with the truth of the gospel. God forbid that we should ever countenance such an approach to singing! On the other hand, said Edwards,

> If the great things of religion are rightly understood, they will affect the heart. The reason why men are not affected by such infinitely great, important, glorious, and wonderful things, as they often hear and read of, in the Word of God, is undoubtedly because they are blind: if they were not so, it would be impossible, and utterly inconsistent with human nature, that their hearts should be otherwise than strongly impressed, and greatly moved by such things.[14]

From this Edwards concluded that "such means are to be desired, as have much of a tendency to move the affections. Such books, and such a way of preaching the Word, and administration of ordinances, and such a way of worshiping God in prayer, and singing praises, is much to be desired, as has a tendency deeply to affect the hearts of those who attend these means."[15]

I completely agree with Edwards. Therefore, my response to the objections raised in the church today to the sort of musical compositions or chord progressions that tend to excite or intensify the affections and feelings of the soul, often with a corresponding impact on the body, is that such are to be desired and sought after if that with which we are affected by them

---

14. Edwards, *Religious Affections*, 121.
15. Edwards, *Religious Affections*, 121.

is truth! If our affections or feelings or emotions or passions are rooted in gospel truth, as given in Scripture, then no objection can be raised to the sort of musical composition that serves to intensify them.

If a song is structured in such a way that my love for Jesus is deepened, then by all means let us sing it! If a song or chord progression is of such a nature that my heart is greatly warmed and my tears flow in gratitude for the grace of God shown to me in Christ, then by all means let us sing it! We should not recoil in fear of any musical composition, assuming its lyrics are biblically orthodox, that tends to intensify our affections or move us into ever-increasing heights of emotional euphoria, so long as they are in response to the glorious revelation of all that God is for us and has done for us in Christ Jesus.

Affections and Emotions: Are They the Same?

I've used the word *affection* with the assumption that you understand what is meant. But perhaps I need to pause and define the term. Some of you are familiar with it only in the context of romantic feelings that pass between a man and a woman. This is not the sense in which I use it here. Jonathan Edwards defined the affections as "the more vigorous and sensible exercises of the inclination and will of the soul."[16] So, are our affections the same as our emotions or passions? I don't think so.

Certainly, there is what may rightly be called an emotional dimension to affections. Affections, after all, are sensible and intense longings or aversions of the will. Perhaps it would be best to say that whereas affections are not less than emotions, they are surely more. Emotions can often be no more than physiologically heightened states of either euphoria or fear that are unrelated to what the mind perceives as true. Affections, on the other hand, are always the fruit or effect of what the mind understands and knows. The will or inclination is moved either toward or away from something perceived by the mind. An emotion or mere feeling, on the other hand, can rise or fall independently of and unrelated to anything in the mind. One can experience an emotion or feeling without it properly being an affection, but one can

---

16. Edwards, *Religious Affections*, 96. See appendix A, in which the experience of Edwards's wife, Sarah, is chronicled. Her "religious affections" were clearly tethered to and awakened by biblical truth.

rarely if ever experience an affection without it being emotional and involving intense feelings that awaken and move the body.

True spirituality, or true religion therefore consists to a large extent in "vigorous and lively actings of the inclination and will of the soul, or the fervent exercises of the heart,"[17] which is to say, in the affections. This is nowhere better seen than in 1 Peter 1:8: "Though you have not seen him, you love him. Though you do not now see him, you believe in him and rejoice with joy that is inexpressible and filled with glory." The apostle tells us about the nature of true faith, grade A faith, faith in its purest and godliest form this side of being glorified in the new heavens and new earth. This is the experience of the believer after he or she has been refined by the fire of suffering, or what Peter called "various trials" (v. 6). What, then, is left when the dross of hypocrisy and insincerity and selfishness and pretense is burned away? To put it simply: love for Jesus, trust in Jesus, and joy "that is inexpressible and filled with glory."

These are among the preeminent affections of the heart that embody the essence of true Christianity. Don't ever think that Christianity is merely about thinking the right thoughts or choosing the right things. Those are certainly involved. But at the heart and soul of our relationship with Jesus is love, unashamed extravagant affection for him; trust, which is to say that we treasure and prize him above all else, entrusting our souls to his care and comfort; and joy that transcends the capacity of the human tongue to articulate, joy that is replete with the very glory of God himself.

Lingering and Loving

Charismatic churches, such as those in which I've been involved for the past thirty-five years, often devote at least thirty minutes (and sometimes considerably more) every Sunday morning to the transforming spiritual power of sustained, uninterrupted singing. My approach to this issue comes not only from my understanding of how the Spirit works but also from Scripture and my own personal experience, as well as the testimonies of others who have spoken to me over the years of what happens during worship.

My desire is that people be exposed to what the Spirit does when we

---

17. Edwards, *Religious Affections*, 99.

linger in his presence. Oftentimes, people who have had little experience with the Spirit will find themselves initially resistant to what they feel is happening in their hearts, only to discover that as they become gradually more at ease and open and vulnerable to what the Spirit is doing, they encounter God in truly life-transforming ways. If I may be allowed to use an old and well-worn charismatic term, the opportunity to *soak* in the Spirit during extended times of singing can bring the increased possibility that genuinely life-changing experiences with God will occur.

My goal is that we might give the Spirit opportunity to awaken the hearts, minds, and affections of everyone to his presence and power. The opportunity to encounter the presence of the Holy Spirit during at least one-half hour of concentrated and focused praise is an experience we long for and trust that God will use to radically impact individual lives.

My prayer is that in our corporate gatherings we will facilitate times in which the affections of men and women, affections of love, joy, peace, hope, white-hot zeal, deep gratitude, awe, reverential fear, sorrow for sin, and delight in the reality of forgiveness will be awakened in their hearts by means of the biblical truth we sing.

My hope is that all who attend church will be overwhelmed with the greatness, beauty, power, and love of our great triune God. Joyful, jubilant, spiritually energetic, vertically oriented worship is key to what we believe God wants to do for us anytime we gather to worship.

I pray that people will be physically healed and emotionally restored during our time of extended singing. In fact, we want to be open to the spontaneous direction of the Spirit during our singing, which may involve the giving of prophetic words or special times of prayer.

So I encourage all believers in Jesus to come to church on Sundays with biblically informed thoughts about God, high expectations for what he might do, and hearts that are overwhelmed with Christ-exalting, sin-killing, soul-satisfying joy for all that God is for is in Jesus.

CHAPTER 16

How Charismatics Worship (2)

The Spirit's Power and Presence

I want to continue our effort to understand the differences between contemporary charismatic worship and more traditional, Reformed approaches to honoring God.[1] I've found the best way to do this is to identify several differing theological beliefs and personal expectations that each group entertains.

Principles and/or Power?

The different approaches to worship are often influenced by whether principles or power are given pride of place. Evangelical cessationists tend to emphasize principles over power and understanding over experience, in which maturity is measured by theological expertise. This often entails a corresponding focus on the intellect and rational inquiry. Knowledge becomes the index of spirituality. The kingdom of God is advanced by the understanding, explication, and wholehearted embrace of truth. The question often heard following their services is "Did you *understand* the sermon today? Do you agree with it?"

Charismatics, conversely, subordinate principle to power,[2] tending to gauge

---

1. A quick reminder: there is nothing inconsistent with being both charismatic and Reformed. The apostle Paul was both—and so am I!

2. Perhaps the most extensive, and certainly the most negative, analysis of the "power" theology among charismatics (and in particular, the third-wave theology of John Wimber) is Martyn Percy's *Words,*

growth by the depth of spiritual experience, and emphasize the affections above the mind. The kingdom of God is advanced by the visible defeat of Satan, often seen in physical healings and other overt displays of divine power. In the absence of such phenomena during a corporate service, some would doubt whether God had truly "shown up." The question most often heard following their services is "Did you *feel* the Lord's presence today? Did he touch you?"

Is it too much to believe that one can *feel* God's tender touch in the sermon and *learn* more of his ways and means during worship? Is it too much to expect that one might return home on Sunday afternoon having both learned and loved, been stretched mentally and emotionally, and been edified by a biblical text and healed of a physical affliction? Dare we hope, strive, and settle for anything less than the thrill of theological insight *and* deliverance from demonic oppression?

Sadly, though, many on both sides are persuaded that the emphases of the other are detrimental, in the final analysis, to what they believe most honors God. Charismatics are willing to think, but not if rational inquiry impedes the activity of the Spirit. Too much doctrine, they fear, threatens to kill "the anointing. They are often heard to say something like, "How can I be entirely open to the work of the Spirit in an attitude of humility and receptivity if I'm busy critiquing every syllable spoken by the preacher or if I'm constantly obsessed with the accuracy of every doctrinal assertion?" Or, "We don't want a theological Gestapo in our church spying out every misstep in the interpretation of Scripture."

Conversely, cessationists are skeptical of the authenticity of any alleged supernatural ministry if it emerges in the context of theological error, however infrequent and insignificant that error may be. If some charismatics are inclined to disparage the mind, some cessationists are nigh unto deifying it. Yes, that's an exaggeration, but the fact remains that an otherwise admirable love for theological accuracy has the potential to harden one's spiritual arteries.

Wonders and Power: Understanding Contemporary Christian Fundamentalism and Revivalism (London: SPCK, 1996). For a more positive and biblical understanding of "power" in Christian ministry, see J. I. Packer, "The Empowered Christian Life," in *The Kingdom and the Power: Are Healing and the Spiritual Gifts Used by Jesus and the Early Church Meant for the Church Today?*, ed. Gary S. Greig and Kevin N. Springer (Ventura, CA: Regal), 207–15; Wayne Grudem, "Should Christians Expect Miracles Today? Objections and Answers from the Bible," in *The Kingdom and the Power*, ed. Greig and Springer, 55–110; and especially Jack Deere, *Why I'm Still Surprised by the Power of the Spirit?* (Grand Rapids: Zondervan, 2022).

One of the primary reasons why contemporary charismatic worship is ridiculed, even if unspoken, is that most charismatics are Arminian. Anyone who is not overtly and proudly Reformed in their theology is immediately suspect in the minds of many. How could anything of value or God-centered come from those who deny unconditional election and irresistible grace? If people hold to a flawed theology of human free will in defiance of God's exhaustive sovereignty, their music must likewise fall short of what is acceptable and Christ-honoring.

I'll illustrate this from an incident involving a former student of mine at Wheaton College. "Mary" (not her real name) was an especially gifted and highly intellectual young lady who had taken several of my courses in various aspects of theology. She was extremely well-read and knew the Bible better than most.

Mary and I were both present at a conference where the primary speaker was openly and decidedly charismatic and Arminian. His message on the night in question was quite good, but he was guilty of a couple of minor theological foibles, neither of which, in my opinion, were deserving of a second thought. Mary had a different opinion.

After the meeting, she approached me, obviously quite upset. Upon hearing what she believed (correctly) to be a misinterpretation of a particular biblical text, she, in essence, "shut down." She found it almost impossible to concentrate on anything else the speaker had to say. Her face was wrinkled with anxiety, concern, and even a measure of sadness. As far as she was concerned, the speaker had disqualified himself as worthy of being heard because he failed to articulate this particular point of doctrine carefully. Mary wasn't interested in or open to his appeals concerning the ministry of the Holy Spirit. His theological indiscretions had virtually incapacitated her. If anything, she was worried that others present would open their hearts to what she was convinced might well be the influence of a false teacher.

People like Mary believe that the slightest exegetical error or theological misstatement invalidates whatever other ministry a person may fulfill. *Surely God would not bless those who are so careless with his Word with power or miracles!* It's as if they think God is so offended by the lack of absolute precision that he would withhold his favor from those guilty of it.

Charismatics, on the other hand, are impatient with what they perceive to be excessive and fastidious concern with accuracy in interpreting texts and theological concepts that bear little practical fruit. It's common to hear them say, "I don't want to be slowed down or distracted from what God is doing by ultimately abstruse doctrinal squabbles." They would point to "Mary" as an example of what happens when the human intellect is elevated above the divine Spirit.

The deeper I dig into what separates our two camps, the more I am convinced that we need an approach characterized by both/and rather than either/or. While some cessationists identify successful worship as singing songs that articulate God's glory, charismatics contend that we should also aspire to encounter God or, in some sense, experience a heightened spiritual awareness of his glory and presence.

Both groups share their conviction that worship must be theocentric: concerned with glorifying God. Where they differ is on the ways and means. Cessationists believe God is most glorified when biblical truths about him are accurately and passionately proclaimed in song, liturgy, and recitation of Scripture. The focus of worship is understanding God and representing him faithfully in corporate declaration. Worship is thus primarily didactic and theological, and their greatest fear is emotionalism.

Charismatics, on the other hand, believe God is glorified not only when he is accurately portrayed in song but also when he is experienced in a personal encounter. Charismatic worship does not downplay understanding God but insists that he is truly honored when he is enjoyed. Their worship is thus emotional, physically expressive, and relational in nature, and their greatest fear is intellectualism.

Admittedly, this characterization is perhaps a bit too tidy. Cessationists would no doubt agree that God should be enjoyed, but they see this as primarily a cognitive experience. Charismatics contend for a more holistic enjoyment. God is not merely to be grasped with the mind but felt in the depths of one's soul. The mind is expanded, but the affections are also stirred (and the body may well move!).

God's Presence

Perhaps the best way to illustrate this difference is the way both groups think of God's *presence* in times of corporate praise. Cessationists view God's presence as a theological assumption to be extolled, while charismatics consider it a tangible reality to be felt. Hymns of the former stress divine transcendence. Songs of the latter stress divine immanence. Cessationists tend to fear excessive familiarity with God. They "know that God's will cannot be confined, let alone reduced, to a calculus of human reckoning and desire."[3] Charismatics tend to fear relational distance. They want nothing to do with an impersonal religion that relegates God to a remote and deistic heaven. Their longing is for the "nearness and now-ness" of God. John Frame speaks to the dangers inherent in both approaches: "Churches that focus on divine transcendence are in danger of making God appear distant, aloof, unfriendly, unloving, devoid of grace. Churches that focus on God's immanence sometimes lose sight of his majesty and purity, his hatred of sin, and the consequent seriousness of any divine-human encounter."[4]

The spiritual atmosphere cessationists cultivate is characterized more by fear and reverence than the charismatic desire for joy and love. Again, the former prizes form, the latter freedom. A cessationist service is somewhat controlled in terms of what is regarded as acceptable physical posture and the length of time devoted to corporate singing. Charismatic worship is emotionally free and tangibly demonstrable, with the characteristic lifting of hands and dancing. And whereas cessationists more often sing *about* God, charismatics prefer to sing *to* him.

There is a humble solemnity in most cessationist services versus the exuberant celebration among charismatics. This invariably elicits criticism from both sides. The cessationist is offended by what appears to be an overly casual, if not presumptuous, approach to God. *Is not our God a consuming fire, holy and righteous?* The charismatic sees in cessationist worship an excessively formal, if not lifeless, approach to God. And without denying that God is holy, the charismatic is emboldened by what he or she believes is God's own passionate longing for relational intimacy.

Ian Stackhouse is quick to acknowledge the benefits of contemporary worship and its focus on "immediacy" and "intimacy" with God. He does not believe, as some within the charismatic movement do, that "contemporaneity" and "theological substance" are irreconcilable. He argues that, in the

---

3. Grant Wacker, "Hand-Clapping in a Gothic Nave: What Pentecostals and Mainliners Can Learn from Each Other," *Christianity Today*, March 2005, 61.

4. John M. Frame, *Contemporary Worship Music: A Biblical Defense* (Phillipsburg, NJ: P&R, 1997), 14.

right context of worship, "spiritual encounter of an ecstatic nature should be positively encouraged."[5]

But Stackhouse also fears that, if left unchecked and not tethered to biblical truth, contemporary worship will be valued only for the interest it can generate or experience it can induce. In other words, worship becomes an instrument for the effects it produces rather than a celebration of God as he is in himself. In such cases "worship takes on an authority of its own so that only in and through the experience of worship, and the way we perform in worship, can grace be appropriated; hence, the pressure to make something happen. Worship as spiritual formation is sidelined in favour of worship as effect."[6]

I must concede that I have encountered this mentality in charismatic churches. One can sometimes sense that the worship leader is working hard at eliciting from the congregation a certain response, a height of emotion, or some physical posture that would indicate they are "fully engaged." Merely to bear witness in song and prayer to God's splendor seems insufficient. A service is "successful" only if "breakthrough" is achieved, singing reaches a certain decibel level, or tears are shed in sufficient quantity. There's nothing intrinsically wrong with any of these responses. In fact, some cessationists, regrettably, are meticulous in ensuring that such reactions never occur! There is a carefully orchestrated "glass ceiling" on what is permissible during worship. On the other hand, charismatics must be careful lest they conclude that God is not honored simply because certain manifest effects are absent.

Stackhouse focuses particularly on the belief in some charismatic circles that revival depends on what happens in the moment of worship. He cites the popular song "Lord, You Have My Heart," in which, he argues, "there is an implicit belief that drawing near to God in worship will bring down the glory of God, and presumably the revival. This is not a celebration of the glory that already inheres within the gospel of Christ, but a further glory, encapsulating all the hopes of a revived land, that can only be uncovered by intensity: the community of feeling that charismatic spirituality has often been identified with."[7]

---

5. Ian Stackhouse, *The Gospel-Driven Church: Retrieving Classical Ministry for Contemporary Revivalism* (Waynesboro, GA: Paternoster, 2004), 45.
6. Stackhouse, *The Gospel-Driven Church*, 48.
7. Stackhouse, *The Gospel-Driven Church*, 53.

I'm only partly in agreement with Stackhouse here. Yes, we should celebrate the glory that "inheres within" the gospel and see that glory and power as the foundation for life, growth, and mission. But this doesn't preclude the need for fresh impartations or anointings of power for present ministry. We are touching here on the delicate tension, but not contradiction, between the "already" of our conversion and reception of the Spirit and the "not yet" of what God offers and invites us to receive.

And let's not too quickly dismiss the importance of "intensity" if by that one means both the individual and collective depth of hunger, desperation, and longing for God to act in ways that will bring honor to his name. Perhaps it is going too far to say that revival is suspended on intensity, but the Scriptures do encourage persistence, struggle, passion, and concentrated, single-minded focus as important elements in the heart's pursuit and search for God (I have in mind the principle underlying such texts as Pss. 63:1–8; 84:1–12; 91:14–15; Jer. 29:12–13; 33:3; and Luke 11:5–13, just to mention a few).

Stackhouse takes direct aim at Matt Redman's song "Lord, Let Your Glory Fall,"

> in which the numinous experience of the priests in the temple in 1 Kings 8 is retold. The tempo of the song reflects the fairly buoyant and upbeat mood that is the hallmark of charismatic musicianship; but what is problematic with this lyricism is the repeated discontentedness of the worshiper with the status quo and an inadequate understanding of the factualities of revelation. In the retelling of the drama, and in the expression of desire for more (again, an entirely legitimate desire [a concession I'm glad to see Stackhouse make!]), the song, nevertheless, inhabits a peculiarly pre-Christian hermeneutic that forestalls on the fulfillment of the promise of glory in the coming of Christ and the Spirit.[8]

I think Stackhouse is both right and wrong in this critique. He's right in pointing out that the "glory" that "fell" at the dedication of Solomon's temple was an adumbration or foreshadowing of the "glory" that came in the person of Christ and in the descent of the Spirit at Pentecost. I myself hesitate to sing those words for the simple fact that I don't believe "glory"

---

8. Stackhouse, *The Gospel-Driven Church*, 53.

will come to the church, in any literal or tangible sense, apart from that which is already ours by means of the indwelling Christ.[9] The "glory" that hovered over the mercy seat in the holy of holies has now taken up residence in the individual believer and in the body of Christ, the church, corporately. Such "glory," in its visible and concrete Old Testament manifestations, will not again be seen and should not again be expected until it appears in the person of our returning Lord at the close of history. See Titus 2:13, where the blessed hope is identified as "the appearing of the glory of our great God and Savior Jesus Christ."

So, yes, from a purely redemptive-historical point of view, the lyrics fail to take note of the way that Old Testament episode found its consummate fulfillment in the incarnation of Christ and the events associated with the day of Pentecost. My point is simply that the "glory" that appeared then, in Solomon's day, now resides in its fullness in the heart of every believer.

On the other hand, I want to defend Redman's intent. Surely his point is that today we long less for the literal and visible coming of such glory and more for its practical and often life-changing operation. This is like our simultaneous affirmation of God's omnipresence and our praying for him to "come" or "draw near" in his "manifest" presence. Christ already lives in and abides with every Christian, but we pray for him to "dwell" in our hearts "through faith" (Eph. 3:17). Other examples could be cited in which an accomplished theological truth may as yet be "released" into our experience in transforming power. I suspect this is what Redman had in mind, and I concur with him.[10]

Were it not for the fact that Stackhouse is a charismatic, this would be a perfect illustration of the differences between our two groups. I can hear the charismatic protest: "This sort of theological nit-picking is precisely what I dislike most about cessationists. I'm trying to love God and engage with

---

9. And yet we must consider Peter's assurance that if we are insulted for the name of Christ, we are blessed, "because the Spirit of glory and of God rests upon" us (1 Peter 4:14).

10. Stackhouse concludes his chapter on worship with this provocative statement: "The loose structure [of charismatic worship] is performed in the name of informality, relevance and immediacy, and is close to the centre of charismatic ideology; it is expressive—we ought to remember—of an understandable mistrust of ritual and form. But the irony is that the loss of distinctive liturgical space, transcending ordinary time, means in fact that no time is sacred. Immediacy and accessibility could mean, paradoxically, worship that is escapist and, strangely, irrelevant. Devoid of all theological ritual, alternative worship may be no real alternative at all, but a mimicking of the culture, and theologically insufficient to sustain Christian faith." Stackhouse, *The Gospel-Driven Church*, 66.

his heart in a tender moment of intimate worship, and all you want to do is exegete the song! For heaven's sake, ease up and enjoy God's presence."

The cessationist is quick to respond: "See, that's just what I mean. You charismatics don't care what you sing as long as it makes you feel good. If you continue in your indifference toward theological accuracy, you could well end up worshiping a false god. Don't forget, we're supposed to worship in both spirit *and* truth!"

Immediacy versus Mediacy

Related to the above is the difference one often sees in how the sacraments are understood. There is certainly no uniform approach to the ordinances of the church among those who are cessationists, but they tend to place more emphasis on the sacramental nature of life than do charismatics. This is due in no small part to the emphasis on "immediacy" among charismatics, as over against the recognition of "instrumentality" among cessationists. The Roman Catholic scholar Yves Congar cites Protestant theologian Gérard Delteil: "The charismatic form of expression seems to be linked to a theology of immediacy—an immediacy of the Word grasped via the text, an immediacy of God's presence grasped through experience, an immediacy of relationship expressed by speaking in tongues and an immediacy that by-passes history."[11]

As a rule, but not without exception, cessationists are more open to the possibility that the physical can be a medium or perhaps even an embodiment of the spiritual. They have a greater appreciation for religious symbolism and are more likely to highlight baptism and the Eucharist in their corporate worship than are charismatics. This is largely due to an incipient gnosticism that permeates much of the charismatic world. Charismatic theology is often characterized by a dualism between spirit and body as well as heaven and earth, in such a way that the beauty of creation and the "physicality" of God's redemptive purposes are diminished.[12]

---

11. Yves Congar, "The Renewal in the Spirit: Promises and Questions," in Congar, *I Believe in the Holy Spirit*, trans. David Smith (New York: Crossroad, 1997), 165.

12. I think the best and most biblical attempt to wed Spirit and sacrament is found in Andrew Wilson's excellent book, *Spirit and Sacrament: An Invitation to Eucharismatic Worship* (Grand Rapids: Zondervan, 2019).

Grant Wacker makes the point that for mainliners, or cessationists, sacramentalism extends beyond the elements of the Lord's Table. Other material objects, such as "stained glass in the nave, [and] carved wood in the chancel—become sites for the intersection of the supernatural and the natural. Mainliners know that Christians experience God with their senses too."[13]

Some are surprised that a charismatic Baptist such as Stackhouse would emphasize the church's sacraments. But he clearly believes that "the loss of the concept of mediation, inherent in a sacramental understanding of religion . . . is central to the diminution of Christian identity" so evident in much of the charismatic tradition.[14] Stackhouse attributes much of this to the fact that it is the musicians, rather than pastors and theologians, who set the agenda for worship in today's churches. Thus, the hallmark of worship today is that it is "immediate, intimate and most definitely non-sacramental (indeed immediacy and non-sacramentality are two ways of saying the same thing)."[15] The result has been a diminishing of transcendence. The loss of the theological notion of mediation means that God is all too near. Thus, what is encouraged is an "ecstatic" rather than "incarnational" view of religion, which can, at times, undermine the genuinely human and material dimension of Christian spirituality.

I'm a bit torn at this point. My love for "immediacy" in contemporary worship was initially provoked by the lifeless formalism of more traditional approaches. I longed for God to be "near." I was done with any form of Christian "deism" that relegated God to a distant and uninvolved transcendence and with classical hymns that enabled me to keep God at a safe distance from my heart. I also appreciate Stackhouse's point. But why must we choose between worship that is "ecstatic" and "incarnational"? Why must we choose between a God who is immanent and transcendent? Is it impossible to formulate a theology and praxis of worship that honors the intimacy of God's nearness and the awe and reverence of his holy otherness? I refuse to settle for anything less.

The strongest element in Stackhouse's call for a retrieval of the sacramental dimension is its ability to sustain focus on the centrality of the gospel of what God has done in and through Jesus Christ and the indwelling

---

13. Wacker, "Hand-Clapping in a Gothic Nave," 60.
14. Stackhouse, *The Gospel-Driven Church*, 125.
15. Stackhouse, *The Gospel-Driven Church*, 127.

Spirit. It does this primarily by evoking "remembrance" of God's movement toward us in Christ. Indeed, "this is the basis of all missiological activity by the church, because it is only out of the church's awareness of the gospel's power to initiate and sustain its own inner life that it can go forth into the world confident of the efficacy of its message."[16]

Stackhouse acknowledges that

according to certain preconceptions, the language of remembrance is inert, dead language that stultifies spiritual growth, in contrast to the vital and pressing language of revival. However, as [Gordon] Fee points out, *anamnesis* [remembrance] is not the recalling of past events for the sake of nostalgia; rather, in the light of the resurrection, it is the recalling into the present the very real and substantial events of death and resurrection, in order that they might be celebrated, enjoyed, even participated in.[17]

In sum,

the deployment of the sacrament of the word, baptism and eucharist, are not the church being overly academic—nor overly liturgical, for that matter—but the church being itself: the church attending to what it has done historically to keep alive truly gospel speech. After all, it is Paul who tells us that the Lord's Supper proclaims "the death of the Lord until he comes." And by retaining this sacrament of grace, the church challenges the reduction of the gospel to method or experience. It is a summons not only to adhere to but also participate in the facticity of the death and resurrection of Christ, initiated by baptism and sustained by communion, with the notion of remembrance central to both.[18]

An additional word of clarification concerning the nature of sacramental theology is needed. Contrary to much Protestant opinion, the sacraments are not barriers between God and man, but bridges. They are not designed to keep God at arm's length or to inhibit our intimacy with him. The very purpose of a sacrament is to mediate the sanctifying, life-changing, powerful

---

16. Stackhouse, *The Gospel-Driven Church*, 135.
17. Stackhouse, *The Gospel-Driven Church*, 137.
18. Stackhouse, *The Gospel-Driven Church*, 149.

presence of divine grace to the heart of the believer. Sacraments are not sub-stitutes for the person of Christ, but the divinely ordained means by which our Lord makes himself and his love and his sin-killing power available to the redeemed.

We should never think of the sacraments, whether the Eucharist, bap-tism, the preached Word, or whatever, as if they stood between us and God to keep the two apart. Precisely the opposite is the case! God ordained them to draw near, make himself known, and bring into present experience the reality and joy of that intimacy with Jesus Christ that his cross secured. I applaud Stackhouse's efforts to make this point and join him in calling back the evangelical world to a biblical appreciation for the classical "means of grace."

Is Worship a Bottom-Up Endeavor or a Top-Down Experience?

Yet another question emerges in our discussion of these two differing approaches to worship. Is worship an exclusively (or at least primarily) bottom-up experience or perhaps also top-down? Many in the Reformed and cessationist camp conceive of worship as what James K. A. Smith calls a "bottom-up" experience. Smith, on the other hand, views it as equally a "top-down" encounter with God. Here is how he describes it:

> Instead of the bottom-up emphasis on worship as our expression of devo-tion and praise, historic Christian worship is rooted in the conviction that God is the primary actor or agent in the worship encounter. Worship works from the top down, you might say. In worship we don't just come to show God our devotion and give him our praise; we are called to worship because in this encounter God (re)makes and molds us top-down. Worship is the arena in which God recalibrates our hearts, reforms our desires, and rehabituates our loves. Worship isn't just something we do; it is where God does something to us. Worship is the heart of discipleship because it is the gymnasium in which God retrains our hearts.[19]

---

19. James K. A. Smith, *You Are What You Love: The Spiritual Power of Habit* (Grand Rapids: Brazos, 2016), 77.

Read that again: *"Worship is the heart of discipleship because it is the gymnasium in which God retrains our hearts."* This is, in part, what distinguishes charismatic worship from what occurs in most cessationist churches. Smith's point is that worship is formative and not just expressive. This doesn't deny that we express our adoration and gratitude in worship. But to think of it exclusively in such terms loses sight of what God does to us when we extol him in praise. In worship we exalt God, but we also encounter him in transformative power. In other words, "there is a reciprocity involved in worship that must be noted."[20] Worship is "not reciprocal in the sense that we the worshipers are also worshiped. But something *is* returned in worship—namely, love. Because God is relational, our worship is not a mere performance of love, but a loving exchange with the God who is love (1 Jn. 4:8, 16)."[21]

Therefore, Frame is correct in stressing that "there is more to worship than teaching. Worship is not merely an educational experience; it is first of all a meeting between ourselves and God. Teaching is one thing God does for us in these meetings. But he also relates to us in all the rich and complicated ways that a loving father relates to his children. Worship is an exchange of love, comfort, peace, encouragement, challenge, and many other things."[22] He further points out that "there is no contradiction between the vertical and the horizontal, between the God-centeredness of worship and the benefits available to the worshipers. For it is that very God-centeredness that blesses us. Meditating on God's greatness and his saving work in Christ is what enables us to grow in our devotion and obedience and thus to experience more and more the blessing of God in our lives."[23]

One of the criticisms of charismatic worship is that it is unduly repetitive. Whenever I hear this, my mind immediately turns to Psalm 136, which I will leave to the reader to search out. Smith contends that viewing worship as a top-down endeavor gives new meaning to repetition:

> If you think of worship as a bottom-up, expressive endeavor, repetition will seem insincere and inauthentic. But when you see worship as an invitation

---

20. Steven Felix-Jager, *Renewal Worship: A Theology of Pentecostal Doxology* (Downers Grove, IL: InterVarsity, 2022), 58.

21. Felix-Jager, *Renewal Worship*, 58.

22. Frame, *Contemporary Worship Music*, 105.

23. Frame, *Contemporary Worship Music*, 15–16.

to a top-down encounter in which God is refashioning your deepest habits, then repetition looks very different: it's how God rehabituates us. In a formational paradigm, repetition isn't insincere, because you're not showing, you're submitting. This is crucial because there is no formation without repetition. Virtue formation takes practice, and there is no practice that isn't repetitive. We willingly embrace repetition as a good in all kinds of other sectors of our life—to hone our golf swing, our piano prowess, and our mathematical abilities, for example. If the sovereign Lord has created us as creatures of habit, why should we think repetition is inimical to our spiritual growth?[24]

What Does It Mean to Worship God "in Spirit and Truth"?

Perhaps the best way to sum up the focus of this discussion on diverse views of worship is to direct our attention to the well-known encounter between Jesus and the Samaritan woman in John 4. What precisely did Jesus mean when he said that the Father is seeking men and women who will worship him "in spirit and truth" (v. 23), and how does this help us in our efforts to find a convergence between Word and Spirit in our celebration of God's glory?

To say that we must worship God "in spirit" means, among other things, that it must originate from within, from the heart; it must be sincere, motivated by our love for God and gratitude for all he is and has done. Worship cannot be mechanical or formalistic. That does not necessarily rule out certain rituals or liturgy. But it does demand that all physical postures or symbolic actions must be infused with heartfelt commitment, faith, love, and zeal.

But the word "spirit" here may also reference the Holy Spirit. The apostle Paul said Christians "worship by the Spirit of God and glory in Christ Jesus and put no confidence in the flesh" (Phil. 3:3). It is the Holy Spirit who awakens in us an understanding of God's beauty, splendor, and power. It is the Holy Spirit who stirs us to celebrate and rejoice and give thanks. It is the Holy

---

24. Smith, *You Are What You Love*, 80.

Spirit who opens our eyes to see and savor all that God is for us in Jesus. It is the Holy Spirit who, I hope and pray, orchestrates our services and leads us in corporate praise of God.

This worship, however, must also be "in truth." This is easier for us to understand, for it obviously means that our worship must conform to the revelation of God in Scripture. It must be informed by who God is and what he is like. Our worship must be rooted in and tethered to the realities of biblical revelation. God forbid that we should ever sing heresy. Worship is not meant to be formed by what feels good but by the light of what is true.

Genuine, Christ-exalting worship must never be mindless or based in ignorance. It must be doctrinally grounded and focused on the truth of all we know of our great triune God. To worship inconsistently with what is revealed to us in Scripture ultimately degenerates into idolatry.

Some prefer to worship only "in S/spirit" but couldn't care less about truth. They think that focusing on truth has the potential to quench the Spirit. The standard by which they judge the success of worship is the thrills and chills they experience. Make no mistake: worship that does not engage and inflame your emotions and affections is worthless. Jesus himself criticized the worship of the religious leaders in his day by saying that whereas they honored God "with their lips" their "heart is far from" him (Matt. 15:8). True worship must engage the heart, the affections, the totality of our being. But any affection, feeling, or emotion that is stirred up by error or false doctrine is worthless.

Others prefer to worship only "in truth" and are offended when they or others feel anything or experience heightened emotions. Not long ago, I heard a prominent evangelical pastor say this: "I often wish that we wouldn't sing or have music, but that I could simply see and say the words or the lyrics that express biblical truth. I don't like being distracted by the emotions that rise up in me when we sing to musical accompaniment." I couldn't believe my ears! By all means, let us sing only what is true. But to do so without affection, feeling, and heartfelt emotion is unthinkable. On the other hand, while emotions are good, they must never lead to self-centeredness or an undue dependence on feelings as a criterion for doctrinal belief or decision-making.

I'd remind you of this statement by John Piper, which I quoted in chapter 7: "True worship comes from people who are deeply emotional and who love deep and sound doctrine. Strong affections for God rooted in truth are the bone and marrow of biblical worship."[25] Many would insist that this is simply impossible. The human soul, they say, can't hold together simultaneously such seemingly conflicting realities. You will eventually default to one side or the other. Some insist that you can't focus on the truths of God's Word without turning into an overly intellectual, arrogant elitist, while others argue that you can't cultivate heartwarming, emotionally uplifting celebrations without deviating from the Bible and falling into unbridled fanaticism. I beg to differ! Better still, Jesus begs to differ! The Bible itself begs to differ! God forbid that we should ever find ourselves individually or as a church failing to worship God in both S/spirit and truth!

Genuine, Christ-exalting worship is the fruit of both heat and light. The light of truth shines into our minds and instructs us about who God is. Such light, in turn, ignites the fire of passion and affection and the heat of joy, love, gratitude, and deep soul-satisfaction. Some people will inevitably conclude that there is too much emotion at certain charismatic churches, while others insist there is too much doctrine. Some will say we're too experiential in our worship, while others contend that we're too theological. Personally, I don't think you can be too much of either, just so long as they are both embraced and God is honored.

None of this means that you must worship the way other people at your church do. If the truth of God's Word moves you to lift your hands, dance, shout aloud, or wave a banner, God bless you. If the truth of God's Word leads you into solemn reverence as you remain seated and immovable, God bless you. We must also remember that "there is a place in the Christian life to ponder complexities. But there is also a place in the lives even of the most mature Christians to ponder the profundity of the simple."[26] We can honor God both with the simplicity of Lynn DeShazo's "More Precious than Silver" and the complexity of Martin Luther's "A Mighty Fortress Is Our God." I love deep theology in our music as much as anyone, but one of the benefits of contemporary music is the way that it takes archaic and incomprehensible language and puts it in the vernacular of modern people.

Scripture neither endorses nor denounces any particular style of music or the genre of songs we sing, be they classic hymnody or contemporary

---

25. John Piper, *Desiring God: Meditations of a Christian Hedonist* (Colorado Springs, CO: Multnomah, 2011), 82.

26. Frame, *Contemporary Worship Music*, 27.

songs. What it does insist upon is comprehensibility and biblical fidelity. We must avoid both musical snobbery that often comes with traditional worship and the trendy, hipster mentality that is often associated with contemporary styles.

I'm not unfamiliar with the criticisms of contemporary worship, some of which are entirely baseless and others with a certain degree of merit. Some critics of charismatic worship contend that it is entirely oriented to the "spirit" but gives little attention to the "truth" of God's Word. Yet another tendency is to condemn all charismatic worship based on false associations. To sing more recent songs, together with the highly expressive style of worship in such churches, must mean, or so I've been told, that one is aligned with the Word of Faith movement, or the so-called prosperity gospel, the seeker-sensitive movement, or the church-growth movement, the marketing of Christianity for personal gain, preaching with a view to meeting "felt needs," a pragmatic approach to Christian living, the power of positive thinking, or any expression of Christianity that is riveted on the personality and charisma of a particular minister. In this way, contemporary worship music "becomes the scapegoat for everything bad in modern Christendom. In my view this kind of argument represents poor logic, theology, and ethics."[27]

I concur with John Frame. To reject contemporary music and the atmosphere of freedom and joy it evokes because some on the fringes of the movement are theologically weak and even misguided is entirely unjustified. Most of the charismatic churches with which I'm familiar and in which I minister regularly would have nothing to do with such aberrant theology. One could easily flip the argument and point to the intellectual pride, hyper-judgmentalism, critical spirit, and legalistic approach to Christian living found in many churches where congregants only sing hymns with hands firmly planted at their sides and where nary a tear is to be seen.

Critics of charismatic worship often point to what they call "Jesus is my boyfriend" lyrics. Needless to say, any overt attempt to sexualize our singing about the relationship between Christ and the Christian must be resisted. But if the Song of Solomon includes a focus on the intimacy of love between Christ and the Christian,[28] there is a reason for this emphasis on the

---

27. Frame, *Contemporary Worship Music*, 70–71.
28. An interpretive approach to the Song that was the dominant perspective in Christianity for its first eighteen hundred years.

affections of intimacy and delight. Jesus does love me, for the Bible tells me so! And the first and greatest commandment is that we love him with all our being. That such mutual affection should elicit elevated feelings of comfort and joy is not unexpected, nor is it to be stifled and suppressed.

What is most important is that whether we sing the profound theology of a classical hymn or the deeply personal contemporary chorus, we are worshiping in both S/spirit and truth! For it is just such people the Father is seeking.

CHAPTER 17

How Charismatics Worship (3)

Prophetic Worship and Singing in the Spirit

Two of the distinctives of charismatic worship that you likely will never find in a church that believes in the cessation of revelatory spiritual gifts, are prophetic worship and singing in tongues.

Filled with the Spirit

We'll look first at prophetic worship, and the place to begin is with Paul's instruction in Ephesians 5:18–21:

> Do not get drunk with wine, for that is debauchery, but be filled with the Spirit, addressing one another in psalms and hymns and spiritual songs, singing and making melody to the Lord with your heart, giving thanks always and for everything to God the Father in the name of our Lord Jesus Christ, submitting to one another out of reverence for Christ. (see also Col. 3:16)

Before we examine the possible differences between psalms, hymns, and spiritual songs, let's consider this phrasing in its context. We should begin by observing the relationship between being "filled with the Spirit" and worship or singing. A few observations are in order. First, being filled with the Holy Spirit is contrasted with being drunk with wine. The issue here is one of influence, control, or power. If you insist on getting drunk, be inebriated with the Holy Spirit! Please note, however, that the force of this exhortation is not that Christians should stagger and slur their speech as those drunk with wine do. This misunderstanding of Paul's language has led to rather bizarre behavior by some charismatics and justifiable criticism from our cessationist friends. The influence of the infilling Spirit is *moral* in nature. The results and tangible evidence of the infilling is the *spiritual and relational fruit* Paul described in Galatians 5. Paul envisioned a community of people (the church) whose lives are so totally given over to the Spirit "that the life and deeds of the Spirit are as obvious in their case as the effects of too much wine are obvious in the other."[1]

Second, notice that Paul did not say, "be full of the Spirit," as though one were full of the Spirit like one is full of wine. He said, "be filled by/with the Spirit." The emphasis is on being filled to the full by the Spirit's presence. Compare this with Ephesians 3:19, where Paul spoke of being "filled with all the fullness of God," that is, being filled up with God himself.

There is considerable disagreement among commentators on the proper translation of the Greek preposition *en* ("by" or "with"). Did Paul mean we are to be filled "with" the Spirit, as if the Spirit is himself the content with which we are filled? Or did he mean we are to be filled "by" the Spirit, the content of which is not clearly specified? Peter O'Brien takes the latter and proceeds to argue that "the earlier uses of the 'fullness' language in Ephesians are determinative for understanding what that fullness is here at 5:18."[2] He points to "fullness" language in 1:23; 3:19; and 4:10 and concludes "that the *content* with which believers have been (or are being) filled is the fulness [sic] of (the triune) God or of Christ. No other text in Ephesians (or elsewhere in Paul) *focuses* specifically on the Holy Spirit as the *content* of this fulness [sic]. It is better, then, to understand 5:18 in terms of the Spirit's mediating the fullness of God and Christ to the believers."[3] O'Brien's view, however, is by no means certain.

The third thing to note is that the verb is imperative, that is, it is a *command*. This is not a suggestion, mild recommendation, or polite piece of advice. Being filled with the Holy Spirit is not optional. It is obligatory. To refuse to heed this command is nothing less than overt disobedience to God.

---

1. Gordon Fee, *God's Empowering Presence* (Peabody, MA: Hendrickson, 2001), 721.
2. Peter T. O'Brien, *The Letter to the Ephesians* (Grand Rapids: Eerdmans, 1999), 392.
3. O'Brien, *The Letter to the Ephesians*, 392.

Fourth, the verb is plural. This is Paul's way of reminding us that the responsibility to be filled is not a unique experience intended only for a privileged few. It is a blessing that comes to all who seek it. In other words, the exhortation primarily concerns community life, the need for God's people to be so collectively full of God's presence that their worship, relationships, and the totality of their lives are transformed.

Fifth, although we must be careful not to read too much theology into a Greek verb tense, there is an equally dangerous tendency to ignore it altogether. The verb here is present tense, possibly suggesting that Paul envisioned a continuous, ongoing experience. This is not so much a dramatic or decisive experience that settles things for good but a daily appropriation that applies to all Christians throughout the course of their earthly lives. So, the mere fact that we are *commanded* to be *filled* implies that a Christian faces the danger of being "low" (but never empty!). We are always in need of refreshing and renewal. Furthermore, in view of this command, we should cease speaking of the "second" blessing and begin to seek God for a "third" and a "fourth" and a "fifth" and countless other infillings of the Spirit.

This brings us to the *consequential evidence* of being filled with/by the Holy Spirit. In Ephesians 5:18–21 we see several things that are the fruit of this experience.

a. *Speaking to one another in ministry* (one of the initial signs of being filled is mutual fellowship and encouragement). Psalms, hymns, and spiritual songs can have a didactic purpose and are designed to instruct believers.
b. *Singing to God* (wholehearted worship in corporate fellowship).
c. *Gratitude* (for all things at all times).
d. *Mutual submission* (as opposed to being self-assertive and demanding).

It is helpful to see the structure of the passage to observe that the filling of the Spirit produces or results in these specified activities:

Do not get drunk	on wine
But be filled	by/with the Spirit,

speaking to each other
with psalms, hymns, and spiritual songs,
singing and making music to the Lord
with your hearts,
giving thanks to God
for all things
in the name of our Lord Jesus Christ.
submitting yourselves to one another
in the fear of Christ.

This brings us to our primary concern in verses 19–20, where Paul spoke of "addressing one another in psalms and hymns and spiritual songs, singing and making melody to the Lord with your heart, giving thanks always and for everything to God the Father in the name of our Lord Jesus Christ, submitting to one another out of reverence for Christ."

The apostle envisioned believers communicating truth, knowledge, and instruction, using these various forms of singing. But what's the difference, if any, between "psalms" and "hymns" and "spiritual songs"? Some insist there is no difference between these items. But what is the point of employing three different words if he meant only one thing? More likely, Paul had a distinction in mind that's important for us to note.

"Psalms" most likely refers to those inspired compositions in the Old Testament book of that name. Luke used the word in this way in his writings (Luke 20:42; 24:44; Acts 1:20; 13:33), and Paul encouraged Christians to come to corporate worship with a "psalm" to offer (1 Cor. 14:26). The Hebrew word literally meant "to pluck" or "to strike or twitch the fingers on a string" and thus could possibly refer to singing with instrumental accompaniment (although we shouldn't restrict it to that).

The word "hymns" would be any human composition that focuses on God or Christ. Hannah's song in 1 Samuel 2 or the Song of Moses in Exodus 15 would qualify, as would Mary's Magnificat in Luke 1. Perhaps the most explicit examples would be the so-called Christ hymns in Philippians 2:6–11; Colossians 1:15–20; and 1 Timothy 3:16.

Why is the third expression of singing designated not simply as "songs" but as *spiritual* songs" (although some contend that this adjective applies to all three)? Could it be Paul's way of differentiating between those songs that are previously composed and those that are *spontaneously evoked* by the Spirit himself? Yes, I think so. In other words, "spiritual songs" are most likely *unrehearsed and improvised*, perhaps short melodies or choruses extolling the beauty of Christ. They aren't prepared in advance but are *prompted by the Spirit* and thus are uniquely and especially appropriate to the occasion or the emphasis of the moment. This isn't to say that psalms and hymns are, for that reason, less spiritual or of a lower quality. They can be composed under the influence of the Holy Spirit, no less so than "spiritual songs."

The primary difference is that these are probably songs we sing under the immediate prompting and infilling of the Holy Spirit. I have in mind spontaneous songs that break out unexpectedly during our worship. In other words, there is a difference between those songs a worship leader rehearses and practices before we gather (the words of which appear on the screen or are found in a hymnbook), and the unplanned melodies and phrases and short choruses that break out spontaneously.

This interpretation strikes many as strange because, outside of charismatic churches, there are virtually no opportunities for expressions of spontaneous praise. The only songs permitted are those listed in the bulletin, the words of which are either in the hymnbook or included in the liturgy. In these churches, singing is highly structured, orchestrated, and carefully controlled (but not for that reason any less godly or edifying). There is typically a distinct beginning and ending without the possibility of improvisation or free vocalization. People are expected to sing what is written in the hymnal or projected on a screen, nothing more and nothing less.

But Paul seemed to envision a "singing" in which individuals are given freedom to vocalize their own passions, prayers, and declarations of praise. Although this may strike some as chaotic and aimless the first time it is heard (it certainly did me!), it can quickly become a beautiful and inspiring experience as the Spirit is given free rein in the hearts of Christ's people. As the instrumentalists play a simple chord progression or perhaps even the melody of a familiar song, the worshipers spontaneously supply whatever words are most appropriate to their state of mind and heart.

Prophetic Singing

On countless occasions, I have been blessed and edified by what some have called "prophetic singing" (so called because it is believed the Spirit reveals something to the person who, in turn, puts it to music). Typically, an individual who is part of a worship team is led by the Spirit into a spontaneous song that may evoke another to respond antiphonally. Such "spiritual songs" can last a few seconds or several minutes. Often, what one person sings will stir up yet another with a similar refrain, which, on occasion, will lead back into a verse or the chorus of a hymn previously sung.

More important still is that such singing, whether psalms, hymns, or spiritual songs, are designed not simply to extol God but to educate his people. Through them we "teach" and "admonish" one another. Paul envisioned biblically grounded and theologically substantive songs that communicated truth and called for heartfelt consecration, repentance, and devotion to the Lord. Let's not forget that Paul described a situation far before the printing press and hymnbooks. Thus, these various expressions of singing were an invaluable means for transmitting and inculcating Christian truth.

Not long ago, one of the men in our church approached me with a concern. He was slightly uncomfortable with how one of our worship leaders would spontaneously deviate from the song list and engage in free vocalization. His objection wasn't theological in nature. He had no qualms about what was being sung, as if it were unbiblical, but only that it was being sung while he perceived others to disengage. "They don't know what to do," he said. "So many of them just sit down." Incorporating such "spiritual songs" in our time of corporate praise was unsettling to him. He asked, "Why can't he do that when he's in his car or somewhere other than in front of hundreds of people who are attempting to follow his lead?"

That's not an illegitimate question. I suspect others were wondering the same thing. So, at the first opportunity, I instructed our people on what one should do when worship took this unexpected turn. I told them that one must resist disengaging on the false assumption that this expression of praise is only for the benefit of the person singing and has nothing to do with anyone else. Instead, I provided several suggestions.

Listen and learn! Note again Ephesians 5:19—"addressing one another . . . spiritual songs." Meditate on what is being sung. Focus on the words. Turn them over again and again in your mind. Ask the Spirit to quicken in your own heart the truth of what is being sung and to stir your affections with joy and love. Be open to being taught in those times of prophetic worship. The Spirit may well have prepared something uniquely for you!

Sing the same song. Listen for recurring phrases and the melody line, and if it lasts long enough, join the singer in whatever "spiritual song" he or she is singing.

Sing your own spiritual song. Take whatever truth about God or Jesus the Spirit has awakened in your heart and put it in your own words, adapting it to the melody of the leader. It may be a short, simple phrase of praise, thanksgiving, proclamation, or prayer. Those, such as yours truly, who possess the spiritual gift of speaking in tongues, will often take advantage of such times to sing in tongues. This is surely what Paul had in mind when he made known his resolve to "sing praise with my spirit" (1 Cor. 14:15; see also Acts 2:11; 10:46). More on this below.

Pray. Use the time to intercede for yourself or others. Or perhaps take the truth of what is being sung and let that shape and form the content of your prayers. Turn the singer's "spiritual song" into your own personal intercession!

Give thanks (v. 20). Spend time thanking God (either in prayer or in song) for all that he has done.

Why do I refer to the singing of "spiritual songs" as *prophetic* worship or prophetic singing? Those who believe the revelatory gifts of prophecy and word of knowledge are no longer being given to the church by the Holy Spirit will obviously object to my use of the word "prophetic." If one does not believe that the Holy Spirit can still communicate to our hearts beyond (but never, ever contrary to) what is already written in Scripture, any notion of prophetic singing is dismissed. But if the Spirit continues to impart revelatory insights or significant spiritual impressions on our hearts, then we may be drawing close to understanding what Paul was saying in this passage.

All genuine, Christ-exalting, Christ-enjoying worship is in or through the Holy Spirit. This is what Paul meant when he said, "For we are the [true] circumcision, who worship by the Spirit of God and glory in Christ Jesus and put no confidence in the flesh" (Phil. 3:3). His point is that the Spirit evokes worship, directs our hearts and minds to Christ in worship, reminds us of all the right reasons for worship, and empowers and energizes us for worship. These are some of the ways in which the Holy Spirit is active in our worship:

- Spirit-prompted prayer in the selection of a set list
- Spirit-empowered rehearsal or practice
- Spirit-sustained unity among the band members
- Spirit-awakened expectations of what God might do during the course of worship
- Spirit-spoken direction in the atmosphere of Christ-exalting praise (Acts 13:2)

So what, then, is *prophetic* worship, and how does it differ from the ordinary or routine expressions of praise, honor, and gratitude that we read of in Scripture?

The most important point to draw from this passage is that Paul understood Christ-exalting worship to be the fruit of having been filled with the Holy Spirit. Apart from the Spirit's empowering presence in us, there can be no Christ-exalting singing of psalms, hymns, and spiritual songs. There may be singing, but it will be of little value if not the result of being filled with the Spirit. Likewise, our giving of thanks to the Father in the name of Jesus must be the product of the Spirit's work in our hearts. Simply put, all worship, and not just what we call "prophetic" worship, together with addressing one another in edifying ways, as well as expressions of gratitude to God in the name of Jesus, must emanate from the overflow of the Spirit's presence in our lives.

In prophetic worship, I'm proposing that just as a "revelation" may be granted spontaneously to a person who then communicates it to the congregation as a whole (1 Cor. 14:29–32), the Spirit may likewise reveal something to a member of the worship band who in turn communicates this through singing. If this is the case, the same guidelines that apply to the spoken prophetic word (judging, weighing, etc.) would apply to the sung word.

Perhaps the most common form of prophetic worship occurs when the worship leader senses the Spirit indicating the need to pause and reflect more deeply on something in a song's lyrics, whether that be prayer or the specific application of some biblical principle to the people as a whole.

The Holy Spirit can often speak or reveal something to a worship leader well before the service. As the leader is praying over a potential set list, the Spirit can provide guidance and impress upon the heart something perhaps only tangentially related to what is contained in the song itself. The singer may then carry this truth or emphasis in his or her heart for days before Sunday arrives, meditating on it, praying it back to God, and asking for additional guidance on whether, when, and how to introduce it into the worship set.

I suspect that many worship leaders have often sensed God giving them a prophetic song days before Sunday worship. They find themselves humming a melody or a specific lyric all through the week, which may be the Spirit's way of prepping them to sing it on Sunday.

Prophetic worship may also be the fruit of writing songs under the influence of the Spirit. I'm not claiming infallible inspiration for a song any more than I claim such when I write a book. But in both composing a song and in writing a book, one can often sense the Spirit's leading, together with suggestions of a particular word or image to employ.

Can prophetic worship be both horizontal and vertical in its focus? Yes. A horizontal focus means that the intent of the "song" or chorus is to communicate something directly to God's people. In Colossians 3:16 Paul envisioned this sort of worship as "teaching and admonishing" others in the body of Christ. A vertical focus means that its primary orientation is toward God in the form of explicit praise or adoration. But most often a prophetic song is a delicate combination of both.

What is the role of *musical instrumentation* in prophetic worship? We saw in our examination of 1 Samuel 16 that music has more than simply a psychological or emotional effect on people. It also has the power to frustrate, drive away, and defeat demonic forces: "Whenever the harmful spirit from God was upon Saul, David took the lyre and played it with his hand. So Saul was refreshed and was well, and the harmful spirit departed from him" (v. 23).

David's music had this effect for only one reason: "the LORD is with him" (1 Sam. 16:18). Don't miss the point: music played or sung by those who love God and are filled with God's Spirit and who devote their talents to the glory of God irritates and agitates the enemy! We read in 2 Samuel 22:1 that "David spoke to the LORD the words of this song on the day when the LORD delivered him from the hand of all his enemies, and from the hand of Saul." It would appear then that David prophesied through singing.

Essential to effective prophetic singing is humble prayer in advance, asking God to sensitize your heart and open your eyes and ears to be alert to his voice and leading. Otherwise, you will end up being led by the flesh, perhaps with selfish, competitive, and ambitious motives. As worship leaders, we must consistently cultivate friendship and intimacy with the Holy Spirit. We must not only know his voice but listen to his voice.

The most effective prophetic songs are those that flow naturally out of what the congregation has just sung. One should, in most instances, resist the temptation to create a diversion from the focus of the set. It is somewhat jolting and unedifying to move instantly out of sweet melodies about God's love into loud and energetic declarations of wrath and judgment. The content or focus of prophetic songs might conceivably cover a wide range of topics, such as these:

- gratitude
- a challenge to God's people to respond
- a prayer of intercession based on the truth of something just sung by all
- a reaffirmation or pressing into the truth of something just sung
- joyful celebration
- encouragement
- a cry for mercy
- a call for repentance

Singing in Tongues as an Act of Worship

A second distinctive of charismatic worship is singing in tongues, or what Paul referred to in 1 Corinthians 14:14–15 as singing "with my spirit."[4] This undoubtedly refers to his regular practice of singing in tongues. Since tongues, whether in spoken words or in song, is the result of the Spirit's empowering presence ("the Spirit gave... utterance," Acts 2:4), it has the

---

4. The following is adapted from my book *The Language of Heaven: Crucial Questions about Speaking in Tongues* (Lake Mary, FL: Charisma House, 2019), 99–104.

potential to be prophetic. In any case, it must be subject to interpretation like a spoken word in tongues would be. And once a song in tongues is interpreted, it is also to be judged or weighed following the instructions we find in 1 Corinthians 14:29 and 1 Thessalonians 5:19–22.

There is a strong likelihood, however, that Paul primarily had in view his regular practice of singing in tongues during private devotional prayer and praise. In such cases, no interpretation is needed since no one else is present. Even though Paul confessed that he did not understand what he was saying/singing (i.e., his "mind [was] unfruitful"), he was nevertheless determined to continue this spiritual exercise.

Several texts lead me to believe that the gift of tongues can be used in worship. We see this from a description of what happened on the day of Pentecost. At that time the disciples spoke exuberantly in human languages they had not previously learned and, in doing so, were heard declaring "the mighty works of God" (Acts 2:11). To proclaim the many miraculous and merciful deeds that God has done is to worship him; it is to make known his gracious acts in delivering his people and in preserving them in times of trouble. The psalmist exhorted, "Sing to him, sing praises to him; tell of all his wondrous works!" (Ps. 105:2). "We recount your wondrous deeds," declared Asaph (Ps. 75:1), and he spoke for himself, saying, "I will ponder all your work, and meditate on your mighty deeds" (Ps. 77:12). Such expressions of praise and honor are found throughout the psalter.

We encounter this same thing in Acts 10 when Cornelius and his Gentile companions spoke in tongues. Whether or not they were "extolling God" (v. 46) in tongues or merely did so in conjunction with their tongues speech is unimportant. What we see consistently in these texts is that often when a person makes use of his or her gift, either the content or consequence of it is the praise and worship of God.

Paul said that the one who speaks in tongues addresses God, not man (1 Cor. 14:2), and this may include more than prayer. Praise is, after all, no less God-oriented speech than is petitionary prayer. But there can be no mistake about the role of tongues as worship when we come to Paul's description of his own personal practice. When he stated his resolve to make use of tongues even though his mind didn't grasp what was being said, he included this affirmation: "I will sing praise with my spirit" (1 Cor. 14:15). The word translated "sing praise" is from the verb *psallō*, which means to touch or strike the strings or chords of a musical instrument. Others render it "to play on a stringed instrument" such as a lyre (or in our day, a guitar) or "to sing with musical accompaniment."

Clearly, Paul's gift of tongues took on more than one formal expression. He didn't merely "speak" in tongues but often would "sing" in tongues as well. What he might say during his prayers he could as easily set to music and worship God in a more melodious and perhaps even poetic manner. There is no escaping the fact that Paul viewed tongues as one way to sing his praises to God. The question we must now face is whether he believed this could or should be done in the corporate gathering of God's people, not merely by himself but in unison with other gifted individuals. And if he believed this was permissible, did it require interpretation in the same way that he insisted when it came to a spoken utterance in tongues? To that question, we now turn our attention.

Is It Permissible for People to Sing in Tongues in Corporate Worship?

One question I'm often asked, for which I don't have a definitive answer, is whether it is ever biblically permissible to sing in uninterpreted tongues in a corporate setting. Many would immediately say no and point to Paul's emphasis throughout 1 Corinthians 14:28: "But if there is no one to interpret, let each of them keep silent in the church and speak to himself and to God [presumably, in private]."

Of one thing, I'm sure. If the corporate gathering in view is an official church service, the point of which is to edify other believers (cf. 1 Cor. 14:26), uninterpreted tongues are not permissible. This accounts for Paul's demand for silence in verse 28. But people will often suggest possible exceptions to this rule. In certain Pentecostal denominations, it is almost standard practice for the pastor or worship leader, at some point in the course of corporate praise, to encourage everyone present to sing aloud in the Spirit, that is, in tongues. Rarely, if ever, is this followed with interpretation. And how could it be? If dozens, perhaps even hundreds of people are singing in tongues simultaneously, it would be impossible for an interpretation of each utterance to be given.

For example, Mark Cartledge, a theologian who specializes in Pentecostal and charismatic Christianity, describes his experience at three separate New

Wine conferences in the earlier years of the twenty-first century, at which anywhere from five thousand to eight thousand people were in attendance. New Wine is a ministry outreach based in the United Kingdom, comprised largely of Anglicans committed to the contemporary validity of all spiritual gifts. According to Cartledge, there was typically a time when the worship leader would sing into the microphone in tongues and encourage others to do so. "It is interesting to observe," says Cartledge, "that I have never heard anyone give an audible message in tongues followed by interpretation."[5] The explanation given to Cartledge for this is that the gathering is too large to facilitate interpretation. Furthermore, the gathering was not a church service but a summer conference at which only believers were expected to attend. Might this be an exception to the otherwise important rule that tongues always be followed by interpretation?

It is not uncommon in charismatic church gatherings for the person leading worship to occasionally break from the song that all are singing in English (or in whatever language they all typically speak) and begin to sing in tongues on his or her own. No one else does. Sometimes it is hardly noticeable, but in most cases, it is obvious what is happening. The leader will typically say that he or she was caught up in the euphoria of praise and very easily and naturally transitioned from singing in English to singing in tongues. Again, though, similar to what happened at the New Wine gathering, there is rarely, if ever, time given to ask for an interpretation.

What should we say if the gathering is one at which only believers are in attendance? What if the purpose of the meeting is not instruction or exhortation but praise and intercession? One of Paul's concerns is that uninterpreted tongues will confuse any unbelievers who may be present (see 1 Cor. 14:22–23). But if the meeting is, if you will, a "believers" meeting, perhaps even a small group gathering in someone's home, that possibility no longer exists. In such settings, the unintelligibility of uninterpreted tongues, whether spoken or sung, is no obstacle to achieving the purpose for which people have congregated and therefore would not violate Paul's counsel.

This is by no means a definitive answer. I also realize that it is, in large measure, an argument from silence. I'm only suggesting that we be cautious

---

5. Mark J. Cartledge, *Charismatic Glossolalia: An Empirical-Theological Study* (Burlington, VT: Ashgate, 2002), 211.

about enforcing the rules of 1 Corinthians 14 in contexts that Paul didn't envision or in circumstances other than those that evoked his inspired counsel. What I'm saying is this. If a meeting was of a decidedly different nature and purpose from that which Paul assumed in 1 Corinthians 14, a meeting, for example, the overt aim and advertisement of which was *not* the instructional edification of the body, a meeting at which the presence of unbelievers was neither encouraged nor expected, the effect of uninterpreted tongues, against which Paul warned in this chapter, *may* well be a moot point (and I emphasize the word *may*). If there was a gathering of Christians exclusively for the purpose of worship and prayer, a gathering in which the circumstances that evoked Paul's prohibition of uninterpreted tongues did not obtain, would the prohibitions stand? Perhaps not.

One more passage in Paul's discussion of this issue should forever put to rest any concern about the substantive and spiritually beneficial blessing that comes from speaking or singing words that one's own mind does not comprehend. In 1 Corinthians 14:14–17 Paul stated without equivocation his determination to both pray in tongues and in the language that he and anyone listening could understand. He called the former praying "with my spirit" and the latter "with my mind." He used the word "mind" to convey the idea that he and others could understand what was being said. It's important, said Paul, that we not only pray with our spirits (i.e., in tongues) but also with our minds: "Otherwise, if you give thanks with your spirit, how can anyone in the position of an outsider say 'Amen' to your thanksgiving when he does not know what you are saying?" (1 Cor. 14:16). Notice carefully what is happening here. The "outsider" is a visitor to the service. Whether Paul intended us to understand this person to be a Christian or non-Christian is unclear. However, since he envisioned this person saying "Amen" to one's words of gratitude, it is probable that he had a born-again person in view. He also said that this person could be "built up" if he or she could understand what you were saying.

But the primary thing I want you to see is that when you "give thanks" with your spirit, that is to say, in an uninterpreted tongue, you truly give thanks! And in giving thanks, you are worshiping and praising God for his many blessings. There is substantive content to your words even though neither you nor the outsider knows what is being said. *God* knows what you're saying. *God* hears your expression of gratitude. But it is far better that when you are in the presence of others in the assembly of God's people that you "give thanks" with your "mind" so that all can hear it, comprehend it, and say "Amen" in response to it.

Paul then added this critically important statement: "For you may be giving thanks well enough, but the other person is not being built up" (1 Cor. 14:17). Do you see the importance of this? We are trying to answer the question of whether it is beneficial or helpful or meaningful to utter or sing words in uninterpreted tongues, words that your mind does not comprehend. Here, Paul said, in effect, "Yes, by all means, it is real and meaningful and substantive. You are truly saying thank you to God. You are expressing heartfelt gratitude for all he has done and will do, although your mind doesn't comprehend it. You are extolling him for the countless ways he has blessed you in Christ Jesus."

Don't race past this verse! When you speak or sing in tongues in your private devotional life, you are truly expressing your appreciation to God for his grace, love, and providential kindness, among other things. Of course, should other people hear you do this without interpretation, they won't benefit from it. That would require interpretation. But the fact that *they* can't be built up doesn't mean *you* can't! You can, and you are!

So, the answer to our question, once again, is this: Yes! Speaking and singing in tongues in private, even without interpretation, is real communication and genuine worship and authentic gratitude to God!

CHAPTER 18

Should We Sing Songs Written by Churches with Questionable Theology?

M y overly simplistic answer to whether we should sing songs written by churches with questionable theology is yes, if the lyrics are biblical and the music is aesthetically excellent. My answer is no if the songs contain questionable theology and are put to bad music. Here I will expand on my answer.

Perhaps you saw an article online in which Mackenzie Morgan, a worship leader at Refine Church in Lascassas, Tennessee, announced that she and her church would no longer sing songs from Bethel Church in California or Hillsong Church in Australia. After examining some of the teaching from both Bethel and Hillsong, she concluded that to sing any song that originated with or was composed by someone from either of these local churches was dangerous.[1]

Morgan insists that when it comes to corporate singing in church, "theology matters." "It matters," she says, "if a song is weak in theology and is not accurately displaying the Holiness of our God."[2] I couldn't agree more.

---

1. Stephanie Martin, "'Theology Matters'—Why One Worship Leader Can No Long Support Hillsong, Elevation, Bethel," ChurchLeaders, July 15, 2021, https://churchleaders.com/news/401523 -mackenzie-morgan-hillsong-elevation-bethel.html. We see the same argument in the article by Scott Aniol titled "Stop Singing Hillsong, Bethel, Jesus Culture, and Elevation," February 21, 2022, G3, https:// g3min.org/stop-singing-hillsong-bethel-jesus-culture-and-elevation/. See also Katelyn Beaty, "Opinion: It's Time to Stop Singing Hillsong Music," The Roys Report, June 16, 2023, https://julieroys.com/opinion -its-time-to-stop-singing-hillsong-music/.

2. Martin, "'Theology Matters.'"

At Bridgeway, the church where I formerly pastored, and Convergence Church OKC, where I currently attend, we are careful never to sing error. If a song is inconsistent with Scripture, we don't sing it, no matter who wrote it or how much we might like the melody.

Morgan is also bothered by the fact that in singing the songs of Bethel and Hillsong, we are allowing "royalties" to be paid to them and thus tacitly subsidizing and spreading "their false gospel message." She continues, "What if the majority of the church is leading its people astray singing music that is less than worthy of a Sovereign and Holy God? Would God be pleased with the lights? With the smoke machines? With the obsession of hands in the air and 'response' from the crowd? With loud worship nights singing songs He doesn't approve of?"[3]

So, let me go on the record in this regard. I don't like the strobe lights that so often are used in church worship sets. We refused to make use of smoke machines. But I'm puzzled by the reference to the raising of hands. Has she not read Scripture's many references to this practice? Has she not considered the deeply symbolic and spiritual nature of this and other physical postures in worship? I'm curious: Does a person's stiff, statuesque posture, with hands firmly at one's side or stuffed into one's pockets honor God more than those lifted in praise?

And should we not expect a "response" from the crowd? I read in Scripture of shouts of joy and declarations of "Holy, holy, holy," and affirmations of thanksgiving, among others. And what is the alternative to "loud worship nights"? Quiet or soft worship days? And as I said, no one endorses songs that God wouldn't "approve."

Be assured of this: In no way do I endorse or turn a blind eye to the scandals that have rocked Hillsong in recent days. In no way do I endorse certain ministry methods employed at various churches that artificially stir up emotions as an end in themselves or manipulate people into behaviors or experiences that lack biblical sanction. Every church, be it Bethel, Hillsong, or Convergence OKC where I now worship (including Refine Church in Tennessee), needs to labor more vigorously to tether their teachings and practices to the inspired Word of God.

But let's go straight to the point. Because Morgan believes that some of

---

3. Martin, "'Theology Matters.'"

what Bethel and Hillsong teach is unbiblical, no other church should make use of the music composed or sung there. She also insists that we should "read their church's doctrine and see what they preach, teach, and believe. But don't stop there. Don't compare it to your traditions or what you think is right. Compare it with Scripture. Scripture is the ultimate authority. Not me, not your pastor, not the world, only God. There are no gray areas in God's Word."[4]

So, I did just that. Bethel's statement of faith is profoundly evangelical, orthodox, and consistent with the historic creeds of Christianity. It affirms the Trinity, the inspiration and authority of the Bible, the incarnation and virgin birth of Jesus Christ, his substitutionary death on the cross, bodily resurrection, and ascension into heaven. It explicitly declares that Jesus is "true God" and "true man."

Bethel further affirms that we are saved by grace through faith in the person and work of Jesus. Bethel was once affiliated with the Assemblies of God, yet their statement on the issue of Spirit baptism differs from that denomination's viewpoint. Here is what they say: "The baptism of the Holy Spirit, according to Acts 1:4–8 and 2:4, is poured out on believers that they might have God's power to be His witnesses."

Nothing is said about speaking in tongues being the initial, physical evidence of Spirit baptism. They do appear to believe that this experience is separate from and subsequent to conversion, but even then the language is a bit ambiguous. And let us not forget that although I and many evangelical charismatics believe baptism in the Spirit occurs simultaneous with conversion, the doctrine of "separate and subsequent" has been and still is embraced by numerous Christian denominations within the Pentecostal world and is ably (even if not persuasively) defended by countless biblical scholars who minister in that tradition. We may disagree with their view, but it is a secondary, perhaps even tertiary, doctrine. It is hardly a hill to die on.

Bethel also believes in the second coming of Christ and the eternality of both heaven and hell. One statement that clearly needs greater clarification is this: "We believe the victorious, redemptive work of Christ on the cross provides freedom from the power of the enemy—sin, lies, sickness, and torment." I also believe this, but the question of when complete freedom from

4. Martin, "'Theology Matters.'"

"sickness" is expected must be clearly stated. But note well: nothing in the statement affirms the Word of Faith movement and its beliefs or the so-called health and wealth gospel. If anyone at Bethel teaches these notions, it is not because they are acting in conformity with the church's official statement of faith.

And there is a lengthy, thoroughly biblical defense in their statement concerning the historic and traditional biblical sex ethic, in which marriage is designed solely for one woman and one man. As for homosexuality and transgenderism, I can't recall ever reading a more clearly defined and thoroughly biblical perspective on those issues.

I'm baffled by how or on what basis Morgan accuses them of preaching a "false gospel." They preach salvation by grace alone in Christ alone through faith alone. They tether their hope of eternal life on trust in the sinless life; sacrificial, atoning death; and bodily resurrection of Jesus.

If some in Bethel or Hillsong believe in the so-called prosperity gospel, they are, of course, in error. But as grievous as that error may be (and is), it is not damning. Those who embrace that view are not, for that reason, consigned to eternal condemnation.

Now, are there other ministry practices that Bethel embraced that I find questionable and without explicit biblical support? Yes. Do they employ a style of ministry that we may find objectionable, even offensive? Yes. But those do not make them heretical or deserving of cynical disdain. If more time were spent by Bethel's critics praying for them than is given to writing hypercritical reviews, perhaps such practices would diminish over time. I'll say, at the same time, that we should pray just as fervently for Morgan and those who agree with her article. I'm reminded of Paul's exhortation to the church in Rome, and we would all do well to heed his counsel: "May the God of endurance and encouragement grant you to live in such harmony with one another, in accord with Christ Jesus, that together you may with one voice glorify the God and Father of our Lord Jesus Christ" (Rom. 15:5–6).

I also followed Morgan's advice and read Hillsong's Statement of Beliefs (I wonder, did she?). And let me clarify that I'm writing this in the immediate aftermath of the egregious scandals that have come to light at Hillsong in recent months. I've watched all the online documentaries exposing the financial misconduct allegedly present among Hillsong leaders, and I am greatly grieved, as I'm sure you are, by the sexual immorality of certain of

Hillsong's (now former) leaders. My aim, however, is to assess the biblical quality of Hillsong's contribution to charismatic worship music.

I discovered by examining Hillsong's statement of faith that aside from one or two minor, secondary, doctrinal differences (Hillsong is affiliated with Australian Christian Churches, a traditionally Pentecostal denomination), it is thoroughly evangelical and orthodox. Do I agree with all that is done in the context of their worship services? No. It may not be my "style" or Morgan's, but that doesn't make them heretical. It just means they are different and perhaps unwise. But in numerous other ways, aren't we all?

Morgan says that she will not sing songs that are not "worthy of a Sovereign and Holy God." Good for her. I agree. And I hope you wouldn't ever sing such songs either. And if songs are composed by someone from Bethel or Hillsong that are beneath the dignity of our great triune God, don't sing them. But I challenge anyone to closely examine the lyrics of these songs, all of which were composed by someone in Bethel or Hillsong or related to them in close friendship or some other ministry alliance (such as Jesus Culture), and tell me they are dangerous, unbiblical, or not worthy of who God is and what he has done. Here is a small sampling:

"Abba"
"All Hail King Jesus"
"Cornerstone"
"Ever Be"
"Fall Afresh"
"For the Cross"
"God, I Look to You"
"Goodness of God"
"Holy Spirit (You Are Welcome Here)"
"Jesus, We Love You"
"King of Kings"
"Lead Me to the Cross"
"Lion and the Lamb"
"Living Hope"
"Man of Sorrows"
"New Wine"
"No Longer Slaves"

"O Praise the Name!"
"One Thing Remains"
"Outrageous Love"
"Raise a Hallelujah!"
"Seas of Crimson"
"Shout to the Lord"
"This Is Amazing Grace"
"Worthy Is the Lamb"

I will go on record and say that God is profoundly honored and exalted by each of these songs.

Oh, but Sam. We disagree with some of their secondary doctrines. Won't our singing of these songs communicate to people that we endorse what some in their churches believe? And we have to pay royalties to sing those songs. Aren't we contributing to the spread of their errors?

No. Folks, I plead with you: Don't let cancel culture come to church! You may differ with Bethel and Hillsong in some (perhaps many) of their ministry practices. So do I. But we will sing with these people around the throne of the Lamb for eternity. They are our brothers and sisters in Christ. Surely you are not prepared to denounce them as unbelievers because they don't toe the line on every secondary doctrine you embrace.

What about Morgan's concern that by singing the songs of Bethel and Hillsong we are paying royalties to these churches? Well, let me ask Morgan and others a question or two. Where will you draw the line on where and to whom you will allow your money to go? I daresay that you will find it difficult to survive in our world if you refuse to participate in or make use of something, be it a song, a book, or a product, simply because you fear that by doing so you are promoting and indirectly subsidizing what you regard as unbiblical.

Should I throw away all the books in my library that Jewish scholars wrote because they reject Jesus as the Messiah? I'm talking about books with profound and instructive insights into the Old Testament and other historical and textual issues. Have you ever purchased such books? Should you?

What about the numerous scholarly resources that greatly help us understand biblical languages, backgrounds, and cultural contexts? Must I dispense with the multivolume *Anchor Bible Dictionary* because a few of its contributors are likely not born again?

Have you refused to do your shopping at Kroger and Target because they are decidedly pro-LGBTQ? Does not your purchase of their products indirectly support that movement?

Have you refused to take your kids to Disney World because of their widely public and visible stance on same-sex marriage?

Do you carefully avoid purchasing gas for your car from those stations that obtain their products from oil companies that fund Planned Parenthood?

Do you continue to read novels and other books written by decidedly non-Christian authors, lest by purchasing their works, you contribute to their unbiblical lifestyle?

Have you stopped singing "A Mighty Fortress Is Our God" because its author, Martin Luther, made horrific anti-Semitic statements in his later years?

Do you make use of Facebook and X, two companies owned and operated by unbelievers who support both LGBTQ and abortion causes?

Do you refuse to use songs written by Matt Maher or John Michael Talbot because they are Roman Catholic?

Should we refuse to sing "It Is Well with My Soul" because the author of its lyrics, Horatio Spafford, eventually denied the existence of hell, affirmed universalism and purgatory, and was guilty of multiple instances of fraudulent financial dealings?

Shall we never again read books by Jonathan Edwards or sermons by George Whitefield because both at one time owned slaves?

If someone within the Churches of Christ wrote an otherwise biblically based worship song, would you refuse to sing it in your church because they affirm water baptism as necessary for the forgiveness of sins?

In no way do I even remotely endorse the errors I've just mentioned, but to refuse to sing thoroughly biblical worship songs written by people who believe differently than we do lest we somehow be tainted or defiled in doing so is both impractical and absurd and will only lead to a legalistic and pharisaical local church culture.

It is virtually impossible in our day not to support in some manner groups, companies, or individuals that violate our biblical standards of truth and morality. If you choose to "cancel" everyone who differs with you on some matter of doctrine or ministry practice, out of concern that your money will subsidize their errors, you will end up encased in your own echo chamber, isolated and alone, pridefully patting yourself on the back for being among the remnant who "get it right."

I, for one, will instead continue to remain rigorously biblical in what I preach and how I sing but do so without castigating and/or canceling other Christians who happen to differ from me on some secondary issue or ministry style.

A Defense of Two Controversial Worship Songs

Much has been said and written about the song "What a Beautiful Name" (written by Ben Fielding and Brooke Ligertwood, the latter of Hillsong) in the past few years, mostly negative.[5] I happen to love the song! But a line in it has caused a few to wonder if we are singing heresy.

The problem comes in the lyric "You didn't want heaven without us." Some have argued that this line suggests that Jesus is needy, that he is, in himself, somehow deficient and less than complete, and only we, his people, can fill up what he lacks. That's why he "didn't want heaven without us." But we know from numerous biblical texts that God needs nothing, that as Creator and providential Lord over the entire universe, he is altogether self-sufficient and independent (see Mark 10:45; Acts 17:24–25; Rom. 11:33–36).

So, does that mean the song is heretical after all? Not necessarily. I don't know what its composers were thinking when they wrote it. But we must ask, "*Why* did Jesus not want heaven without us?" If the answer is because he was lonely or needed us or was incomplete without our presence, then we have false doctrine. But that doesn't necessarily follow from the statement that Jesus "didn't want heaven without us." Consider what Jesus asked of his Father in his prayer in John 17. There we read, "Father, I desire that they also, whom you have given me, may be with me where I am" (John 17:24). Clearly Jesus "desires" or "wants" his people to be with him, where he is, in heaven. But we can't stop with the first half of the verse. We must read the rest. In other words, when we ask, "*Why* does Jesus desire that we be with him, where he is?" the answer is immediately forthcoming: "Father, I desire that they also, whom you have given me, may be with me where I am, *to see my glory that you have given me because you loved me before the foundation of the world."*

When Jesus said, "I desire that they also . . . may be with me," it wasn't so that he could receive something we can give, but in order that he might give something that we desperately need. Jesus lacks nothing. His desire for us to be "with" him is so that he can show us his "glory" and in doing so fill up what is lacking in us, not something that is lacking in him. What you and I need most and what Jesus will supply us with forever is the sight and the savoring of his eternal glory.

So, when I sing this glorious song and declare, "You didn't want heaven without us," I will sing it with the understanding that it is because Jesus desired to supply us with what will bring to our hearts the greatest imaginable joy: the sight and savoring of his own eternal and majestic glory!

So, whether or not this was in the composers' thinking as they wrote the song, it is in my thinking as I sing it! And continue to sing it, I will.

Is God's Love "Reckless"?

Yet another extremely popular worship song has come under scrutiny: Cory Asbury's "Reckless Love." We sing it regularly at my church, and I encourage you to do so as well.

I was surprised when a few people pushed back, wondering if it was biblically and theologically appropriate to speak of God's love as "reckless." Then I was informed that others around the country were raising similar questions.[6] Some even suggested it insulted God to speak of his saving love in this way. So, what should we do? Stop singing the song? No!

As I read or sing these lyrics (and I would encourage you to look them up if you're unfamiliar with the song), it appears evident from them alone what the composer had in mind and why he would speak of God's love as reckless. I take the word *reckless* to mean that God's love defies all human categories of how love ought to operate and express itself. God loves sinners in the most unconventional and seemingly unsophisticated manner possible. His love is

---

6. See John Piper, "Should We Sing of God's 'Reckless Love'?" Desiring God, November 21, 2020, https://www.desiringgod.org/interviews/should-we-sing-of-gods-reckless-love.

contrary to how we typically love one another. As Cory Asbury himself said in explaining the background to this song, God's love for us isn't crafty, slick, or cunning. God isn't concerned with what it might cost him in terms of his reputation among people. He isn't concerned with the consequences that might come his way when those he loves don't love him in return. God's love is anything but cautious.[7]

When Jesus chose to welcome into his presence and company both prostitutes and tax collectors (Luke 15:1) he knew the Pharisees were watching. He knew they would mock, revile, and sling mud on his reputation. *Why love people like that? What can they possibly do for you in return? Have you no regard, Jesus, for how this might come back to bite you?*

At this point in Luke 15, Jesus told the parable about the one sheep that wandered from the fold. "What man of you, having a hundred sheep, if he has lost one of them," asked Jesus, "does not leave the ninety-nine . . . and go after the one that is lost, until he finds it?" (v. 4) Well, sadly, the answer is, probably a lot of men. Many, maybe most, would ignore the one who wandered off. That would seem to be the wise and prudent thing to do. Take care of the ninety-nine who weren't dumb enough to stray.

To seek after the one and leave the ninety-nine seems so disproportionate, so careless. *For heaven's sake, Lord, let the silly one go. After all, that's what he or she deserves. You've got ninety-nine others who need your attention and care.* A love that isn't "reckless" might reason like that. But not Jesus. His love is of a different order.

All too often, human love is conditional: if you will first love me, then I'll love you back. But God's love doesn't operate in that way. It is reckless because he loves those who have done nothing to warrant or justify his affection. He loves those who "can't earn it" and certainly "don't deserve it." Every time you try to squeeze God's love into a human mold for what is acceptable and reasonable, he shatters it!

Do you passionately and consistently love your enemies? In this song, we hear of a love that "fights" on behalf of the one who was God's "foe." Isn't this what the apostle Paul said in Romans 5? It was "while we were still weak"

7. See Asbury's response to criticism at "The Power of Love–God's Reckless Love," Good News Fellowship, April 17, 2019, https://gnf.ca/blog/2019/04/17/the-power-of-love-gods-reckless-love-liturgy-service/. Steven Felix-Jager provides an insightful analysis of this song in *Renewal Worship: A Theology of Pentecostal Doxology* (Downers Grove, IL: InterVarsity, 2022), 171–75.

(v. 6) that God loved us in Christ. God's love isn't reserved for the "strong" who can do things for him to merit his love and affection. He loved those who spit in his face and nailed him to a cross. Christ's love was for the "ungodly" (v. 6), not the righteous. Indeed, "God shows his love for us in that while we were still sinners, Christ died for us" (v. 8). It was while "we were enemies" that God demonstrated his love for us (v. 10). Who among you loves like that?

Does that sound like the sort of love that you would expect? Or does it sound entirely unreasonable and even unwise? Looking at things from a human perspective, I would describe someone who loved like that to be incredibly "reckless"! Aren't they just asking for trouble?

Consider the parable of the prodigal son. It was contrary to all custom and rules of human behavior that a father would set aside his personal dignity and risk his reputation by running down the road to welcome home and bless his wayward son. Talk about reckless! Talk about a love that couldn't care less what others might think of how it behaves!

God's love for us doesn't square up with our expectations of what we think is fitting and proper and wise. He shatters the mold! He breaks all the (human) rules for how love should act and on whom it should be showered. It even strikes us as dangerous that God would love people who continually fail and resist him and consistently refuse to give him thanks. But that's God for you! Such a reckless lover he is. And how eternally blessed we are for it.

So, the next time you sing this song, or perhaps when you sing it for the first time, remember that God's way of loving isn't always our way of loving (praise God for that!). His motivation and the manner in which that love comes to expression will shock you and take your breath away! If it doesn't, you haven't understood it. Just when I think God has every reason in the world not to love me, he loves me anyway! Just when I think his love ought to conform to my love or that his love should observe the same rules and regulations as mine, he turns everything on its head.

When I read about God's love in Scripture and then consider how I, a hell-deserving sinner, have been the recipient of it, my initial reaction is to say, "God, I don't mean to give you advice. After all, you're infinitely wise. But this is nuts! You shouldn't love people like me. You won't reap the benefits you deserve. Surely you ought to love only those who first love you. Don't take this personally, Lord, but you appear to be acting somewhat recklessly!"

God's love typically comes to us without regard for how it makes God look in the eyes of sinful humanity. It colors outside the lines. It strikes us as foolish and ineffective. Yet such is God's love for sinners like you and me: reckless, defiant, extraordinary, and determined to bring a blessing to its objects when all they deserve is condemnation.

And on top of it all, God's love is "endless." Not ours. We often stop loving as soon as the object of our devotion ceases to be lovely. We turn our affection away from the one who refuses to reciprocate. Not God. His love is endless, yes, and gloriously, majestically, graciously, and sovereignly "reckless"!

Oh, the overwhelming, never-ending, reckless love of God!

Conclusion

I seriously doubt that I can say anything of substance in this conclusion that I haven't already said in the preceding eighteen chapters. To try to sum up in just a few sentences what it has taken me this long to unpack and explain would undoubtedly prove futile. But there is one thing that continues to weigh heavily on my heart as we press into this issue of what genuine worship is and how best to engage with God in our praise of him: the lingering divisions and often bitter strife that pit Christians against one another when it comes to worship. It pains me each time I come across yet another article, book, or blogpost in which one professing Christian ridicules and eventually rejects another because of their dislike of the style in which the other chooses to extol our great and glorious God.

I do believe, however, that one thing unites us all: our expressed desire to "glorify the God and Father of our Lord Jesus Christ" (Rom. 15:6). This is something on which charismatics and cessationists can all agree. Whether you are a Baptist, a Presbyterian, an Anglican, a Methodist, or a nondenominational believer in Jesus, we are of one mind and heart when it comes to the goal of our worship. We all want to declare and display the glory of our great triune God. Although it may strike some as overly idealistic, the apostle Paul made his appeal to the church in Rome that they, both Gentile and Jewish believers, might "live in such harmony with one another, in accord with Christ Jesus, that together you may with one voice glorify the God and Father of our Lord Jesus Christ" (Rom. 15:5–6).

Paul's aim in this marvelous and deeply theological epistle (and in most of his other letters) was to encourage and facilitate unity among all God's people when it came to worship. Is it too much for us today, some two thousand years later, to live in harmony with one another, and together, with one voice, honor and extol God for who he is and what he has been and is doing? Must we continue to let differences in taste, style, instrumentation, and physical posture keep us apart? Is not the immeasurable beauty and all-sufficient splendor of our great God enough to overcome our petty and secondary differences about the best way to make him known?

If you've persevered long enough to reach this point in the book, you can see how I prefer to worship Christ Jesus. I have personal preferences, just as you do. There are songs I love to sing that, in many cases, differ from the ones you enjoy. I'm probably more physically expressive than a lot of you are. I enjoy extended times of uninterrupted, sustained singing of songs that awaken and stir up heightened affections of love, joy, peace, hope, delight, awe, and any number of other ways in which my love for God can be expressed. We may never agree on any one approach or style or definition of worship, but surely we can "live in harmony with one another" and together, "with one voice," glorify God.

That is my hope as I bring this long book to a close. You may think it is a baseless hope with little chance of coming to fruition After all, one sits while another stands. One weeps while another does not. One worships with raised hands while another doesn't. And the differences, as we have seen, are many and varied. But I have enough confidence in the power of the Holy Spirit to believe that the people of God, from every tongue, tribe, people, and nation, regardless of style or song selection, can, with one unified voice, declare the greatness and goodness of our majestic triune God.

> May the God of endurance and encouragement grant you to live in such harmony with one another, in accord with Christ Jesus, that together you may with one voice glorify the God and Father of our Lord Jesus Christ. (Rom. 15:5–6)

Affections of the Heart in the Experience of Sarah Edwards

A mid the ongoing debate about the proper role of affections, passions, and emotions in the Christian life, especially when we engage in the worship of Christ Jesus, I can think of no more instructive illustration than what occurred in the experience of Sarah Edwards (d. 1758), wife of Jonathan Edwards (d. 1758).[1] I'm including her story in this book to shed what I believe is helpful and encouraging light on the nature of Spirit-wakened, heartfelt, and wholly Christ-exalting affections in the experience of a believer in Jesus Christ.

While Jonathan was engaged in ministry away from Northampton, Massachusetts, Sarah, the mother of their eleven children, experienced a visitation of the Holy Spirit unlike anything I've ever known. When Edwards returned home, he was so struck by the sincerity and reality of what his wife had experienced that he prevailed on her to write it down. He initially published the account without disclosing who it was, most likely to protect his wife from unwanted and unjustified scrutiny. A few excerpts from her story will suffice to make my point.

Sarah's experience began with a renewed sense of the assurance of her salvation, evoked by a meditation on Romans 8:34. The day was January 20, 1742.

---

1. The full text of Sarah's testimony, on which the following is based, is found in S. E. Dwight, *The Life of President Edwards* (New York: Carvill, 1830), 171–86, emphasis added. The revised version in which Jonathan replaces the first-person pronoun with "the person" in order to hide Sarah's identity can be found in Jonathan Edwards, *The Great Awakening*, ed. C. C. Goen (New Haven, CT: Yale University Press, 1972), 331–41.

When I was alone, the words came to my mind with far greater power and sweetness; upon which I took the Bible, and read the words to the end of the chapter, when they were impressed on my heart with vastly greater power and sweetness still. They appeared to me with undoubted certainty as the words of God, and as words which God did pronounce concerning me. I had no more doubt of it than I had of my being. I seemed as it were to hear the great God proclaiming thus to the world concerning me; "Who shall lay anything to thy charge," and had it strongly impressed on me how impossible it was for anything in heaven or earth, in this world or the future, ever to separate me from the love of God which was in Christ Jesus. I cannot find language to express how certain this appeared—the everlasting mountains and hills were but shadows to it. My safety and happiness and eternal enjoyment of God's immutable love seemed as durable and unchangeable as God Himself. *Melted and overcome by the sweetness of this assurance, I fell into a great flow of tears and could not forbear weeping aloud.* It appeared certain to me that God was my Father, and Christ my Lord and Savior, that He was mine and I His.

Under a delightful sense of the immediate presence and love of God, these words seemed to come over and over in my mind, "My God, my all; my God, my all." The presence of God was so near and so real that I seemed scarcely conscious of anything else. God the Father, and the Lord Jesus Christ, seemed as distinct persons, both manifesting their inconceivable loveliness and mildness and gentleness and their great and immutable love to me. I seemed to be taken under the care and charge of my God and Saviour, in an inexpressibly endearing manner; and Christ appeared to me as a mighty Saviour, under the character of the Lion of the tribe of Judah, taking my heart, with all its corruptions, under His care and putting it at His feet. In all things which concerned me I felt myself safe under the protection of the Father and the Saviour; who appeared with supreme kindness to keep a record of everything that I did, and of everything that was done to me, purely for my good.

The peace and happiness which I hereupon felt was altogether inexpressible. It seemed to be that which came from heaven; to be eternal and unchangeable. I seemed to be lifted above earth and hell, out of the reach of everything here below, so that I could look on all the rage and enmity of men or devils with a kind of holy indifference and an undisturbed tranquility. At the same time I felt compassion and love for all mankind, and a deep abasement of soul, under a sense of my own unworthiness. . . .

I continued in a very sweet and lively sense of divine things, day and night, sleeping and waking, until Saturday, Jan. 23. On Saturday morning I had a most solemn and deep impression on my mind of the eye of God as fixed upon me to observe what improvement I made of those spiritual communications I had received from Him. At night my soul seemed to be filled with an inexpressibly sweet and pure love to God and to the children of God, with a refreshing consolation and solace of soul which made me willing to lie on the earth, at the feet of the servants of God, to declare His gracious dealings with me and breathe forth before them my love and gratitude and praise.

[Much of what Sarah describes below was her experience under the ministry of a Mr. Buell, a visitor to Northampton who had come to preach the gospel.]

At 3 o'clock in the afternoon a lecture was preached by Mr. Buell. In the latter part of the sermon one or two appeared much moved, and after the blessing, when the people were going out, several others. To my mind there was the clearest evidence that God was present in the congregation on the work of redeeming love; and in the clear view of this, I was all at once filled with such intense admiration of the wonderful condescension and grace of God, in returning again to Northampton, as overwhelmed my soul, and immediately took away my bodily strength.

This was accompanied with an earnest longing that those of us, who were the children of God, might now arise and strive. It appeared to me that the angels in heaven sung praises for such wonderful, free and sovereign grace, and my heart was lifted up in adoration and praise. I continued to have clear views of the future world, of eternal happiness and misery, and my heart full of love to the souls of men. On seeing some that I found were in a natural condition, I felt a most tender compassion for them; but especially was I, while I remained in the meeting-house, from time to time overcome, and my strength taken away by the sight of one and another, whom I regarded as the children of God and who, I had heard, were lively and animated in religion. We remained in the meeting-house about three hours, after the public exercises were over. During most of the time, my bodily strength was overcome; and the joy and thankfulness which were excited in my mind as I contemplated the great goodness of God led me to converse with those who were near me in a very earnest manner.

[When Sarah speaks of her "bodily strength" being "overcome" or "taken away" she is describing her experience of falling down. Today, many would call this being "slain in the Spirit." Neither Sarah nor Jonathan ever used such terminology, but her experience is still somewhat similar to what many in our day experience.]

When I came home, I found Mr. Buell, Mr. Christophers, Mr. Hopkins, Mrs. Eleanor Dwight, the wife of Mr. Joseph Allen, and Mr. Job Strong, at the house. Seeing and conversing with them on the divine goodness, renewed my former feelings and filled me with an intense desire that we might all arise and with an active, flowing and fervent heart give glory to God. The intenseness of my feelings again took away my bodily strength. . . .

And while I was uttering the words, my mind was so deeply impressed with the love of Christ and a sense of His immediate presence that I could with difficulty refrain from rising from my seat and leaping for joy. I continued to enjoy this intense and lively and refreshing sense of divine things, accompanied with strong emotions for nearly an hour; after which, I experienced a delightful calm and peace and rest in God until I retired for the night; and during the night, both waking and sleeping, I had joyful views of divine things, and a complacent rest of soul in God.

I awoke in the morning of Thursday, Jan. 28th, in the same happy frame of mind and engaged in the duties of my family with a sweet consciousness that God was present with me and with earnest longings of soul for the continuance and increase of the blessed fruits of the Holy Spirit in the town. About 9 o'clock these desires became so exceedingly intense, when I saw numbers of the people coming into the house, with an appearance of deep interest in religion that my bodily strength was much weakened, and it was with difficulty that I could pursue my ordinary avocations. About 11 o'clock as I accidentally went into the room where Mr. Buell was conversing with some of the people, I heard him say, "O that we, who are the children of God, should be cold and lifeless in religion!" and I felt such a sense of the deep ingratitude manifested by the children of God, in such coldness and deadness, that my strength was immediately taken away, and I sunk down on the spot. Those who were near raised me and placed me in a chair; and from the fullness of my heart, I expressed to them in a very earnest manner the deep sense I had of the wonderful grace of Christ towards me, of the assurance I had of His having saved me from hell, of my happiness running parallel with eternity, of the duty of giving up all to God, and of the peace and joy inspired by an entire dependence on His mercy and grace.

Mr. Buell then read a melting hymn of Dr. Watt's concerning the loveliness of Christ, the enjoyments and employments of heaven, that I leaped unconsciously from my chair. I seemed to be drawn upwards, soul and body, from the earth towards heaven; and it appeared to me that I must naturally and necessarily ascend thither. These feelings continued while the hymn was reading and during the prayer of Mr. Christophers which followed. After the prayer, Mr. Buell read two other hymns on the glories of heaven, which moved me so exceedingly and drew me so strongly heavenward that it seemed as it were to draw my body upwards, and I felt as if I must necessarily ascend thither. At length my strength failed me and I sunk down; when they took me up and laid me on the bed, where I lay for a considerable time, faint with joy while contemplating the glories of the heavenly world. After I had lain a while, I felt more perfectly subdued and weaned from the world, and more fully resigned to God than I had ever been conscious of before. I felt an entire indifference to the opinions and representations and conduct of mankind respecting me.

I was entirely swallowed up in God, as my only portion, and His honour and glory was the object of my supreme desire and delight. At the same time, I felt a far greater love to the children of God than ever before. I seemed to love them as my own soul; and when I saw them, my heart went out towards them with an inexpressible endearedness and sweetness. I beheld them by faith in their risen and glorified state, with spiritual bodies re-fashioned after the image of Christ's glorious body and arrayed in the beauty of heaven. The time when they would be so appeared very near, by faith it seemed as if it were present. This was accompanied with a ravishing sense of the unspeakable joys of the upper world. They appeared to my mind in all their reality and certainty, and as it were in actual and distinct vision; so plain and evident were they to the eye of my faith, I seemed to regard them as begun. These anticipations were renewed over and over, while I lay on the bed, from 12 o'clock till four, being too much exhausted by emotions of joy to rise and sit up.

I continued in a sweet and lively sense of divine things until I retired to rest. That night, which was Thursday night, Jan. 28, was the sweetest night I ever had in my life. I never before, for so long a time together, enjoyed so much of the light and rest and sweetness of heaven in my soul, but without the least agitation of body during the whole time. The great part of the night I lay awake, sometimes asleep, and sometimes between sleeping and waking. But all night I continued in a constant, clear, and lively sense of the heavenly sweetness of Christ's excellent and transcendent love, of His nearness to me, and of my dearness to Him; with an inexpressibly sweet calmness of soul in an entire rest in Him.

I seemed to myself to perceive a glow of divine love come down from the heart of Christ in heaven, into my heart, in a constant stream, like a stream or pencil of sweet light. At the same time, my heart and soul all flowed out in love to Christ; so that there seemed to be a constant flowing and reflowing of heavenly and divine love, from Christ's heart to mine; and I appeared to myself to float or swim in these bright, sweet beams of the love of Christ, like the motes swimming in the beams of the sun or the streams of His light which come in at the window. My soul remained in a kind of heavenly elysium. So far as I am capable of making a comparison, I think that what I felt each minute, during the continuance of the whole time, was worth more than all the outward comfort and pleasure which I had enjoyed in my whole life put together. It was a pure delight which fed and satisfied the soul. It was pleasure, without the least sting or any interruption. It was a sweetness which my soul was lost in. It seemed to be all that my feeble frame could sustain, of that fullness of joy which is felt by those who behold the face of Christ and share His love in the heavenly world. There was but little difference whether I was asleep or awake, so deep was the impression made on my soul; but if there was any difference, the sweetness was greatest and most uninterrupted while I was asleep.

This lively sense of the beauty and excellence of divine things continued during the morning, accompanied with peculiar sweetness and delight. To my own imagination, my soul seemed to be gone out of me to God and Christ in heaven, and to have very little relation to my body. God and Christ were so present to me and so near me that I seemed removed from myself. The spiritual beauty of the Father and the Saviour seemed to engross my whole mind; and it was the instinctive feeling of my heart, "Thou art; and there is none beside Thee." I never felt such an entire emptiness of self-love or any regard to any private, selfish interest of my own. It seemed to me that I had entirely done with myself. I felt that the opinions of the world concerning me were nothing, and that I had no more to do with any outward interest of my own than with that of a person whom I never saw. The glory of God seemed to be all, and in all, and to swallow up every wish and desire of my heart.

Mr. Sheldon came into the house about 10 o'clock, and said to me as he came in, "The Sun of righteousness arose on my soul this morning, before day;" upon which I said to him in reply, "That Sun has not set upon my soul all this night; I have dwelt on high in the heavenly mansions; the light of divine love has surrounded me; my soul has been lost in God, and has almost left the body." This conversation only served to give me a still livelier sense of the reality and excellence of divine things, and that to such a degree, as again to take away my strength, and occasion great agitation of body. So strong were my feelings, I could not refrain from conversing with those around me, in a very earnest manner, for about a quarter of an hour, on the infinite riches of divine love in the work of salvation; when, my strength entirely failing, my flesh grew very cold, and they carried me and set me by the fire.

As I sat there, I had a most affecting sense of the mighty power of

Christ, which had been exerted in what He had done for my soul, and in sustaining and keeping down the native corruptions of my heart, and of the glorious and wonderful grace of God in causing the ark to return to Northampton. So intense were my feelings, when speaking of these things, that I could not forbear rising up and leaping with joy and exultation. I felt at the same time an exceedingly strong and tender affection for the children of God, and realized, in a manner exceedingly sweet and ravishing, the meaning of Christ's prayer in John 17:21, "that they all may be one, as thou Father art in me, and I in Thee, that they also may be one in us." This union appeared to me an inconceivable, excellent, and sweet oneness; and at the same time, I felt that oneness in my soul, with the children of God who were present. . . .

So conscious was I of the joyful presence of the Holy Spirit, I could scarcely refrain from leaping with transports of joy. This happy frame of mind continued until 2 o'clock, when Mr. Williams came in, and we soon went to meeting. He preached on the subject of the assurance of faith. The whole sermon was affecting to me, but especially when he came to show the way in which assurance was obtained, and to point out its happy fruits. When I heard him say that those who have assurance have a foretaste of heavenly glory, I knew the truth of it from what I then felt: I knew that I then tasted the clusters of the heavenly Canaan; my soul was filled and overwhelmed with light and love and joy in the Holy Ghost, and seemed just ready to go away from the body. I could scarcely refrain from expressing my joy aloud, in the midst of the service. I had, in the meantime, an overwhelming sense of the glory of God, as the Great Eternal All, and of the happiness of having my own will entirely subdued to His will. I knew that the foretaste of glory, which I then had in my soul, came from Him, that I certainly should go to Him, and should, as it were, drop into the Divine Being, and be swallowed up in God. . . .

In the evening, I read those chapters in John which contain Christ's dying discourse with His disciples, and His prayer with them. After I had done reading and was in my retirement, a little before bedtime, thinking on what I had read, my soul was so filled with love to Christ and love to His people, that I fainted under the intenseness of the feeling. I felt, while reading, a delightful acquiescence in the petition to the Father—"I pray not that thou shouldst take them out of the world, but that thou shouldst keep them from evil." Though it seemed to me infinitely better to die to go to Christ, yet I felt an entire willingness to continue in this world so long as God pleased, to do and suffer what He would have me.

After retiring to rest and sleeping a little while, I awoke and had a very lively consciousness of God's being near me. I had an idea of a shining way or path of light between heaven and my soul, somewhat as on Thursday night, except that God seemed nearer to me, and as it were close by, and the way seemed more open, and the communication more immediate and more free. I lay awake most of the night, with a constant delightful sense of God's great love and infinite condescension, and with a continual view of God as near, and as my God. My soul remained, as on Thursday night, in a kind of heavenly elysium. Whether waking or sleeping, there was no interruption, throughout the night, to the views of my soul, to its heavenly light, and divine, inexpressible sweetness. It was without any agitation or motion of the body.

I was led to reflect on God's mercy to me, in giving me, for many years, a willingness to die; and after that, for more than two years past, in making me willing to live, that I might do and suffer whatever He called me to here; whereas, before that, I often used to feel impatient at the thought of living. This then appeared to me, as it had often done before, what gave me much the greatest sense of thankfulness to God. I also thought how God had graciously given me, for a great while, an entire resignation to His will, with respect to the kind and manner of death that I should die; having been made willing to die on the rack, or at the stake, or any other tormenting death, and, if it were God's will, to die in darkness: and how I had that day been made very sensible and fully willing, if it was God's pleasure and for His glory, to die in horror. But now it occurred to me that when I had thus been made willing to live and to be kept on this dark abode, I used to think of living no longer than to the ordinary age of man. Upon this I was led to ask myself, Whether I was not willing to be kept out of heaven even longer; and my whole heart seemed immediately to reply, "Yes, a thousand years, if it be God's will, and for His honour and glory."

and then my heart, in the language of resignation, went further, and with great alacrity and sweetness, to answer as it were over and over again, "Yes, and live a thousand years in horror, if it be most for the glory of God; yea, I am willing to live a thousand years a hell upon earth, if it be most for the honour of God."

After I had felt this resignation on Saturday night, for some time as I lay in bed, I felt such a disposition to rejoice in God, that I wished to have the world join me in praising Him; and was ready to wonder how the world of mankind could lie and sleep when there was such a God to praise and rejoice in, and could scarcely forbear calling out to those who were asleep in the house, to arise and rejoice and praise God. When I arose on the morning of the sabbath, I felt a love to all mankind, wholly peculiar in its strength and sweetness, far beyond all that I had ever felt before. The power of that love seemed to be inexpressible. I thought, if I were surrounded by enemies who were venting their malice and cruelty upon me in tormenting me, it would still be impossible that I should cherish any feelings towards them but those of love and pity and ardent desires for their happiness. At the same time I thought, if I were cast off by my nearest and dearest friends, and if the feelings and conduct of my husband were to be changed from tenderness and affection, to extreme hatred and cruelty, and that every day, I could so rest in God, that it would not touch my heart, or diminish my happiness. I could still go on with alacrity in the performance of every act of duty, and my happiness remain undiminished and entire. . . .

The same lively and joyful sense of spiritual and divine things continued throughout the day—a sweet love to God and all mankind, and such an entire rest of soul in God, that it seemed as if nothing that could be said of me, or done to me, could touch my heart or disturb my enjoyment. The road between heaven and my soul seemed open and wide, all the day long; and the consciousness I had of the reality and excellence of heavenly things was so clear, and the affections they excited so intense, that it overcame my strength, and kept my body weak and faint, the great part of the day, so that I could not stand or go without help. The night also was comforting and refreshing.

This delightful frame of mind was continued on Monday. About noon, one of the neighbours who was conversing with me, expressed himself thus, "One smile from Christ is worth a thousand million pounds," and the words affected me exceedingly, and in a manner which I cannot express. I had a strong sense of the infinite worth of Christ's approbation and love, and at the same time of the grossness of the comparison; and it only astonished me, that anyone could compare a smile of Christ to any earthly treasure. Towards night, I had a deep sense of the awful greatness of God, and felt with what humility and reverence we ought to behave ourselves before Him. Just then Mr. W_____ came in, and spoke with a somewhat light, smiling air, of the flourishing state of religion in the town; which I could scarcely bear to see. It seemed to me that we ought greatly to revere the presence of God, and to behave ourselves with the utmost solemnity and humility, when so great and holy a God was so remarkably present, and to rejoice before Him with trembling.

In the evening, these words, in the Penitential Cries,—"THE COMFORTER IS COME!"—were accompanied to my soul with such conscious certainty and such intense joy, that immediately it took away my strength, and I was falling to the floor; when some of those who were near me caught me and held me up. And when I repeated the words to the by-standers, the strength of my feelings was increased. The name—"THE COMFORTER"—seemed to denote that the Holy Spirit was the only and infinite Fountain of comfort and joy, and this seemed real and certain to my mind. These words—"THE COMFORTER"—seemed as it were immensely great, enough to fill heaven and earth.

On Tuesday after dinner, Mr. Buell, as he sat at table, began to discourse about the glories of the upper world; which greatly affected me, so as to take away my strength. The views and feelings of the preceding evening, respecting the Great Comforter, were renewed in the most lively and joyful manner; so that my limbs grew cold, and I continued to a considerable degree overcome for about an hour, earnestly expressing to those around me, my deep and joyful sense of the presence and divine excellence of the Comforter, and of the glories of heaven.

It was either on Tuesday or Wednesday, that Mr. W_____ came to the house, and informed what account Mr. Lyman, who was just then come from Leicester, on his way from Boston, gave of Mr. Edwards's success, in making peace and promoting religion at Leicester. The intelligence inspired me with such an admiring sense of the great goodness of God, in using Mr. Edwards as the instrument of doing good, and promoting the work of salvation, that it immediately overcame me, and took away my strength so that I could no longer stand on my feet. On Wednesday night, Mr. Clark, coming in with Mr. Buell and some of the people, asked me how I felt. I told him that, I did not feel at all times alike, but this I thought I could say, that I had given up all to God; and there is nothing like it, nothing like giving up all to Him, esteeming all to be His, and resigning all at His call. I told him that, many a time within a twelvemonth, I had asked myself when I lay down, How I should feel if our house and all our property in it should be burnt up, and we should that night be turned out naked; whether I could cheerfully resign all to God; and whether I so saw that all was His, that I could fully consent to His will, in being deprived of it? and that I found, so far as I could judge, an entire resignation to His will, and felt that, if He should thus strip me of everything, I had nothing to say, but should, I thought, have an entire calm and rest in God, for it was His own, and not mine....

After the people had retired, I had a still more lively and joyful sense of the goodness and all-sufficiency of God, of the pleasure of loving Him, and of being alive and active in His service, so that I could not sit still, but walked the room for some time, in a kind of transport. The contemplation was so refreshing and delightful, so much like a heavenly feast within the soul, that I felt an absolute indifference as to any external circumstances; and, according to my best remembrance, this enlivening of my spirit continued so, that I slept but little that night.

The next day, being Thursday, between 10 and 11 o'clock, and a room full of people being collected, I heard two persons give a minute account of the enlivening and joyful influences of the Holy Spirit on their own hearts. It was sweet to me to see others before me in their divine attainments, and to follow after them to heaven.... While I was thus listening, the consideration of the blessed appearances there were of God's being there with us,

> affected me so powerfully, that the joy and transport of the preceding night were again renewed. After this they sang a hymn, which greatly moved me, especially the latter part of it, which speaks of the ungratefulness of not having the praises of Christ always on our tongues. Those last words of the hymn seemed to fasten on my mind, and as I repeated them over, I felt such intense love to Christ, and so much delight in praising Him, that I could hardly forbear leaping from my chair and singing aloud for joy and exultation. I continued thus extraordinarily moved until about 1 o'clock, when the people went away.

I don't know how else to explain what Sarah Edwards experienced in those days other than to cite the words of Peter, who spoke of joy inexpressible and full of glory (1 Peter 1:8)! Knowing the negative and critical response that would inevitably come, Jonathan Edwards appended this statement to his wife's story:

> Now if such things [as Sarah experienced] are enthusiasm [Edwards's word for "emotionalism"], and the offspring of a distempered brain, let my brain be possessed evermore of that happy distemper! If this be distraction, I pray God that the world of mankind may all be seized with this benign, meek, beneficent, beatific glorious distraction!

Do Christians and Muslims Worship the Same God?

In a book that insists the only legitimate worship is that which has the triune God of biblical Christianity as its sole focus, something should be said about where that leaves non-Christians, like Muslims. Do they worship the same God we do? I am constantly amazed that this question is still being asked and even more amazed that some Christians respond by saying yes. May I remind you of a few important things that Muslims believe, or conversely, don't believe?

Muslims deny the truth of the Trinity, that the one eternal God exists in three coequal persons: Father, Son, and Holy Spirit. Muslims also deny the incarnation. We are told in John 1:14 that the eternal Word, or second person of the Trinity, "became flesh," a notion that is abhorrent to all Muslims. Yet Muslims also do their best to speak highly of Jesus. He is given a prominent place in the Qur'an. He is called the Messiah, the virgin-born Son of Mary, Messenger, Prophet, and Servant. He is revered by Muslims much in the same way as are Abraham, Moses, and Muhammad. But Jesus, so say all faithful Muslims, is not himself God.

The death of Jesus on the cross as a substitute for sinful men and women, followed by his bodily resurrection from the grave, is the very heart and soul of Christianity. There is no gospel, no good news, indeed no Christianity, apart from the sinless life, atoning death, and bodily resurrection of Jesus. But Muslims deny that Jesus died on the cross. And since he never died physically, he never rose from the dead. Someone disguised as Jesus suffered crucifixion, while Jesus was taken up into heaven by God.

There was an interesting billboard on Broadway Extension, here in

Oklahoma City, for quite some time. On the right side of the sign, in huge letters, was the word ISLAM. On the left side, under the title One Family, were the names of Abraham, Moses, Jesus, and Muhammad. No! We are not one family with those who deny that Jesus is God. Abraham and Moses are two of the great saints of the old covenant, but they lived in anticipation of the coming of Jesus. Their words, deeds, and prophetic utterances pointed forward to the coming Son of God, the one true Messiah, Jesus. To suggest that Jesus is merely one of a long line of revered prophets that includes Abraham, Moses, and Muhammad, is blasphemous. Worse still, it is damning. To believe this lie is to consign your soul to eternal death.

In John 5 Jesus clearly and unmistakably claimed to be equal with God the Father and to be God himself. In fact, he said in John 5:23, "Whoever does not honor the Son does not honor the Father who sent him."

Consider how this speaks directly to whether people of other religions worship the same God as do Christians. That question is easily answered: Do they believe Jesus is the incarnate revelation of the second person of the Trinity? Do they honor Jesus Christ as such? Do they acknowledge who he is? Do they believe and affirm that he is the Word who became flesh and made a sacrifice for the sins of men and women? Do they know and celebrate Jesus as the true Messiah? Do they honor and praise him for being equal with God the Father in deity, glory, and majesty? If they don't, then they don't honor the Father either. Clearly, if you don't honor the Father, you don't worship him, you don't know him, you have no relationship with him.

So, let me speak directly to the question: Do Christians and Muslims worship the same God? No! Definitely and decisively, no! Muslims do not honor the Son. They deny about Jesus everything he himself claimed to be. They reject his being the Son of God. They reject his atoning sacrificial death on the cross. They repudiate any notion of his bodily resurrection. And any suggestion that only through faith in the person and work of Jesus Christ can someone be saved is abhorrent to them.

John the apostle wrote much the same thing in his first epistle: "Who is the liar but he who denies that Jesus is the Christ? This is the antichrist, he who denies the Father and the Son. No one who denies the Son has the Father. Whoever confesses the Son has the Father also" (1 John 2:22–23). The "liar" par excellence, the one who embodies and gives expression to the spirit of the Antichrist himself, is the person, be it male or female, who denies that Jesus is the Christ, the Son of God who has come in human flesh (see 1 John 4:1–6).

The reason why I expressed my continual shock that knowledgeable Christians would persist in asking the question, Do Christians and Muslims worship the same God? is because of the simple yet profound declaration in 1 John 2:23. "No one who denies the Son has the Father." If you do not "have" the Father, you do not know him, you cannot honor or worship him.

My prayer is that any who are reading this short appendix, be they Muslim or atheist, who deny the Son, may by the grace of God open their eyes to the true identity of Jesus of Nazareth. He is the Word who became flesh (John 1:14). He is the one whom we must honor and adore with the same passion and conviction with which we honor and adore his Father.

Regulative, Normative, Both, or Neither?

A book on worship wouldn't be complete without addressing the debate over whether we are obligated to observe what is known as the regulative principle, or the normative principle, or neither, or perhaps both. I touched on it briefly in chapter 9, but it calls for more extensive analysis.

In his excellent book on worship, John Frame points out that Roman Catholics, Episcopalians, and Lutherans contend that we may do anything in worship except what Scripture explicitly forbids (the normative principle). Those of the Reformed faith who subscribe to the Westminster Confession of Faith operate based on what is called the regulative principle. Thus, Presbyterian and Reformed churches and many Southern Baptists argue that whatever Scripture does not command is forbidden. "Scripture must positively require a practice, if that practice is to be suitable for the worship of God."[1] The Westminster Confession defines the regulative principle as follows: "The acceptable way of worshiping the true God is instituted by himself, and so limited by his own revealed will, that he may not be worshiped according to the imaginations and devices of men, or the suggestions of Satan, under any visible representation, or any other way not prescribed in the holy Scripture."[2]

---

1. John M. Frame, *Worship in Spirit and Truth*: A Refreshing Study of the Principles and Practice of Biblical Worship (Phillipsburg, NJ: P&R, 1996), 38.

2. Westminster Confession of Faith, 21.1. Consider chapter 22 of the Second London Confession of Faith, "Of Religious Worship, and the Sabbath Day," article 1, which states, "The Light of Nature shews that there is a God who hath Lordship, and Sovereignty over all; is just, good, and doth good unto all; and is therefore, to be feared, loved, praised, called upon, trusted in, and served with all the Heart, and all the Soul, and with all the Might. But the acceptable way of Worshipping the true God, is instituted

According to the regulative principle, the essential elements of worship are regulated by what is explicitly taught in Scripture, while the "circumstances" of worship are left to "the light of nature, and Christian prudence."[3] The latter include the time and place of worship, as well as the content of prayer and songs. But as Frame rightly points out, "Scripture is silent about many things that we do in worship."[4] Frame struggles with the way in which the regulative principle is applied, and so do I. The most serious problem he finds in it "is that there is no scriptural warrant for it! Scripture nowhere divides worship up into a series of independent 'elements,' each requiring independent scriptural justification. Scripture nowhere tells us that the regulative principle demands that particular level of specificity, rather than some other."[5]

For example, how does one differentiate between what is "essential" and what is "circumstantial"? There is no biblical text to which one might appeal to make this distinction. There is no text that tells us which so-called circumstances of worship are allowed and which are not. And without any explicit biblical instruction, how would we know? Who is to say whether musical instruments, which are nowhere mentioned in the New Testament, are included as "circumstances" that may or may not be employed depending on "the light of nature and Christian prudence"? Who is to say, and on what basis, whether a dramatic enactment designed to illustrate biblical truths is permissible or not? Did not Jesus tell stories (parables) to provide concrete insight into deep theological principles? If so, why can we not do so today in a form that is suitable to the twenty-first century? Although I favor verse-by-verse expository preaching, where in the Bible are we told that it is the only acceptable form of communicating the Word on a Sunday morning? Is it permissible to make use of a single text, a sentence, or a paragraph, or perhaps even preach an entire book of the Bible in one setting? On what biblical basis is this decision relegated to "circumstance" and "Christian prudence"? As best I can tell, notwithstanding my personal preferences, no particular method of preaching is mandated in the New Testament.

by himself; and so limited by his own revealed will, that he may not be worshipped according to the imaginations, and devices of Men, or the suggestions of Satan, under any visible representations, or any other way, not prescribed in the Holy Scriptures."

3. Westminster Confession of Faith, 1.6.
4. Frame, *Worship in Spirit and Truth*, 40.
5. Frame, *Worship in Spirit and Truth*, 53.

Several individuals in my church give expression to their joyful adoration of God by waving banners during worship. Is this outside the bounds of what the Bible explicitly prescribes, or does it fall within the domain of circumstances or Christian freedom? And who is to make that judgment, especially given the fact, once again, that we have no explicit biblical text that endorses either view? I'm quite sure all of us would agree that worshiping with a banner on which was emblazoned a pentagram or the Nazi swastika would be entirely wrong and sinful. Likewise, any banner that displayed a rainbow pride flag would be entirely impermissible.

You may wonder, in the absence of any explicit affirmation of the regulative principle, why do so many in the Reformed world insist upon it? Although they may well disagree with my answer, I think it has much to do with their disdain for the more emotionally expressive and physically demonstrative ways in which charismatics and Pentecostals worship. It may also be that the regulative principle appeals to many evangelicals because it gives the appearance of holding to and defending a high view of the functional authority of Scripture. I'm certain another reason is that the regulative principle enables them to exclude those elements that undermine or detract from the centrality of Christ. On that point, I'm in agreement with them. But I don't need the regulative principle to tell me what is and is not permissible in such cases. I only need the Bible and the basic rules of interpretation. That is how I know that the Catholic practice of withholding the cup from the laity during the celebration of the Eucharist is wrong. It is how I know that baptizing infants is outside the parameters of what is acceptable worship (recognizing that my paedobaptist friends would disagree). It is how I know that restricting the term *priest* to an ordained member of the clergy is wrong. Could it be that the regulative principle was developed at the time or immediately after the Reformation primarily to justify the elimination from worship of the many trappings and rituals of the Roman Catholic Church, many of which undermined the truth of God's sovereign grace and the priesthood of the believer?

I've often wondered why some in the Reformed camp (and I, too, am a Calvinist!) believe it is important (or at least permissible) for the pastor to preach while wearing ornate robes or vestments. Where is that in the New Testament? It is yet another example of the countless things we do in worship that are not explicitly mandated or forbidden in the Bible. I have no problem with robes. I've worn them while preaching in churches that requested I wear them. My problem is the arbitrary way in which a decision is made about what is and is not essential, what is and is not circumstantial.

One advocate of the regulative principle suggests that "many do not believe Scripture sets forth such parameters for worship as is argued by the regulative principle."[6] But when he then cites Scripture to support his assertion, he lists Isaiah 29:13; Matthew 15:8–9; Mark 7:6–7; and Colossians 2:23. The first three of these texts all say the same thing, that to worship with a disengaged heart is unacceptable. But what are the "commandments of men" in these texts? Does gathering for worship in an ornate church structure, rather than in someone's home, constitute a "commandment of men"? If not, why not? Who decides? And on what basis? He then argues that Scripture is sufficient for our worship and must not be amended, citing Deuteronomy 4:2; 12:29–32; 2 Timothy 3:16–17; and Revelation 22:18–19. These texts tell us that we must not add to or detract from the inspired canon. But no one who follows the normative principle advocates eliminating certain texts or adding to the sixty-six books of the Bible.

Do those Southern Baptist churches that install the senior pastor as the lone elder, as over against the plurality of elders so clearly taught in Scripture, violate the regulative principle? In my opinion, yes. I'm unaware of any biblical text that prescribes Sunday school classes based on age or argues for a designated youth ministry. Why would these be "circumstances" but not "essential" elements in the life of the local church? I don't typically make use of the sign of the cross, but on what biblical grounds would it be forbidden? None. Opposition to it is because of its use in the Roman Catholic Church. But must we necessarily never do what Catholics do? If so, why?

Jesus declared that he is "the light of the world" (John 8:12). John echoed

---

6. J. Ligon Duncan, III, "Let God Teach You How to Worship Him: An Introduction to the Regulative Principle of Worship," June 13, 2022, www.thegospelcoalition.org/article/god-teach-you -worship/. See also J. Ligon Duncan, III, "Does God Care How We Worship?" in *Give Praise to God: A Vision for Reforming Worship: Celebrating the Legacy of James Montgomery Boice*, ed. Philip Graham Ryken, Derek W. H. Thomas, and J. Ligon Duncan III (Phillipsburg, NJ: P&R, 2003), 17–50. Likewise, Kevin DeYoung, "The Freedom of the Regulative Principle," February 14, 2012, www.thegospelcoalition .org/blogs/kevin-deyoung/the-freedom-of-the-regulative-principle/; and Jonty Rhodes, *Reformed Worship* (Phillipsburg, NJ: P&R, 2023). For a more rigorous defense of the regulative principle, see D. G. Hart and John R. Muether, *With Reverence and Awe: Returning to the Basics of Reformed Worship* (Phillipsburg, NJ: P&R, 2002); and Ryan Speck, *Trembling Joy: A Biblical Defense of Traditional Worship* (Lancaster, PA: Alliance of Confessing Evangelicals, 2022).

this truth, declaring that "in him was life, and the life was the light of men. The light shines in the darkness, and the darkness has not overcome it" (John 1:4–5). Jesus, said John, is "the true light" that gives light to all (John 1:9). So, on what basis do some advocates of the regulative principle insist that it is inappropriate to employ candles to illustrate this truth, especially during advent season as we prepare our hearts for the celebration of the incarnation and birth of the Messiah? Nowhere are we explicitly commanded to make use of candles in this way, but neither are we forbidden from doing so. The question, it seems, is whether we find them helpful in facilitating our grasp of the truth of the coming of Christ and driving home to our hearts the work of spiritual enlightenment he accomplished.

Baptist John Dagg said, "When the finger of God points out the way, no place is left to us for human preferences."[7] I agree. When God's finger specifically calls for a particular form or expression of worship or Christian living, there is no place left for our human preferences, especially if they run contrary to God's stated will. But what should we do when God's "finger" is silent? Such advocates of the regulative principle insist that unless a practice is found in the canonical Scriptures, it is not to be permitted. But I believe that no one can consistently live with this principle, given the multitude of practices, rituals, and activities most churches embrace that are nowhere found in the Bible.

Again, the regulative principle insists that to incorporate any activity in our worship requires biblical warrant. According to Ligon Duncan, "That warrant may come in the form of explicit directives, implicit requirements, general principles of Scripture, positive commands, examples, or things derived from good and necessary consequences."[8] Based on this definition, I quite honestly don't know what could be reasonably excluded from Christian worship. I believe I could easily justify virtually any expression of praise and celebration based on the principles he articulates. Of course, there are certain things that would be clearly precluded by the Scriptures, such as worshiping any "god" other than the God of the Bible, singing songs that deny any clear teaching of Scripture (such as celebrating salvation by

---

7. John Dagg, "Duty of Baptists," in *Manual of Theology*, vols. 1–2 (Charleston: Southern Baptist Publication Society, 1859), 300.

8. Ligon Duncan, "Let God Teach You How to Worship Him," The Gospel Coalition, June 13, 2022, https://www.thegospelcoalition.org/article/god-teach-you-worship/.

works), or portraying in any way the Lord Jesus Christ such that his glory and power and saving grace are distorted. Any form of dancing as an expression of worship that displays sexual acts or nudity would be excluded. Certainly, we would all agree that to celebrate the Eucharist as a re-sacrifice or propitiatory offering of the once-for-all death of Christ on the cross would be excluded, as would water baptism as effecting regeneration and the forgiveness of sins. Preaching a sermon in tongues without interpretation would be in direct violation of Paul's instruction in 1 Corinthians 14, as would soliciting an offering with the assurance that if people give generously, God will bless them with untold financial wealth.

But aside from those obvious examples, it would prove exceedingly difficult, if not impossible, to judge, based on the light of prudence and wisdom, what is and is not appropriate. When Duncan speaks of "implicit requirements" and "general principles," I wonder how and by what objective biblical standard such distinctions are to be adjudicated. What is implicitly required by one person may be explicitly forbidden by another, based on their interpretation of what is a "general principle" in God's Word.

Surely, if the Bible is sufficient, and I believe it is, we would expect it to provide explicit indications of how to differentiate between the so-called essentials of worship and those elements that are but "circumstantial," if such a differentiation were important for our determining what is and is not acceptable worship. But the all-sufficient Bible does no such thing. On what basis, then, aside from one's own personal preferences or denominational traditions, does an advocate of the regulative principle insist on that distinction? As a strong believer in the sufficiency of Scripture, the absence from the latter of this differentiation prompts me to avoid making any attempt to draw dogmatic conclusions that the Scriptures decline to make. Simply put, if the Bible doesn't explicitly draw a distinction between what is essential and what is circumstantial, what right do I have to do so?

So, if all worship is "limited" by God's "own revealed will," on what grounds does anyone justify the countless expressions of worship and ministry in the contemporary church, none of which are explicitly revealed and mandated in Scripture? My point is simply that the regulative principle, so stated, is impossible to observe. Everyone violates it and then does their best to justify such practices based on this arbitrary distinction between essentials and circumstances.

I'll cite other examples. Why do we identify one particular Sunday each year as Easter and celebrate it as unique? Of course, some advocates of the regulative principle would argue that we shouldn't. On a related note, why do we observe the events of Holy Week leading up to Good Friday and Easter Sunday? These are nowhere prescribed in Scripture. The same could be said of Pentecost Sunday and Christmas. Is it a violation of the regulative principle to focus on such special days, insofar as nowhere in Scripture do we read of the New Testament church doing so? It strikes me as singularly arbitrary either to forbid such celebrations, on the one hand, or to identify them as mere "circumstances" or "applications" on the other. Personally, I believe Christians and local churches are free to worship God in accordance with the Christian calendar, or not. Nothing in Scripture regulates either choice.

When my wife and I were for a short season part of an Anglican congregation, we observed Ash Wednesday and, like virtually all others in our church, received the sign of the cross on our foreheads. Nothing in Scripture either commands or prohibits such a practice. Although we no longer engage in this ritual on Ash Wednesday, I believe we are entirely free to do so. If we did, would this be participating in something not prescribed in the Scriptures and thus outside God's "revealed will"? Not being a part of God's "revealed will" does not necessarily mean it is contrary to God's will. I have a friend who, during Lent, refrains from writing anything on his otherwise excellent blog site. Is such a practice forbidden by the regulative principle, or is it permissible? And who makes that call, and, again, on what basis?

In chapter 10 under the section "Further Reflections on Feasting: The Extinction of Intinction," I argue for the "extinction of intinction" when it comes to how the Eucharist is to be observed. Is the way the elements of the Lord's Table are served mandated in Scripture, or is this left to Christian prudence and personal preference? Nowhere in the New Testament are we told who may serve the elements. May women? May laymen? If only ordained clergy are permitted to oversee the Lord's Table and water baptism, on what scriptural basis is such a decision made?

And where in Scripture is "ordination" explicitly commanded? And where does Scripture regulate how often the Lord's Supper is to be celebrated? Narrative sections in the book of Acts portray the early church as engaging in Communion on a weekly basis, most likely in conjunction with a corporate meal. Is every church, then, obligated to follow suit, or is there freedom in determining how these features of worship are to be implemented? Must one use only unleavened bread, or, for the sake of those who suffer from celiac disease, is gluten-free bread also permitted? And must we always employ wine when we serve the cup, or is grape juice permissible, especially given the struggles that recovering alcoholics face? What about the common cup? Most have abandoned it out of health concerns during the COVID pandemic. But should we? May we?

One author seeks to prove that God cares greatly about how we worship by appealing to the provisions for tabernacle worship in Exodus 25–31 and 35–40, as well as in Leviticus. But those chapters only tell us what God required of those who lived under the dictates and terms of the Mosaic covenant. They say nothing about what God requires of those who now live under the provisions of the new covenant. And it is quite clear that neither this author nor any other advocate of the regulative principle lives in accordance with those Old Testament texts. How, then, can they be cited as proof of the legitimacy of the regulative principle?

I don't need the regulative principle to tell me what is permissible in the worship of the local church. As noted above, a close reading of the New Testament clearly indicates that teaching or preaching of the Word is standard practice, as is singing to the Lord and teaching and admonishing one another in psalms, hymns, and spiritual songs. The public reading of Scripture and prayer are two additional features of worship that all churches should regularly observe. Likewise, celebration of the ordinances of the Lord's Table and water baptism, as well as the enforcement of church discipline, are fundamental to the life of the local church and its worship of the Lord.

Beyond this, it seems arbitrary and baseless to insist that other expressions cannot be approved unless there is some explicit biblical precedent or command. If we were to consistently apply such a principle, we would have to do away with church buildings, budgets, cafés that serve coffee, church bookstores, Sunday school, ministry restricted to and divided according to the age of youth, announcements, the distribution of a weekly bulletin, livestreaming of our services, the sharing of personal testimonies from the platform, making the church facilities available to a local blood drive, setting aside one week each summer for vacation Bible school or some equivalent ministry, and countless other things we do in the pursuit of ministry.

To casually dismiss these many expressions of church life as merely "circumstances" or "applications" feels unjustified and, again, entirely arbitrary, largely grounded in personal preference and cultural norms. Who decides, and on what biblical basis, that such things are either permissible or prohibited? If one should insist that these many expressions of Christian life and ministry are "derived from good and necessary consequences," on what basis, biblical or otherwise, is such a judgment made? What strikes some as "good and necessary" will likely be found "bad and optional" by others.

I'll appeal to one more example of the inconsistency of trying to orchestrate church life and worship based on the regulative principle. Some Southern Baptist churches who say they abide by the regulative principle do not admit to the Lord's Supper a Christian who has not yet been baptized after coming to personal faith in Christ. In other words, those only "baptized" as infants are prohibited from receiving the bread and the cup. Again, the regulative principle states that we are not free to do anything that is not explicitly revealed in the Scriptures. So, where in Scripture does it say that a person must be baptized in water as a believer before they can partake of the Lord's Table? The answer is, nowhere.

The same concept applies when it comes to whether water baptism is necessary for a person to be admitted into formal membership in a local church. Many who embrace the regulative principle insist the answer is yes. But again, where in Scripture is it explicitly stated that if you haven't been baptized in water, you can't be a functioning member of a local church? The answer again is, nowhere. But if nothing is to be done in worship for which we don't have explicit precedent in the Scriptures, something to which the Lord's "finger" clearly points, on what basis can an advocate of the regulative principle deny church membership to an unbaptized believer? None, so far as I can tell. Should all believers be baptized? Absolutely yes.

Contrary to what some proponents of the regulative principle might say, my opposition to it is not because I don't believe the Bible addresses how church life is to be pursued and practiced. I believe the principles of church government, for example, are clearly taught in the New Testament and that we are not free to deviate from those established rules. Other advocates of the regulative principle contend that God has clearly given us instruction on the nature and parameters of corporate worship. And yet perhaps the only (or at least the clearest) example of corporate worship in the early church is Paul's statement in 1 Corinthians 14. But—and here is the supreme irony of it all—most who insist on the regulative principle intentionally exclude the very elements of worship described in that chapter, be it prophetic ministry or the exercise of tongues with interpretation. It is an even greater irony (or dare I say overt inconsistency) that one of the clearest commandments of the apostle regarding public worship, "Do not forbid speaking in tongues" (1 Cor. 14:39), is regularly disobeyed. Virtually all noncharismatic churches believe they should "forbid speaking in tongues," in direct contradiction to what Paul required.

The bottom line is that the decisions by which the regulative principle is enforced are not rooted in explicit biblical instruction. This so-called principle is therefore largely useless as a way to provide direction for what is and is not permitted in worship. The Bible most certainly supplies us with the theological and ethical standards by which we decide on the propriety of anything that is either included or excluded in Christian worship. But given the paucity of explicit instruction on what must be practiced (aside from those elements I cited above), it is better to allow each church to determine, under the guidance of the Holy Spirit, how best to worship God.

Yet another advocate of the regulative principle argues that "at least with the regulative principle we can come to worship knowing that nothing will be asked of us except that which can be shown to be true according to the Word of God."[9] What does that mean? Does "shown to be true" mean there must be an explicit biblical precedent for a practice to be permitted today? Or does it mean that all practices/styles and so on simply must be theologically consistent with and not contrary to what is stated in Scripture? My point, yet again, is that the regulative principle is simply unworkable.

As I said before, this does not mean that "anything goes," as the only things that "go" are those that one can reasonably demonstrate reflect the truths revealed in God's Word or do not overtly conflict with those truths. Thus, the Bible continues to exert a functional authority over how we worship but also permits freedom regarding those features that are nowhere explicitly endorsed or denounced in its pages.

Perhaps the best way to formulate my response to this question is to say that in worship, we *must* do what Scripture commands, and that we *may* do what is not forbidden as long as whatever we do (1) is not in clear violation of biblical principles, (2) proves instructive and edifying to God's people, (3) and serves to honor and extol the Lord Jesus Christ.

---

9. DeYoung, "The Freedom of the Regulative Principle."

Subject Index

Scripture Index

Ancient Sources
2 Baruch

2 Maccabees